.

Development, Values, and the Meaning of Globalization:
A Grassroots Approach

Gasper F. Lo Biondo, SJ
Rita M. Rodriguez

Results of the Woodstock Theological Center's
Global Economy and Cultures Project
In Collaboration with Jesuit Social Centers

**A free downloadable electronic version of this text
is available online at: *woodstock.georgetown.edu/gec***

THE WOODSTOCK THEOLOGICAL CENTER
at Georgetown University • Washington, DC

Woodstock Theological Center
Georgetown University, Box 571137
Washington, DC 20057-1137
woodstock@georgetown.edu
http://woodstock.georgetown.edu

Book and eBook production manager: Matthew Gladden

Cover photo: Shanti and Manjhu, in front of the coal mine encroaching on
their village in Agaria Tola, Jharkhand, India; photo courtesy of Tony
Herbert, SJ.

Cover design by Keelan Downton and Matthew Gladden

Photos from the Global Economy and Cultures project's International
Consultations and of the narrative mosaic tiles were provided by Woodstock
Theological Center staff; photos of the narrative protagonists in their home
towns were provided courtesy of Tony Herbert, SJ (*Chapters 5-6*); Leonard
Chiti, SJ (*Chapter 7*); Josep Mària, SJ (*Chapter 8*); David Velasco Yáñez, SJ
(*Chapter 9*); Rev. Tianzhi Peter Chen (*Chapter 10*); Bernard Lestienne, SJ
(*Chapter 11*); AXJ Bosco, SJ (*Chapter 12*); Robin Schweiger, SJ (*Chapter 13*);
Chong-Dae Kim, SJ (*Chapter 14*); and Rev. Raymond B. Kemp (*Chapter 15*).

ISBN 978-0-578-09942-2

10 9 8 7 6 5 4 3 2 1

**A free downloadable electronic version of this text
is available online at: *woodstock.georgetown.edu/gec***

To the Protagonists of this book's narratives,
on whose shoulders we stand.
With the hope that development practitioners
will value their wisdom.

CONTENTS

PREFACE

This book was born out of the hope that Jesuits around the world could build a network based on shared experience of the plight of poor people caught in the throes of economic globalization. It is addressed to all those who work in any way to help achieve sustainable development and confront the challenges of deep-seated poverty. The book, which features eleven people whose lives were altered by globalization, is the result of the work done in the Global Economy and Cultures (GEC) project at the Woodstock Theological Center (WTC) at Georgetown University in Washington, D.C. in collaboration with Jesuit social centers from around the world. The GEC project, in turn, can trace its origins directly to the sessions of the 34th General Congregation (GC-34) of the Society of Jesus – the 34th "constitutional assembly" since the founding of the Jesuits in 1540 – which was held in Rome in 1995 and was composed of about 200 Jesuits selected from around the world by other Jesuits.

Among the participants at the GC-34 was a group of about fifteen directors of Jesuit social centers from around the world who decided to get together after hours to discuss topics of mutual interest. James Connor, SJ, at the time the director of the Woodstock Theological Center and also participating in the deliberations of the Congregation, met with them. These discussions gave voice to a desire to do something together and Connor offered to coordinate the effort. Woodstock is a theological center, not a social center per se, but it wanted to be of service to the social centers. Back in Washington, Connor approached the then Senior Woodstock Fellow Gasper Lo Biondo, SJ, and shared the results of that meeting by reporting on the themes that were of interest to the social centers for future collaboration and networking. These revolved around economic development issues and the impasse that everyone was feeling. "Globalization" as such had not been named in their discussion, but it seemed to underlie the issues they had in mind. In fact, in addressing the subject of globalization of the world, the official documents by the Congregation seemed to be referring to the concerns expressed by the directors of the social centers:

> In our times there is a growing consciousness of the interdependence of all peoples in one common heritage. The globalization of the world economy and society proceeds at a rapid pace, fed by developments in technology, communication and business. While this phenomenon can produce many benefits, it can also result in injustices on a massive scale: economic adjustment programs and market forces unfettered by concern for their social impact, especially on the poor; the homogeneous "modernization" of cultures in ways that destroy traditional cultures and values; a growing inequality among nations and – within nations – between rich and poor, between the powerful and the marginalized. In justice, we must counter this by working to build up a world order of genuine solidarity, where all can have a rightful place at the banquet of the Kingdom.
>
> **—Thirty-Fourth General Congregation of the Society of Jesus (GC-34), Decree 3, No. 7**

This text reflected concerns that existed among many others at the time of GC-34. As the 1990s progressed, the cry of the poor had begun to echo around the world. The wave of economic globalization initiated in the 1980s was taking shape and creating strong opposition among people in many nongovernmental organizations (NGOs). Many development practitioners dedicated to improving the standard of living of the poor, especially those involved with faith-based projects, were growing increasingly negative in their assessment of the processes associated with globalization.

Among those who were discontented with globalization were many Jesuits around the world whom Woodstock was coming into contact with through the center's international outreach. Thus the vision of an international Jesuit social research network dedicated to understanding and addressing problems associated with the global economy emerged with a good deal of enthusiasm among Jesuits and their associates in many cultures. The vision was one of realizing the enormous potential of a global network of grassroots development practitioners. This interest on global networking among Jesuits continues to this day, as manifested by a major presentation by Father Adolfo Nicolás, SJ, Superior General of the Jesuits, in March 2010 on the topic of global networking among Jesuit universities. Woodstock has faithfully pursued this continuing emphasis on networking with the hope that universities and social centers might work together more closely.

The GC-34 documents also provided the other major component to our way of thinking about globalization. GC-34 insisted that the mission of the Society of Jesus, the service of faith of which the promotion of justice is an integral element, is possible only when cultural and religious dialogue is involved. The local cultural context in which economic globalization was taking place needed to be addressed explicitly if we wanted to understand what was happening among the poor in the globalization process.

We now had the main elements of the GEC project that produced this book: the global economy, local cultures, and the beginnings of a Jesuit network of development practitioners. It had also become clear that merely descriptive accounts of the effects of globalization would not reflect the creativity of people involved in the process of attempting to rebuild their lives in the new global context. We wanted to come up with something to say that had explanatory power related to how human values are capable of shaping the world. By September 1999, Woodstock had conceived a way to relate globalization, cultures, and development. It was based on a Jesuit spirituality rooted in the dynamic process of decision-making in the *Spiritual Exercises* of St. Ignatius of Loyola and the insight of GC-34 that the Jesuits' social mission is not possible without cultural and religious dialogue. In response to an invitation to participate in a joint project around this concept, fourteen representatives from Jesuit social centers from around the world convened at Georgetown University in Washington D.C. There, at the First International Consultation of what later was to be known as the Global Economy and Cultures (GEC) project, the GEC project was launched.

But the authors' involvement with the subject of this book, in fact, can be traced to something much earlier than the 1990s. For the authors, the roots of this Woodstock project date back many decades and lie in their personal journeys in a variety of countries like Chile and Cuba, in settings that bridged seemingly incompatible sets of human relationships. One set was the world of economic poverty and of direct involvement in action to address it. The other was the complex world of macroeconomics and business decisions in the context of personal experience of grassroots friendships and relationships. Dreams born of frustration at sensing a lack of connection between those two sets are the lifetime energy source of this book. Would it be possible to integrate the values of good friends on each side of the divide? The desire grew.

Lo Biondo had engaged in grassroots research on microenterprise development, which was deeply rooted in a concern for its impact on the common good. His work in microfinance heightened a sense of a void that local development practitioners experienced. While the practitioners kept sharpening their technical tools, the tools at hand for detecting cultural values were still too dull to detect or cut through the rich data surrounding their grassroots commitments. At the same time, the experience of economist Rita Rodriguez in teaching and policy-making work in the area of international finance had led her to sense a lack of connection between the field of international finance and poverty as experienced at the grassroots level. They both felt a strong need to address the poverty and injustice that persisted, and was even created by globalization, while many others could increasingly enjoy its benefits.

Since the GEC project was launched at the First International Consultation in 1999, the elaboration of this book has taken over a decade. Two main reasons account for this length of time. One is grounded in the nature of the core narrative methodology, the other on the limitations on the resources available relative to the scope of the project originally envisioned. The core methodology, relying on the traditional Jesuit approach to spirituality, required the creation of new research tools along the way that would provide more adequate qualitative analysis of the rich narratives. At several junctions in the project, the research team at Woodstock realized that the research process still lacked the conceptual tools for achieving its goal of understanding the meaning of globalization as seen through the eyes of the poor in their local cultural context. Until those tools could be developed the results of the project were doomed to fall short of the explanatory power that we had envisioned for it. Gradually, through a painstakingly slow consultative process, the essential tools took shape. At the resource level, soon after 2000, the Woodstock team had to move from full-time dedication to part-time work on the project. However, contact with people working on a limited number of selected narratives continued to yield results. Gradually, with these dedicated partners, we painstakingly created tools that would yield the kind of explanation we sought. We are delighted that these tools can now be made available to the world of development research and practice.

Given the number of years that this project has taken, our narrative approach to the search for the meaning of globalization has focused on information that is historical in character. However, we believe that this fact does not detract from our goal. The fact that the narratives are not current does not affect the deeper ethical issues that we are addressing.

Before concluding this preface, it is worthwhile to point to the connection between this book and another major effort by the Jesuit order in the area of globalization. Around 2004, Jesuit Superior General Peter Hans Kolvenbach convened an international task force to pull together the best thinking of Jesuits around the world on the topic of globalization and marginalization. This task force, headed by Fernando Franco, SJ, and in which Lo Biondo participated, produced a beautifully constructed report that was made available to all the Jesuits in the world. It is our hope that the results reported in this book will complement the task force's report by bringing in something additional that, we believe, is essential for development practitioners. It makes available to them tools of theological reflection.

In making these tools available, this book provides a service to grass-roots researchers who want to pay closer attention to the ways in which people's values operate in their decisions related to phenomena associated with globalization and development. Our efforts will be successful if readers gain from this book two things: insights into their own way of working, and inspiration to locate critical wisdom in the valuing process that guides poor people's decisions. However, it must be said that while we have focused on these decisions, we realize that they are part of a much larger picture of the economy and society. We believe that poor people's choices, together with those of all the "agents of development," including private sector and public sector actors, are what shapes development.

In all of this, we have here a project that reflects the mission of the Woodstock Theological Center: theological reflection on the burning issues of our day. It provides research tools that theology needs, tools that grew out of partnerships involving multidisciplinary cooperation rooted in personal experience. But the project also serves as a stepping stone in the progressive globalization of Jesuit education and social research. With this book, Jesuits can contribute to something bigger than any of our local efforts. We can take the Jesuit spirituality of decision-making, and the theological tradition that integrates value ethics, and translate them into other fields, such as development. We hope that this unique angle of research will inspire researchers and other professionals in the development area to build on the Woodstock approach. If this book provokes new questions and sheds some new light on sustainable development efforts, it will have in some small way achieved its hoped-for outcome.

ACKNOWLEDGMENTS

The list of those people without whose inspiration, support, and assistance this book would not have materialized is very large. We run the risk of overlooking some names in attempting to recognize all of them. Nonetheless, we wish to acknowledge a few individuals to whom we feel especially indebted. First, we wish to single out three men whose contributions, encouragement, and moral support were central to the development of the GEC project and the writing of this book. They are James L. Connor, SJ, Juan Floriani, and John P. Hogan. James L. Connor, SJ, Director of the Woodstock Theological Center from 1987 to 2002, provided inspiration, leadership, and patience without which the Woodstock GEC project never would have begun. Juan Floriani, an economist at the time recently retired from the Inter-American Development Bank, contributed insights, hard analytical work, experience, and personal commitment to the work of the Jesuits; this work played a major role in the shaping of the design of the GEC project. Juan worked closely and traveled with Gasper Lo Biondo from the mid-1990s until 2002. Finally, John P. Hogan, former Associate Director for International Operations of the Peace Corps, brought to bear his experience in economic development, cultures, and religion to the project and was essential to the design and implementation of the cultural analysis of the narratives. His contributions permeate every area of the project as he offered constructive criticism on every facet of the project throughout the years.

In the administrative support area, we owe much to Allegra Da Silva and Theresa McCaffrey Beatty, who served in different periods as the GEC Project Managers, and to Jennifer Holst, special assistant to Gasper Lo Biondo during the early years of the project. They took care of the administrative side of the project and maintained the voluminous amount of data generated by the project in an accessible manner – even after they were no longer associated with the project. They were also extremely successful administrative officers for the several international consultations and regional meetings the project held. Their dedication, flexibility, and enthusiasm for the project and its participants kept the project humming, even during difficult times. We are also thankful for the assistance that Georgetown University summer interns provided to the project. In particular, we wish to mention Sean Burke for his contribution to synthesizing narrative data into the short stories that appear in the narrative chapters in this book.

Many other people served as research assistants, consultants, and regional experts over a number of years. They provided invaluable support in helping frame the issues and process the narratives, and assisting with the international consultations. Among these, we want to make special mention of those who spent time in residence at Woodstock Theological Center working on the GEC project. Prominent among these are Mark Allman; Terry Armstrong; Jaime Badiola, SJ; Perianayagam Devanesan; Munhumeso Manenji (deceased); Carlos Esteban Mejia; Odomaro Mubangizi, SJ; Victor Pacharoni, SJ; Mario Serrano, SJ; and Johannes Wallacher. Among the regional experts, those who supported our various project international meetings include Mark Allman in the United States; Jean-Yves Calvez, SJ (deceased) in Europe; Jorge Cela, SJ, in Latin America; Jose Mario Francisco, SJ, in East Asia Eugene Goussikindey, SJ, in Africa; and James Redington, SJ and A. Joseph Xavier, SJ in India.

Along the way, particularly during Phase I of the project, we benefitted from the guidance provided by the GEC Advisory Board. Throughout the years, the membership of the Advisory Board included Stephen J. Callahan; Maryann Cusimano-Love; Oscar Echevarria; Juan Floriani; John P. Hogan; John M. Kline; William Lewis; William Rickle, SJ; British Robinson; Jim Stormes, SJ; John D. Sullivan; and Marcia A. Wiss.

As draft chapters of this book began to emerge, we also profited from the contribution of several reviewers who provided very valuable comments. Among these, John P. Hogan stands out, having provided comments on every chapter of the book. Peter Bisson, SJ, and Neil Ormerod made significant contributions in developing the Phase II methodology chapters in the book. We are also very thankful to Peter Albert; Nelle Temple Brown; Ilia Delio, OSF; Eugene Goussikindey, SJ; Daniel F. Hartnett, SJ; and Gerard Whelan, SJ, for the comments they offered on the introductory chapters as well as sample narrative chapters.

For the final stages in the publication of this book we owe much to Paula Minaert, who copy-edited the book; Matthew Gladden, who designed the electronic and print versions of this book; and Georgetown University students Jane Bullock, Corey Linehan, and Kelly Olson, who assisted with formatting and proofreading. Paula Minaert, by insisting that she herself have a clear understanding of the text, went well beyond the traditional exercise of her professional talents as a copy editor. As for Matthew Gladden, were it not for him, this book might have never appeared as an e-book. He opened our eyes to the immense possibilities that electronic publishing offers. He did so at the conceptual level, as well as at every step, as he designed and managed the production of this book.

A large project like this would not be possible without substantial financial support from donors. Among these, we owe a great deal of thanks to our largest donor, who wishes to remain anonymous and whose foundation provided a three-year grant of $100,000 per year at the inception of the project. The continued commitment of this Catholic foundation to those who serve the poor and marginalized around the world is itself a matter for the highest thanks and praise.

Other major donors who made this project possible were, first, the Maryland Province of the Society of Jesus, whose initial grant, thanks to James Stormes, SJ, Provincial at that time, strengthened the life of the project at a crucial moment in its early life. Substantial early support was also contributed by the Kimsey Foundation. Then, as the project moved along, we received strong financial support from the U.S. Jesuit Conference, the U.S. Conference of Catholic Bishops, the Raskob Foundation, and several anonymous donors. At a later stage, Charlotte Mahoney and Peter Albert, long-time friends of the Woodstock Center, committed to the completion of this book and Vito Germinario to its publication. Their personal interest and support meant a great deal. We are also indebted to a long list of faithful Woodstock donors who through the years have earmarked their donations in support of our project. Among these, we give special thanks to Mr. and Mrs. Theodore A. Schwab, whose consistent support has spanned nearly a decade. Without the resources and patience of all these donors, large and small, the GEC project and this book would have never materialized.

Finally, the GEC project and this book result from the enthusiastic participation of the many Jesuits and associates who are the backbone of the project. They are the ones who personally know the protagonists of the narratives in the project and in this book. They are the ones who opened themselves to the search for a better understanding of what was happening within these protagonists as global forces entered their lives. They are the ones who, despite their busy ministry schedules, were willing to find the time to spend very long hours developing the data, answering questions from the WTC researchers and, for many of them, then engaging in a communal reflection at the project's international meetings. This book is as much theirs as the authors' at Woodstock, particularly the narrators who contributed the life stories contained in this book. Because the Jesuits and associates who participated in the GEC project are so numerous, we have chosen to list their names in the table that follows.

Jesuits and Lay and Religious Associates Who Contributed to the GEC Project

In the chart below, **E** = regional expert consultants, including meeting participation; **N** = contributed a narrative or essay *and* participated in the project's meetings; and **P** = participated in the project's international and/or regional meetings.

The Narrators whose Narratives are Featured in This Book

(N)	Xavier John Bosco, SJ	India
(N)	Rev. Peter Chen	China
(N)	Leonard Chiti, SJ	Kenya; Zambia
(N)	Tony Herbert, SJ	India
(N)	Francois Pazisnewende Kabore, SJ	Burkina Faso
(N)	Rev. Ray Kemp	U.S.
(N)	Chong-Dae Kim, SJ	South Korea
(N)	Bernard Lestienne, SJ	Brazil
(N)	Josep Mària, SJ	Spain
(N)	Robin Schweiger, SJ	Slovenia
(N)	Jean Jacques Tene	Cameroon
(N)	David Velasco Yáñez, SJ	Mexico

Regional Expert Consultants

(E)	Mark Allman	U.S.
(E)	Jean-Yves Calvez, SJ (deceased)	France
(E)	Jorge Cela, SJ	Dominican Republic

(E)	Joseph Christie, SJ	India
(E)	José Mario C. Francisco, SJ	Philippines
(E)	Eugene Goussikindey, SJ	Kenya
(E)	James D. Redington, SJ	India; U.S.
(E)	A. Joseph Xavier, SJ	India

Others who have Contributed to the Global Economy and Cultures Project

(N)	Antonio Abreu, SJ	Brazil
(N)	Victor Adangba, SJ	Côte d'Ivoire
(N)	Mathew Aerthayil, SJ	India
(N)	D. Albert, SJ	India
(N)	Xavier Albó, SJ	Bolivia
(P)	Bruce Anderson	Canada
(N)	Terry R. Armstrong	U.S.
(N)	Sosai Arokiasamy, SJ	India
(N)	Edward Arroyo, SJ	U.S.
(N)	Piotr Aszyk, SJ	Poland
(N)	Shay Auerbach, SJ	U.S.
(N)	Marcello Azevedo, SJ	Brazil
(N)	Jaime Badiola, SJ	Spain
(P)	Tiberius Barasa, SJ	Kenya
(P)	Alvaro Barreiro, SJ	Brazil
(N)	Antoine Berilengar, SJ	Chad
(P)	Carlos Rafael Cabarrús, SJ	Guatemala
(P)	John Carroll, SJ	Philippines
(P)	Drew Christiansen, SJ	U.S.
(N)	Afiawari Chukweyenu, SJ	Nigeria
(N)	Lucio Cirne, SJ	Brazil
(P)	Bishop Francisco Claver, SJ (deceased)	Philippines
(N)	Thomas Colgan, SJ	U.S.
(N)	Perianayagam Devanesan	India

(N)	John Donahue, SJ	Lebanon
(P)	Michael L. Doss, SJ	India
(P)	Yvon Christian Elenga, SJ	Congo
(P)	Oscar Alberto Espinosa de Rivero	Peru
(P)	Ricardo Falla, SJ	Honduras
(N)	Thomas Fernandez	India
(P)	Fernando Fernández Franco, SJ	Italy
(N)	Alfredo Ferro, SJ	Colombia
(N)	Thomas Florek, SJ	U.S.
(N)	Jojo Fung, SJ	Malaysia
(N)	Thomas Gannon, SJ	U.S.
(N)	Thomas Giblin, SJ	Ireland
(P)	Wilfredo González, SJ	Venezuela
(P)	Gabriela Gorjón Salcedo	Mexico
(N)	Michel Guéry, SJ	Cote d'Ivoire
(P)	Francis Guntipilly, SJ	India
(N)	Bernardo Haour, SJ	Peru
(N)	Peter Henriot, SJ	Zambia
(N)	Francis X. Hezel, SJ	Federated States of Micronesia
(N)	Robert Hillbert, SJ	U.S.
(N)	Ando Isamu, SJ	Japan
(P)	Carlos James dos Santos, SJ	Brazil
(N)	Francis Jayapathy, SJ	India
(P)	D. Samuel Jesupatham	India
(N)	Jim Joyce, SJ	U.S.
(N)	Mike Kennedy, SJ	U.S.
(N)	Z. Kujinga	Zimbabwe
(P)	Savarimuthu Lazar, SJ	India
(N)	Thierry Linard de Guertechin, SJ	Brazil
(N)	Christopher Llanos, SJ	Jamaica
(N)	Lancy Lobo, SJ	India
(N)	Lucas López, SJ	Paraguay

(P)	Prakash Louis D'Montfort, SJ	India
(N)	Sosthenes Luyembe, SJ	Tanzania
(P)	Adrian Lyons, SJ	Australia
(P)	Maria-Merce Mach-Piera	Spain
(N)	José Magadía, SJ	Philippines
(N)	Kudzai Makoni	Zimbabwe
(N)	Richard Malloy, SJ	U.S.
(N)	Munhumeso Manengi (deceased)	Zimbabwe
(P)	I. John Soosai Manickam, SJ	India
(N)	Pedro Marchetti	Honduras
(P)	M. Marialouis, SJ	India
(N)	Carlos Mejia	Colombia
(N)	Peter McIsaac, SJ	Jamaica
(N)	Janice McLaughlin	Zimbabwe
(N)	Pablo Mella, SJ	Dominican Republic
(N)	Tony Mifsud, SJ	Chile
(P)	Paul Mike, SJ	India
(P)	Odomaro Mubangizi, SJ	Uganda; Cameroon
(N)	Ferdinand Muhigirwa, SJ	D.R. Congo
(N)	Emanuel Mumba, SJ	Zambia
(N)	Alex Muyebe, SJ	Zambia
(N)	Yves Nalet, SJ	Taiwan
(N)	Paul Nicholson, SJ	United Kingdom
(N)	Peter Norden, SJ	Australia
(N)	Stanisław Obirek	Poland
(N)	Victor Pacharoni, SJ	Argentina
(N)	Antony Palackal, SJ	India
(N)	Mathew Pampackal, SJ	India
(N)	Francis Mun-su Park, SJ	South Korea
(P)	Hilary Pereira, SJ	India
(N)	Etienne Perrot, SJ	France
(P)	James Pierce, SJ	U.S.
(N)	Ambrose Pinto, SJ	India

(N)	James Profit, SJ	Canada
(N)	Pierre-André Ranaivoarson, SJ	Madagascar
(P)	John Rapley	Jamaica
(P)	Fulgence Ratsimbazafy, SJ	Madagascar
(P)	Sr. Jane Remson, O. Carm.	U.S.
(N)	William Ryan, SJ	Canada
(N)	Léon de Saint Moulin, SJ	D.R. Congo
(P)	C.S. Saravanan	India
(N)	Juan Carlos Scannone, SJ	Argentina
(N)	Dieter B. Scholz, SJ	Zimbabwe
(N)	Mario Serrano, SJ	Dominican Republic
(N)	Peter Masatsugu Shimokawa, SJ	Japan
(N)	Sr. Bina Stanis	India
(N)	Budi Susanto, SJ	Indonesia
(N)	Joel E. Tabora, SJ	Philippines
(N)	Sahayaraj Thangasamy, SJ	India
(P)	Katarzyna Iwona Tomczak	Poland
(N)	Dominique Tyl, SJ	China
(N)	Jesús Vergara Acevez, SJ	Mexico
(N)	Johannes Wallacher	Germany
(N)	Noel Keizo Yamada, SJ	Japan
(N)	Debi Yomtou, SJ (deceased)	Chad
(N)	Rodrigo Esteban Zarazaga, SJ	Argentina

PART I

FRAMEWORK AND METHODOLOGY

Chapter 1

An Introduction

Globalization is a "big" story and there are many ways of approaching this kind of story. The purpose of this book is to acquire a deeper personal and communal knowledge of how the global economy – what drives the big story – functions, specifically as it is seen through the eyes of the poor and the marginalized, from their cultural and religious perspective. Looking at it this way means seeing the world from the standpoint of other people's cultures and values, as well as our own. What we have written here helps us understand the meaning that the rapidly-changing globalized world has for the poor. In the process of acquiring this understanding, we hope to learn about the values that guide their lives in this different world. As such, this book is also about the researchers themselves, who are finding new perspectives that may lead to new approaches to development policy. Ultimately, this book is an invitation to the reader, especially development practitioners, to test our tools so they may gain insights from the perspective of the poor and the values that motivate them. These insights have a bearing on how we approach development policy. We hope that others will build on what we have begun.

The chapters of this book are the result of our applying a methodology that immerses us in the lives of poor people. We attempt to understand our own understanding of the world in which they live. Our immersion is based on narratives that make more accessible the lives and culture of specific individuals, most of them economically poor. The stories come from around the world. They relate what was happening in the lives of these specific individuals, the protagonists, as their countries increasingly adopted market-driven policies and opened themselves to the global forces of foreign trade and investment in the 1990s and early 2000s. The narrators of the stories are Jesuits (with the exception of two diocesan priests) and their partners in ministry, most of whom work at local Jesuit social centers around the world. These narrators, in effect, are local development practitioners working in local nongovernmental organizations (NGOs) that function as part of one of the oldest global enterprises in the world, the Society of Jesus – the Jesuits. The authors of this book, who partnered with the narrators in the research effort, are Senior Research Fellows at Woodstock Theological Center (WTC) in Washington, D.C., also a Jesuit institution. WTC's mission is to engage in theological reflection on contemporary issues.

Our goal is to understand how the protagonists of our stories came to know their changing reality and how they made decisions and acted on the basis of that knowledge. The socioeconomic environment often limited the choices they had, but they did actively make decisions within those constraints. In particular, we want to know more about the values that these poor people cherish, which guided their decisions. For we argue that this energy can be harnessed and put into the service of truly sustainable development. Thus, the novelty of our methodology is that it provides tools to reflect on the protagonists' decision-making process and the values that seem to have guided this process. Using these tools offers a window into the protagonists' understanding of the meanings and values of what was going on in their world. The perspective from this window, in turn, has the potential of changing both the perspectives and the practices of those who look through it. Such change has practical implications for development policy. Policies informed by the meanings and values that people hold are more likely to produce sustainable development than policies that ignore them.

Our approach is not aimed at a judgment of whether globalization and prevailing socioeconomic structures have been, overall, good or bad. Although our methodology does provide the tools to do so, such a goal would require a much larger sample and different objectives than what we have in this research. Nonetheless, even within our small sample of narratives, it is difficult to ignore the challenges that globalization has brought to the protagonists. Nor it is possible to discount the barriers that existing political and socioeconomic structures have imposed on the development of these people. The suffering that the narrators witness among the protagonists of the narratives was too palpable for us to remain blind to these forces – although evaluating them was not our main objective.

This book makes available to others the knowledge we have gained and the research tools we have developed to see globalization through the perspective of the poor. These others include, in the first instance, Jesuit social centers and Jesuit institutions of higher education, but also other professionals involved in development at the local, regional, and country levels. We believe such professionals will find our approach to understanding poor people and generating policy to be of interest, for we also believe that seeing the world in this way enhances development policy and practice.

Our method can provide new insights into the world of the people whose lives development professionals are trying to improve. Even though some of the insights that we gained will appear intuitive to those who have been working at the local level for any significant period of time, we believe the approach itself will open horizons for development professionals at all levels. For professionals who find that development efforts "from the top" do not fully reach their mark, this book presents an indispensable aspect of the approach to development "from below," which can at least be complementary. In this "from below" perspective we are forced to appreciate decision-making by the poor in a holistic fashion and within the cultural, moral, and religious contexts in which they live and in which they are motivated to decide and act the way they do. Understanding poor people in this way enables the practitioner to pursue policies in which the poor are empowered to drive the development process, guided by their own values. In doing so, there is hope for a more sustainable development.

We also hope that in the future this knowledge will be made available to people locked in poverty in ways that they can use to work together with others – from the world of business, government, and civil society – to create sustainable development alternatives from below. By participating in popular education approaches, people who are poor can understand their own voice. So, speaking for themselves, they can work "from below" in new ways. We can then accompany them as they, in their own voice, articulate what is going on in their lives to people outside of their environments. The tools we designed and apply in this book, tools of basic interpretation, can support this communal, cultural discernment.

In the following three sections of this chapter, we describe the globalization process and the notion of culture that informs this book and then we introduce the reader to our approach to economic development. The chapter then provides the highlights of how our research methodology unfolded and we built the necessary tools. It concludes with a description of the structure of the book.

OUR FOCUS IN LOOKING AT THE GLOBALIZATION PROCESS

For the purposes of our research, our point of reference is the economic aspect of globalization. In general, globalization refers to the intensification and acceleration of an ever more open flow of communication and movement of people, technologies, money, goods, images, and ideas across national borders. This cross-border interaction links individuals, organizations, countries, and cultures into a global economy. The economic globalization process that is the focus of this book began in the late 1980s and early 1990s. Similar to preceding waves of globalization, there have been reductions in barriers to international trade that led to an increase of trade in goods such as machinery. But, in addition, this wave has been characterized by a large increase in the international trade in so-called services, such as banking, telecommunication, media, and transportation. In addition, there has been an unprecedented growth in the flows of capital and people across national borders. The reduction in barriers to the flow of trade and capital in this globalization wave was accomplished mainly through international trade agreements, in particular the Uruguay Round of trade negotiations reached in 1995, but also through regional agreements such as the North American Free Trade Agreement (NAFTA).

Supporting this most recent globalization wave is a sea change in economic philosophy worldwide that affected both international and domestic economic policy. This has been particularly the case since the fall of the Soviet Union and its communist system in the early 1990s. Around the world, and with only rare exceptions, the belief in a state-driven economic system that had prevailed in many countries was superseded by a new belief in a market-driven system. The change in philosophy also was accompanied by a historical reality: the old state-directed economic systems in many non-communist countries culminated in major financial crises in the 1980s and 1990s. As these countries searched for a way out of the crisis, the support available from the international financial community (the World Bank and the International Monetary Fund, as well as various regional development banks) came accompanied by a "conditionality," which demanded the adoption of the new market-driven economic philosophy and a "structural adjustment" of the borrowing countries' economy.

While economic philosophy worldwide was changing, an unprecedented explosion in electronic communications technology was also taking place, in the form of such developments as the cellular phone, the personal computer, and the Internet. This new technology made it possible to evade previously existing restrictions; for example, cellular telephones could circumvent the failures of government-owned telephone companies and even efficient established telephone companies. It also enabled the newly-liberalized economic forces to flow at an ever-increasing speed and reach unprecedented levels. The result has been a never-before realized network of national market economies. It is an integrated and interdependent global economy, with huge flows linking countries through increasing volumes of trade in goods and services and – especially characteristic of this wave – finances. Moreover, this global economy saw new electronic technology increase the proximity of, and connections between, faraway peoples and countries.

At the local level, the new economic philosophy, with its reduced role for the state in the economy, meant an increase in the role of the private sector. Privatization of state-owned assets became a major feature. Countries opening to the rest of the world meant people's exposure to new things: to new products they could now consume at lower prices; to competition from workers who could produce more efficiently abroad; to new media and other countries' lifestyles; to new political ideas and civil society institutions; to non-governmental organizations (NGOs') agendas around the world; to the new ways of learning and social structures that the Internet now made possible. This represented a confrontation between the traditional values of the society and the values embedded in the new global forces. For the individual, such as the protagonists in our narratives, this globalization required a reevaluation of what is considered good, worthy of being pursued, in the whole spectrum of socioeconomic, cultural, and personal possibilities.

OUR NOTION OF CULTURE

This book's notion of culture is empirical, not normative. This approach affects the way we see the relationship between the global economy and cultures. In our empirical approach to culture, we see how people do not live in isolation; they are part of a local society and culture and that local culture evolves as its individuals search for meaning and carry out the business of living their lives. Both the material (art, craft, technology) and the non-material (values, attitudes, beliefs) aspects of culture are essential elements of human life. They make up the framework within which communities function. They give common meaning (interpretative function) and value (normative function) to their economic, social, political, and religious activities. Moreover, they operate through institutions (family, church, market, government, voluntary associations) whose processes can either develop or break down over time: generate progress or decline.

In this project, we adopted the following definition of culture:

> … the way in which a group of people live, think, feel, organize themselves, celebrate, and share life. In every culture, there are underlying systems of values, meanings, and views of the world, which are expressed, visibly, in language, gestures, symbols, rituals, and styles.

> **—Thirty-Fourth General Congregation of the Society of Jesus**
> **(GC-34), Decree 4, No. 1**

As a country opens itself to market forces and the global economy, its citizens are affected not only as individuals, but through its social and cultural institutions. The whole local culture is exposed to change, and social tensions emerge between what is valued in the tradition and the new forces for change. People manage these tensions from the core of their inherited ways of understanding and valuing their world – from within their local cultural context. It is from within their own culture that they are affected by and respond to the changes brought about by globalization – changes often initiated outside their local culture.

Institutions associated with the global economy bring new meanings and values into local cultural settings. International trade and investment, as well as modern communications media, transportation, and tourism disseminate ideas and behavior that alter people's daily life. Local cultures are exposed to new production methods, consumption patterns, and leisure opportunities, as well as to new points of view. These new points of view include things such as consumerism and emphasis on productivity, but also notions in which, for example, it is acceptable for human rights to include gender equality and for government to involve democratic processes.

Because the new ideas come from outside and carry the momentum of common global attraction, an individual easily feels the tension between what the tradition values and the new ways brought about by global forces. On the one hand, a person can reassert herself through the rejection of everything new associated with globalization. On the other hand, this person can uncritically assimilate the "global culture." Between these two extremes, this person can reinterpret and reevaluate the traditional and new ways of life and doing business, and seek a variety of alternative ways of taking responsibility for adapting and changing. This is the process that we study as we analyze the values that drive the decisions of the protagonists in the narratives.

Successful adaptation depends on the extent to which people can forge a new consensus on how to reinterpret and adapt their inherited meanings and values. As they open themselves to interaction with other cultures, a certain pluralism develops within the culture itself. Given the growing openness of cultures and the uneven ways in which they interact and influence one another, these public discussions take place among cultures as well as within them. In a world of cultural pluralism, each culture has a voice and no single culture can make itself normative for the others. We all must find the norm in the moral and religious values that inform our global interaction. In this situation, the higher viewpoint of the global common good can result only from inter-cultural dialogue that deals with tensions between market and society in economic policy discussions.

OUR APPROACH TO ECONOMIC DEVELOPMENT

We view economic development as a complex process that is both economic and philosophical. As stated in the tradition embodied in papal documents like *Populorum Progressio,* "Development…must be integral" (par. 14).

First, we acknowledge that economic development is an integral part of human history and the evolution of the human species. When human history moves forward to the common benefit of the whole earth, we consider it progress. Economic development, therefore, is an aspect of progress that overcomes the evils of human misery.

Secondly, economic development is an integral aspect of the evolution of human knowledge and human consciousness. As such, it results from human initiative, is under human control, and serves human purposes. Technological and theoretical advances pave the way for improved standards of living and the economic systems that make them possible. Hence, our understanding of economic development goes beyond an exclusively material perspective. Development in human history involves "significant qualitative change usually building up incrementally" (Jane Jacobs, *The*

Nature of Economies, 2000, p. 15). The accumulation of ideas and knowledge is an integral part of development.

Thirdly, economic development has what we might call a redemptive aspect to it. In other words, it is a dynamic force that results in the reversal of the trends that work against human progress. In this sense, it moves humanity in the direction of greater freedom by replacing patterns of human thought and conduct that act as impediments to people's capabilities.

In this general framework, development professionals will appreciate the need for an approach to economic development that goes beyond traditional ways of thinking in economics. Thus, the methodology we have developed to analyze the narratives in this book addresses two common biases found in more traditional approaches to development. We believe these biases often undermine the efforts of the development community to alleviate the poverty and the misery of the masses who live at the bottom tier of the world's economies. The first bias we call the *technical economism bias.* This measures development primarily, and often exclusively, by socioeconomic achievements, ignoring that people also have other values critical to their lives. The second we call the *victim bias.* In it, poor people are seen primarily, if not solely, as victims of the prevalent political and socioeconomic structures, thus ignoring the fact that poor people are also authors of their own history and agents of development.

The Technical Economism Bias in Addressing Development

Development, normatively considered, involves the realization of potentialities, the flourishing of human beings. Traditionally, development has focused almost exclusively on the technical issues associated with economic growth and institution building; and it has been measured by social variables such as income per capita, education level, and health achievements. We argue that there is more to human development. We believe that sustainable development cannot be measured solely in terms of GNP per capita and the achievement of sociopolitical objectives — essential as these goals are. We believe that development objectives should acknowledge the following:

1. People need "meaning" in their lives, and they need a sense of belonging and of being appreciated — the stuff of which culture is made.

2. People need a sense of their lives being about "doing the right thing" – about being morally good.

3. People need to make sense of life's great mysteries: love, suffering, death.

A development program that focuses solely on GNP per capita, socioeconomic statistics, and institution-building can easily ignore the cultural, moral, and religious values that guide people's lives. Certainly, if it were possible to increase income – and the availability of food, shelter, and health that income can buy – without tapping into what people value culturally, morally, and religiously, it would be easy to ignore all these other values. But that is not the case. All these values are interrelated in practice. Water to a tribal woman in India can be more than a source of hydration; it can be a source of cultural and religious meaning when the water comes out of the village's ancestral spring. Work to an active union member can be more than power to bargain with management; it can be self-fulfillment in obtaining justice for others. Development policies and strategies that ignore what human beings desire beyond economic and social values are problematic.

Most directly, they run the risk of not even achieving the intended higher income and better quality of life. Furthermore, even when economic and social progress are achieved, there is a risk of a decline in other areas in the society; i.e., people having a higher standard of living, but feeling alienated as they see everything that gave meaning to their lives being destroyed. Ultimately, this cultural, moral, and religious decline will undermine economic and social progress in a way that political solutions will not be able to fix. Deeply-held values need to be addressed in all spheres of life – not only at the economic and social levels. Thus, development in this book refers to development in the larger context of "value ethics," in contrast to other ethical approaches to development.

Viewing development exclusively in terms of socioeconomic values essentially assumes that addressing technical economic and institutional problems – such as low income and lack of education – by itself will generate progress, and that this is enough. In our more integrated approach, addressing these technical problems is necessary, but not sufficient. Even when socioeconomic variables might be improving, decline, instead of progress, of that society might occur. That would be the case if cultural, moral, and religious values were decaying. If the "way of life" of the society becomes meaningless, if "doing the right thing" becomes totally self-serving and unjust, and if participation and commitment cease to be valued, disintegration at the cultural, moral, and religious levels will take place: the community will break down. In a culturally and morally disintegrating society, economic and institutional values will ultimately falter. They are inextricably linked. The large sweeps in history of expansion and decline of empires are testimony to these relationships. The same is true at the local community, regional, and country levels. But it is not an inexorable cycle: economic and social recovery can reappear in the midst of decline when attention is given to cultural, moral, and religious values. In religious terms, God's grace is always available.

To be clear, we are not arguing that development should put any less emphasis on improving the material lot of the millions who live in abject poverty, disease-ridden, and without access to even the most basic education. We are arguing for explicit attention to those values of people that go beyond economic and institutional ones, even when pursuing only basic economic and social goals. We believe that development programs that take place at the expense of people's motivations in the cultural, moral, and religious spheres will not achieve their potential and will ultimately not be sustainable. We should also point out that consideration of cultural, moral, and religious values can take place within a macro-economic structure that supports the efficient, although probably not unfettered, operation of markets.

The Victim Bias in Working with Poor People

It is easy to see poor people as victims of sociopolitical structures that have kept them from meeting even basic needs for food, shelter, health, and education. Poor people often are victims of these structures. From a moral point of view, we can also say that the poor are victims of our personal and institutional indifference – in fact, victims of human rights violations. But we believe that poor people are much more than victims. They also are conscious and intelligent beings with human dignity. They find meaning in their world and their actions, in spite of the limitations imposed by their environment, and they are guided by what they value. Their energy, like any other human being's, lies in these meanings and values. Failing to understand them undermines the goals of any development policy.

If we are serious about the importance of cultural, moral, and religious values in the development process, by necessity we must also be serious about involving the people who can best speak about their meanings and values as development policy is planned and implemented. Great progress would be made in discussing development policy by always engaging anthropologists, ethicists, and religious leaders to throw light on the communities' larger values. But we argue that we must go even further. The development process produces changes that affect the whole range of meanings and values that people hold. A need often emerges to make tradeoffs within traditional values and between what the tradition values and the new values that the development process brings with it. We argue that, as a matter of principle, the poor people who would be most directly affected by the changes have the right not only to be fully informed but also to be the ones who ultimately decide to enter into the bargain that development involves.

It is often said that poor people cannot be involved in planning, let alone implementing, the process of development because they really are unsophisticated and do not understand. This is clearly the case if one has in mind asking them (or, for that matter, most of the population in a developed country) technical questions; e.g., the most appropriate size of the government's fiscal balance. However, we firmly believe that poor people are capable of intelligent decision-making within the boundaries of their own experience. If they can be properly informed, if the technical questions can be translated into the language of their own experience, they can in turn not only inform the planning process but also suggest creative alternatives. Policies that do not involve the poor in their formulation not only disrespect these human beings whom they purport to help; they are likely to fall short of the goals they pursue on behalf of the poor. Much has been written along these lines by experts in development ethics.

Our "bottom-up" approach to development, in contrast to the more traditional "top-down" one, implies a different attitude and approach towards the poor. It is a subtle difference, but it is a very important one. It has been advocated by many development experts, such as Paulo Freire (1921–1997), and pioneers such as Louis Joseph Lebret (1897–1966) and Denis Goulet (1931–2006), as well as policymakers such as David Ellerman (*Helping People Help Themselves,* 2005). This approach is about "being with" the poor as fellow human beings who can make intelligent decisions within their own world, instead of "doing for" the poor as victims who are objects of our concern. We can know the reality of someone as a human being only within the actual context of that person's life, where he or she is at home, within the particular local community and culture where that person lives and acts upon his or her values. It is about the development practitioner learning by seeing through the eyes of the people who are supposed to benefit from the intended development – learning what is important to people, learning and respecting their values, letting them help lead the process in the context of a dialogue among all the actors. We believe that a true sensitivity to people's meanings and values can be obtained only when we ourselves come to know them more intimately in a form of civic and cultural friendship, finding a way of personal empathy.

Central to our position is the belief that we must get to know how the poor, as real people, understand their situation, rather than treat them as statistics; we must look at them as subjects who are capable of shaping their own destiny, rather than as objects – problems to be solved. Unless we do these things, we run the risk of solving the wrong problem and endangering the achievement of sustainable development for the poor. If we treat poor people only as victims, we run the risk of perpetuating their victimhood without ever empowering them.

Before leaving the subject of what we have called the *victim bias,* we should mention that this bias often has a mirror bias in how we look at the other sectors in society. This bias shows itself when these other sectors are seen exclusively as perpetrators. As much as we do not want to see the poor cast only as victims, we do not want either to run the risk of casting other actors only as victimizers or perpetrators. We believe that in practice sustainable development policy requires an understanding of the motivation of the other actors and, even more, these other actors' reflections on the life of poor people and the development process. The planning stage of the development process should provide a venue for the various participants to interact with the poor and with one another. Only then can all the parties, including the poor, come to appreciate the aspirations, values, as well as complexity and institutional constraints that each participant brings to the process. Sustainable development requires engaging *all* relevant parties in building community for the common global good.

RESEARCH METHODOLOGY HIGHLIGHTS

Now that we have considered our approach to globalization, culture, and development, we turn to a brief description of the research project that led to this book. This description includes the researchers who participated in the project, as well as a consideration of how our research unfolded historically as we built the tools we needed.

Network of Researchers Locally Grounded

Structurally, a major highlight of the methodology used in this book is that it is based on the results of a joint effort of more than fifty Jesuit social centers worldwide that collaborated with the Woodstock Theological Center (WTC) – the principal researchers – in the Global Economy and Cultures (GEC) research project. The Jesuit social centers brought with them the grassroots experience of the project participants: Jesuits and their partners who live and work closely with poor people throughout the world – and who themselves often are native to the countries and cultures where they work. In addition to the Jesuits, two diocesan priests participated in the project. Thus, the project participants embodied a unique combination of rich diversity and a common framework. Each of the project participants was part of, and lived in, a different local culture – often one into which they were born – and which they shared with the narrative protagonists. However, they had in common the Jesuit training and spirituality that made it possible for them to have a common language and discernment methodology in the project. Even the two diocesan priests had had the experience of making the Spiritual Exercises of St. Ignatius. The Jesuit approach and spirituality held in common came accompanied by the unique understanding of a culture that only a local person can have. The cooperative effort between the stories' narrators, who worked at these Jesuit social centers, and the WTC researchers was interactive and took two major avenues: (1) electronic exchanges using e-mails, without which this project would have been practically impossible; and (2) a series of international and regional one-week long conference meetings. The list of Jesuits and others who participated in the GEC project appears in the Acknowledgements section at the beginning of the book.

Narrative Tools of Research Globally Shared

In order to see the global economy through the eyes of poor people, from the beginning the project's main research tool was narrative stories that were rich in local details. Beyond that starting point, however, our research tools can best be seen as building blocks that emerged as earlier tools were found insufficient to reach our goals in understanding the meanings and values of poor people as they encountered the global economy. The major tool building blocks in our methodology fall into two phases.

Phase I: Tools for Data Gathering
(in Close Interaction between Narrators and WTC Researchers)

1. Gathering of the original narratives

2. Enrichment of the original narratives to differentiate the events directly related to the country's greater reliance on the market economy from pre-existing conditions; also enrichment to include other actors

3. Cultural analysis of what was happening with the protagonists and their communities along six traditional development themes: consumption, production, migration, social relations, political power relations, and religious experience and expression

4. Moral reflection on the changes observed in the protagonists and their communities with elements involving spirituality

A detailed description of the methodological tools used during Phase I of the project appears in Chapter 3, "Research Methodology, Phase I: Narrative Data Gathering, Cultural Analysis, and Moral Reflection."

During Phase I, the participating social centers around the world began by selecting a "narrator" (a Jesuit in most cases) to gather narratives that documented the lives of specific local poor people – the protagonists of the narratives – and their communities as they were touched by the economic globalization taking place in the 1990s and early 2000s. From the approximately fifty original narratives, twenty were selected for data enrichment and further development. Then, from among those twenty narratives, ten were selected to conduct an in-depth cultural analysis, in which the narrators began by answering questions prepared by WTC researchers. The cultural analysis continued in a dialogue and consultation between the narrators and WTC researchers. That culminated in the Third International Consultation meeting, which featured a moral reflection on the narrative data gathered up to that point for the ten selected narratives. After that came further work on the ten selected narratives, the substitution of one of the narratives, and the addition of another one (thus bringing the total of selected narratives to eleven). Phase I concluded with the Fourth International Consultation meeting of about forty of the project participants, including the narrators of the final eleven selected narratives. In that meeting, there was an opportunity for all the project participants to share the insights they had gained and compare and contrast the experiences of the protagonists of the eleven selected narratives. In the eleven narrative chapters in this book, the first two sections – "Narrative" and "Cultural Analysis" – were written based on the data and analysis derived from applying the methodological tools of Phase I.

It should be noted that the historical context of our narratives is the late 1990s–early 2000s. Our intent was to capture and analyze what was going on with the protagonists of the narratives at that moment in time. We did not intend to follow the developments since then, so there was no attempt to update them. The fact that the narratives are dated does not detract from our research objectives.

As we sat down at WTC to prepare to publish the results of the project of what we now call Phase I, we realized we were not yet satisfied that we had a good understanding of the meaning that globalization had for the protagonists and the values that guided them. We had collected a great deal of information on the protagonists and their communities, and the events that were taking place in the culture. But, although already focusing on the decisions that the protagonists of the stories had made, we were still looking at them primarily from our own perspective – the perspective of the narrators and WTC researchers. We were seeing the protagonists through a combined set of lenses. First was the lens worn by the narrators, the Jesuits telling the story and interacting with both the WTC researchers in the electronic dialogue and the other participants attending the International Consultations. Second was the lens worn by the WTC researchers in framing the questions about narrative facts, guiding the cultural and moral analysis, and interpreting the results. We still understood our protagonists primarily through our own eyes – and still saw them primarily as victims. We needed a more direct tool to get to what was going on within the protagonists themselves.

Phase II: Tools for Reflection

1. Understanding the protagonists' meanings and values by inference from the actions they took: what was happening in their consciousness and what values motivated them

2. Researchers' reflection on their own knowledge of the protagonists before and after gaining a better knowledge of the protagonists' meanings and values

3. Consideration of development policy implications

Chapter 4, "Research Methodology, Phase II: Finding the Protagonists' Meanings and Values," describes in detail the conceptual framework and approach behind the tools of Phase II methodology.

The tools of Phase II methodology begin by trying to deconstruct what might have been going on in the protagonists' consciousness as they moved from experiencing in their own lives the encounter with the global economy to the actions that we captured in the narratives. That is, we try to deconstruct the protagonists' knowledge of what was transpiring, even if they were unable to articulate it. More specifically, the tool was designed to detect the values driving the decision and the adjustments in those values required by the observed actions. The application of this tool to the narrative data gave us the perspective we had been seeking. Furthermore, our reflections showed that our attitudes and values towards the protagonists and the development process had begun to change.

The Phase II methodology was applied to six of the narratives. In five of these narratives we worked closely with the original narrators. This analysis is presented in Chapter 6 and the sections in Chapters 7-10 entitled "The Protagonist's Meanings and Values as Reflected in Her Decisions" and "Researchers' Reflection." In one other narrative, we conducted an experiment by introducing a new "narrator," who was asked to reflect on the protagonist of the narrative before and after applying the Phase II methodology. This experiment is reported in the Appendix to the final chapter, Chapter 17. Because of time and resource constraints, the Phase II methodology was not applied to the remaining five narratives that are presented in Part III of the book.

The application of Phase II methodology to the five narratives presented in Part II of the book was done with a level of detail that we hope will be useful to those wishing to apply the methodology themselves to their specific development situations. For the reader who is working among poor people, this presentation provides an illustration of how to see through a new lens the life of people for whom they might be service providers. It shows the questioning process and provides a guide for the practitioner to search for answers among the people with whom he or she works. That might affect how they approach development policy. Of course, this methodology is not limited in its application to people who are poor, although that is the context in which we use it in this project.

Early in Phase II of the project, we at WTC also came to the realization that in our approach to research we, the principal researchers, were also part of the subject to be researched. We found out we needed to scrutinize what we ourselves had been thinking and doing at each stage of the project, lest our preconceived views of development filter what we were learning about the protagonists of the narratives as well as the narrators who generated the narratives. To preserve our objectivity in working with the narrative data, we had to begin questioning what it was that we were doing at each step of the project in order to counter our biases, of which we were now more aware. We had been on a journey together with both the protagonists of the narratives and the narrators. We had to reflect not only on how the protagonists were creating new meanings and values, but also on how we ourselves were finding new meanings and values along the research trail. We had to apply to ourselves the same approach to understanding what had been going on in *our* consciousness that we had to apply to the protagonists of the narratives. Our own decisions in the course of the project became research data, as much as the data provided by the narratives. If we believe in the centrality of engaging poor people in a truly open fashion in order to learn from them, chances are that we ourselves, and therefore our approach, will be changed. We were changed and this Introduction itself reflects those changes in the authors.

STRUCTURE OF THE BOOK

This book is divided into four parts. Part I goes beyond this introductory chapter to provide a detailed framework for the research that led to this book. Chapter 2 presents an introduction to our theological framework. Chapters 3 and 4 provide a detailed exposition of the research tools that were created for developing the narrative data and carrying out our cultural and value analysis of the narratives. These chapters were referred to in the preceding section, which provided the highlights of our research methodology. Chapter 3 covers the tools developed during Phase I of the project and Chapter 4 presents the tools applied during Phase II.

The heart of the book is presented in Parts II and III. Part II contains the narratives to which both Phase I and II methodologies were applied; Part III presents the narratives which, because of resource constraints, were analyzed using only the Phase I methodology.

By looking at the last section of the corresponding narrative chapters in Parts II and III, it is possible to compare our reflections after applying only Phase I methodology with our insights after applying Phase II. Under the heading "Interpretation," the last sections in Chapters 11-16 in

Part III contain our reflections on the narratives after applying only the Phase I methodology tools. The sections entitled "Researchers' Reflections" in Chapter 6-10 present the understanding that we gained from applying the tools of both Phase I and II methodologies.

Finally, in Chapter 17 in Part IV, we provide a retrospective view of all the narratives, and offer a broader viewpoint from which the narrative analyses can be viewed. From this broader viewpoint, we also offer comments on implications of our findings for development policy.

Chapter 2

Theological Framework

In Chapter 1 we introduced three concepts central to understanding the research scope behind this book: our special focus on globalization, our notion of culture, and our approach to economic development. In this chapter we go further by offering an opportunity for the reader to acquire a deeper understanding of the overall framework within which the authors operate. Here we highlight two related areas: our approach to theology and religion, and the elements of Jesuit pedagogy in our research methodology. This chapter is intended to provide those who may be curious with a brief view of how the authors of this book understand their own relationship to religion, cultures, and Jesuit pedagogy. We hope this will help others involved in development understand our approach to religious, moral, and cultural values. However, adherence to the religious tradition that we come from is not a necessary prerequisite to engaging in the kind of development research we are presenting. Furthermore, our approach is philosophically compatible with other intellectual traditions. But the reader for whom religion and theology are not relevant may want to consider skipping this chapter.

OUR APPROACH TO RELIGION AND THEOLOGICAL REFLECTION

We refer to religion as a practical matter, and theology as the discipline that deals with religious belief and practice. Religion can be defined as a set of beliefs and practices relating to faith and worship of a supernatural power accepted as the creator and governor of the universe. Theology is a branch of knowledge, one of whose functions is to bridge belief and practices rooted in religious faith and their cultural framework. Theological reflection, since the Second Vatican Council of the Roman Catholic tradition (1962 – 1965), has emerged as an experience-based way of carrying out this role of theology. While this book does not require theological reflection in the strict sense, it emerges from an understanding of the relationship between religion and theology.

Friedrich Heiler, in his article in *The History of Religions* (edited by M. Eliade and J. Kitagawa, 1959), found a number of commonalities in many world religions, such as Taoism, Buddhism, Hinduism, Zoroastrian Mazdaism, Islam, Judaism, and Christianity. These common features allow us to see how diverse beliefs and practices can be construed in a global context. Bernard Lonergan, SJ, in his book *Method in Theology* (1971), says that these features are implicit in the human experience of being in love in an unrestricted way, that is, with someone who is transcendent. According to this broad notion, religious beliefs and practices carry the overarching meaning and values of our lives, our meta-narrative or "big story" experience, of being in love in an unrestricted way. They become the ultimate touchstone for all our other values and involve a human response to the facts of good and evil, progress and decline, and the character of the universe. This response is expressed in pluralistic ways.

Judaeo-Christian beliefs, understood according to the radical reforms of the Second Vatican Council, are the setting for our theology in this book. Those reforms marked a watershed in the Roman Catholic tradition's approach to theology and its integral relationship to experience and practice. In this tradition, as well as in the traditions that Heiler studied, religion is a general life orientation open to transcendence and is an essentially positive and dynamic force in the world. While religious experience can be institutionalized in ways that are divisive of human community, our view is that in the long run, religious faith plays a positive and meaningful role in societies when it is world-affirming and based on self-donating love. It is thus an expression of the human search for goodness; it is essentially a creative and healing force and not a violent and destructive one.

This particular theological tradition – the Roman Catholic one – from which we reflect on development and culture takes a positive view of the universe. It believes that we human beings find ourselves in an essentially friendly universe in which good overcomes evil through love. Moreover, our approach to religious belief and theology views the history of the universe as an open system that is *evolutionary*. It seeks to understand the tensions between good and evil in the interplay of three vectors or forces. One is *progress*, the pattern of development that occurs when people are true to themselves as originators of value and cooperative with the goodness of creation. The violation of this pattern we call *decline*, when biases distort objectivity and lead to valuing that disregards the long-term good of others: it supports destructive and unjust patterns of behavior. The third vector is *redemption*, the healing force of self-sacrificing love, whose role is to undo the mischief of decline and restore the cumulative process of progress. It is a divine gift that is offered universally and always available, always at work. Because these three vectors interweave throughout the history of human development, they are relevant to the way we approach issues of development.

This approach to religion and theology, which we have briefly described, is embedded in our approach to economic development. As discussed in Chapter 1, our view in this book is that if we learn more about the religious, moral, and cultural values that guide the lives of poor people, we will be in a better position to understand what goes on – as well as contribute to policies that result in sustainable development – than if we were to operate with what we have called the *economism bias*. This broader way in which we approach development we call theological reflection. This is the framework that allows us to discover the religious, moral, and cultural values that guide human decision-making. However, it is not necessary that the reader be a professional theologian to follow this approach.

Carrying the process of theological reflection means taking all human experience and trying to understand it from the highest possible viewpoint. In the Christian tradition, this means understanding development (progress) from the perspective of non-violent, self-sacrificing love (redemption through the Cross) that reverses the evil of personal and systemic injustice (decline). It leads us to commit to what is most authentic in that experience. The higher the viewpoint with which we approach any phenomenon, the more likely we are to come closer to the truth about it. So when we speak of theology and "theological reflection on the human problems of our day" (phrase used by Pedro Arrupe, SJ), we mean several things. A closer look at five characteristics of our theological framework will elucidate this.

First, this theological framework is more than the kind of academic discipline that applies doctrine to existing human concerns. It starts with experience, not with the consideration of religious values in the abstract. It is a sustained attempt to understand the relationship between human beings and their creator or higher power, God. Those genuinely engaging in reflecting on the human problem can benefit from the fruits of that reflection, even if they do not share that worldview. The starting point of this sustained attempt is the stance of those who desire and seek wisdom, the deepest meaning of life, in whatever ways this relationship takes place; the stance of those whose concern is with the total human situation.

Secondly, this theological framework involves operating from a perspective that genuinely seeks the global common good, believing that good is attainable in the light of either religious faith in a divine creator or, if not religious belief, in the light of the conviction that we live in a basically friendly evolutionary universe. Although this conviction can be a non-religious one, our approach understands it to be compatible with the notion of a God, a higher being who embodies the highest values beyond imaginable goodness and love. From this vantage point, our approach to theological reflection focuses not simply on religious values requiring doctrinal adherence to a particular religious faith, but rather on what actually happens to people – to individuals, groups, nations, and cultures in the light of human values that are shared by non-religious as well as religious people. In other words, without demanding that one hold the religious values on which this book is grounded, our approach to theological reflection in a pluralistic world respects all people of good will.

Thirdly, our approach to religion and theological reflection in our pluralistic world is open to all development practitioners who want to research the values operative in other people's religious experience and who seek a deeper understanding of how those values play a significant role in their particular cultural setting. Hence it should be clear that the point of view from which we approach theological reflection seeks to discover and reflect upon the vital energies that drive people's decisions. It does not require that the development practitioner and researcher share the religious experience of either the authors of this book or of the subjects of our narratives.

Fourthly, and consequently, the only thing required for the development practitioner to find our approach of interest is to accept that religious values are an important source of vital energies for many people; that religious values color everything these people do and that these values are reflected in their cultures. The premise of this book is that sustainable development is possible only if our strategies and policies highlight the importance of religious, moral, and cultural values to the subjects whom we accompany. If religious values are viewed by development practitioners as impediments to development, a great deal of money and human effort will be lost.

Finally, in order to accomplish this, our theological reflection also needs to be interdisciplinary because it takes seriously what goes on both in the economy and in the changing culture. Globalization is a historical process involving economic, social, cultural, and political relations with varying degrees of emphasis.

These five characteristics of our theological framework underpin our approach to globalization and cultures. If religion plays a major role in cultures, then we need to understand how our own religious experience relates to the cultures and religions of others. In this sense, theological reflection is the lens through which we look at the role of religious belief in the cultures of others as well as in our own.

OUR APPROACH TO RESEARCH METHODOLOGY: JESUIT PEDAGOGY

Our approach to grassroots research in this book, not surprisingly, can be understood within a Jesuit framework. The Jesuit pedagogy in this research provides us with a consistent way to handle the kinds of research questions that we face. Historically, Jesuits developed a pedagogy or approach to education that broke with traditional pedagogies of sixteenth-century Europe. They embraced Renaissance humanism. Now they have brought this humanist tradition into the twenty-first century by embracing modern science. One of the characteristics of this pedagogy is that it helps us improve our capacity to read the hidden signs of development that are embedded in the decisions of the protagonists of our narratives. They help us to see the global economy through the eyes of the poor. (We should note that for the purposes of this book the terms *Jesuit* and *Ignatian* can be used interchangeably. The term *Ignatian* is an adjective coming from the name Ignatius [of Loyola], the founder of the Jesuits.)

The foundations of the contemporary Jesuit framework for our approach to research are found in the official documents of the Jesuit Order generated between 1975 and 2008. In these documents, the approach to the Jesuit mission of the service of faith through the promotion of justice integrates both cultural and religious value considerations into everything Jesuits do, including research: Jesuits will say, "finding God in all things." This integration turns out to be the foundation for a new and creative framework that characterizes the approach taken in this book.

We can consider the pedagogy of our approach to research as comprising three building blocks. These building blocks form an integrated approach. However, many constitutive parts of these building blocks also can be found in secular works in the fields of anthropology and economic development. In describing our approach to research in this section, we will make reference to some of these secular authors.

The three building blocks of Jesuit pedagogy in our approach to research are:

1. *Spiritual:* referring to a personal disposition of "interiority" that is essential to the Jesuit spirituality of the *Spiritual Exercises* of St. Ignatius of Loyola

2. *Anthropological:* our approach to human nature and the notions of culture and value

3. *Intellectual and educational:* practically related to the Ignatian or Jesuit structured approach to knowing, imparting knowledge, and putting knowledge into practice

First Building Block: Jesuit Spiritual Framework

In order to understand what is at the heart of the Jesuit intellectual and educational tradition and what shapes our anthropological approach to grassroots research, we must first turn to the Jesuit spiritual framework. In our research enterprise, this spiritual framework shapes the way we perceive and work with data about what goes on within the person. Simply put, our interest in this kind of data comes directly from the approach to human knowing that is embedded in the *Spiritual Exercises* of St. Ignatius. For Jesuits, human knowledge includes all kinds of knowledge: scientific knowledge, spiritual knowledge (wisdom rooted in carnal knowledge), and self-knowledge (the result of sustained reflection on what goes on within one's mind and heart).

Three key terms, involving three aspects of our methodology, are embedded in the Jesuit spiritual tradition: radical personal/social transformation (called *conversion*); reflective decision-making from within (called *discernment*); and heightened awareness of the process of knowing (called *interiority*).

Conversion, discernment, and interiority relate to one another within the context of spiritual freedom. Freedom, conceived in this non-materialistic way, is the capacity to decide for oneself what one wants to make of oneself, regardless of the external constraints that one experiences. From a religious point of view, this kind of freedom can only be achieved with divine assistance – the action of divine love.

Let us now examine how conversion, discernment, and interiority reflect Jesuit pedagogy. We will first dwell on the process of conversion at greater length, establishing its relationship to economic development.

Conversion

In economic terms, conversion refers to the practice of exchanging one type of financial instrument, such as stocks and bonds or currency, for another. It involves a change from owning one thing to owning another. However, this kind of change is limited to the material world. It is "out there" and does not ordinarily involve a change within the persons who are engaged in the transaction.

We can note another use of the term conversion in economic thought. In *Development as Freedom* (1999), Amartya Sen uses conversion to refer to the enhancement of human capabilities and the elements that go into the opportunity to pursue what is good. Sen says that "account would have to be taken not only of the primary goods the persons respectively hold, but also of the relevant personal characteristics that govern the conversion of primary goods into the person's ability to promote her ends" (p. 74). Here the term conversion refers not only to a change in the material world, but also a transformation that goes on in the individual who goes from the state of not having to the state of acquiring and using primary goods. Before the conversion, the goods were not able to be "humanized." After the conversion, they become part of the person's power to pursue higher values and effectuate good both for herself and for others. Sen adds this new dimension to the economic term conversion when he relates it to his creative new human capability theory.

In a Jesuit framework, we understand Sen's approach to conversion to be integral to the work of development practitioners. Development practitioners are participants in the conversion, as defined by Sen, when they accompany the poor. As we explained Chapter 1, in the section "Our Approach to Economic Development," along the lines of Sen, our approach to development is not restricted to the materialistic aspects of development. However, the Jesuit approach to conversion takes the notion embodied in Sen's capabilities approach to development one step further. Our contribution rests on emphasizing development as the accumulation of knowledge *within* people, as well as the existence of roads, bridges, energy grids, electronic communications infrastructure, etc. *around* people. This emphasis on the accumulation of knowledge in the process of sustainable development would seem to require some degree of conversion in development agents. The kind of change needed for a situation to carry the dynamics of sustainability requires a transformation of a person and her/his world, one involving a change of course and direction.

We can now spell out how our approach to grassroots research involves a transformation process within the mind, heart, and spirit of a person or a group that goes beyond the one referred to by Sen above. Our reasoning is simple. What Sen describes as the relevant personal characteristics that govern the conversion of primary goods into a person's ability to live and survive (her vital values), also govern the other dimensions of value. That is, they govern the good things that correspond to belonging to a community (her social values), finding meaning and value in one's way of life (her cultural values), being respected and respecting others (her moral values), and loving and being loved (religious, or what we call ultimate values). In fact, these same relevant personal characteristics hold for all the parties involved in development – not only the poor. (The concept of value and its five dimensions are elaborated further in the section that follows, "Second Building Block: Anthropological Approach.").

From the development perspective, the transformation of human goods into a person's ability to enjoy them involves a change in the person's way of thinking as well as a change in the situation surrounding those goods. If we take this notion of transformation one step further, into the realm of spirituality, we can see that the processes that go on wherever there is genuine human development correspond to the processes that people associate with spiritual awakening.

Our approach in this book invites the reader, as potential or actual researcher, to intimately connect to the search for truth and to be open to experience a change in outlook that may translate into changes in development strategies and policies. Bernard Lonergan's understanding of the Jesuit angle on this provides the normative framework of human integrity and authenticity. In this context, one enters the process of radical change of conversion when:

1. New questions for research arise in the search for truth, and the researcher begins to become free of destructive biases in the process of data collection of each situation (*intellectual conversion*).

2. New questions arise so that the claim to moral respect for the dignity of the poor begins to include respect for all their capabilities and their capacity for self-determination (*moral conversion*).

3. New questions arise in search of genuinely human values that are grounded in a universe that is open to a transcendent or higher power, and in which love and self-sacrifice become the highest value (*religious conversion*).

Discernment

Discernment refers to the kind of evaluation of possibilities that goes on when one is making a decision. The decision need not be a religious one. But it always involves value judgments. The kind of conversion that we are talking about in relation to sustainable development hinges on crucial judgments and decisions on the part of the carriers of development. Thus, decision-making is central. St. Ignatius of Loyola, author of the spiritual handbook entitled *Spiritual Exercises*, discovered the dynamics of decision-making in his own life and reproduced them. The focus of our research on decisions in our narratives is one of the most significant ways in which the Jesuit approach to research is put into practice in this book. People such as the protagonists of our narratives arrive at decisions through a process of making value judgments and weighing the consequences of their decisions in light of the trade-offs, the pros and cons of the alternatives – even when this process is not fully articulated in the person's consciousness. However, just as stocks and bonds must be convertible in order for exchange transactions to take place, so people also need to be "convertible" for their conversion to take place. This capacity for convertibility is embodied in the process of deliberating that precedes decisions. The Jesuit tradition refers to this as discernment in the context of faith-based decisions. However, the same psychological process occurs in all big human decisions.

Interiority

The term interiority carries both philosophical and theological meanings, although it is most commonly used in the context of spirituality. Interiority, broadly conceived, refers to a person's awareness of what goes on within that person's mind (capacity to understand, reason, and make judgments), heart (capacity to be altruistic, cooperative, and to love without necessarily getting *quid pro quo*), and will (capacity to make free decisions and to act on them). We propose this broadly conceived definition, though we rely on the philosophical approach to interiority that Lonergan puts forth in *Method in Theology*. (Lonergan's approach also involves awareness of what one is doing when one is knowing and the ability to differentiate various operations by whether they carry common sense or theoretical meaning.) Our approach to interiority is *evolutionary*, as is our approach to religion and theological reflection presented earlier, as well as our approach to anthropology to be presented in the next section. Taken in its evolutionary framework, interiority pays attention to the emerging new forms of human consciousness that are developing as we evolve towards a world of justice, peace, and love.

Our interest in describing this core element in our Jesuit approach – interiority – is to help the reader better understand why we approach our narratives in the way we do. When someone is in the process of discerning whether to take one course of action or another, she comes to a decision when she is more at peace with one option than with another. In relation to good and evil, some call this peace "a clear conscience." In any case, when we talk about interiority – the "within" where people sift through what is moving them to make decisions – we are talking about what goes on within a person. In this realm of spirituality, people experience the inner dynamics of their own psychological and spiritual processes. This is where they can integrate their culture, their morality, and their religious faith (or their higher ideals, if religious experience is not relevant for them). Grassroots research, if it has the right research tools, can explore data in this realm of "the within of people."

In the next two chapters on methodology we will go into greater detail as we describe the research tools we have created in an attempt to gather the data of people's consciousness. This data involves what goes on when people make decisions and take action. Once we isolate a protagonist's decision, we can ask questions about the process of how she came to that decision. These questions yield what we refer to as the *data of her consciousness.*

When a researcher operates with what we might call "the research tool of the realm of interiority," she reflects on what is going on, in much the same way as those who go through the Ignatian spiritual retreat reflect on themselves. The researcher uses her own data of consciousness to learn about the consciousness of the protagonist. Consequently, one of the basic characteristics of this powerful spirituality tool is that it is empirical. It follows the same sequence of operations that any empirical study would follow. In the *Spiritual Exercises* of St. Ignatius, where St. Ignatius insists that all the steps of the meditations be done in sequence, one begins with the basic data of the scriptural narrative under consideration. Basic data comes in through hearing or reading the story. Next, one tries to understand the text and then reflect on it, making some judgments of fact and value. All this occurs in the quiet realm of one's inner self – one's interiority. We follow this pattern of experiencing, understanding, judging, and then deciding and acting as we find it in the *Exercises*. This method involves a recurrent process in which the pattern yields cumulative and progressive results, new developments. It can even result in spiritual renewal; the enhancement of one's freedom to love.

In the Jesuit spiritual framework, our method of research allows us to be "contemplatives in action." For the researcher, this means there is "a constant interplay between experience, reflection, decision, and action in line with the Jesuit ideal of being contemplative in action" (GC-34, Decree 4, No. 73). For development practitioners, this idea translates into maintaining a balance between action and reflection.

Finally, for those interested in the theological framework of this book, Jesuit spirituality seeks to foster an interior process of personal and social renewal. Renewal is what happens when sustainable development takes place. Because it is interior as well as external, theology refers to it as the work of the Spirit, from within, from below, and working horizontally. In theological terms, this reference to God as Spirit is the *pneumatology* (theology of the Spirit) on which the religious rationale of this book is based. The implications for our grassroots research methodology are huge. If, according to our religious belief, God the Spirit is present and active in all creation, then, with the eyes of faith, we can find God working in the midst of the lives of the poor in new and creative ways. However, because love embraces suffering for the good of the other through empathy, access to the kind of data that we are looking for in the narratives is possible only through friendship. The success of the very gathering of narratives hinges on whether the researchers are friends with the poor or not. All seasoned development practitioners know that if we do not have personal relationships and friendships with people who are poor and marginalized, research and economic development policies will not yield results that genuinely serve the interests and needs of the poor.

Second Building Block: Anthropological Approach – About Culture and Value

The notion of culture in our research, which was presented in Chapter 1, is intimately associated with a Jesuit approach to grassroots development. That is to say, when a Jesuit social center in any part of the world dedicates itself to ameliorating the situation of those who are at the margins of development, the Jesuits and their partners characteristically immerse themselves in the lives of those people. They become experts with firsthand knowledge of what people are experiencing. This firsthand knowledge, coupled with a view of human nature that sees it as essentially good and cooperative, is at the heart of the Jesuit approach to research related to culture.

Our definition of the term culture, as presented in Chapter 1 and set forth in official Jesuit documents of the 34th General Congregation (1995), coincides with the anthropological language of Clifford Geertz (*The Interpretation of Cultures*, 1973), who approaches culture in its broadest and most concrete sense, i.e., as an .entire way of life. This narrative approach to grassroots research emphasizes the fact that our understanding of the particulars of people's cultures involves interpretation of the meaning they give to what they do. Moreover, like Geertz, in our research we seek the meaning of our stories through "thick description," as contrasted with "thin description," which uses abstract categories to capture meaning. In this book, throughout our interpretations of the narratives, we seek the meaning of the narratives of people through the thickness, the concrete particularities, of their situations. Using Geertz's approach, we assume that in the particularity of the thick description at the heart of a situation, we will discover the meaning that our protagonists give to their decisions and actions. The application of the concept of thick description is explained in more detail in Chapter 3, "Research Methodology, Phase I: Narrative Data Gathering, Cultural Analysis and Moral Reflection."

We go beyond Geertz when we do this in relation to basic human values, as suggested in earlier sections. Assuming that there are basic human values that are common to our species, we are able to find deeply embedded in the particulars of people's stories elements that have universal significance. This is the basis for our claiming in this book that by qualitatively analyzing our narratives, we can provide practical insights for development practitioners around the world.

The term value, as we use it in this book, also involves the human capability for attaining goodness of one sort or another. Values (as a noun) are what human beings intend to strive for when they are seeking every form of goodness. To value (as an action verb) involves the human capability of judging between good and bad, appreciating what is worthwhile, and deciding to act accordingly. In other words, values involve both: (1) the good achieved with the acquisition of any specific goods; and (2) the capability and process of choosing courses of action that lead to that achievement. In this sense, we build on the work of Amartya Sen. In *Development As Freedom,* Sen introduces the term capability as an essential component of development. For Sen, "essential" human freedom enjoyed by all people can become "effective" or realized only when impediments to all their human capabilities are removed. A grasp of this dynamic approach to the term value is important for a full understanding of this book and its policy implications. Chapter 4, "Research Methodology, Phase II: Finding the Protagonists' Meanings and Values," will explain in greater detail these concepts of value.

As already suggested, the anthropological approach to culture and value that we espouse involves a nuanced theological way of talking about what is valued, that is, what is considered good. Our view is that human values are not limited to one (univocal) dimension of goodness. Rather, they correspond to five aspects of what we consider worthwhile, valuable, and good: to live and survive, to belong to a community, to find meaning and value in one's way of life, to be respected and to respect others, and to love and be loved. These five good things are called economic (vital), social, cultural, moral, and religious values. These five "good things" of life evoke corresponding dynamisms in people's consciousness that allow them to spontaneously raise questions that orient them to understand and pursue their specific goals. If theology is going to be meaningfully related to development, this five-fold differentiation must be maintained. In our tradition, grace does not work in a parallel with material development; rather, grace is integral to all human activity – including economic activity. When these five levels of the good we seek are placed in the framework of a faith-based approach to development research and practice, this approach reflects a *theological anthropology* – an understanding of what it means to be human based on the Judaeo-Christian faith tradition and open to other faith traditions.

Third Building Block: The Jesuit Intellectual and Educational Tradition

In the framework of the four hundred and fifty-year-old Jesuit intellectual and educational tradition, our approach to grassroots research involves an approach to discovering new knowledge that has been embodied in the pedagogy of Jesuit schools and that is faith-based without being sectarian. It respects truth wherever it is found. In a current expression of this tradition, John Haughey, SJ, says this:

> The line of demarcation in this regard is not between Catholic and non-Catholic faculty members, but between those who ask questions and those who do not, between those who strive to make the connections their particular areas of competence have prepared them to make, and those who do not. The strivers are contributing to the upbuilding of the "noosphere," as Teilhard de Chardin liked to describe the sphere of mind and spirit that surrounds the earth.

> —*Where is Knowing Going? The Horizons of the*
> *Knowing Subject (2009), p. 148*

Our approach to grassroots research is rooted not only in our theological anthropology, but also in this way of relating it to the Jesuit intellectual and educational approach to knowledge. According to this tradition rooted in Aristotle and Aquinas, human knowing boils down to empirical method, taken in its most general sense. When we know that we know something, we are actually experiencing a normative pattern of recurrent and related operations. These operations involve paying attention to data, analyzing the data and understanding its meaning, testing it and arriving at a reasonable judgment of fact, and finally of deciding what to do. The results are usually cumulative (we build on insights we already have) and progressive (we move in a direction that we can call development).

OUR VISION

Finally, a word about our vision is in order. The vision that drives this book is rooted in contemporary official Jesuit documents and in recent Jesuit educational developments. Inspired by Jesuit sources, we envision the kind of world community in which everyone will be able to sit at the same table. It includes people of all cultures, all religious traditions, all genders, races, economic and political levels, and all agents of development, including those most marginalized from policy decisions. In religious terms, Christians call this the "banquet of the Kingdom of God." The vision of justice, peace, ecological renewal, and love that we carry "requires that we get at the attitudes of people embedded in their culture and we create communities of solidarity. Solidarity, in order to have its full meaning, must engage all of the actors" (GC-34, Decree 3, No. 7 and No. 10).

This kind of vision is not so utopian that it fails to recognize the reality of tensions that exist among opposing forces in society. But we envision the balancing of these tensions through the establishment of cooperative ventures that seek greater equality and harmony of interests among those who represent these forces. Thus, we envision cooperative ventures among those who are affluent and those who lack life's necessities; those who are responsible for order in society and those who carry creative solutions to problems; those who adhere to cultural traditions and those who value self-determination; those whose dignity is protected and those whose dignity is denied; and those who believe in closed religious traditions and religious people who favor dialogue.

Inspired by recent Jesuit educational developments ranging from informal education to higher education, we envision a whole new approach to global education through networking both inside and outside the walls of schools. For those who are at the margins of formal economies, our vision is of a world in which they learn of the complexities of local, regional, and global markets so they can bring their creative insights to bear on policies. For those who own or manage vast resources and who make decisions affecting the lives of millions of people, as well as the development practitioners who work with them, our vision is that they be educated to the ways in which poor people make their decisions and incorporate essential values into their lives. Our vision is that this kind of ongoing multi-faceted educational task, when translated into training programs for development practitioners, will give new direction to a global economy in which attention is paid to people's cultural, moral, and religious values – not only their socioeconomic values. We envision, above all, a new approach to economic development that has as its normative goal the inclusion of all people in a dialogue of cultural, moral, and religious values. We hope this book contributes to moving this vision towards its realization.

Chapter 3

Research Methodology, Phase I: Narrative Data Gathering, Cultural Analysis and Moral Reflection

The Global Economy and Cultures (GEC) research project is based on dialogue and collaboration. The dialogue took place among the researchers. They were, on the one hand, the researchers and primary authors of this book at the Woodstock Theological Center (WTC), who also developed the methodological approach and coordinated the effort. On the other hand were the Jesuits (and two diocesan priests) and their partners in the Jesuit social centers around the world, who knew the protagonists of the narratives personally. They interacted in bilateral discussions and in international and regional meetings that were held during the project, and these interactions form the heart of the methodology. The more specific methodological tools used in the project evolved as it progressed.

This chapter describes the tools that the researchers applied to all the narratives during Phase I of the project: the development of the narrative stories, their cultural analysis, and the interpretation of these data by the WTC researchers. In Parts II and III, the narrative chapters, we see the final product of the Phase I methodology in two sections in each chapter: "Narrative" and "Cultural Analysis." For the narratives in Part III, to which only this Phase I methodology was applied, the WTC researchers reflect on the narrative and the cultural analysis in the final section entitled "Interpretation." This reflection was reviewed by the narrators and incorporates their comments.

THE ORIGINAL NARRATIVE

In the first stage of the GEC project, the narrator wrote a *narrative*, about five pages long, telling the true story of the experience of a real local person, the *protagonist* of the story – someone the narrator knew personally. The story was to relate the changes that had occurred in the life of this protagonist since the current form of globalization entered his or her life. The narrator was instructed to make the narrative a story, not an analysis. The purpose of the narrative was not to argue against the harms of globalization or in favor of its benefits. Instead, the purpose was to present simple narrative data showing the changes in the protagonist's life associated with the effects of globalization. The objective was to understand the people's direct experience of what was going on in the local culture. Others would decide for themselves the effects of globalization.

These were the narrators' specific instructions:

> Describe an event, something that happened, that reflects an experience of changes due to globalization. What happened? When, what day, month, year? In what concrete place? What did specific people in the narrative say and do? What was done to them? How? Let the narrative take its readers into the heart of the experience of the main characters from the perspective of their local culture. Please tell the story with as much rich local detail as possible. These concrete colorful details about what the people in the narrative say and do will carry the local culture, with its values (both good and bad), with its seeds of despair and its seeds of hope, both of which will be intermingled in the concreteness of the events that are narrated. Describe also what the main characters' lives were like before globalization came to their village, town, or city. What changed in their way of carrying out basic economic activities? How did the main characters decide to deal with the changes?

The foundation for our anecdotal style is what the anthropologist Clifford Geertz calls a "thick description" of reality in the first chapter of his book *The Interpretation of Cultures* (1973).

ENRICHING THE ORIGINAL NARRATIVE

The original narratives, more than fifty, were gathered and then discussed at one or more meetings that followed. These were the First and Second International Consultations, held at Georgetown University in Washington, D.C. in September 1999 and October 2000, and three subsequent Regional Meetings. These discussions led to the realization that the narrative data needed enrichment, which was subsequently done before conducting the remaining Regional Meetings. A brief history of these meetings appears in the appendix to this chapter, "Early GEC Project History: Consultations and Regional Meetings." This enrichment took two primary forms. First, in each narrative, a country benchmark year was established: this was the year of the critical shift in the country's policy towards a greater opening to the global market economy. The choice of this benchmark year was based on aggregate socioeconomic data. Selecting a benchmark year allowed a sharper distinction between, on the one hand, the conditions already prevailing at the time of the economic changes; and, on the other hand, the changes associated with the new economic policies. Second, the WTC researchers engaged in an exhaustive dialogue with each of the narrators about every actor who might have been relevant to the narrative, whether or not already mentioned, and how their behavior and relationships had changed under the new policies. The narrators, however, were not always sufficiently familiar with these other actors; in these cases, resource constraints did not allow pursuing this additional data. But this dialogue did generate a great deal of additional information to complement the original narrative. The "Narrative" section of the narrative chapters of this book reflects this additional information, as well as subsequent analysis.

Participants in the First International Consultation (1999)

Participants in the Second International Consultation (2000)

NARRATIVE CULTURAL ANALYSIS

Cultural Traits

The cultural analysis of each narrative began with identifying cultural traits of the protagonist's local culture. These traits were first identified by independent anthropologists, or professionals familiar with the local culture, and then discussed with the narrator and sometimes modified after these discussions. Defining these cultural traits raised the narrators' consciousness of their own culture and provided a framework for both the narrators and the WTC researchers to do the cultural analysis proper. This analysis included an interview with the protagonist.

Cultural Analysis Proper

Narrator's Interview of the Protagonist. Before the interview, the narrator and the WTC researchers jointly identified the principal decision(s) that the protagonist had had to make in the new environment. In the actual interview, the narrator then asked the protagonist to discuss: (1) the options available at the time of the decision; (2) the advantages and disadvantages of each option; (3) the reason why the particular option was chosen; and (4) how the decision fit with the values this person learned in his or her childhood. The narrators were asked to report the protagonists' answers without trying to interpret them. The WTC researchers wanted to hear the protagonists' voices directly. An edited version of this interview appears in each narrative chapter in the box that follows the listing of local cultural traits.

Narrator's Cultural Analysis. In order to engage the narrators in a cultural reflection, each narrator was given a questionnaire, tailored to the specifics of the narrative, to reflect on the impact on the local culture of the changes brought about by the opening of the economy. The questions were grouped into six traditional socioeconomic development topics, which we call analytical themes. These themes look into the changes in patterns of: consumption, production, migration, political power, social relations, and religious experience and expression. These themes were defined as follows:

> ***Consumption.*** Economic goods such as food, clothing, shelter, travel, entertainment, health care, etc. that an individual buys and uses.

> ***Production.*** What an individual makes when he or she does any kind of work such as farming, factory work, housework, selling, etc. Production takes place both in the formal and informal sectors of the economy.

> ***Migration.*** The movement of a person from one geographical location to another, such as from a rural to an urban area, or from one country to another country. Migration can be permanent or temporary and takes place for economic and/or sociopolitical causes.

> ***Political Power Relations.*** The structure of the relationships between the individual and institutions with political power. These include the relationships of the individual with his or her government, both national and local, and focuses particularly on

the participation and representation of the individual in that government. It also refers to the relationships with social groups such as organized labor, nongovernmental organizations (NGOs), and multilateral organizations such as the World Bank, as well as the relationships among these organizations.

Social Relations: The relationships among and within social groups to which the individual belongs. These social groups include the family, male and female groups, elders, and marginalized minorities. Among social groups we also include media institutions and relationships with the physical world.

Religious Experiences and Expression: How the individual and the community experience and express their spirituality in relationship to the Divine.

Matching Cultural Traits with Interview Data and Narrators' Cultural Analysis. Finally, the WTC researchers used the local cultural traits identified earlier in each narrative to sift through and interpret the interview information and the narrators' answers to the cultural questionnaire. For example, could a protagonist's decision be seen as influenced by a particular cultural trait? Could it have been affected by an element in one of the six identified socioeconomic analytical themes? How did the changes in those themes reflect the cultural traits? The result of this matching and interpretation provided the basis for the texts in the Cultural Analysis sections in the narrative chapters.

NARRATIVE MORAL REFLECTION: THIRD INTERNATIONAL CONSULTATION

The effort required to enrich the original narrative data also resulted in the practical necessity to reduce to ten the number of narratives on which we worked actively for the rest of the project. The narrators of these ten narratives, the WTC researchers, and six regional experts with professional experience in various fields such as anthropology, met at the Third International Consultation, held at Georgetown University in Washington, D.C. in July 2003. This consultation began with sessions conducted along each analytical theme – consumption, production, etc. For each theme, each narrator first worked independently with his or her own narrative. Then the narrators from a given region, plus the regional experts, discussed the theme. Finally the theme was discussed in plenary session.

During the narrators' independent work, each narrator first was asked to verify that the facts identified by the WTC researchers (and presented along the six analytical themes) as significant changes in the protagonist's story were accurate. Then the narrators were asked to discuss: (1) the protagonist's affective reaction to the changes in her situation; (2) any other values of the protagonist, beyond those identified as local cultural traits, relevant to understanding the protagonist's situation; (3) whether the narrator thought the protagonist, having made the decision elicited by the global changes, was or was not "at peace" with herself; and (4) the protagonist's religious values, as defined by the culture, that are consistent and inconsistent with the protagonist's decision.

Towards the end of the consultation, the participants also prepared action plans to take back to their social centers. These were designed to facilitate empowering the protagonists of the narratives, as well as their communities, to better negotiate the new economic global environment. This consultation ended with a two-day meeting among the regional experts and the WTC researchers to reflect on the narrative discussions held during the preceding week of consultation.

Participants in the Third International Consultation (2003)

*GEC experts debrief at the Woodstock Theological Center after the Third
International Consultation (2003)*

THE GLOBALIZATION MOSAIC:
FOURTH INTERNATIONAL CONSULTATION

At this final international GEC consultation, held in September 2004, a much larger group of researchers again discussed the individual narratives, which now included the product of the full cultural analysis and the moral reflection of the Third International Consultation. Thirty Jesuits, two diocesan priests, and their partners, representing thirty Jesuit social centers in twenty-three different countries, gathered together with the WTC researchers at Georgetown University in Washington, D.C.

Participants in the Fourth International Consultation (2004)

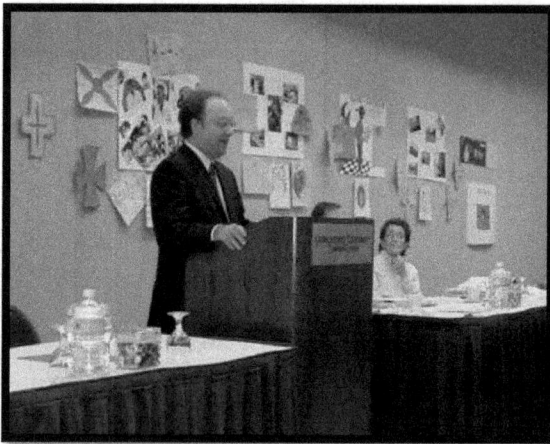

Georgetown University President John J. DeGioia addresses participants at GEC's Fourth International Consultation (2004)

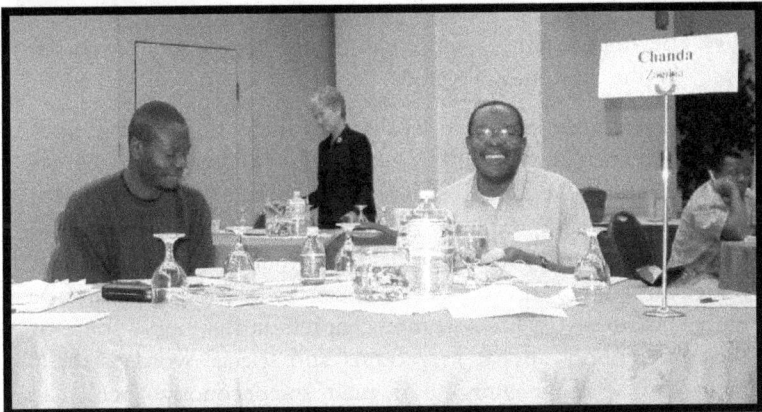

Participants discuss narratives at the Fourth International Consultation (2004)

In preparation for this consultation, the WTC researchers took the narrative data that had been collected throughout the project, together with the knowledge gained during the cultural analysis and the three preceding international consultations, and edited them. These became, essentially, the short narratives that appear after the introductory "Summary" section, in the narrative chapters in this book. This discussion of the stories provided validation for the editorial work that had been done. In addition, to facilitate looking at the stories through a different prism, the WTC researchers presented the narrative data in terms of certain common organizing concepts, or metaphors. The organizing metaphors were:

Threshold metaphors: These represented the tensions in the life of the protagonist, created when one or more of the person's cultural traits was affected by the changes in values from before to after the economic opening.

Bridge/moat metaphors: These represented the variable(s) behind the protagonist's response to the change in his or her situation. It could be a cultural trait, but it also could be something else like "consumption" or Western values. A variable identified by this metaphor helps the protagonist to address the tensions in the threshold metaphor. In doing so, the bridge can:

- Help the protagonist to creatively integrate his or her old tradition with the new situation (a true bridge)

- Become the source of resistance to any integration with the new situation (a moat)

- Be nonexistent, because the protagonist is just overtaken by the new cultural values

Mosaic metaphors: These represented the particulars that connect the protagonist's "little story" with the "big story" of the region, nation, the global economy, Christianity, etc. They provided us with unique pieces, like "mosaic" tiles; that helped to differentiate one protagonist from another and enhanced our understanding of the larger "mosaic" or kaleidoscope of the global economy. In the narrative chapters in this book, some of these metaphors appear as refrains and special words, usually presented at the beginning of each socioeconomic analytical theme such as consumption, production, etc.

At the Fourth International Consultation, the participants were organized first in small regional groups and then blended into small international groups. Small group discussions were always followed by presentations and plenary discussions. During these meetings the participants worked to compare and contrast the narratives and produced artwork for each narrative – the "narrative" mosaic tiles. Then they discussed the "mosaic" of globalization experiences among the poor that emerged from juxtaposing the narratives in a grand "mosaic of the global economy". The group also reflected on their own experience of the research process. In particular, the narrators in the group explored "the bridge," the relationship, between them and the protagonists and other actors in the narratives.

The major contribution of this Consultation was to understand how the pivotal metaphors of each narrative were uniquely tied to its specific cultural context, and how the uniqueness of each narrative was enhanced by juxtaposing it with the larger regional context and the other narratives from around the world. As a result, a kaleidoscopic picture emerged, in which the unique characteristics of each narratives were put next to each other in the region and in the world: a visual "mosaic" of the global economy. However, we also realized we had not yet arrived at sufficiently fine-tuned results.

Examples of the artwork with the "narrative mosaic tiles" are presented in this chapter and the corresponding narrative chapters. The "mosaic of the global economy" is partially reproduced in Chapter 11, on p. 406ff.

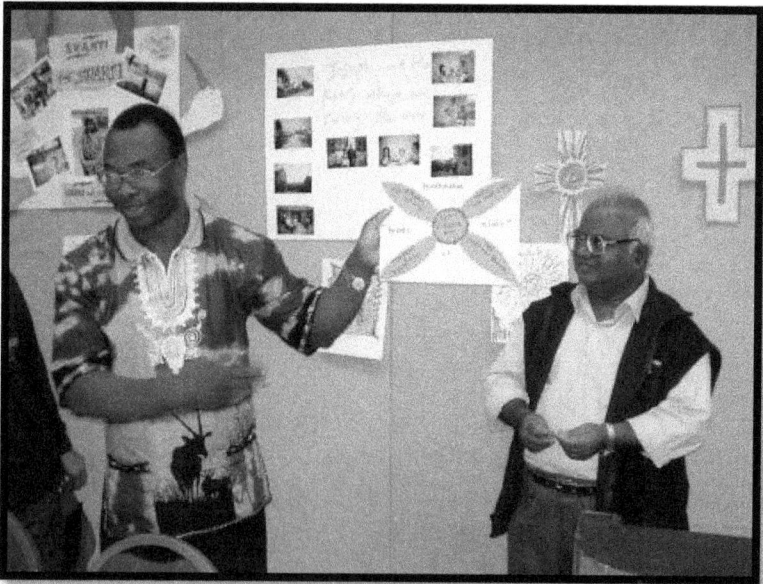

GEC project participants present the "mosaic tiles" for their narratives'
protagonists, at GEC's Fourth International Consultation (2004)

WOODSTOCK RESEARCHERS' ANALYSIS

Based on the materials developed and the discussions held by the GEC project from its inception and through the Fourth International Consultation, the WTC researchers undertook a reflection or interpretation for each narrative. This reflection had two components. In one component we looked at the macro-economic situation. In all the narrative chapters in the book, this appears under the heading "Country's Economic Globalization and the Protagonist." In the other component, we looked at the protagonist of the story as a subject: as someone actively involved in making choices in her life. In the narrative chapters in which only Phase I was applied – Chapters 11-16 – the analysis of the protagonist appears under the heading "Protagonist as a Person." However, as we proceeded to write these reflections on the protagonists, we realized that we had not quite succeeded yet in seeing the world through the eyes of the protagonists. This gave rise to the development of the methodology of Phase II, which is discussed in the next chapter.

REFLECTIONS ON PHASE I METHODOLOGY

The GEC project has been an ongoing process of trying to understand how the global economy is functioning from the perspective of the poor, in their culture – always looking at that basic goal. Even during Phase I of the project, it has also been a process of designing new research tools to explore the lives of the protagonists and the local cultures portrayed in the narratives.

Especially during Phase I of the project, the rich experience of the reflection and discussion at the various meetings also resulted in the development of regional networks of committed participants who are carefully examining the impact of the global economy on local communities "from below." Participants have found great value in being able to form linkages with others in their region, in order to continue the exchange of ideas well beyond the scope of the GEC project. A list of the participants in the GEC project appears in the Acknowledgements section at the beginning of the book.

APPENDIX: EARLY GEC PROJECT HISTORY –
CONSULTATIONS AND REGIONAL MEETINGS

As described in the Preface and earlier chapters, the foundation of the Global Economy and Cultures (GEC) project can be found in the meetings of the 34th General Congregation (GC-34) of the Society of Jesus. Following that GC-34 meeting, some members of social centers responded to an invitation letter to attend Woodstock Theological Center's First International Consultation, held at Georgetown University in Washington, D.C. in September 1999. At this consultation, twenty-two representatives from fourteen countries worldwide brought narratives from their countries to the table and shared them. A main finding of this consultation was that we lacked the research tools needed to accomplish the task of understanding the cultural dimensions of the narratives. As a result, the meeting was limited to reflecting in general on positive and negative impacts of globalization. It focused minimally on concrete narrative data. To overcome this difficulty, the WTC researchers prepared a set of common questions that asked the narrators to comment on cultural aspects and other actors relevant to their narratives.

At the Second International Consultation, held at Georgetown University in Washington, D.C. in October 2000, twenty-one representatives from fifteen countries held an in-depth discussion of eight selected narratives that incorporated the new data. They searched for similarities and differences among the narratives to find the ways in which the global economy was affecting the ways of life of the protagonists of the stories. Out of these comparisons, participants forged a list of core themes and further questions for enhancing the narrative data. We realized that we needed to go from description to explanation. If we stayed at the level of narrative description, we would not really get at a deeper understanding. We realized we had to develop tools for explanation. Finally, we outlined a long-term plan of the project, to hold six regional meetings to be followed by a Third International Consultation.

At the first three regional meetings we held in 2001, we attempted to write "explanatory texts" that would embody the findings. But, once again, we ended up talking about the narratives, in a very general descriptive language that tried to promote justice directly for the protagonist. After looking at the explanatory texts, the participants felt that they could not take them any further or deeper. We discovered that we still lacked adequate research tools that would get us beyond aggregate descriptions that reflected only socioeconomic generalizations. We decided we needed to ask more questions, in order to deepen the narratives before trying to explain what was happening in them.

So we went back to the narrators from East Asia and Africa, the two regions yet to conduct the anticipated regional meetings, and asked many more questions. (See the section "Enriching the Original Narrative" in Chapter 3.) These questions tried to do three things: (1) identify the macro socioeconomic conditions in the countries; (2) establish a sharper distinction between the changes produced by the global economy and pre-existing conditions in the life of the protagonist; and (3) systematically identify all the other actors and their roles in the life of the protagonists of the stories.

The narrators worked very hard responding to the questionnaires in preparation of the meetings. So when we held the Manila and the Nairobi Regional Meetings in 2002 we worked on four narratives in depth in each of the meetings, using the newly gathered data. We made progress. In these meetings we also tried to get at metaphors that would enhance our understanding. But we learned that the metaphors we were using were too large: for example, land and ocean as metaphors for mother. Those metaphors did not help us extract any more meaning from the narratives.

GEC Regional Meetings: 2001-2002

Latin America and the Caribbean Regional Meeting – September 2001: Thirteen participants from nine countries met in Brazil at the Centro Cultural de Brasília

South Asia Regional Meeting – October 2001: Nineteen participants from India met at the Indian Social Institute in Bangalore

U.S. and Canada Regional Meeting – December 2001: Five participants from the USA and Canada met in Camden, New Jersey at the Romero Center

East Asia and Oceania Regional Meeting – April 2002: Ten participants from eight countries met at the East Asian Pastoral Institute in Manila, Philippines

Africa and Madagascar Regional Meeting – June 2002: Fourteen participants from eight countries met at Hekima College in Nairobi, Kenya

Note: The sixth planned regional meeting, to be held in Europe, never took place.

Contemplating the additional work involved with the new questionnaires, we also decided we needed to concentrate on fewer narratives and look at them in much greater detail, now through the lens of their local cultures. From among all the narratives, we selected ten and developed a cultural questionnaire for each of them. (See the section "Narrative Cultural Analysis" in Chapter 3.) In this questionnaire we identified the critical decisions that the opening of the country's economy had forced upon the protagonist and asked the narrator to interview the protagonist and record their answers. In addition, we asked the narrators how the protagonist and the culture were responding to the changes brought about by globalization along six socioeconomic themes. These themes are: consumption, production, migration, social relations, political power, and religious experience and expression.

GEC's South Asia regional meeting in Bangalore (2001)

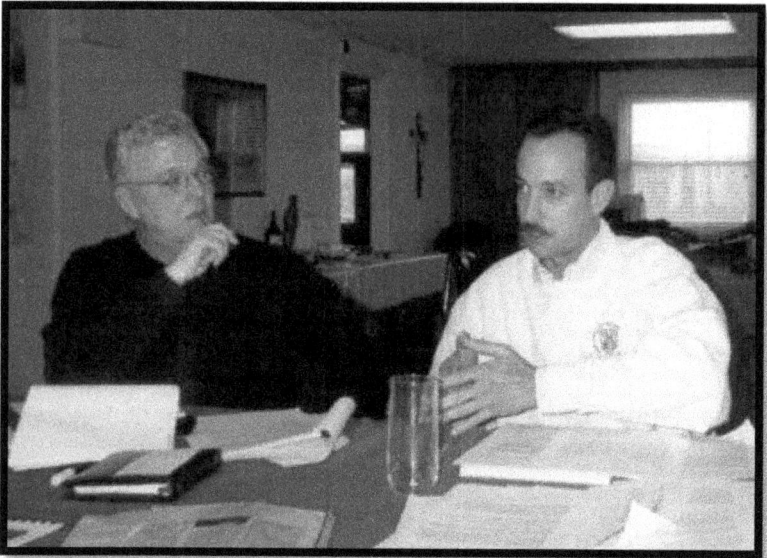

The U.S. and Canada regional meeting in Camden (2001)

The East Asia and Oceania regional meeting in Manila (2002)

The Latin America and Caribbean regional meeting in Brasilia (2001)

*Left: Victor Adangba, SJ and Ferdinand Muhigirwa, SJ at the Africa &
Middle East regional meeting in Nairobi (2002); right: Sosthenes Luyembe, SJ at
the regional meeting in Nairobi*

Chapter 4

Research Methodology, Phase II: Finding the Protagonists' Meanings and Values

In the preceding chapter, we presented Phase I of the project. We outlined the methodology we originally used to develop the narratives and their cultural analysis and to interpret the data. This methodology immersed us in the lives and cultures of the protagonists of the narratives. However, after writing our interpretation of these data, we realized that this approach was not fully achieving our goal, which was to see the world through the eyes of those protagonists. We realized we were not yet fully seeing globalization in terms of the protagonists' own meanings and values. We needed to go further. We needed to understand more deeply how the meaning of the protagonists' world changed as this world itself changed with the forces of globalization entering into their lives. We also needed to go beyond cultural traits to understand better the values that motivated their lives and how these values changed in the protagonists' encounter with the new global economy. We needed a better understanding of how the protagonists came to know and live in this new world as agents of change of their own history. This chapter describes the project's Phase II methodology, which we developed to accomplish this goal.

Empirically, Phase II methodology is anchored in two reasonably objective facts that we know in each narrative story. We know a lot about how the global economy entered into the lives of the protagonists, and what they first experienced. We also know some of the actions that they took in response to those experiences. If so, then we can deduce what their decisions were. Because there is no evidence in our narratives that the protagonists were coerced or not in their right minds, we can conclude that their actions flowed from their own decisions.

For example, in the story of Chanda, we know that the Zambian government, in 1994, withdrew agricultural support from the village where he lived, as part of its economic restructuring. We also know that, partly because of the hardship this caused, the village elders sent Chanda to live in the capital, Lusaka, to help support his family. This is how globalization entered Chanda's life. We also know that Chanda stayed in Lusaka and became a cigarette vendor. This is his action. If so, we also know the decision that led to his actions, because he acted in relative freedom; he was not forced to do anything. His action to sell cigarettes was based on his own decision, even though the scope for his decision-making was very limited.

The Phase II methodology was designed to help us make inferences about how the protagonists moved from their initial experiences of globalization to making decisions in this changed environment, and on to how they implemented those decisions (i.e., the actions that we had observed). In other words, the objective of Phase II methodology is to deconstruct the protagonists' knowledge of what was occurring. By understanding this process, we can also expect to delve deeper and to answer questions such as: What values drove them? How did they negotiate the tensions caused by the meeting of their traditional values and those embedded in the new global forces?

We saw that the protagonists addressed these tensions by using what they knew. They decided and acted out of the core of their inherited ways of knowing and valuing from their own culture. But in the process of facing their changing world, they adapted their values in light of their new experiences and created new meanings. We see this, for example, with Marie in Cameroon. She adapted how she interacted with her extended family, and created a new meaning of family for herself, after her experience of losing her job and having to look for another way of making a living. Phase II tries to shed light on these new meanings and values as the protagonists developed as human beings and, often, forged a new identity as well.

The roots of the Phase II methodology can be found in the process that takes place in every human being who has a minimum of natural intelligence and who is conscious when he or she acts. This process, essentially, consists of responding to specific questions; the answers to which, in turn, generate new questions. We naturally raise questions as we experience new things and wonder what to do about this experience. When we try a new product or somebody addresses us, we want to know more about it. Who or what is it? Why? How does it work? The answers to these questions provide an understanding of the changing world in which we live. This understanding then becomes the context in which we ask ourselves what to do and bring to bear what we care about, what we value.

This questioning process is a universal built-in permanent dynamism that functions in every human being independently of time and place and cultural, religious, and personal characteristics. It is the questioning process the protagonists, as human beings, had to follow to get to know their changing world and act in the ways that we observed. This questioning in most cases was not explicit and the protagonists might have never verbalized it, but it was implicit in the actions that we observed. Our methodological task, in essence, was to pose these questions explicitly and then surmise the answers from the observed actions.

Our Phase II methodology relies on three major building blocks, which will be explained in more detail later in this chapter:

1. Dynamics of the human process of knowing. This is the universal process by which all conscious human beings come to know, find new meanings, decide, and act in their world.

2. Humans' scale of values (at five different levels, to be explained). This is what people care for, what fires and drives their lives.

3. Tensions within and among these levels of values.

These building blocks are the research tools. They help us see the world of the protagonists in light of their own meanings and values, and help us see as well how the protagonists adapted these meanings and values as their world was exposed to new global forces. The pillars for the development of our methodology are the works of Bernard J.F. Lonergan, *Method in Theology* (1971); Brian Cronin, *Value Ethics: A Lonergan Perspective* (2006); and Neil Ormerod and Shane Clifton, *Globalization and the Mission of the Church* (2010, Chapter 2, "Theology of History"), which draws from Robert M. Doran, *Theology and the Dialectics of History* (1990).

Finally, we would like to point out that the "Cultural Analysis" section of the narrative chapters reflects the earlier, Phase I, methodology. There we report on the narrators' interviews with the protagonists about some of their decisions. So, we already addressed in that section many of the actions that later on we analyze using Phase II methodology. However, the interview questions, which were performed using the Phase I methodology, were of a different nature than the ones contemplated by the Phase II methodology described in this chapter. Chapters 5 and 6 of this book present in great detail the application of the two phases of the methodology to the story of Shanti in India. Chapter 5 shows the product of applying the Phase I methodology: the narrative and our cultural analysis. Chapter 6 shows the results of applying the Phase II methodology: getting to Shanti's meanings and values as reflected in her choices. Chapters 7-10 present the other narratives to which Phase II methodology was applied. In addition to these chapters, the Appendix to Chapter 17 presents the application of Phase II methodology in an experiment in which a third party applied the methodology.

DYNAMICS OF THE HUMAN PROCESS OF KNOWING: SOME ROLE-PLAYING

Reaching a Decision: From Experiencing to Deciding

Before discussing this process more formally, and how we used it to discern the protagonists' meanings and values in their own reality, we will do some role-playing and introduce some terminology. We owe the conceptual framework used in this and the following section to Lonergan's interpretation of the transcendental method. See Bernard J.F. Lonergan, *Method in Theology* (1971).

Let us put ourselves in the role of having received the news that we have been fired from the job we have had for years and on which we depend for our livelihood. We are told that new global competition requires the plant to increase productivity and function with fewer, more productive, employees and we are not to be one of the employees retained.

Experiencing. First, we hear the news that we have been fired and perhaps we utter a verbal outburst. We immediately *feel* rage, denial, befuddlement, and horror at the thought of losing the one source of our livelihood. We remember relatives who in the past became unemployed. We *experience* the event.

Understanding. Then we attempt to *understand*. Eventually we calm down a bit, and this initial experience soon leads to asking ourselves questions, such as: how is this possible? What is this global competition management is talking about? What are the real reasons for management firing us? What are we to do? What are our options? In essence, by asking questions, we are trying to understand the new employment situation in which we find ourselves. It probably would not be easy to answer many of these questions with certainty and some answers would conflict.

Judging. At some point, this process leads us to *judge the facts* of the situation. We reflect on the answers we get to our initial set of questions and try to establish whether each particular one is correct. Do we have reason to believe that management is firing us out of greed? Do we have evidence to support management's contention of low productivity on our part? How realistic is it for us to find a comparable job elsewhere? How probable is it that an organized labor protest would lead management to reverse their decision? The answers to these and other similar questions would lead us to reach some conclusions, or a judgment of the facts as we know them: yes, new imports are creating more competition for the company, but we also believe that management is greedy. No, we cannot think of productivity deficiencies on our part as a reason for being fired. Yes, it would be very difficult to find a comparable job; and, yes, an organized labor protest, and even some violence, might make management reverse their decision. Now, our judgment of the facts might not be correct. All the facts often are not available to us and reality can be more complex than what we perceive. We often do not search for answers in a dispassionate way, or have the intelligence to ask all the relevant questions. But those positive and negative answers would remain our judgment of the facts until the source of the error is corrected. Those answers would be how we come to understand the global economic forces in our own new reality, the meaning of these global forces to us.

Deciding. The next step, after reaching these conclusions about the facts, is to *decide* what to do. (Note that this is not the action itself, not the carrying out of the decision: it is simply making the decision.) Our judgment of the facts of the situation already embodied an urge to decide what we are going to do about our newly-found predicament. The rationality behind our conclusions about the facts actually begins to suggest a decision: organizing a labor protest might succeed in changing management's position. Still, we have doubts and we would soon question ourselves whether this decision is the right one. Is the protest worth the risks that we will be taking? What would it mean in terms of people we care about? How unlikely, really, is it for us to find a comparable job? We would be evaluating the alternative decisions we could take, and this is where values enter the picture. In evaluating, we would be guided more or less explicitly by the values we cherish. Our values will enter as arbiters of our decision. Our conscience would be calling us to decide what is the right thing to do, given the way in which we understand our world. We essentially want to be moral people.

Reaching a decision as to what to do may prove very difficult. Many of the values and associated feelings we have would be consistent with what our community values – they would be part of the traits of our culture, discussed in Chapter 3, "Research Methodology, Phase I: Narrative Data Gathering, Cultural Analysis and Moral Reflection" – but the possibility does exist for our deciding to disregard, or even oppose, those values. Not everybody in a culture interprets cultural traits in the same way in specific situations. We are also part of many subcultures, like family, co-workers, and neighborhood. We may belong to a very active labor community at the same time that we belong to a general traditional culture that tends to be submissive and avoid confrontation. Our judgment of the facts points to organizing a protest and confronting management. Such a decision would be supported by the labor community. But our family and neighbors might argue that accepting management's decision to fire us and finding another job is the right thing to do. They believe that management ultimately would win out and only harm to ourselves and others could come out of a confrontation. But we feel indignant at the injustice. There will be a lot of tension created in our trying to reach a decision. There is a conflict between the decision that is best for the labor union, what is best for the family I love, and even what is best to satisfy my desire for vengeance. There will be a lot of back and forth among competing alternative decisions and their supporting values. But eventually we will reach a decision that reflects what we consider to be the best thing to do under the circumstances and one that leaves our conscience at peace. It is a decision that takes into account all that we value. In the process of reaching that decision, we also would have begun to change to some degree. The meaning to us of work, of our relationship with management, of other workers, and of our community will have changed somewhat in the process.

Below is a diagram of the stages of consciousness in reaching a decision, from experiencing to deciding:

Reaching a Decision

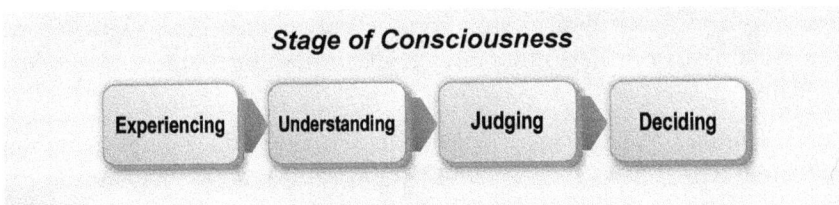

Stage of Consciousness

Experiencing ▸ Understanding ▸ Judging ▸ Deciding

Implementing the Decision: From Deciding to Acting

One might think that having decided to, say, become a labor protest organizer is the end of the story. But all that we have decided is that the protest is the best course of action. We have not moved into action yet. There is still more to do before our decision becomes an action. As we know from our own experience, there is a big difference between deciding to do and doing. As we move to implement our decision, we need to confront the implications of the decision and the new way in which we see things. We need to integrate this "new way" with the "old way" of our life. At any point in the process, we may even decide not to put this decision into action. In essence, we go through a similar process to the one we followed to reach the decision (from experiencing to deciding). But the focus of the process now is not the new situation we experience: it is the decision itself, and the process moves through the same stages, but in reverse order: *deciding, judging, understanding, experiencing* (the action).

Deciding. We start with the *decision.* We begin by questioning the decision itself. Is this the right decision? Are we really willing to put the decision into action? We decided that it was the best course of action, but are we really prepared to work and be known as a protest organizer and confront management openly?

Judging. We would also wonder again about the facts on which we based our decision: the new management of management and labor unions. We used to consider management worthy of trust. Is it true that they are basically greedy and that the increased competition does not support the alleged need to increase productivity by using fewer employees? Have the facts as we used to know them really changed? How does our decision change the *judgment of the facts,* their *meaning,* in our life?

Understanding. Then, we would need a new *understanding* of our day-to-day life and how our decisions would change it. How would our decision work in practice? What would it mean in terms of legal responsibilities for actions taken, access to medical assistance when dismissed for cause, how to go about actually organizing a workers' union? If the answers to these questions and other similar ones still support going ahead with the implementation of our decisions, our very last question would emerge. Will we actually do it?

Experiencing. Answering affirmatively, we would be doing something that itself represents a new *experience* for us: call out the first meeting to organize the labor protest. Start to be known as a confrontational labor organizer. Globalization for us now truly means losing our job because of unfair management as well as confronting this management and making all the changes in our lives that this requires. We would be changing how we value management and labor unions and our views of how they fit in our community and how we make a living.

Below is a diagram of the whole process from initial experience to the experience of acting that results from the decision:

Reaching a Decision

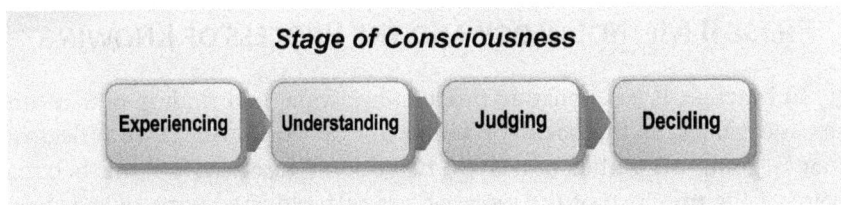

Stage of Consciousness

Experiencing → Understanding → Judging → Deciding

Implementing the Decision

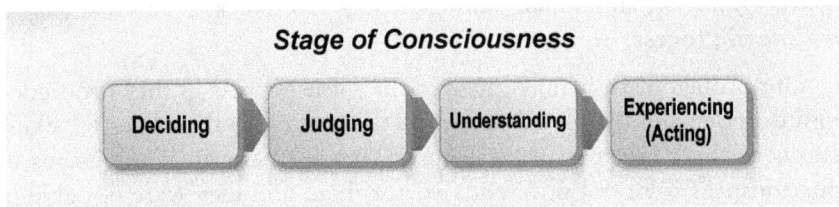

Stage of Consciousness

Deciding → Judging → Understanding → Experiencing (Acting)

We have presented in somewhat stylized form the basic structure of how we might go about understanding the changes in the reality of our working life, deciding what to do, and taking the necessary steps to implement that decision into explicit action. We differentiated and explored separately each stage in the process; and we had each stage neatly suggested by the preceding one in a linear progression. In practice, the process is not nearly so orderly. The differentiation in the stages of knowing is more evident in the field of scientific research, which proceeds from data gathering, to experimentation, to hypothesis verification, and to conclusions; and which is followed by a process of integrating the findings with the existing body of knowledge. However, in everyday life, the initial four stages are often going on without any clear conscious distinction among them until an acceptable decision is reached. Also, action often takes place while we are still integrating our new ways with the old ones and some-times the integration is not fully realized for a long time, as it happens with migrants who remain living in two worlds for more than a genera-tion. In real life, whether in scientific research or everyday life, the process of finding out what are the true facts of a situation and then deciding and acting in function of that truth – the process from experience to action – is not a one-shot straight-forward operation. In reality, this dynamic pro-cess moves back and forth in both directions and is often performed in a changing context.

PHASE II METHODOLOGY AND THE PROCESS OF KNOWING

In practice, it is a dynamic process: knowing, and finding new mean-ings and values, as the basis for acting in our world. But if we reflect on what is going on within ourselves, if we look carefully, we will become aware of the presence of the more or less differentiated parts of the struc-ture we have described. This is particularly so for important decisions. We would be conscious that we are engaged in the process of *experiencing, un-derstanding, judging,* and *deciding* and each stage would be a different *stage of consciousness* process.

Our protagonists were engaged in the same process as they proceeded from experiencing the global forces that entered into their lives to taking actions in the context of these forces. This is true even if the stages of consciousness were not differentiated for them and they were not able to articulate the process. That is how they came to define the meaning of globalization for themselves. Our objective is to understand the protago-nists at this level. Thus, in our research we have attempted to deconstruct the process, which was undifferentiated within the protagonists. We ad-dress separately each of the stages of consciousness that must have been involved and ask explicitly the questions that would have been proper at that level. We deduce the answers from the actions we know the protago-nists took. Interestingly, in the process we follow for understanding the protagonists' meanings and values, we ourselves as researchers undergo a comparable process. We start experiencing and understanding the protag-onists in a new way. As a result, we begin to raise questions regarding de-velopment policy – the researchers' decision point.

To get to the protagonists' questioning process, and in order to em-ploy the methodology in each of the narratives consistently, we construct-ed a generic template of guiding questions for the narrators and the WTC researchers to ask themselves. The template begins by identifying a significant action the protagonist (P) took in response to the global economy. Then, for each identified action, it raises specific questions designed to deconstruct P's processes of knowing that culminated in the observed action.

Note that questions A and D directly address what is going on within the protagonist, as deduced from her particular action. Questions B, C, and E go more deeply and explore what is happening in terms of the protagonist's meanings and values. Note, too, that in terms of time, A, B, and C focus on the process of reaching a decision: moving from experiencing to deciding. Questions D and E focus on the process of implementing the decision, as P then evaluates her decision and moves to put it into action.

Phase II Methodology Template

What is the significant action the protagonist (P) took in response to global forces?

Based on that action, deconstruct P's processes of knowing by asking questions.

A. What can we infer goes on within P as she *experiences the new economy and moves on to decide* to take this action? What questions may P have been raising and what answers seem consistent with her decision?

B. What values appear to drive P's decision? What are the good things that she seeks?

C. How does P's new knowledge and decision change the horizon of meanings in her world?

D. Given P's new horizon of meanings, what can we infer goes on within P *as she moves to implement her decision?* What questions may P have been trying to answer as she puts her decision into action? What values of P are engaged in this implementation?

E. Do we detect changes in the relative weights P now places on different values *within* a given level of values and *among* different levels of values? [This will be explained more fully later.] Does P seem comfortable with her decision and action?

Stages of Consciousness in Reaching a Decision: From Experiencing to Deciding

Our introductory role-playing illustrated in general the structure that we use to answer the template questions and referred to the various stages of consciousness involved in the process of experiencing, understanding, judging, and deciding. In this section and the next, we summarize what happens at each one of these stages of consciousness. At each stage, a different part of our human capabilities – senses, intellect, reason, or conscience – plays the central role in informing our consciousness, although our whole being is involved at each stage. In this summary we also pose characteristic questions raised at each stage of consciousness.

First, a diagram of the process of reaching a decision, from the process of experiencing to the process of deciding, and the human capability that is most engaged in each stage:

Reaching a Decision

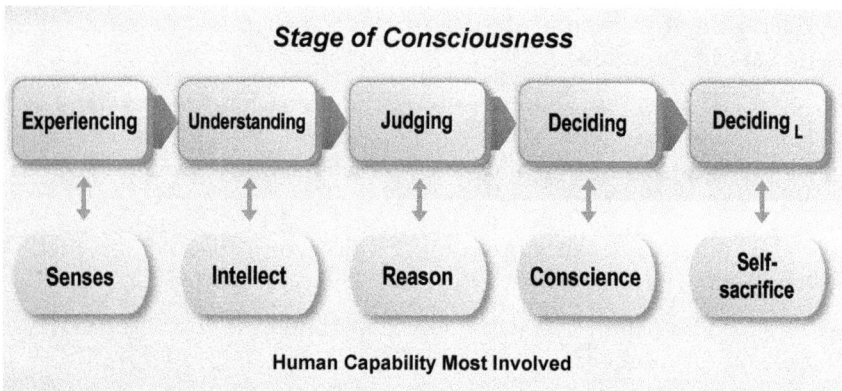

Stage of Consciousness

| Experiencing | Understanding | Judging | Deciding | Deciding $_L$ |

| Senses | Intellect | Reason | Conscience | Self-sacrifice |

Human Capability Most Involved

1. Experiencing – empirical consciousness. At this stage, our *senses* are the primary source of our experience consciousness: touching, smelling, seeing, hearing, imagining, and remembering. It is being conscious of hearing we have being fired from the job on which our livelihood depends and we feel rage and fear.

2. Understanding – intellectual consciousness. At this stage our *intellect* is heavily involved in an attempt to understand our experience. We ask why, how, and when, with regard to our experience. It is being conscious of questioning why management fired us and developing viable alternative responses.

3. Judging – rational consciousness. At this stage we ask questions that engage our *reasoning* powers to sift through the evidence in order to reach a conclusion about the facts of our situation. What is the truth? It is being conscious of choosing one among alternative hypotheses to answer why we were fired; e.g., we come to believe that although there is more import competition for the company, management is acting out of greed and lack of productivity on our part is not a good reason for our being fired.

4. Deciding – moral consciousness. At this stage we ask what the best thing to do is and we deliberate the course of action to take, given the facts and knowledge we have developed. We engage our *values and our conscience and take responsibility* for choosing what we believe to be the best course of action to follow. It is, first, being conscious of responsibly establishing priorities among our values, goals, and targets; second, considering the consequences of all the alternatives (protest or move on) and, finally, deciding to commit to an action (e.g., it would be worthwhile to organize a labor protest).

Now we introduce an additional dimension to the deciding stage, which we will identify as Deciding $_L$.

5. Deciding – being-in-love consciousness. This stage of consciousness also takes place during the deciding process but, arguably, it is of a different nature. It brings to bear a different, higher, type of values. It is what happens when in the deliberations leading to a decision we go beyond asking, "What is the right thing to do?" and instead ask, "What is the right thing for me to do for the one(s) I love?" We ask things such as, what will really help my children? Will I choose out of love, even if I must sacrifice myself, or will I hold back, withdraw? It is being willing to engage our *capacity for self-sacrifice, service to others*, etc. out of love. It is being conscious of establishing priorities, considering consequences, and *deciding in the context of love*. This happens frequently when we decide out of love for our children, for our parents, for our spouse. For many people, however, it can also mean deciding out of love for neighbor or even humanity. Finally, for the religious person, this ultimate stage of consciousness also engages the capacity of humans to be open to the possibility of a loving God (the Transcendent) intervening in their lives. It is the consciousness of reaching a decision to organize a labor protest because we care for the people who are being fired together with us and/or we want to be faithful to the merciful God who we believe loves us and whom we love in return.

Our understanding these stages of consciousness helps us to answer Questions A through C in the template.

Answering Question A in the template (page 87). Question A asks us to infer what was happening within the protagonist as she experienced the new global forces and, eventually, reached a decision. For example, we can see the first stage of consciousness of our protagonist in Mexico, Jorge Enrique, when he experiences hearing that management is closing the factory and he is fired: he feels fear and anger. We also see the other stages at work in his efforts to understand and evaluate the new situation and in his eventual decision to ally himself with the protesters, rather than accept the liquidation money offered him.

Answering Question B in the template (page 87). Once we infer what is happening within the protagonist, we have the basis for answering Question B: what are the values that appear to drive the protagonist's decision? We are going deeper. We discern, in Jorge Enrique's case, that the value that he places on staying with his family and his religious faith are major drivers in his decision. He is also motivated by what he considers to be a "good job." (The section "Humans' Scale of Values and the Stages of Consciousness" later in this chapter will also help answer Question B.)

Answering Question C in the template (page 87). Understanding the protagonist's stages of consciousness also helps us to appreciate how the person's new knowledge and decision signify new meanings: this is the answer to Question C. The protagonist's horizon of meanings changes in the process of reaching a decision. For Jorge Enrique, management and the labor union both take new meanings for him as he reaches the decision to become an active member in the union protesting management actions.

Stages of Consciousness in Implementing the Decision: From Deciding to Acting

However, making a decision is not the end of things. Now we face the challenge of putting the decision into action. To succeed in this task, and in order to remain at peace, we must reconcile the meanings and values of our new world that required the decision, influenced by global forces, with the meanings and values of our old world, the world of our local culture. If we do not succeed in this reconciliation, we will not be at peace – we will not be able to maintain our integrity – as we act on our decision. Signs of not being at peace would manifest themselves, on the one hand, in the form of alienation from our local society or, on the other hand, inability to function in the new environment.

Below we summarize what happens at each stage of consciousness as we move from deciding to acting. This process is similar to the first process we undertook, when we moved from experiencing to deciding. It engages the same stages of consciousness, and corresponding parts of our humanity, as the earlier process that led to the decision. But now, the object of the questioning at each stage becomes the decision itself, instead of the initial experience that led to the decision. Analytically, the sequence appears in reverse order. It begins with a question about the value of carrying out the decision itself and ends with the experience of expressing the decision in an explicit action.

Here expressed in a diagram is the process of implementing the decision from the process of deciding to the process of experiencing, and the part of our humanity most engaged at each stage of consciousness:

Implementing the Decision

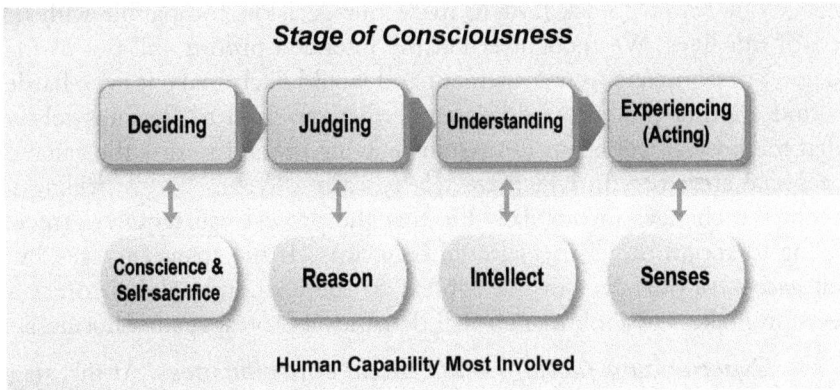

Stage of Consciousness

Deciding	Judging	Understanding	Experiencing (Acting)
↕	↕	↕	↕
Conscience & Self-sacrifice	Reason	Intellect	Senses

Human Capability Most Involved

6. Deciding – moral consciousness. At this stage we once again engage our *values,* our *conscience,* and our capability for *self-sacrifice,* and raise questions. But this time the question is not, "What is the best course of action to take?" Rather, the question becomes, "Do we really want to follow through with our decision?" We are conscious of wondering if this decision is consistent with our moral and ultimate values. Answering "yes" means we accept responsibility for the consequences of our decision, and also the changes within ourselves that will be necessary. It makes the decision operative; it becomes the foundation for how we will proceed. For example, we decide to go ahead and do what is necessary to implement our decision to organize a labor protest.

7. Judging – rational consciousness. At this stage we engage our *reason* to question the reasonableness of the decision. Referring to the situation above, we ask if our decision is consistent with the facts. Is management's motivation greed? If so, we become conscious that our view of management has changed, both from the view we had before and from the view others may still have. Is the conclusion specific to the management of this company at this time, or does it apply to all company managements at all times? Do we have sufficient reasons to go ahead with the intended protest? If we answer "yes," we are saying it is reasonable to continue with the protest. We are also saying that is reasonable to adjust our views of management and unions and what they mean in our community. So our cultural values have changed. We now *judge* that global economic competition unleashes management's greed and we have to oppose it.

8. Understanding – intellectual consciousness. At this stage we engage our *intellect* to ask how to make our decision compatible with the rest of our lives. We recognize that the intended protest will put us in a position antagonistic to management and would likely make it even harder to find another job. We are conscious that we need to find answers to what the protest will mean for earning a living in the future – the value of the social structure on which we rely to earn a living. Are we willing to accept the changes in our daily life that the protest will require? Are we willing to accept the changes in old behaviors? If the answer is "yes," we will *understand* ourselves in the context of the economic global forces as decision-makers in a job market that demands a protest against business.

9. Experiencing (acting) – empirical consciousness. At this stage we talk, write, and meet others. We engage our *senses*, in order to take the necessary steps to implement our decision. We answer affirmatively that we want to move on to action. This action communicates to the rest of the world a new view of ourselves, because we experience ourselves differently. We have a new identity: someone who finds it reasonable to engage in the protest and to adjust our way of life accordingly. Also, this experience of calling a labor protest is very different from the work experience we had before, up to the point when we were fired. It is our new experience of work in the global economy.

Answering Questions D and E in the template (page 87). Understanding the workings of the four stages of consciousness as we move from deciding to acting helps us answer Question D in the template. Now we can infer both what was happening within the protagonist during this process (between deciding and acting), and also the values that were engaged and had to be adapted. This then allows us to answer Question E, which summarizes the changes in weight given to different values that seem to have taken place in the protagonist. These adjustments in values sometimes are just changes in preferences among similar values. At other times, the change is much broader, leading us to appreciate the world in a way very different than before.

The terminology we use to talk about values is elaborated in more detail later in this chapter, in the sections on "Humans' Scale of Values and the Stages of Consciousness" and "Tensions Within and Among Levels of Values." The answer to the final question under Question E, whether the protagonist is comfortable with her action, helps us to corroborate whether the protagonist was relatively free and in charge of her choices, and not just acquiescing to the changes in circumstances.

Practical Constraints and Universality of the Process of Knowing

The different stages of consciousness are structurally interrelated and the quality of each stage depends on the achievements of the preceding one. At the judging stage, we will not be able to make good judgments if we have not fully understood the situation – which happens in the earlier, understanding stage: if, say, we don't have access to data to answer our questions, or if we don't ask enough questions. By the same token, if we don't reach accurate conclusions about the data in the judging stage, we won't be able to make good decisions about it in the deciding stage. Our actions will not reveal an integrated identity if we do not question the implications of our decision for who we are, its reasonableness, or the necessary adaptations in how we relate to our world. The reverse is also true. Good analysis of data leads to good judgments and good judgments lead to better decisions; good questioning of the implications of the decisions lead to actions backed by an integrated decision-maker.

The quality of the decision-making process also depends on the decision-maker's freedom from biases. In real life we have many *biases* that frustrate the questioning process and get in the way of making good decisions and taking proper actions. Some of these biases arise from our own selfishness; we want to please our desires without recognizing the interests of others. Other biases are more generalized and we share them with our group in society, such as when a society believes in the inferior role of women. Other biases are based on the way things usually work in a society and are seemingly supported by practical common sense often shared by the culture. But they truncate a deeper inquiry that may provide a better understanding of reality. For example, sometimes farmers are reluctant to change the way they have traditionally grown their crops, despite new information. In our research we try to be mindful of our own biases and the biases that the protagonists might have brought with them to their process of getting to know their new reality.

We all carry biases with us. Despite their presence, however, we always find in human beings the outlines of the dynamic questioning process that we have described. It will just not work as well. It won't produce as good decisions as it could without biases. The only requirements for this process to be operative are for the person:

1. To be conscious, in the most basic sense of being awake;

2. To have a minimum degree of natural intelligence;

3. To be rational, in the sense of being in his or her right mind;

4. To be emotionally balanced, able to reach out to others.

The decision may be an unimportant one that does not require a lot of pondering or one that we make out of habit – but the steps, even if in a very limited form, will be there whether or not we intentionally take them. We may decide out of selfishness or passion, instead of what we believe to be the right thing to do. But, as long as we are conscious, in control of ourselves, and capable of thinking of others when we reach a decision, we will not be able to avoid engaging in the human development process that we have described – even when we make a "bad" decision.

The spontaneous questioning arises from the dynamism of a process that is a given in our human nature, despite our incomprehension and errors. It is powered by a human being's natural drive to ask questions, to understand, to find out the truth. We want to respond to the demands of our intelligent, rational nature by acting responsibly according to our conscience – the dynamism of being a conscious human being. The context in which a person is capable of doing this might be limited to the practicalities of everyday living, but the basic process of questioning and wanting to act responsibly will be there nonetheless. The questions often are not posed explicitly in an internal Socratic dialogue. But what we do in getting to know, making decisions, and taking actions, implicitly does try to answer questions – the answers to which, in turn, generate new questions. Sometimes we do it superficially; but if the decision is important it tends to be done in a very thoughtful manner. As we try to understand what goes on within our protagonists, the meaning of the new globalization to them, and the values they bring to bear, our task is to raise these questions explicitly and surmise the protagonists' answers from the actions we observed in the narrative. As researchers, we also will be asking similar questions of ourselves as we come to understand the protagonists in a new way.

The basic assumptions of our Phase II methodology are: 1) actions are a person's ultimate answer to a series of questions; and 2) our protagonists meet the minimum human requirements mentioned above for the human process of knowing to operate. The methodology relies on the strength and universality of this questioning process. In our research we raise questions and speculate on the answers, based on the understanding of the protagonists and their world we gained from developing the narrative and conducting the cultural analysis. That work is the counterpart of the knowledge that a development practitioner would gain working on the ground. This analysis was done in cooperation with the narrators, but it could not be verified directly with the protagonists, with whom we did not have direct contact any more at this stage of the project. Therefore, some of our inferred answers might lack in accuracy. Still, we found the process of trying to see the protagonists' world through their own eyes very illuminating. The development practitioner working on the ground would not encounter the same difficulties we had in verifying the analysis.

HUMANS' SCALE OF VALUES AND
THE STAGES OF CONSCIOUSNESS

The second major building block in our Phase II methodology is humans' scale of values: what people care for, what fires and drives their lives. Values play a role in the process of knowing that we explored in the preceding section. Brian Cronin, following on Lonergan's path, provides the foundation for our approach to the scale of values. See Brian Cronin, *Value Ethics: A Lonergan Perspective* (2006).

Values appeared explicitly in Questions B and E of the Phase II methodology template on page 87. Values drive the process of reaching a decision. They also are the focus in the integration process that takes place between deciding and acting. In this section we describe the process of valuing more fully and explore the different levels of values to which we alluded earlier.

By values we mean what human beings value, what they desire because they believe it to be good and worthwhile. The process of valuing is part of all areas of life. Values underlie all human decisions, from things as fundamental as the food we eat and the music we like to our ideas of justice. And people everywhere, in all societies, are driven by values as they make decisions.

Human behavior, of course, does not always seem to seek the "good." People do not always seek healthy food; they do not always fight for justice. Biases enter into our decisions. But we can assume that in any decision we make, we are seeking what we consider to be the better choice. This might involve self-sacrifice but also could entail selfish motives. But, whatever the motivation, it is what is most desirable to us, given available information, cultural inclinations, personal and social passions, etc. From another point of view, it might not be the best decision for us or for our society, but it is where our energies are.

We value things at every level of life. At the most basic level, that of survival, we value, say, food that is flavorful. This is the *vital* level. As we come together in social groups, we value a good educational system for our children. This is the *social* level of values. At another level, what we value is embedded in our culture. So we value some food, music, and traditions not just for any physical need they meet, but also because they make us feel at home and provide a sense of belonging. These are *cultural* values. At a higher level, we find *moral* values, such as freedom and justice. And at a still higher level is the good we seek when we act out of love for another person. For the religious person, this would include an experience of the sacred. These we call *ultimate* values. At each level in the scale of values, then, we are seeking a different type of "good."

At each level in the scale of values, a different human capability is dominant in the valuing. We are at a different stage of consciousness. The stages of consciousness we presented earlier have a corresponding value in our scale of values. For example, when we search for good food it is our senses that most inform our consciousness of whether that food is good. Here is a diagram containing the scale of levels of values, with the corresponding stages of consciousness and the human capability most engaged at each stage.

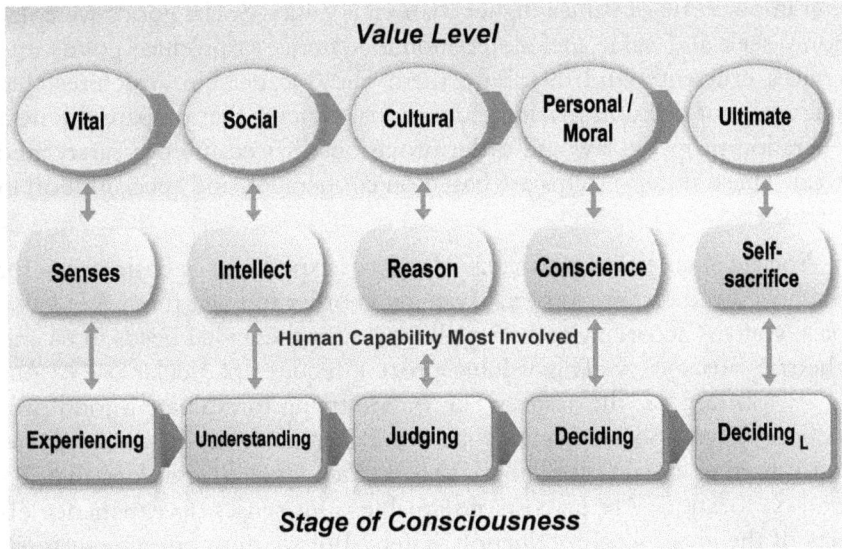

A summary of the five levels of values follows.

1. Vital values: what we value as good in things needed for basic existence. Valuing at the experiencing stage of consciousness. When we seek something that is good for satisfying physical and psychological needs basic to our human existence, we are seeking something we value at a vital level – a vital value. Thus, we seek food and water, which we value by how they meet our need for sustenance; shelter, which we value for how it protects us from the elements; sleep, which we value for how it restores our energies; security, which we value as protection from danger, etc. The individual seeking a vital value still uses his or her intelligence to, say, understand the content of food, and judge whether a particular food is healthy (good). But what dominates when a person seeks to satisfy a basic human need is the individual's consciousness of *sensing* and *experiencing*. When we value food, for example, we are engaging our basic sensual experience of that food to value it. Does it nourish? Does it taste good? This applies to anything we consume.

2. Social values: what we value as good in social structures (good of order). Valuing at the understanding stage of consciousness. When we seek something that is good at the social level, we are seeking the good in social systems. We value them according to how they help us meet vital needs – basic survival needs – that we could not easily meet on our own. We are seeking a social good. Our social values are at a level in our scale of values higher than vital values. Social goods we commonly seek and value include economic systems to produce goods and services efficiently and distribute them fairly, leadership structures that facilitate joint decision-making, educational systems that prepare the next generation properly, law and order provisions that ensure our safety, and so on. These social systems are based on cooperation and specialization in our society.

Social values encompass vital values, our experience of basic needs for which we need to rely on social systems in order to meet them. We value social systems according to how well they meet these vital needs in us and others in our society. This valuing process requires particular use of our *intellect* to *understand* the system. Say we are trying to evaluate a food production system. So we ask, is food readily available or do some people find it hard to obtain? Is it good or is it often spoiled, and does that depend on location? Are its costs reasonable? Our senses do experience effects of the given food production system. But we must engage our intellect more than our senses in order to understand how it functions, who decides what food will be produced, how it is priced, how farm income is distributed – i.e., to evaluate it. It is our intellect that plays the larger role when we value a social system.

3. Cultural values: what we value as good because our culture gives it meaning. Valuing at the judgment stage of consciousness. When we seek what is good at the cultural level, we are seeking what gives us a sense of belonging in the larger society that we respect and in which we live. We are seeking the publicly shared meanings, values, and beliefs of our way of life in our society. This way of life includes social structures and ways of satisfying our vital needs. Our cultural values are at a higher level in our scale of values than our social and vital values. Cultural values influence how we value things at the social and vital levels. We actively seek what we value as good culturally when we choose one set of meanings over an alternative set of meanings for the same thing; for example, the meaning of the role of elders in a society. In some societies they are accorded great respect as a source of wisdom; in others, they tend to live on the margins of society and are given little consideration. The culture expresses what it values in its myths and stories, its customs and traditions, and in its laws and institutions. Cultural values are a society's shared operative assumptions about how we are expected to interact in our daily activities. These values include the food we eat, the type of dwelling in which we live, how we interact with different members of society, and so on. But at this level we value these things not because of the sustenance or shelter they provide, or the social contribution they make, but because of their meaning to us in our society. Rice, for instance, holds a particular cultural meaning in Asian society, a meaning that is more than rice as food and is associated with family, ritual, and religion. Cultural values also tell us the acceptable ways of behaving in society. For example, some cultures value punctuality; to be late for an event is considered very rude. In other cultures, it is seen as rude to break off an encounter with one person in order to adhere to a schedule.

Cultural values encompass social and vital values. Family, for example, is valued at the social level as an economic and social system with the practical purpose of helping raise children and providing mutual support to family members at the vital level. But, beyond this value of the social and economic system, family is also a cultural value, whose meaning varies in different cultures. Family means one thing in African cultures, with obligations to a very extended family; something different in American culture, with its nuclear family; and something different yet again in Asian cultures.

Our cultural values form the basis of what we commonly believe to be true, our shared politics, and our view of human nature. Our common expectations rest on them. They are socially accepted assumptions on which we base our trust of one another so that we can interact with some degree of spontaneity, in the midst of the practicalities of making a living, raising a family, etc. We receive cultural values through education and socialization. We internalize these values as we grow up, but we can also question them when they seem at odds with our other values.

The human faculty most engaged when we value something in our culture is *reason*. With cultural values, we still experience them with our senses and understand them with our intellect − the faculties predominant in the vital and social levels of values − but we use mostly our *reason* to *judge* that we identify with these aspects of our culture. For example, if we are looking for a way to make a living, we look for a good job: one considered prestigious in our culture. I want the culture to validate the worth of my job. This is a cultural good.

4. Personal/moral values: what we value as good because we see it as being "right" and not "wrong." Valuing at the deciding stage of consciousness. Personal/moral values spring from a conviction of our innate human dignity, both our own and others', a dignity based on the recognition that each person has a conscience and must act as a free and responsible individual within a society. Our conscience guides us in deciding the "right" thing to do. When we act responsibly, according to our conscience and moral values, we are seeking a moral good. Our moral values are at a higher level in our scale of values than cultural, social, and vital values. Our moral values influence how we value things at the cultural, social, and vital levels.

When we seek moral values, we operate at all levels of consciousness; we still experience, understand, and judge the situation. But we are most conscious of deliberating and *deciding* about what our *conscience* considers morally good, of accepting responsibility for ourselves and for others in our decisions. Our conscience helps us in *deciding* the best way to be true to ourselves as a person in society, for the good of one's self (not selfishness) and the good of others.

When we seek moral values, the dominant human capacity engaged in this activity is our conscience. And while we use our conscience and sense of responsibility when we seek the good at the other levels of values, it is when we seek the higher moral values that human responsibility is most profoundly expressed. There is responsibility involved in choosing to eat healthy food; but it is in choosing to be fair to others, even at great cost to us, that the greater responsibility for the moral good lies. And in seeking to be fair to others I will be enhancing the way in which I seek the vital good of food. For example, as a result of moral values, I may eat more healthily because there is a cost to society if my health is not good. Seeking moral good and deciding in favor of good moral values make a person who the person really is and wants to become.

Personal/moral values encompass cultural, social, and vital values. Healthy moral individuals and societies affirm the rights, dignity, and respect of all individuals and groups of individuals (women, different ethnic groups) in the context of the larger society. Society's myths and traditions often suggest explanations for how respect and dignity are doled out. For example, a society's myth may suggest that if a person belongs to an inferior caste, she is therefore less worthy of respect. An individual's conscience would go along with the culture if she agrees that a lower-caste person is inferior, but her conscience will rebel against this cultural value if her personal belief is that all human beings have the same dignity, regardless of the caste into which they are born. Her conscience will also affect how she values the social structures that discriminate against the lower caste; i.e. her social values.

5. Ultimate values – what we value as the ultimate good motivating our lives. Valuing at the deciding stage of consciousness when based on love. This is the highest level of values. When we evaluate alternative choices in the context of what is good for others, even at our own expense – in other words, in the context of love – we are pursuing the ultimate good. What we consider the ultimate good permeates the search for all that we value as good. When we pursue these values we are searching for the ultimate truth, goodness, beauty, peace, joy, and sense of unity and harmony with the rest of the universe. That search may be in the context of love for our family, but also for the benefit of neighbor or even humanity at large.

For religious people, the love context of ultimate values is found in a higher power that can be called God. For Christians the ultimate value is found in the love of a God who creates, supports, and redeems all creation in Christ, and in a sense of our ultimate moral impotence and need for outside help to maintain integrity. But for both religious and nonreligious people, our being in love is always mediated by the goodness and love of others – parents, mentors, friends – towards us. And when we fall in love, this influences everything we do and our life is qualitatively different. These ultimate values, embedded in love, set our horizon and open our closed world to a complete fulfillment of the human questioning that thrusts us beyond ourselves.

Ultimate values encompass moral values; they too involve the *conscience*. But they go beyond moral values to demand that our *decisions* be based on *love*, mercy, and compassion. Ultimate values guide us in deciding what is "the right thing to do," moral values; but not all moral values have an ultimate dimension. When we restrain ourselves from retaliating against the manager who fired us because we value the human dignity (even the dignity of a corrupt manager) that demands a lawful process, we are seeking moral values. When we do it out of love for neighbor – even the enemy – it is the fulfillment of that love that we are seeking. When we not only restrain ourselves but actually forgive the manager because we have also been forgiven by our God, it is God's love that guides our decision. In the last two instances we are seeking ultimate values; a secular and a religious version of love for others. Many would refer to the sacred version of ultimate values as religious values. We have chosen the term *ultimate* value instead of *religious* value to make it clear we are referring to how we value the experience of the Transcendent in our lives, in contrast to what might just be a cultural value; such as the secular celebration of Christmas, with the lighting of a Christmas tree.

The five levels in the scale of values are all structurally interrelated. Each value level provides the conditions for enhancing the following level, and this happens in the order in which we presented them above. So seeking the good at one level enhances the possibility of achieving the good at the next level up. The reverse is also true: achieving the good at a higher level of value makes it possible to reach a fuller realization of the good at lower levels. For example, if the individuals in a society have a developed moral sense, it makes for a culture where human rights are observed and where good social structures are created to address vital needs. Achieving what we value as the ultimate good enhances what we value morally. Furthermore, once we reach a decision by choosing according to our ultimate values, these values become the guiding principle for how we integrate the new decision with our old world as we move to implement the decision into action. Ultimate values will guide how we readjust what we consider good at the various levels of value.

Finally, we must acknowledge that the possibility exists for our choosing the opposite of value, of choosing what is not good or choosing a "disvalue." We all value honesty, but people can convince themselves that being dishonest (perhaps only this one time) is justified. It requires a certain level of rationalization, but the newspapers give witness to how often people can convince themselves in this manner.

TENSIONS WITHIN AND AMONG LEVELS OF VALUES

The final building block in the Phase II methodology is the set of tensions that exist within and among levels of values. In introducing our approach to dealing with these tensions, we draw on Neil Ormerod and Shane Clifton, *Globalization and the Mission of the Church* (2010, Chapter 2, "Theology of History"). Their framework, in turn, has its origins in Bernard J.F. Lonergan's work as elaborated by Robert M. Doran, *Theology and the Dialectics of History* (1990).

In the previous section, we described the five levels of values and discussed how they are interrelated, so higher levels encompass the lower levels on the scale. There, we described each level in a rather static fashion. But there are dynamic tensions at work within each level, which we discuss in this section. These dynamic tensions also generate movements among levels of values.

By tension we mean an active, ongoing energy between two poles: stability and tradition on the one hand, and change and development on the other. The first pole encourages harmony and integration and calls for agreement in the community and compliance with tradition. It has difficulty dealing with development. The second pole, however, encourages development. It calls for adopting new ways, which threaten the cohesiveness of the community and the continuity of tradition. There's always a creative energy flowing between these poles, an energy that pulls in opposite directions, between inherited values on the one hand and the forces of change on the other.

In a stable situation, there is a balance between the pull of these two poles at each level in the scale of values. It is when that balance is disturbed that problems arise. Many of these imbalances arise within us, especially in the process of our growing up and maturing as individuals. For example, say a person is brought up believing that going to church regularly is the proper expression of religious values, or ultimate value. At the cultural level, parents and society both reinforce this idea; going to church is a value at the cultural level; and this cultural value has implications for the church social structures that this person values. But as an adult, this person may begin thinking that her relationship with God is not defined by going to church. At the cultural level of value, she knows that those around her approve of church attendance, it is part of their way of life, and so are the associated church structures. So with these new thoughts, an imbalance emerges between wanting to belong, on the one hand, and wanting to develop in her experience of God, on the other. An imbalance has been created and the person's situation is not stable any more.

In the preceding example, the force for change comes from within the individual. But change can also come from external sources. When a country's economy opens to the global market, foreign trade and investment introduce much more than just new products and production technologies. It also brings new ways of valuing food and consumer goods. It brings different types of relationships, both at work and in the community. The market economy also brings a greater reliance on personal responsibility, as opposed to tradition. Previously, there had been a balance in the tensions at each value level between the two poles of stability/harmony and change/development. But the entrance of the global economy breaks that balance at each level of values in favor of change and development. This outcome often appears attractive to the outsider, but unfortunately, it is not sustainable without further adjustments. With the balance broken, instability grows, in both individuals and communities, and the new situation becomes unsustainable.

For the new situation to become sustainable, the balance between the two poles will have to be restored, at each level of value. Failure to do so will break social cohesion (social value level), create alienation within the community (cultural value level), develop psychopathological individuals (personal/moral value level) and eventually frustrate development – regardless of positive socioeconomic indicators in the early stages.

In looking into what was going on within our protagonists as they reached decisions (after experiencing the effects of the new global economy), we are identifying the tensions between the values of the old stable and socially cohesive system and the values of the forces for change introduced in their lives by the new global economic forces. In looking into what was going on within the protagonists as they implemented their decisions, we are looking into how they worked towards restoring balance in the tensions between the two poles of stability and change.

The next page provides a diagram representing these relationships.

Reaching a Decision

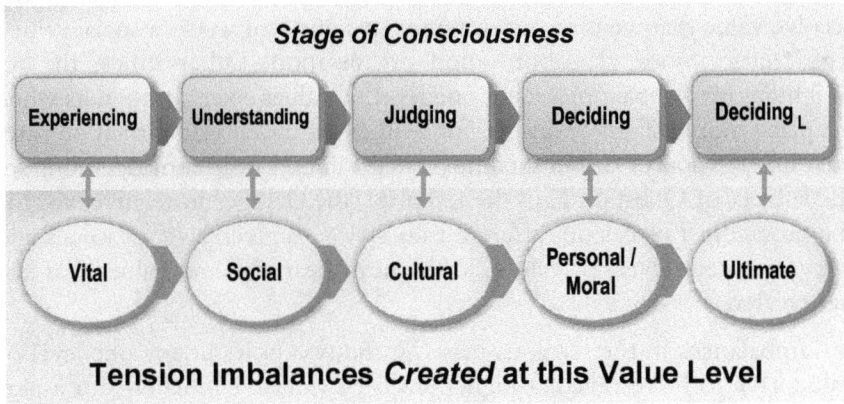

Stage of Consciousness

Experiencing	Understanding	Judging	Deciding	Deciding L
↑	↑	↑	↑	↑
Vital	Social	Cultural	Personal / Moral	Ultimate

Tension Imbalances *Created* at this Value Level

Implementing the Decision

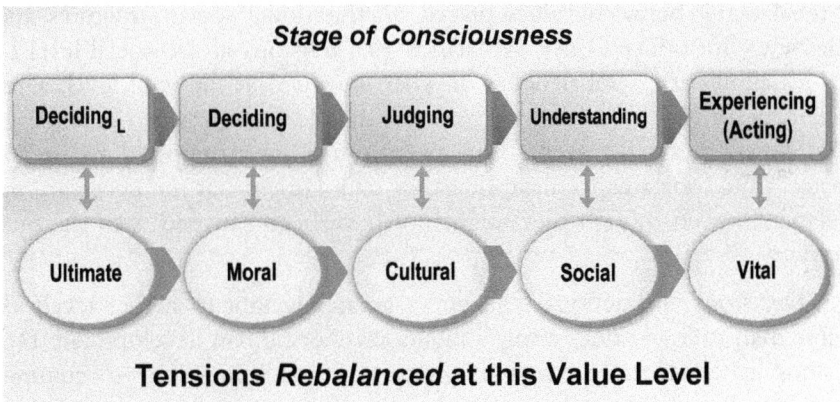

Stage of Consciousness

Deciding L	Deciding	Judging	Understanding	Experiencing (Acting)
↑	↑	↑	↑	↑
Ultimate	Moral	Cultural	Social	Vital

Tensions *Rebalanced* at this Value Level

When a new situation is introduced, the person goes through a process: from experiencing the new situation, to understanding it and then judging it before reaching a new decision. This process reveals imbalances between the two tension poles at each value level in the scale of values, imbalances created by the new situation. Once a decision is made, a rebalancing of these tensions must take place if the decision is to be implemented into an action that is sustainable. A re-weighting of values must happen in order to achieve this rebalancing. Some of the re-weighting of values takes place within the same level of values, as when we change the relative value that we place on different structures of work (a social value); e.g., factory work vs. labor union organization. Other times, the re-weighting involves emphasizing one level of values over another, as when we place more weight on justice for workers (a moral value) than on safeguarding the source of our income (a vital value). These considerations are the subject of Question E in the template, the changes in relative weights the protagonist places on different values *within* a given level of values and *among* different levels of values, in the new meanings and values that she has created.

Imbalances in the tensions between the two poles at any one level of value have to be resolved at higher levels of values. Ultimately, for a person to be "at peace", the rebalancing has to be consistent with the highest levels – the religious and moral levels of values. Sorting values at the religious and moral levels allows for a rebalancing at the next lower level, the cultural; it allows a rebalancing between traditional cultural values and the new meanings and values. In turn, a balancing of tensions at the cultural level of values allows for a rebalancing of what is valued at the social level: a rebalancing between values placed on traditional social structures and the newly introduced ones. A balancing of tensions at the social level of values allows for a rebalancing of what is valued at the vital level; a rebalancing of the values that we place on the old in contrast to new things that satisfy our vital needs. Our protagonists were reported to be "at peace." We took this to mean that they had worked out the necessary rebalancing, even though they might not have been satisfied with the outcome.

Decisions and actions that give a greater weight to higher levels of value than to lower ones imply a higher level of human development. Decisions in which more weight is given to moral values than to cultural, social, and vital values imply a higher level of human development than decisions that have the opposite relative weights. When the value driving the decision and action is one of the lower levels of values, such as subsistence, there is a regression in human development.

Something we must note here is that we did not fully develop our understanding of the concept of tensions between two poles at each level of values until late in the research process. From early in the development of Phase II methodology, we focused on the importance of recognizing the shifts in weights the protagonist placed within and among levels of values.

But we only recognized the full power of the resolution of imbalances between the poles of tension after we looked at all the narratives together, toward the end of the research. In the narratives to which we applied the Phase II methodology, the language used to discuss the shifts in weights resulting from the tensions between old and new values does not fully articulate the issue as we have presented it in this chapter. It is not until the final chapter, Chapter 17, that we fully use this language of tensions between two poles consistently. Our methodology, in essence, was evolving, and so did this chapter.

THE RESEARCHERS' OWN PROCESS OF KNOWING

Though the way people express themselves can be culturally different, the process by which human beings go about knowing is universal. The researchers of this project, both the narrators and the WTC researchers, went through the same process to get to know the protagonists as subjects of their history. In applying the Phase I methodology, we first *experienced* the protagonists through the initial narratives that the narrators submitted. Then we attempted to *understand* the protagonists and their situation, by the WTC researchers engaging in a dialogue with the narrators. This dialogue enhanced the narrative data. The WTC researchers asked questions about the economic situation in the country and asked the narrators about the why and how of the protagonists and other actors in the narrative. The questioning and dialogue went further in the context of the cultural analysis. The answers to these and related questions took us to some conclusions about the external facts, a *judgment of the external facts*. This judgment was of the protagonists' situation before they encountered global forces and after they did, all within the context of their own culture. The questioning that we have discussed in this chapter under Phase II methodology takes us to a new kind of judgment of facts, this time a *judgment of the facts of the protagonist as an agent of change*.

In the final section of the narrative chapters in Part II, where Phase II methodology was applied, we as researchers reflect on the new understandings gained from studying how the protagonists came to know their new world, their meanings and values, as reflected by their actions. We came to know the protagonists in a much deeper way than we had done before, in a new way. In our research, from early in the project, we identified the "before globalization" and "after globalization" facts in the life of the protagonists. In the final section of the narrative chapters in Part II we focus on the researchers' own "before" and "after applying Phase II methodology," thus getting to know the protagonists in the new way. We too have been changed; the protagonists' new data give globalization a new meaning for us. When we see the protagonists as capable of being authors of their own human development, we also see new potentialities for development policy. Thus, these narrative chapters that applied the Phase II methodology conclude with some implications of our new knowledge for development policy.

In the final chapter of the book, Chapter 17, "Stepping Back and Looking Forward," the authors reflect on the changes in meanings and values they experienced throughout the research project as a whole.

PART II

NARRATIVES TO WHICH BOTH PHASE I AND II METHODOLOGIES WERE APPLIED

As described in Part I of this book, this book is based on the analysis of eleven narrative stories. In Part II, we present the five narratives to which both Phase I and II methodologies were applied. To provide more detail for one narrative, the case of Shanti in India is presented over two chapters. In Chapter 5, "Shanti in India: Where Will She Go?," we present Shanti's final narrative and our cultural analysis, both performed by applying the tools of the Phase I methodology. In Chapter 6, "Getting to Know Shanti Through Her Own Eyes," we apply the tools that we developed during Phase II of the project in order to deduce her meanings and values from the actions that we observed.

Chapters 7-10 present the remaining four narratives to which both Phase I and II methodologies were applied: Chanda in Zambia (Chapter 7), Núria in Spain (Chapter 8), Jorge Enrique in Mexico (Chapter 9), and Joseph in China (Chapter 10).

Part III presents the other six narratives to which limited resources allowed only for the application of Phase I methodology.

Chapter 5

Shanti in India: Where Will She Go?
(Phase I Methodology)

Shanti in her home village of Agaria Tola, India

NARRATOR: TONY HERBERT, SJ

Associate, Prerana Resource Centre
With the assistance of Sr. Bina Stanis
Hazaribag, Jharkhand, India

Narrative Summary and Economic Background

Shanti was born in Agaria Tola, Jharkhand, in northeast India, to a family who had lived in the same village for generations. They used the forest for food and medicine and lived a subsistence lifestyle. They were Bhuiyas, one of India's tribal groups. Shanti's village was nestled between two coal mines that opened when Shanti was a child. Globalization entered the lives of Shanti and her village through these mines. With the increasing demand for energy in India, the mines had been expanding and were now encroaching on the village. The village lands actually had been acquired by Coal India Limited under Indian law and the village might be relocated to accommodate the mine expansion. If the relocation comes to pass, Shanti, now in her fifties and living with her younger children and her sister's family, does not know where she and the others will go or if she will receive any compensation. As a woman, she has no legal claim to the land where she lives, since both her father and husband have died.

After independence in 1947, India's economic growth was characterized by state-driven economic policies and high protection against imports. Also, a significant share of the economy was directly controlled by the government, including ownership of one of the mines encroaching on Shanti's village. These policies led to unsustainable fiscal deficits and total depletion of the country's foreign exchange reserves, culminating in a financial crisis in 1991. In response, India launched a program of economic liberalization. It devalued its currency and reduced government subsidies in various sectors, including agriculture. It also began to dismantle the social policies of earlier decades and let market forces play a larger role. In 1995, with the implementation of the Uruguay Round Trade Agreement, India reduced its import tariffs and further opened the country to foreign investment. The reduction forced Indian coal mines to improve efficiency in order to compete with imported Australian coal and respond to the increasing demands for energy.

NARRATIVE

When Shanti Was a Child

The laughter of her friends greeted Shanti as she walked down the path to the spring. She was carrying her mother's pots to collect water in and the others were there already with their mothers. It was a time of day that the girls loved, when they played, bathed, and refreshed themselves. For their mothers, it was a time to meet and chat, to gossip about their families, to bathe, and to draw the day's supply of water.

The spring was a natural perennial spring near their village of Agaria Tola. It never dried up. The villagers had put a wall around it to protect it, and had built a platform around it for bathing. It was precious to them, and they called it *naihar*. Shanti spent some time there before turning back up the path to the village, splashing the water over the edges of the pots as she walked.

In addition to providing essential fresh water, the natural spring at Agaria Tola was a vibrant center of village life, where women met and socialized and children played together

Back at her home, Shanti waited for her parents to return from the fields. Three of her sisters were also there. They had been in the family's field gathering potatoes and in the forest collecting wood. The children spent a lot of time in the forest. In the monsoon months, Shanti would go there with her friends looking for mushrooms. They also often brought home sag, green leaves that her family would eat. None of them went to school. That thought did not cross Shanti's mind.

Their parents worked as sharecroppers for the local landowner, and her mother went twice a week to the bazaar to barter some of the food she grew in exchange for other necessities. Watching them as they walked up to the house, Shanti thought her father seemed especially tired and her mother had a sad look about her. About a week and a half ago, Shanti's new baby brother had died. Even though they had already lost three other sons as infants, the death of another one was no easier for them.

The parents and their four daughters finished the evening with a quiet dinner of rice and vegetables. Hanging from the roof above them was a burning *dibri*, a small bottle of kerosene with a cloth wick. It gave off a flickering light. Though the nearby Facodih village had electricity, Shanti's village did not.

Agaria Tola is in the Damodar River Basin, in northeastern India. The soil there is rich and the subsoil even richer: it is deep with coal. That night, the family slept inside their hut, unaware of the unseen depths of coal beneath them.

One morning later that week, Shanti heard a loud rumbling sound coming from the forest. She and her sisters ran down to see what was happening. There they saw a large yellow machine tearing the trees down. None of them had ever seen a machine like that before. Captivated, the girls could not help but marvel and delight at this entertaining spectacle and the power of the machine as it trampled and flattened the forest.

Their parents already knew of the coal mine a few miles away — the TISCO West Bokaro mine, owned by Tata Steel, a private Indian steel company in the distant city of Jamshedpur. The Tata Company had obtained a mining lease from the government to mine coal for its steel plant. Shanti's family learned later that their own village's land to the south was in the area targeted for mining.

Shanti was excited about the mining. She and her sisters and a few of their goats went again and again to the forest to enjoy the sight of the big machine with the shovel doing its digging.

For the grownups of Agaria Tola, the mining brought both apprehension and optimism. They were Bhuiyas, one of India's many indigenous groups, or tribals, who had lived in the forest long before the Aryan and Muslim settlers came to India. Now they had to watch as their forest was being razed. They still used the forest's resources for many things: for fuel, for food, for medicine. It had been sustenance for them for generations. More than that, though, the forest was the center of their religion and was intertwined with their culture and identity. It contained the *sarna*, the sacred grove of trees where the Bhuiyas worshipped. To tear all this down was like cutting away at the spirit of the people.

Yet it was not the first time that something had been taken from them. Centuries ago, the Bhuiyas had been small subsistence farmers. Then the Hindu Aryans arrived in Jharkhand and gradually became dominant, taking most of the Bhuiyas' land and making them work it for the newcomers. Since then, the Bhuiyas survived mainly by working for their higher-caste landlords, either in their fields or in their houses.

Along with their land, they also lost some of their identity. They felt they had to please the landlords, who dominated them and, as time passed, the Bhuiyas began to emulate their masters. Eventually the Bhuiyas were assimilated into the Hindu caste system and were categorized as untouchables, or Dalits. They learned to look up to, depend on, even to want, a powerful patriarchal figure to give them security, even though this meant servility and exploitation.

Shanti had always been taught that the upper castes were strong, noble, and intelligent; she, her family, and her community were weak, worthless, and stupid. Bhuiyas were inferior to the higher castes. She was also taught that as a woman, she was inferior to men. She accepted this; it was simply the way things were. There was not much they could call their own; the Bhuiyas had even adopted the high-caste Hindu cultural festivals and celebrations. But the Bhuiyas also continued to revere their primordial ancestor, Tulsi Bir. Shanti's family considered the ancestors as much a part of the community as they themselves were, and Shanti felt that wherever she went, her ancestors would be with her.

As the Bhuiyas watched their forest being razed to make room for the mine, it seemed that nobody cared about what the forest meant to them. The Tata steel company had the support of the government. The unvoiced thinking in both the company and the government seemed to be, "They are only tribals; it doesn't really matter." Without the power to prevent or even have a say in the destruction of the forest, the villagers hesitantly began to adjust to the shift in their lives. On the positive side, the coal mines did offer more work to the people and also introduced new technology and machines to the area. In fact, after TISCO's first year of digging under their former fields and forest, Shanti's father got a job with the company as compensation for land lost to the mine.

Some Years Later

The southern village lands were now a huge gaping chasm: the TISCO quarry. Shanti could see hardly any woods on the other side of the vast hollowed-out ground. The desolation she felt seeing the dreary quarry only added to her sadness at the deaths of yet another brother – the fifth one to die – and her father a few months earlier. She felt numbed by the loss. Her father had died of tuberculosis. He had spent day after day working in the dust-filled quarry and it didn't take long before he became sick. He had lived long enough to have a family, but had been devastated by the deaths of his sons, who were to carry on his name. He had pinned all his hopes on this last one.

Shanti had lost her father and the last of her brothers, but soon afterwards she gained a husband. Still a young teenager, she married a man named Lallo. As is the custom, it was an arranged marriage. Her community and her family circumstances dictated who her husband would be and where she would live. Shanti accepted these conditions; it was the way things were done. Because there were no longer any men in her immediate family, she did not go to live in her husband's village. Instead, Lallo moved to her village as a *ghar damad* to live with her and support her. All of her sisters except one, Manjhu, had already moved out to live with their husbands in their in-laws' villages.

Lallo was able to get his father-in-law's job with TISCO. He began working in the blasting section, filling holes with explosives. A few years were enough for the explosions to take their toll on Lallo's body and he too contracted tuberculosis. He and Shanti already had several small children. Concerned about his family as his health declined, Lallo decided to sign up for the company's Voluntary Retirements Scheme. This ensured that Shanti would receive a regular pension when he died.

A security guard watching the coal mine

To help support her family, Shanti would spend her days scavenging for coal and her nights turning it into coke, a coal byproduct. Other women did it, too. After rising early in the morning to get drinking water for her family, Shanti and the other women would sneak to the coal mine. She took a route that she hoped would keep her hidden from the company guards who watched over the mine. Still, the men would often spot her and hurl taunts at her as she passed. Moving through the quarry, Shanti searched for pieces of coal she could take and carry back with her. Some days, she could not avoid the guards on her way out of the mine. They would never hit or strike her, but they would try to snatch or turn over her basket of coal. She fought back with fierce verbal attacks.

Every evening, Shanti stacked the coal she had taken and lit it. It burned into the night, the red-hot embers releasing a cloud of thick smoke that filled the air and made it difficult to breathe. The process turned the coal into coke. The next morning, Shanti put the coke in bags, and her sons would wheel the bags on bicycles to the main highway and sell them to passing trucks. The trucks would carry the coke to distant towns, where it brought fairly good money – more than what they paid Shanti and her sons. Every week the police would come and take *haftah*, a bribe to allow this illegal activity to continue; that was not a problem. But the process of turning the coal into coke was hazardous. Once Shanti burned her right arm badly and was left with a big scar. Out of embarrassment, to this day she hides it with the end of her sari.

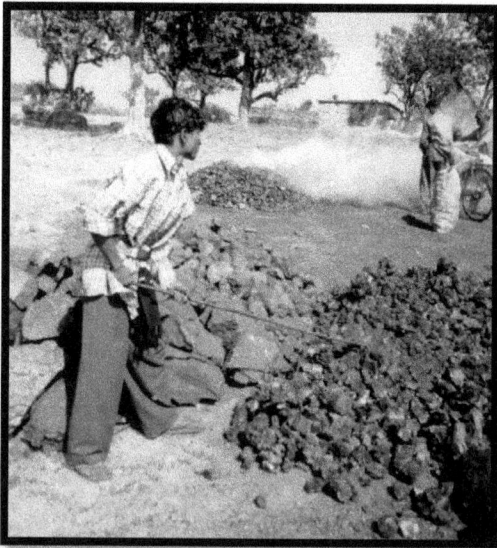

Villagers turning gathered pieces of coal into coke

When Lallo died from the tuberculosis, Shanti was left with five children, two boys and three girls, to support. Together with her sister

Manjhu's family, Shanti and her sons and daughters lived then in a three-room mud hut with a mud-baked tile roof.

The TISCO quarry was now getting closer and closer to the village spring. Finally the bulldozers began to cut into the earth around it. This was too much for Shanti. Uncharacteristically for a Bhuiya woman, she decided to take action. She gathered together the village women who came regularly to the spring and they organized a protest to protect their *naihar*.

Shanti and the other women fought to convince the officials to save the spring. But they were outmatched by company representatives: the defiant demonstration failed to stop the company's inexorable progress. Dejected and defeated, Shanti stood by as the bulldozers chewed into the earth that for centuries had given her people living water. Their *naihar* was destroyed. In exchange, the company promised to build a replacement well. But when it was eventually built, the well often ran dry in the hot summer months.

Digging a new well to replace the destroyed natural spring

By this time, TISCO had mined the whole southern part of the village's lands and had left a moonscape. And, as if this were not enough, now the East Parej mine expansion was approaching the village from the east. That mine was owned by Coal India Limited, a government-owned company that had received a large loan from the World Bank to upgrade and expand the mine. The purpose of the loan was to increase the mine's efficiency so it could compete internationally. However, this expansion eventually ate up even more of the natural resources that Shanti and her people had survived on for generations.

The mines changed more than Shanti's physical environment and source of livelihood. They also brought other new things to her life, such as currency and electricity, and Shanti liked those changes. She received money from Lallo's pension and she no longer had to barter goods and wait for the harvest of her vegetables to buy basic necessities like salt and cooking oil. Also, she eventually was able to build a brick house, a *pakka*, and, having electricity now, could get a fan and a television. Packaged foods and small luxuries were available now as well and she enjoyed them when she could afford them.

Shanti worried, though, about her children. They were not developing the same attitude to work that Shanti and the other Bhuiyas had. They were happy to stay at home watching TV while their mother went scavenging for coal. They preferred to eat packaged foods like biscuits and *paw-roti* for breakfast and despised the traditional *gutha kundi*, which was made out of a tuber and was much more nutritious. They were already forgetting the traditional dances and songs that Shanti had been brought up on and actually looked down on them. They liked better what they saw on TV.

The village *sarna*, almost miraculously, was still standing and Shanti remembered the rites they had had there, but she was aware that her children would never know them. She herself had begun to go to the Hindu temple up on the main road to worship the way the higher-caste people worship their gods.

Besides the people directly associated with the mines, other people had also arrived in Shanti's village. Seeing everything the mines were doing, several nongovernmental organizations (NGOs) had begun to help Shanti's village to confront the problems caused by the new economic development. One of them was CASS, an NGO run by Catholic medical mission sisters. After seeing the effects of the coal mining on the people,

CASS began to advocate on behalf of the villagers. The Prerana Resource Center, a Jesuit NGO, also offered resources.

The Present

Today Shanti has been out with the other women, collecting coal that has fallen from passing trucks. She has started doing this now. Dealing with the guards who tried to stop her gaining access to the mine pit had become too much. Now she walks slowly back to her village. As happens every afternoon, explosions ring in her ears and hazy clouds of smoke and soot hang in the air above the quarry.

She stops briefly at home and then goes out again to collect water. Since the newly-built well dried up early in the summer, the coal company has arranged to truck water in by water tanker. It's the third day of the week, so the water truck is parked nearby, pouring water into cement troughs made in the village for that purpose. One time when it came, the water had smelled of kerosene and the words HIGHLY FLAMMABLE were on the side of the old tanker, painted over but still visible. But today Shanti calmly fills a bucket of water, barely exchanging a word with the other women standing there.

On her way home from collecting coal, she had passed the front-end loaders and dumpers of East Parej mine. The closer they come, the more Shanti worries. After years of encroaching on the edges of the Bhuiyas' village, the mine expansion has finally come to their houses. The country's demand for coal, its relentless development, is not going to stop for these people. Soon it will force them to leave, on the company's terms, whether they like it or not. Some relocation and compensation plan will be offered. But Shanti, a woman, has no legal claim to her land, and does not know if she will receive any compensation at all. She feels she has no options.

Husbandless, landless, and feeling powerless, Shanti shares her cares with her CASS friends. They quietly discuss her concerns. Shanti has a strong will to survive and a determination to provide for her family. She has done it ever since Lallo died, doing what must be done.

But with the looming relocation, she does not know how she will endure. "Shanti, where will you go?" they ask. Her eyes fill with tears. She does not know what to say. She seems resigned to her fate. After some time she answers, "Like the people of East Parej, we too shall go here and there. Where the people of this village will go, there I will go."

CULTURAL ANALYSIS

Shanti's Traditional Culture

Shanti's roots go back to a culture thousands of years old: the Bhuiya people, a tribal group. But about a hundred years ago, they also formally became part of the Hindu caste system. The Bhuiya culture today, then, is somewhat of a mixture; their own tribal traditions exist side by side with the Hindu traditions they have adopted over the years.

1. *Caste system.* Everyone's basic identity is rooted in this system. Each person belongs to a specific caste within the system, and each caste is defined and given a particular status. The individuals who are part of the system internalize and accept the identities assigned to them and to others. The Dalits, among whom the Bhuiyas are classified, are the untouchables or outcasts. They exist at the periphery of the caste system and do jobs considered unclean.

2. *Sense of community.* There is a focus on sharing and mutual support. The community provides support for people when they cannot function alone. The community, rather than individuals, has traditionally made decisions. There is no real feeling of individuality in the Western sense, although this is changing rapidly with urbanization.

3. *Strong family bonds.* There is a clearly delineated network of kin, including extended family, and a sense of loyalty to it. Roles are spelled out very specifically. Marital relationships are seen as long-lasting and elders are respected.

4. *Patriarchal social order.* Women are assigned a subordinate role and are expected to be submissive to men.

5. *Sense of divine in nature.* The tribal people have a reverence for all forms of life, human and non-human, and see the divine in the earth, rivers, and so on. The land is one's place on the earth. It has a religious value and to destroy it, as the mining is doing, is a desecration.

6. *Spiritual outlook on life.* Religion is the lens through which tribal people see life, as opposed to, for example, the lens of reason or science. This does not mean that people are more spiritual, but that religion is the common idiom, much as it was in medieval Europe. This trait serves as a real anchor for people in hard times. "God has given me birth, so he will look after me" is often heard.

7. *Fatalistic and stoic outlook on life.* There is an easy resignation to what is seen as destiny. This is not a religious belief in divine control, but helplessness in the face of overwhelming situations. Patriarchy and the caste system are seen as just "the way things are." Related to this trait is a tendency to look up to a king figure, to someone seen as superior, who is expected to take charge and rule to solve all problems.

8. *Simplicity and resilience.* The people work hard, make little, and can survive with very little in the way of material things. Hard times and devastating events are accepted as the way life is and people do what they must to carry on.

Shanti's Critical Decisions

1. She decided to lead the other women in a protest to protect the naihar from the mining company.

What were her options? She could have simply accepted the company's actions without complaint.

What cultural values lay behind her decision? She was outraged at the destruction of the spring. Water, symbol and sustenance of life, was being taken away.

What cultural values were reflected in the reactions of the other people in her life to this decision? The women who joined in her protest must have shared her sense of outrage at the mining company's actions. The village leaders and company officials probably felt outrage at a woman and a Bhuiya stepping outside her station in life.

2. She must decide what she will do when the mining company takes her house.

What are her options? She thinks of people she has seen working for daily wages wherever they can. She also wonders about the rumors that if they are relocated, the company would provide land for building a house in the new place, or give cash to the villagers. But she says she'll go with her family wherever the rest of her village goes.

What cultural values might lie behind her decision? She wonders what will happen to her family and cannot imagine living anywhere but in her village community.

What cultural values might be reflected in the reactions of the other people in her life to such a decision? We have no information about this, but can assume that the villagers will try to stay together when they go.

Note: Shanti's tribal culture does not encourage individual decision-making. The group is all-important. Her *sense of community* is such that she does not perceive herself as capable of making decisions; rather, it is the community that acts. The arena within which she feels she can make decisions is limited, so providing a verbal answer to the questions on the decisions we had identified was impossible. Also, behind all that Shanti does and does not do is her place in the *caste system* and within *patriarchy*: it is a place of inferiority. But despite these things, in the loss of the spring we have a glimpse of what is important to her and where she truly draws the line. When she led the protest, we can see a measure of her *spiritual outlook on life* and her *sense of the divine in nature*. In her thinking about her future and her reaction to a possible relocation – following the others in the village – we can see both *resilience* and the strong bonds of *family* and *community*. We also see the tendency to *fatalism*.

Changes in Shanti's Life

Globalization entered Shanti's life through the mines' expansion. It was not a one-time event with a clearly-defined beginning and end; instead, it has been the result of a long process. It has been a long-term destruction of her environment that started when Shanti was a child and then progressed in stages, with a sharp acceleration associated with the economic liberalization measures in the 1990s. It comes to a climax for Shanti in the early 2000s with the possibility of the village being relocated.

Consumption

> *Pet chalani rozi:* food for today and maybe tomorrow. *Rozi* means one's daily bread. Along with water – which nowadays is not always available or of good quality when it is available – it is the basic need. Shanti's people focus on these basic needs and lead lives of great simplicity. They have few material things and can get by on very little.

In Shanti's hamlet, she and the other villagers no longer have access to most of the forest and the planting fields – natural resources that had provided most of their consumption needs in the past. Shanti gets paid in cash now instead of forest products, so she has more flexibility to acquire things than she did before. But the actual amount of cash is small, so she still has little buying power to purchase the new consumer items that now fill the village shops.

Shanti has made some new consumption choices with her new limited income. She built a brick house to replace the mud building where her family had lived before. There is electricity in the village now, so she bought a fan and a television set for her new house. She and her family now sit in plastic chairs instead of floor mats and they wear more clothes made out of synthetic fibers instead of cotton. In the old days, they used to eat what they themselves grew, foods such as beans, lentils, and chick peas, which are rather coarse but nourishing. Now they eat more packaged and processed foods. Shanti is happy that she can buy these things because she feels they improve her family's life.

Shanti and the villagers are being exposed to new consumer items through media advertising. Shanti sees that people value things with "style" now, things that are modern. Entertainment now is often not self-created; people play music tapes and like disco instead of their own traditional dances. Shanti's children watch Bollywood movies. Shanti would like to be able to buy more of these new things, but cannot afford most of them and sometimes feels dissatisfied. At the same time, she feels sorrow about the loss of the forest and the natural spring, which had provided so much of what she used when she was a child.

Production

> *Bhuiya:* people of the earth. The word *Bhuiya* comes from the Sanskrit root *bhu*, meaning earth. The Bhuiyas are the original

land settlers, they are the saviors of the land (as in their mythology), and they are people who live and work close to the soil.

With the establishment and expansion of the TISCO and East Parej coal mines, most of the forest and agricultural lands in Shanti's village were taken and the people's whole source of livelihood changed.

When Shanti was a child, her family worked in the fields of a local landowner. They also gathered many things from the nearby forest. They bartered for whatever other goods they needed. But now the mines, rather than the land, are the means of survival.

This has been a big change for the villagers as a whole. "Having a job" is a foreign idiom to the Bhuiyas; traditionally, tribal people prefer the independence of living off the land, even when working for a landlord, to other kinds of work.

Now Shanti survives on a small amount of money she receives from her deceased husband's pension. She also works with other women picking up coal to turn into coke. They used to pick it up from the mines. But now the guards are making that much more difficult, so they pick up coal that has fallen from trucks. In addition, she raises maize and vegetables on the little plot of land attached to her house. Her pension is not much, but it is steady money.

Shanti is determined to help support her family. She is happy to get cash from selling the coal and the food that she grows, and from her husband's pension. She prefers it to the old way of bartering. But now everything will change when the village has to move. Shanti has no idea how she would earn any income in a new place and she is fearful.

Migration

> *Mazbur:* fatalism, an easy resignation to destiny. This has little to do with religion and is more the attitude that this is the way things work out, so this is the way things go. People live for today, as it is, and do not think much about making choices or changes.

In India, there is a large flow of seasonal migration as people move all around the country, following the crops with the changing seasons. Estimates of the number of such migrants range up to twenty-five million people. But this is not part of Shanti's experience. For her, migration is still only a threat. If it does happen, though, it could become a permanent way of life for her. For the moment the mines provide enough work for the people, but it seems very likely that a mass relocation will take place in the future.

When the mines first came to Agaria Tola, the people were assured that their village would not be subject to relocation. But now officials say that relocation is possible, and the villagers believe they will have no say in the decision. On the other hand, if the people do not have to relocate, it will be because the company stops digging for coal — but then it will have no more jobs for the people. The village will be an island of land between two coal pits that have been filled in with rocks and earth that cannot be tilled. If this happens, there will be no real way of making a living there, either by mining or farming.

If they do relocate, the villagers will probably be given a choice between receiving either a small plot of land (not large enough for future generations to build houses on) or a one-time compensation. This is not certain, however. All Shanti — and the other villagers — can do is wait for the coal company to act. There seems to be nothing they can do to affect the outcome of this situation. She feels uncertain and worried.

Social Relations

Chacha, phupha, mamu, and *mausa*: four words for uncle. Shanti's people distinguish between father's brother, father's sister's husband, mother's brother, and mother's sister's husband. The names encapsulate specific relationships. They point to a family bonding that supports the people and helps them preserve their identity.

Shanti's loyalty to her family remains unchanged and kinship groups in the village are still strong. These groups provide a great deal of social security for people, because they are the ones who take care of the sick, the elderly, and small children. Shanti lives with her children and her sister Manjhu and her family. They are economically interdependent, relying on each other for support.

But some cracks have appeared in Shanti's relations with her children, as they stay home watching TV while she continues working very hard to collect coal. She also observes that the unity of some other families in the village has been threatened by infidelity; more people are having extramarital affairs.

Between families, things have changed as well. The village used to be marked by cohesion and sharing. But the arrival of the mines has caused new friction between people. Some people in the village have jobs with the mine and are better off than those who do not, and resentment and jealousy are affecting families' relations with each other.

The presence of the mines also has meant the arrival of strangers in the village, new people with whom Shanti and the villagers are interacting. Some are connected directly with the mine, such as mine workers and security guards. Others are associated with religious groups and nongovernmental organizations who are trying to help the villagers. All this has changed relationships in the village. Some of the changes are negative; for one thing, girls have been seriously teased and some even molested. But some changes are positive. The people from the religious groups and the NGOs have been working with the villagers and trying to help them in many different ways. One example of this is the women's self-help group that existed in the village for a while; it was started by one of the NGOs. Shanti belonged to it. It collected money for small loans and helped support people as they struggled to cope with the changes caused by the coal companies. It allowed women to handle their own money and to be economic actors, which had not happened before. Shanti was glad to be part of it.

One thing, however, has not changed: the caste system, which continues to dominate Shanti's life. As an untouchable, a Dalit, she continues to be looked down upon and scorned; the higher castes do not hear her voice or allow her a real say in any decisions, even those that directly affect her. The actions of the mines have only reinforced her tribal/Dalit sense of inferiority. Along with that self-perception, she continues to have the Dalit deep sense of fatalism, a feeling that she cannot do anything to improve her lot.

Political Relations

Neta: king figure. The Bhuiyas learned to look to a powerful patriarchal figure for security, even if it meant servility and exploitation. Today, the government is the foremost king figure and the government-owned mine has the aura of the government. After the government, the next king figures are the coal company officials and employees and World Bank representatives. They are higher-caste and seen as more powerful and intelligent. The villagers look to them for help, even to solve problems the higher castes themselves cause. At the same time, they fear and resent them.

The changes in Shanti's hamlet brought new institutional actors: the coal companies, the World Bank, some NGOs, and some religious organizations. There are other actors as well, unseen to the hamlet, primarily India's consumer class. The energy needs of this class help drive the actions of the coal companies. Shanti has seen that when conflict arises between the village and these other actors, as in the struggle over the destruction of the people's spring, the local government sides with the companies against the wishes of the people, who traditionally have not held any political power. In a sense, politically, the needs of Shanti and the villagers are being overridden by the needs of the consumer class in the city and the businesses that cater to those needs.

It is true that the villagers now have a voice that they didn't before, facilitated by some of the new institutional actors. They have participated in some discussions with representatives of the coal company, the World Bank, and other actors. And some of the NGOs are working with the villagers as they try to make their needs known. So, in theory Shanti has more access to the political system because of this dialogue — yet in practice, she perceives that nothing has changed. None of this has had any real impact; it has not helped the villagers improve their position in their dealings with the coal companies. The villagers feel they have no effective voice in these affairs that touch their lives so deeply. In that sense, there has been no change.

In general, historically, the government and the Indian political structure have been irrelevant in the lives of Shanti and the villagers. This irrelevance continues in spite of the social and political changes. It is, rather, in the caste system and the local community that the villagers find political meaning, and little has changed in those arenas. As an untouchable, she is looked down upon by the higher castes, the landlords and the mine owners.

Beyond the villagers' lack of political power against the mines' intrusion, Shanti is a tribal woman. She received her identity from her father and her husband, when they were alive, and now she receives it from her children. She is not allowed to own property in her own name; her sons own the house and the land where she lives. And her tribal culture does not encourage individuals to have their own opinions or take actions.

Despite these strictures, Shanti is more active in politics than her parents were. Shanti is disturbed by what is happening with the mines, but there is an attitude of cynicism in the village. "This is just the way that officials are," people think, and they have given up believing what the establishment says. They know they are being manipulated by it and they expect nothing else from it.

However, out of character for a tribal woman, Shanti stepped out to be a leader in her community when she organized protesters to try to prevent the destruction of the village's spring. That was a change.

Religious Experience and Expression

> *Naihar:* a woman's childhood home, her mother's home, a place she goes for refreshment and comfort: the permanent spring that gave the villagers water.

> *Sarna:* the sacred grove where they worshipped. The Bhuiyas revere nature; it is the core of their religion. The nearby forest was a physical extension of their very selves. It provided sustenance, created their culture, formed their world view, and shaped their identity. It was what made them distinctively tribal.

For Shanti, the razing of the land surrounding the village has meant that the foundation of her faith — the forest, the spring — no longer exists. She can no longer worship as she did before. The villagers have been told that they could worship at the Hindu temple nearby, but it's not the same. Shanti does go there to worship, but temples are not part of her tribal religion; they are part of the Brahmanical Hinduism of the higher-caste people. Her children watch the popular Hindu epic stories that are shown on the television. But the stories of their tribal faith do not appear there. The people are also now more inclined to call in a *pandit*, a religious leader from the higher castes, instead of a *pathan*, one from the tribal group, for their rites.

When Shanti looks around her, she sees only the religious symbols of a less familiar tradition: Brahmanical Hinduism. Although the village's *sarna* still stands, most of the ancient tribal symbols she knew are gone. Her children will never know them. The expansion of the mines accelerated the gradual Sankritization of the Bhuiyas' tribal religion, a change that was already under way. All this leaves her feeling bewildered.

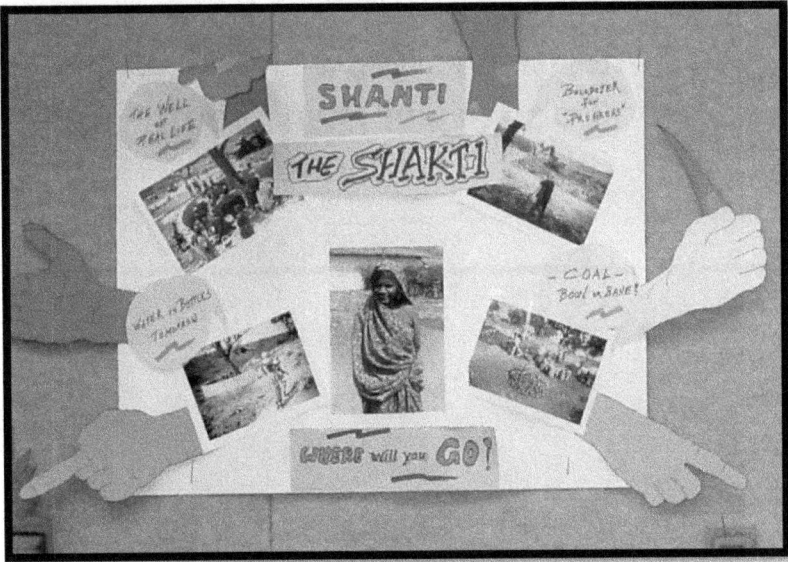

Shanti's mosaic tile from GEC's Fourth International Consultation

Chapter 6

Getting to Know Shanti Through Her Own Eyes (Phase II Methodology)

Shanti and her sister Manjhu, with the encroaching coal mine in the background

NARRATOR: TONY HERBERT, SJ

Associate, Prerana Resource Centre
With the assistance of Sr. Bina Stanis
Hazaribag, Jharkhand, India

Chapter 5 reflects our understanding of Shanti at the end of what we now call Phase I of the project. At this point, we had developed the narrative and conducted our cultural analysis. These had given us a good deal of knowledge about Shanti's life and the culture in which she lives and how both had been affected by globalization in India. We even had identified some decisions Shanti had made and Tony Herbert, the narrator, had discussed them with her. But we were not satisfied that we had a good understanding of the meaning of globalization for Shanti and the values that guided her decisions. We were still looking at Shanti from our own perspective – the perspective of the narrators and the WTC researchers. We began to feel an urge to go deeper into what was going on within Shanti as she experienced and responded to the changes brought into her life by globalization. These root feelings are what motivated us to develop the tools that we call Phase II methodology, which is described in Chapter 4. This chapter presents this methodology in the context of Shanti's story.

The focus of this chapter is two main actions that we observed Shanti taking in her narrative story, presented in Chapter 5. There we identified two major decisions, which the narrator discussed with Shanti. (See box in Cultural Analysis section in Chapter 5.) In this chapter, based on subsequent dialogue, we try to understand Shanti's meanings and values by focusing on one of the decisions identified earlier, the protest, and one other observed action. These are:

1. Shanti changes the way she collects the coal she uses to make coke, which is how she earns a living.

2. Shanti organizes a protest against the destruction of the spring by the coal mine.

Below we analyze these actions, using the methodology and template we presented in Chapter 4, "Research Methodology, Phase II: Finding the Protagonists' Meanings and Values", p. 78ff. (The questions template appears on p. 87.) Our analysis was reviewed by the narrators, but could not be verified with Shanti herself, since we did not have contact with her any more at this point in the project.

SHANTI'S MEANINGS AND VALUES
AS REFLECTED IN HER CHOICES

Action 1: Shanti changes the way she collects the coal she uses to make coke, which is how she earns a living.

A. What can we infer goes on within Shanti as she experiences the new economy and moves on to decide to take this action? What questions may Shanti have been raising and what answers seem consistent with reaching that decision? (Note: This refers to the stages of consciousness, from experiencing to deciding; see Chapter 4, p. 88ff.)

Shanti encounters guards who try to stop her gaining access to the coal mine pit. She feels frustration, and even despair, at contemplating this threat to her livelihood. These feelings lead her to wonder about alternative sources of coal, and she remembers the coal she has seen lying on the road after falling off the transport trucks. Perhaps she also has seen others in the village picking up this coal before. She *experiences* both the restrictions on her access to the mine pit and the availability of an alternative source of coal. These experiences lead her to ask herself if she can circumvent the guards at the mine, if she keeps trying to go there. She also asks what might be involved in picking up the coal on the road. Will the truck drivers be hostile to her, like the mine guards? How hard will it be? Can she do it by herself, or does she need to join other women who perhaps are already doing it? If others are doing it, will they welcome her? Will the guards harass her less on the road? Can she gather as much coal there as she did before from the mine pit?

In answering these questions she comes to *understand* that circumventing the guards at the mine is not an option and that picking up coal on the road is not very different from the gathering in the forest that she and others used to do before the mines destroyed the forest. She also realizes that picking up this coal involves more work because it is less predictable where to find it; but hard work has always been part of the life of the Bhuiyas. On the other hand, on the road there is less harassment from the guards than at the mine pit. With this understanding, she then asks herself whether the coal on the road indeed can be a substitute for what she has been picking up at the mine pit. In giving a positive answer based on her understanding of the facts, Shanti *judges* it to be so. Finally, she deliberates whether it is right to pick up this coal.

In pondering all these considerations, she reflects on the hard work involved, and perhaps even thinks of giving up. But then where will the income to support her family (*vital value*) come from? Shanti remembers how she and her siblings gathered food in the forest when they were children. Picking up coal is very different. She enjoyed going to the forest; wandering along the roads to pick up coal feels different, humiliating. If others in the community are already picking coal off the road, it might make it more acceptable (*social and cultural values*); but there might also be some concern as to whether this coal belongs to them and would she be stealing from them (*moral value*). However, there is no evidence that either Shanti or others object on moral or religious grounds to her picking up this coal. Collecting the coal enables her to make the coke she needs to help support herself and the family she loves, even though she will have to work harder – an *ultimate value* is brought to bear. She is deciding in a context of love. So Shanti in effect *judges* the alternative source of coal to be *morally good*. Absent moral objections, Shanti *decides* it is worthwhile for her to start picking up the road coal, despite the additional work involved and the negative feelings she has about doing this. She decides not to give up on making a living by selling coke and instead takes advantage of the next best opportunity available to find the coal she needs.

B. What values appear to drive Shanti's decision? What are the good things that she seeks? (Note: This refers to the scale of values; see Chapter 4, p. 95ff.)

Her motivation to pick up coal is the need to generate income to support herself and her family. Picking up coal is part of the work arrangement that she values – a *social good*. She values it primarily because it helps her and her family to survive, her *vital values*, but working conditions are also important in her evaluation of work. Her achieving this *social value* also enhances her sense of belonging in her community, which expects family members to take care of one another – a *cultural value* – and her own sense of being responsible for supporting her family – a *moral value*. This may conflict with her sense of lacking personal dignity – another *moral value* – in this kind of work. But her *ultimate value* of love for her family prevails.

C. How does Shanti's new knowledge and decision change the horizon of meanings in her world?

As Shanti reaches her decision, a change in how she envisions earning a living begins to take place: earning a living takes on a new meaning. She is no longer at the mercy of the mine guards to earn a living and this leads to her viewing her work in a different light. She is prepared to add "gathering coal off the road" to the long line of adaptations she has made in her life from when she gathered food in the forest. Her new decision introduces a new perspective. She is no longer indifferent to the coal on the road. With her decision, it has become part of her livelihood. The transport trucks also are now part of her coke-making arrangement. Before, the trucks and this coal were just part of what came along with the mines; now they are a solution to the door that was closed by the mine guards. Shanti deems this to be good in terms of supporting herself and her family. She has expanded the horizon of how she can use her environment to obtain the raw material that she needs. Picking coal off the road has a new meaning. Perhaps her sacrificing her sense of dignity in order to support her family also has a new meaning.

D. Given Shanti's new horizon of meanings, what can we infer goes on within Shanti as she moves to implement her decision? What questions may Shanti have been trying to answer as she puts her decision into action? What values of Shanti are engaged in this implementation? (Note: This refers to the stages of consciousness, from deciding to acting; see Chapter 4, p. 90ff.)

A change in Shanti's perspective on work has taken place, and with it new questions arise. She still has to decide whether or not her decision is worth carrying out. Is this really what she wants to do? Can she see herself walking the roads to pick up coal? After some soul-searching, Shanti answers her question in the affirmative. She finds her *decision worthy* to be carried out and put into action. Because she is thinking of what is good for her family, and her conscience seems at peace, this decision to go ahead is consistent with her *moral values*, even though she might be sacrificing her sense of personal dignity. From here on, Shanti's new point of view and the values that shaped it become the foundation for how she will explore the meaning of her new arrangement and how she understands earning a living in the new world. Particularly if picking up coal from the road is new in the community, Shanti will question again whether this makes sense. Had there been any history in her community of looking down on picking up coal, Shanti would have to question whether her need to earn a living and support her family can be reconciled with what she values and gives *meaning* to her life in the village, her *cultural values*. Happily, there does not seem to be a conflict in this case, and working hard is part of her Bhuiya tradition. Nonetheless, Shanti's new perspectives confer a new meaning on the transport trucks that drop coal onto the road. They are no longer foreign things that make noise and are owned by the mine. They have become important to the community's earning a living. There is a modification of her *cultural values* when she *judges* that yes, it is *meaningful* to pursue this new work arrangement, which depends on the trucks.

Next, she must question how she will actually go about implementing the decision. Is there a schedule to the transport trucks that she needs to understand? Can the timing for picking the coal off the road be reconciled with her duties to her family? What will her children say as she makes the necessary adjustments? Are there risks on the road that she needs to worry about? The answers to these questions will provide Shanti with a *new understanding* of her situation and how she earns a living in the village, an *adjustment of her social values*, the value she places on working arrangements. In valuing this new work arrangement she accepts the implications for blending her decision with the rest of her life. Finally, she moves into action and picking up this coal provides a *new experience* for Shanti. What she values as a good source of work has been altered by this new experience. It will affect how she looks at the possibilities of her generating income in the future, a *social value*, and what she values in the village way of life, her *cultural values*.

E. Do we detect changes in the relative weights Shanti now places on different values within a given level of values and among different levels of values? Does Shanti seem comfortable with her decision and action? (Note: This refers to the tensions within and among the levels of values; see Chapter 4, p. 102ff.)

There has been a deterioration of the conditions in Shanti's work, but there is probably no change in what she understands as a valuable source of work. However, she has come to *understand* and value the road coal and the transport trucks in a different way. They now are part of Shanti's *cultural and social values* in a different way. However, there is no evidence that the new work arrangement is a bigger part of her life, or that the weight she puts on her other levels of values has changed. She seems comfortable with her changed work arrangement – even if she would prefer to pick up the coal at the mines, as before. She has taken responsibility for the changes.

Action 2: Shanti organizes a protest against the destruction of the spring by the coal mine.

A. What can we infer goes on within Shanti as she experiences the new economy and moves on to decide to take this action? What questions may Shanti have been raising and what answers seem consistent with reaching that decision? (Note: This refers to the stages of consciousness, from experiencing to deciding; see Chapter 4, p. 88ff.)

Shanti first sees the bulldozers approaching the spring and hears rumors about their intended use. She might even have heard a representative of the company announcing the date when the demolition would take place. She also talks with the other women, who are equally horrified at the possible loss of the spring. She *experiences* all these things. She also experiences her own and other women's feelings of fear and rage, provoked by images of the impending loss of a spring that is central to their life physically, culturally, and spiritually.

She asks herself and others questions: Why would the mines want to destroy the spring? What, if anything, can be done about it? The answer to the first question is clear for her and the community: the mine's greed for coal-rich land is driving the destruction of the spring. The answer to what to do about it is much less clear. However, Shanti comes up with the idea that organizing a protest against the mines might dissuade the mine from taking over the spring, or at least give expression to the anger they feel at the spring being taken from them. Her answers give Shanti an *understanding* of the mine's actions and they also seem to make room for the village responding to the situation. She *judges* that making their feelings known in a protest might help protect the spring.

But nobody in the village is taking any action, so Shanti begins to wonder if she should instigate the protest. Contemplating such a decision produces great conflicts within her. Confronting the power of the mines is frightening. In addition, her organizing a protest would also confront the village's male hierarchy − a hierarchy that seems to remain passive in the face of danger while still objecting to women taking leadership roles. On the other hand, it is an outrage for the mines to take over and destroy the spring, which for centuries has been a central part of the daily life of the village and a place where the village experiences a sense of the sacred *(social, cultural, and religious values)*. Where will she and the other women go for water? For their social gatherings? For the experience of the sacred? There is a conflict, then, among her values. The village traditions, which Shanti values, her *cultural values*, decree that women should not challenge authority and should not act as leaders. But her *moral and ultimate values*, which guide her life, impel her to act in the face of the threat to the spring.

She is also afraid that the mines could take reprisals against the village and the men working in the mines; they might even run over her and other villagers with their bulldozers if they stood in their way. But Shanti *judges* that the potentially calamitous consequences of the destruction of the spring justify exposing herself and others to the consequences of challenging the cultural traditions. Her *conscience* tells her that the proposed mine action is *morally* unfair and wrong. She *decides* to organize the women in a protest against the mines destroying the spring, thus accepting *responsibility* for a decision that would not be sanctioned by the elders and others in her village.

B. What values appear to drive Shanti's decision? What are the good things that she seeks? (Note: This refers to the scale of values; see Chapter 4, p. 95ff.)

The loss of the spring clearly represents a loss of clean water for drinking and domestic needs, a *vital value*, as well as the loss of the focus of a significant part of her social and village life, *social and cultural values*. But in organizing the protest, Shanti is also challenging the power structures of the mines and the traditional role of women in her society. She is challenging the order of her society. Shanti seeks more than what is good in her vital and social values. She is driven by moral outrage at the injustice of the mine destroying the spring that has a sacred meaning to the village. She is being guided by what she values morally, her *moral and religious (ultimate) values*, and in pursuing these values she is willing to challenge some of her cultural norms about the role of women and the attitude towards the power of the mines.

C. How does Shanti's new knowledge and decision change the horizon of meanings in her world?

Once she makes this decision, something happens to Shanti. Her horizon expands. She begins to look at her world in a different way. Life in the village has a new meaning. The decision to try to save the spring has become a source of new energy. There begins to be a change in her old view that the villagers have no power against the mine. Perhaps even more significantly, there begins to be a change in the belief that a tribal woman must wait for the male hierarchy in the village to lead the way. In these new possibilities, one could even say that her new horizon is qualitatively different, on a different plane, from before. This new horizon challenges the core cultural values that mandate how tribal women relate to the male hierarchy and their access to economic power. Being a tribal woman has a new meaning for Shanti.

D. Given Shanti's new horizon of meanings, what can we infer goes on within her as she moves to implement her decision? What questions may she have been trying to answer as she puts her decision into action? What values of Shanti are engaged in this implementation? (Note: This refers to the stages of consciousness, from deciding to acting; see Chapter 4, p. 90ff.)

In reaching the decision to protest, a perhaps not-so-small change has taken place in Shanti; what her world means to her is different. But she still has questions to answer. Does she really mean to go ahead with her decision to organize the protest? Does she feel good about it, though scared? Is she really willing to confront the power of the mines? Is she really willing to accept the criticism from the village male hierarchy for her leadership role in organizing the protest? She answers these questions in the affirmative. She *judges* it *worthwhile* to pay the price − the consequences for nontraditional behavior − to address the perceived injustice.

When she answers in the affirmative, she begins to truly own her decision and take *responsibility* for it and what it means for the changes in her. She begins to envision herself actually doing it. She begins owning her new point of view that the mines can be challenged and a tribal woman can act in nontraditional roles. It appears her conscience is at peace, so her carrying out the decision to protest is consistent with her *moral values* as to what is right for her and her community. The new horizon and the values that guided it now become foundational for how she re-examines what is meaningful in her culture and how she understands her world. Next she will question whether indeed she is willing to own the *changed cultural values* resulting from her leading the protest. In answering affirmatively, she *judges* that the traditional patriarchy and the power of the mines are not absolute. It is *reasonable* to challenge them when basic rights of the community are threatened. Next she asks: What does this mean in practice in terms of the rest of her life? What will it mean when attending the village gatherings? Will the mines make it more difficult to pick coal off the road? Will the other women accept her socially? It would be difficult for her to answer these questions in advance with any certainty, but considering them would have led her to a new *understanding* of her reality as a tribal woman in her community, as well as a new understanding of the injustice the mine perpetrates in destroying the spring. With this new understanding there will be an *adaptation of her social values*, what Shanti values in her social relations. On the basis of this new understanding she proceeds to *act*: she organizes the protest. The next time that she has to deal with the power structures of the mines and the village's patriarchal system, she will have a different disposition than she had before she organized the protest. The next time that the mines, or perhaps other external forces, threaten the villagers' rights, Shanti will be readier to consider a similar act of civil disobedience. Shanti's decision to organize the protest implies changes in what she values on the whole scale of values. What she considers good has shifted.

E. Do we detect changes in the relative weights Shanti now places on different values within a given level of values and among different levels of values? Does Shanti seem comfortable with her decision and action? (Note: This refers to the tensions within and among the levels of values; see Chapter 4, p. 102ff.)

There is a heightened appreciation for the value of the spring water per se, as well as for the activities and social gatherings around it. It is a greater appreciation of the *vital, social, cultural, and religious values* associated with the spring, which they are about to lose. But this heightened appreciation does not imply a change in the relative weights she puts on each of these levels of value. However, she has also come to *understand* and value the power of political organization, a *social value,* as an outlet for her own and others' anger and as a vehicle to stand up to the forces of the mine. She is willing to put more weight on this social value. She also shifts weights between her cultural values, on the one hand, and her moral and religious values, on the other. Her *moral and religious values* lead her to address the perceived injustice of the destruction of the spring that has religious significance to the village. These values trump and reshape some of her *cultural values.* At least with regard to saving the spring, traditional values that in the past guided Shanti's behavior in relation to the power of the mines and the male tribal hierarchy have taken second place to the value she puts on justice and being in the presence of the Transcendent.

RESEARCHERS' REFLECTIONS

India's Economic Globalization and Shanti

The mine expansions that have affected Shanti's life are framed by the changes in India's economy launched after the financial crisis of 1991. At the time, India concluded that the old economic model was not viable anymore and, in its place, introduced the so-called New Economic Policy (NEP). The NEP placed greater reliance on the market and sought to dismantle many of the constitutionally-supported social policies of earlier decades. The stated objective of the Statement of Industrial Policy in 1991 was the "dismantling of the regulatory system to facilitate increasing competition for the benefit of the common people."

The policies touched Shanti's life primarily through increased demand in India for the energy associated with the new economic growth. This growth fueled the need for expansion of the TISCO and the East Parej mines surrounding Shanti's village. The more liberal regulatory environment certainly facilitated the mining companies' obtaining the necessary permissions to encroach on the village land, including a possible relocation of the village. It also made it easier for the government to waive local employment requirements, such as the earlier ones that had enabled Shanti's father to get a job in the mines as compensation for the village's losses.

The Indian policies of greater reliance on market forces and the opening to global markets have succeeded in providing a faster rate of economic growth in the country. But the way these policies have been implemented, such as in the case of the coal mines in Shanti's narrative, leaves much to be desired. The new economic structure has created jobs in the village and brought in a greater flow of cash exchange in the local market and new consumption choices. Shanti herself says that now it is easier to provide for one's family. But the benefits that Shanti now enjoys have come at a great cost to her environment – including a likely relocation away from the land on which her tribal people have lived for centuries.

Shanti and the villagers bear most of the external costs of the mine expansions, and they are high. But neither the Indian government nor the coal mines have helped them much to address these costs. The opening of the Indian economy and the mine expansion did not establish any new social or political structures to listen to and address the villagers' concerns. There were only the existing structures: the caste system, the power of those with land and capital, the political alienation of the lower castes, and possibly the corruption of government officials. Those structures enabled those with the most power and potential for economic gain to run the system to their advantage, at the expense of the powerless like Shanti and the other Bhuiyas in the village.

Neither the Indian government nor the coal companies even consulted with the villagers – the people most affected by the mine expansions. This was not due to mere paternalism, because they also failed to create any safety net to help the village cope with the easy-to-anticipate negative side effects of the expansions. Even the agreements with the World Bank about the treatment of Shanti's people appear not to have been implemented properly. There appears to be a total disregard for the lives of Shanti and her people, who have lost the environment that gave meaning to their lives. Even information about an impending relocation is not available to them. Some of this disregard has ancient roots in the caste system, but market forces cannot be a justification for continuing this disregard in the name of economic development. Viewing people in this light is never acceptable.

Getting to Know Shanti: Our Journey

When we first met Shanti, and even while working on the narrative's cultural analysis, we felt pity for Shanti and we felt anger at the system that had taken away so much of tribal life. We were outraged that things that gave Shanti's life meaning and value as a tribal had been taken away from her by the mines. The forest had been bulldozed, the spring destroyed, and now she might have to be relocated and leave her home. We could see that, in many ways, she did not understand what was happening to her. Important decisions deeply affecting her life were being made by people far away, people who live a lifestyle she could never dream of, with large energy needs and profit motives. Shanti saw only the repercussions of these decisions. It seemed to us that her natural tribal reaction to these events was one of fatalism: things simply happen, are imposed by external forces, and there is nothing she can do to change them. We tended to see her as leading a life of passivity and even acquiescence to the mines' expansion. From this point of view, Shanti was simply a victim.

And Shanti, indeed, is a victim of multiple socioeconomic structures. She has lived all her life at the bottom of two imposing hierarchies: as a Dalit in the Indian caste system, which considers her "an untouchable"; and as a woman in the tribal patriarchal system, which treats her as inferior to men and does not even give her property rights. And now, in the mines and their financial backers, she was also confronting very powerful social and economic interests. These structures do impose severe constraints on Shanti's development and on her choices and opportunities to order her own reality. So much so, that it seemed to us that the idea of Shanti making decisions by herself was almost foreign to her. But a different picture began to emerge when we started trying to identify some of her decisions and analyze what might have been going on within her as she reached and acted upon these decisions, small and limited as they might have been. We began to see that Shanti *did* deal with the global forces that were transforming her life. And she did so in pursuit of her human desires and values.

Our initial understanding of Shanti's ability to earn a living was focused on the caste system and on what the mines did or did not do to her. The caste system and the mines indeed do dominate how she goes about earning a living. But when we looked into her decision to pick up coal from the road, we realized that she is capable of responding creatively to the coal companies' actions. She can think about and evaluate the new conditions and then decide how to adapt to them. In doing so she is guided by her love for family and her cultural and other values. She has gone from being a gatherer in the forest, to making coke from coal she took from the mine and, when that was not possible anymore, from coal that fell from the transport trucks. She even learned to appreciate the advantages of cash over a barter system – a big change that permeates much of what she does. In the process, she might have had to sacrifice some of her sense of personal dignity, but she has been able to fashion work to meet her vital needs, even under very difficult and changing conditions. Shanti is capable of understanding the changes in her world, in her working conditions. Within the strong limitations of her world, she is able to apply her values and judgment and decide the best way to adapt to these conditions and earn a living. We have a new understanding of Shanti's intelligence and values. We have a better appreciation of the lengths she is willing to go to in order to support herself and her family.

Before getting in touch with what was going on within Shanti as she organized the protest, we tended to see her as a passive individual, incapable of deciding anything independent of the village. For some time in the project, we didn't even pay much attention to the significance of this incident. Her personal moral values were not part of the picture we had of her. The inquiry into her decision to lead the protest provided a new understanding of her. The protest showed her capable of standing up to the major power structures in her life: the mine, with its association with the caste system, and the patriarchal village structure. In this situation, Shanti's conscience provided a moral compass that overruled the cultural and social values of her tradition.

Having delved into Shanti's decision to organize the protest, we began to see that it was perhaps the most exposed action we saw Shanti take in response to the demands of her conscience; but it was not the only one.

The environment created by the mines exposed Shanti to people beyond her immediate circle of family and village, and to situations beyond the traditional roles imposed on women by her village society. We could now see that she had responded creatively. In these new relationships, her responses were those of a moral human being capable of placing moral values above traditional social and cultural values. She has been part of a women's self-help group. She does not shy away from making her views known to the NGOs, trying somehow to reach out to others who might address her concerns. As Shanti comes to understand new situations, she is capable of juxtaposing the traditional cultural pattern of power and patriarchy on the one hand, and her needs and those of her community on the other. In these cases, she judges it worthwhile to counter tradition in favor of those needs. As a human being, she assumes responsibility for her nontraditional actions. We could now recognize that, if Shanti perceives an action as morally good, she is capable of negotiating her cultural values. In our new understanding, Shanti's moral values drive who she chooses to be, an understanding far from seeing her primarily as a victim.

The Shanti story that the narrator, Tony Herbert, provided, as well as the cultural traits of her community, pointed to Shanti's values. She is a loving person with strong family bonds and sense of community. She has a sense of the divine in nature, as in the village forest and the spring, and she has a spiritual outlook on life. We brought these values to bear on trying to understand Shanti's decisions. This helped us see that her love of family and community, of the god of the forest and the spring, all motivate her to open her world to new possibilities. What is more, we could see that these possibilities go beyond her personal self-interest when there is a conflict among her values, as in the protest. This is the context in which she decides and chooses who she really wants to be. As she implements her decisions, that love and sense of the sacred also guide the adaptation of her values to the new world.

Shanti decides in favor of being somebody who is open to new things, to new ways of earning a living and to new relationships. She redefines justice in a way that values it differently from obedience to traditional cultural mandates for a tribal woman in her society. At the point of deciding, Shanti could have chosen to do so out of selfishness. But she does not.

By looking directly into how Shanti's ultimate values guide her decisions, we came to see how these values helped her forge a new horizon for herself. She does not appear so passive anymore; within this new horizon she makes decisions in which all her other values find new expressions. As a result, she creates a new future for herself and for others in her world in the global economy. Within the strict limitations imposed by the socioeconomic structures in her life, she is not necessarily better off. But we see Shanti's decisions as a story of progress that takes place in the midst of her sorrow and in a village with a very uncertain future. We came to see her as somebody capable of processing her new experiences to find meaning in them; somebody capable of deciding and adapting in a context of love and her sense of the sacred, even when there are costs to her.

Our getting in touch with Shanti's personal development as an active decision-maker does not detract from the fact that this development takes place in the midst of great losses in her life. She and her community have had to abandon the worship in the forest and the gatherings around the spring. Her whole sacred environment has been desecrated by the mines. We may even say that there is a certain dehumanization in her picking up coal along the road. But Shanti does not break down. She adjusts. She goes on with her life, remaining centered on her family and the village. One can say that her rootedness in a sacred world and love for family and village still guides her, but in a new way. For a believer, Shanti finds the Transcendent in her search for what is good and this imparts a new meaning to her life in a changing world which does not appear to take her interests at heart. In the words of Tony Herbert, the narrator:

> "When Shanti is presented with a locked door, instead of lamenting that loss, she looks for another door to go through, and another if that is also locked. We are looking at her creativeness in searching at her inner spirit, the new way she finds. We see how she draws on values and meaning, and searches for new ones... But there [is the] question about the locked door – why is it locked, who has the key, who gains the benefit of it being locked?

> "I have learnt something I already had an inkling of, the incredible resourcefulness of the subsistence living person... I have seen how when the traditional world falls apart, she has shown a strong sense of the value of today itself...I also get an inkling in another direction, seeing Shanti as a 'Beatitudinal person' – the people of the Beatitudes are on the margins, be it because of economic class factors, or social (caste/race) factors. There is a locus of wisdom here, they are stripped of the pretences that so many of us take to ourselves. Blessed are the coal scavengers."

Development Policy Implications of Knowing Shanti in This New Way

Our journey in getting to know Shanti has taken us from seeing her primarily as a victim to seeing how much she is capable of in reaching decisions and adapting her world to implement those decisions, limited as those decisions might be because of the big constraints the socioeconomic structure imposes on her. How can we tap into this creativity in order to further her and her village's economic development? Tony Herbert best summarizes the approach suggested by seeing Shanti in this new light:

> "Keeping her centre stage in planning, a lot more listening to her, adapting our way to integrate her ways, being more flexible, having her people do the teaching, not outsiders. Just spending a lot more time with her, not doing activities for her, more being with... It suggests special efforts to integrate [Shanti and the villagers] into the programmes as subjects of their own uplift, not as beneficiaries of others' efforts."

The relocation is still a pending issue and one clearly central to the future of the community. NGOs have been active in advocating on behalf of the village. Efforts are already being made to engage in collective action on behalf of the villagers. The new way of seeing Shanti suggests making efforts to bring her face-to-face, not through NGOs, with the remote persons making the decisions that affect her life. We would have to help her and the others in the village to articulate what is in their minds and hearts and we would have to find an appropriate venue and facilitate the encounter; but Shanti and the villagers should be able to speak in their own voice.

There are also obvious economic development activities that need to take place in the village. There is a need to diversify their local economy away from the traditional subsistence agriculture and daily-wage labor. They need some small income-generating projects, such as small shops. To do this, they need access to education to teach them skills that generate more income. Their youth need better technical training. They need access to some capital for small projects and marketing support to sell their products. The question, though, is how, with the new understanding that we have of Shanti, would we support these activities. Tony Herbert's answer to this question is:

> "Form village-level groups of people on the basis of ... some strongly-felt need, whatever issue touches them."

Although he notices:

> "This is not easily done; they do not so easily come together on social or development issues, even on the issue of displacement. They do come together more easily on the basis of caste identity, but this has the negative effect of fragmenting the village community."

But there are some precedents upon which we could build these groups. For example, in the past Tony Herbert found that "women's savings groups" have been effective. One such group existed in the past in Shanti's village and it could be restarted. Others could be started in nearby villages. Once they are functioning, one could call an area meeting of representatives of those groups, initially to go through their savings accounts with them. But then the meeting could be expanded to discuss other issues such as health or men's drinking – issues of immediate interest. Eventually, the group could evolve to address more ambitious economic development projects.

These groups would be a good venue for facilitating a discussion in which the villagers could get in touch with, and learn to articulate, what they value, as reflected in decisions they have already made or things to which they aspire. On this foundation, then, a consensus on an agenda for development activity might emerge from the group. In this agenda, the job-creation policy would center on Shanti's and the other villagers' ideas for developing and implementing ways to make a better living. By analogy, associated education and health policies would be built on the same foundation: the preferences of Shanti and the other villagers. Once an agreement to pursue certain development activities is reached by the group, then our task would be how to help marshal the necessary resources. Traditional advocacy with the government, the World Bank, and the mining companies on behalf of the village now would be guided by the decisions of the group.

We have seen that Shanti is capable of supporting changes in the village culture that she believes serve a good purpose. So in establishing the development agenda, it is important to get Shanti to understand the benefits of any new emerging policy, as well as the changes in the tradition that it will bring about. She starts from a tradition in which she says that "enough for today is okay, why do you need all these things? We will get by." But we also have grounds to believe that she will not oppose change blindly. If she comes to decide that the improvement in the village is worth the change in traditional behavior, she can become an engine for change not only in her own life, but also in her community. If she cannot see the benefit of the envisioned change, chances are that even a conceptually good idea will not translate into sustainable development.

These and other similar changes in approaches to development policy would help to empower Shanti and her village to have a seat at the development decision-making table. Our goal is to give tools to the development practitioner to do so. But we must not ignore this: for many decisions critical to the development of Shanti's community, other actors will also have to be engaged. This probably will require addressing the current power structure of the caste system, the mining companies, and the government so that a newly-empowered Shanti and her village may be heard. Ultimately, it will require a system in which the country considers alternative energy possibilities, and in which the environmental costs of the mines do not fall only on Shanti and her village, but are accounted for explicitly in calculating the net profitability of these mines and the compensation owed to Shanti's village in the form of land, training, and jobs.

Chapter 7

Chanda in Zambia:
No Chitenge Yet for His Mother

Chanda selling cigarettes in Lusaka

NARRATOR: LEONARD CHITI, SJ

Director, Jesuit Centre for Theological Reflection (JCTR)
Lusaka, Zambia

Narrative Summary and Economic Background

Chanda's life changed dramatically in 1994, when he was sixteen. He left his village in the Chongwe Rural District, where he was a student helping farm his family's land, and went to Zambia's capital, Lusaka. In Lusaka he became the family's breadwinner and sold single cigarettes on the streets. He went there to help support his family when the government withdrew agricultural supports from the village as part of its Structural Adjustment Program (SAP). Without those supports, his family could no longer eke out a living by growing maize, as they had done for generations. He went to the city as a matter of survival. All his meager income now, years later, still goes to support his family, both his sister's family in the city and the family back in the village.

An economic crisis had been building through the 1980s, growing out of an inefficient economic system, a decline in world copper prices – Zambia's major export – and a protracted drought. The situation had led to unsustainably high government fiscal deficits and international debt levels, and a major economic crisis erupted in the early 1990s. In 1992, under the guidance of the World Bank and the IMF, the new government of the Movement for Multiparty Democracy (MMD) implemented an SAP, thus opening Zambia much more to market economic forces. Subsidies were reduced drastically. The government board that had been established after Zambia's independence in 1964 to provide agricultural and credit subsidies to increase agricultural production, NAMBOARD, was abolished. Agricultural production dropped by nearly two-thirds. Chanda's family could no longer subsist on what they grew. With the dire economic conditions, unemployment increased above its already high levels. In urban areas, privatizations drove it even higher. Jobs became even scarcer than they had been in the 1980s, especially for the many people like Chanda who were moving to the city looking for work. The service sector in the informal economy became the only source of employment for them.

NARRATIVE

Chanda sat patiently in his home. His parents had left earlier that morning, assuring him they would be back before long. They had gone for advice to the village elders about Chanda's future because the family was going through hard times. After much discussion, his parents and the elders decided it would be best for Chanda to move to the capital, Lusaka, to stay with his sister and look for work there. Maybe he could find a good job and even continue his studies there. In the past, the village had sent young men to work in the mines, or the city to make money, but Chanda was only sixteen. So the decision was made. Chanda's parents returned home and told him the plan for his future and their future...

Growing up in the Village

Chibwe Chanda was born in Chaasha village, in Chieftainess Nkomeshya of the Lenje tribe, in Chongwe Rural District. Life there revolved around the family and clan, around the traditional religion, and around the land.

The villagers respected the wisdom of the elders and gave them absolute, and unquestioned, authority. They were the ones people turned to in times of trouble. The elders were revered because they knew the history of the clan. Chanda and the other young people always looked forward to the end of the day, when they would gather around the elders and listen to their stories of what had gone on before. They knew that the lessons from the past would stand them in good stead in the future.

Chanda was very excited when he came of age and it was time to be initiated into adulthood. This was when the elders taught him how to deal with the challenges of life, as they knew them. During the initiation ceremonies, the cumulative wisdom of the clan was imparted to young people before they assumed adult roles. Like the people who had gone through this ceremony before him, Chanda thought he now was prepared to tackle the usual challenges that members of the clan were expected to encounter.

The villagers' religion centered on the ancestors. Chanda was taught to revere the family's relatives who had died and to maintain a connection with them. In times of trouble, the villagers called on the ancestors for help. Chanda watched them make sacrifices as part of their appeal, including brewing beer for them. He especially liked that in good times the ancestors were invited to celebrate with the family and clan. Even in ordinary activities such as sharing drinks, people poured a little of the beer onto the floor as an offering to the ancestors before they drank.

Chanda's family grew maize on a small piece of land; they had done this for years. He was a student, but when he came home from school, he went out to help in the fields. The government helped by providing supports such as subsidized financing and marketing assistance. So his family had food for their needs and enough maize left over to sell in the market. They used the money they made for things like the children's education and medical expenses. They lived not much above a subsistence level, but they had some security.

Chanda's home village of Chaasha

Hard Times in the Village

In 1992, when the new government implemented the SAP to address the ongoing economic crisis, it created serious problems for Chanda's family. The cost of fertilizer and seeds went up, they lost financing from the government, and no commercial bank would lend to them because they were small farmers. They also lost their former reliable marketing arrangement, because the government stopped buying from them.

The economic reforms were meant to increase people's incomes. But Chanda's family had lost the only source of livelihood they knew and found themselves starving. This was the dire situation that led to Chanda moving to Lusaka in 1994 to look for work, even though it meant he had to leave school before he finished his education.

In Ng'ombe Township

Chanda joined his older sister and her family in Ng'ombe Township, a slum in Lusaka. It was home to 100,000 people, mostly non-skilled workers. At first, he was enthusiastic about his new adventure. He had been brought up with a strong sense of loyalty to his family and his clan and he wanted to help them. Unfortunately, he couldn't find employment in the city because he had no job skills; he had not even finished eighth grade. Besides, many companies were closing. There was a harsh business environment prevailing at that time and many workers had lost their jobs.

Frustrated by not finding a good job, Chanda began selling single cigarettes, on the streets during the day and in bars at night. He thus became a muchanga boy: doing something that people did not consider a real job. He was ashamed that that was all he could do, especially because he made very little money from it. Then something happened that made things even harder for him: his sister's husband died, leaving Chanda the main provider for her and her two children — in addition to his duties to his parents in the village.

The house of Chanda's sister, in Lusaka

Family Obligations

Chanda struggles with this new role as family provider. He doesn't make enough money to meet all the needs of his sister's family as well as his village family. He needs money to buy food, charcoal for cooking, and candles for light. He must pay rent for the two-room house where they live: 50,000 Kwachas, or U.S. $10, a month. Every day he worries about survival; there is never a moment when he thinks of other things. At the end of the month, when workers get paid, he has one or two days when he brings home as much as 60,000 Kwachas, or U.S. $12. But most other days he makes much less.

In the city, he finds it is almost impossible to stock up on food; it has to be bought every day. It was very different in the village. There, a man could fill his granary with produce and take care of his family until the next harvest. Chanda remembers that it used to be possible, before the economic changes, for city people to go to the village at the onset of the rainy season to plough their fields and plant maize, and this would provide them with food. But now, without the government subsidies, it does not make sense to do this. So Chanda has to depend on the little cash he earns each day to buy food — and he knows that it is considered the greatest humiliation for a man if his family goes hungry, even for a single night.

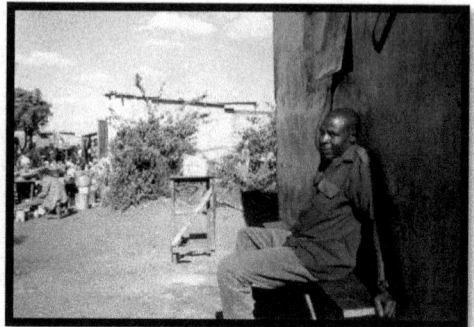

Left: Chanda selling cigarettes; right: one of Chanda's customers, at the market

Chanda also has to use his meager income to pay for his sister's two children to go to school. He does not have children of his own (having put off marriage to concentrate on supporting his family) but still is expected to help educate hers. Mindful that he had to leave school, he does not want the same thing to happen to them.

He is also responsible for helping weaker members of his extended family. Sometimes he has as many as ten extra relatives seeking his help. It strains his resources but he feels bound to adhere to the old custom of sharing the little he has with others. He is angry because he doesn't even have enough money to buy a *chitenge*, a piece of cloth, for his mother – the traditional gift from sons to their mothers, to be bought with the first money the son earns. It symbolizes the cloth in which the mother wrapped the son when he was a baby, and is his mark of thanks for the gift of life that he received from God through her.

Chanda consoles himself with the knowledge that he has earned the esteem of his family and the village elders, who appreciate his commitment to help them in their precarious situation. But the pressures on Chanda are immense. He fears disappointing his family in the village with his marginal job. He would like to look after his own interests, such as searching for a wife, but feels he cannot do this at the expense of the family welfare. He also would like to do some of the many things he sees in the city, like watching Hollywood films and wearing fashionable clothes, but he is forced to put them off. He feels sad missing out on all the new things. While he can and does acquire some things, like blue jeans, he gets them in the Salaula stands that sell second-hand clothing imported from

Europe and the U.S. at low prices. Chanda even dreams of owning a big hi-fi radio system like the ones he has seen in the stores and in the movies. This would indicate a certain level of success that would be recognized even in the village. But these are just dreams.

Political Alienation

Chanda feels that political decisions are often imposed on him. This is not a new thing. His village was not consulted or even informed about the economic reforms introduced in 1992. In the city, he has not met any of his political representatives. He attends local Development Committee meetings, but feels his ideas are never taken seriously.

Every time Chanda goes back to the village, he meets his village headman and consults with the elders for advice. He esteems their wisdom but finds that it's not very relevant in the city. For example, the elders cannot give him any useful advice about how to find formal employment there.

Politicians in the city, Chanda believes, pretend to play the role of elders, but aren't really interested in the welfare of the people. His sister has to walk long distances to fetch water because the local municipal authority has refused to provide potable water on the grounds that the slum is an illegal settlement without official recognition. The slum also needs roads and electricity. The political leaders promise at election time to bring these services, but it has not happened.

Chanda believes that the government is responsible for protecting weaker members of the community, like his family. But so far his family has not received any protection whatsoever. He feels powerless to do anything about these things, partly because he finds it difficult to approach political leaders, even in his own neighborhood. He was brought up to trust them and refrain from criticizing them. But he feels that these leaders have betrayed him. They promised that life would get better but it has become worse and he feels alienated from the whole process.

Changes in the Religious World

In the city, Chanda sees that local shrines have disappeared and therefore he finds it difficult now to call on his ancestors to help him in difficult times. He can't even offer them traditional beer anymore, because people in the city don't brew their own beer but instead drink beer brewed by a foreign company. So the role of the family spirits in Chanda's life has diminished, and he feels alienated from them and from the Deity. At the same time, he still has a strong sense of connection with them and is afraid of offending them. He knows that if he doesn't appease them, he would bring a curse on him. All the same, he rebels against some of the traditional practices. For instance, having missed the funeral of a relative, Chanda — according to tradition — could not approach the person's grave unless he presented an offering of traditional beer to appease the spirits. He was further required to find someone not from his clan to escort him to the grave, and to bring a white chicken as an offering to the spirits. All this annoys him; he doesn't see why he can't approach the grave without fulfilling these conditions.

Also, he gives much less credence to indigenous diviners and priests because he sees them exploiting people. Chanda's brother has psychological problems and neither modern medicine nor prayers helped him. Under pressure from some influential villagers, the family consulted a diviner and was forced to make a down payment of 25,000 Kwachas, U.S. $5, before treatment could begin. But his brother's condition did not improve, and the family was still expected to pay for the treatment in full.

Things like this have disillusioned Chanda. Sometimes he does not like the belief that ancestral spirits can impose sanctions on people and cannot see what wrong his clan has committed to be suffering such hardships. So now he is not taking all the traditional religious beliefs so seriously.

After being in the city for a while, Chanda began attending Christian services with a mainline Protestant congregation, The New Apostolic Church. Later he joined an evangelical Christian group, Receive Miracles Healing Ministry, which places a heavy emphasis on personal piety, as opposed to working for social change. He goes "to pray to God and learn about God, and not to communally solve problems." His relationship with God in these churches focuses exclusively on worship.

Chanda's Struggles

These days Chanda often finds it hard to determine the right thing to do. For example, he cannot tell whether it is right to have a girlfriend in the city sense — someone with whom one has sexual relations. In the traditional system a young man was expected to refrain from having sexual relations with a woman who was not his wife. Chanda is faithful to clan values but feels uncomfortable with some of them, such as the traditional practice of performing rituals every time a bad thing happens in the family. He sees that these practices lead to abuse, as happened with his brother. He has begun to think that hard work and luck, instead of rituals, might someday let his family escape their predicament.

Chanda can't rely on the old ways to cope, because much of what he learned in the village is of no use in the city. His initiation did not teach him how to deal with the harsh realities of the global economy. In the past, if there were something new in the village, the elders would teach the young ones about it. But today, who can teach Chanda about using new technologies such as the Internet, which he sees educated young people using? He has not even touched a computer.

These are some of the questions that trouble Chanda and cause him unhappiness. He does not enjoy life in the city and wonders if it was a big mistake to come. He is proud that he is meeting his responsibilities and that the village values him and can count on him. But he feels trapped by these responsibilities and sometimes he despairs. At his lowest, he feels he has failed in practically everything he has attempted to do with his life.

A Day in the Life...

Chanda's back aches from the long day of standing and selling cigarettes. Once again, he wishes he could be more than a *muchanga* boy. He passes the street vendors and movie theaters and, feeling wistful, again resists the urge to treat himself to a movie or a new shirt. He stops in a doorway and counts the day's earnings: 50,000 Kwachas (U.S. $10). It is the end of the month and this was a very good day. This will be enough to pay the month's rent. But once again there is not enough to buy a *chitenge* for his mother and he stamps his foot in anger. Chanda uses part of the money to buy dinner for the night. He brings the food home, thankful that he can at least provide a decent meal. He thinks briefly about the village and part of him longs to go back. He knows that some new opportunities have opened up there: vegetable gardening, fishing, quarrying, and employment with Agriflora (a new private company growing flowers for export to Europe). But he cannot return empty-handed.

CULTURAL ANALYSIS

Chanda's Traditional Culture

The world into which Chanda was born and where he spent his first sixteen years is the one of the traditional Zambian culture of his village. This culture is what he brought with him to the city.

1. *Vertical culture.* There is an ordered sense of hierarchy, authority, and respect for elders. Young people frequently turn to elders for advice, and are expected to comply with their instructions. Related to this respect for elders is a reluctance to criticize authority. Even when a person feels that the elders have erred, one is expected to avoid criticizing them, at least in public.

2. *Ancestral culture and importance of the past.* Ancestors are respected and there is a strong sense of the "spirits" world. Many people feel connected to the dead and the ancestors, who are considered part of the life of the family or clan and are invoked to take part in many ordinary family activities.

3. *Solidarity.* Community values often prevail over individual values. The interests of the family, clan, and even tribe take precedence. The community, through the elders, can intervene in an individual's life if there is a need to correct errant behavior.

4. *Strong family values.* An individual's primary duty is to the extended family; those responsibilities must be met before tending to his or her own affairs. Responsibility for the family and younger siblings starts very early, forcing people to work at an early age to help the family. As a person matures, he or she is expected to take personal initiative to do something for the family and the clan.

5. *Strong sense of belonging.* As a result of the close family and community ties, the individual has a distinct place in a larger web of ancestors, ethnic group, and family.

6. *Time is valuable but not in a monetary way.* In pre-colonial days, people did not have to go far to cultivate their lands, hunt game, or gather berries and wild fruits. Therefore, they had no sense of urgency and time was never a problem. This

sense of time still permeates village life in Zambia. The focus is on the present, rather than on looking to the future. In fact, there is no word for the future in Chanda's language.

7. *Perseverance.* This virtue is highly valued and is expected to be rewarded with eventual success. In times of crisis it helps to prove the person's worth.

Chanda's Critical Decisions

1. He decided to accept the elders' decision to drop out of school in the village and go to Lusaka to look for a job.

What were his options? Realistically, Chanda did not have much of a choice. The elders, though, could have advised him to: look for a job with one of the more prosperous local farmers, take up farming by himself on a small plot of land, or even take a short farming course run by a mission.

What cultural values lay behind his decision to accept the elders' advice? The wisdom of adults is highly esteemed. The village elders and his parents thought Chanda needed to go to the city and it would have been very difficult for him to go against their instructions. Also, in Zambia, it is the dream of village boys to move to the city, land a good job, and make money for themselves and their families. But Chanda's move was a matter of expediency, caused by the new difficult economic situation.

What cultural values were reflected in the reactions of the other people in his life to this decision? Chanda's family and the elders, as well as the other people in the village, expected him to follow the elders' lead. At the same time, they were apprehensive about him leaving because he was so young.

2. Once in the city, he decided to start selling cigarettes.

What were his options? Chanda had little education and few job skills, so he could not get a regular job; that was not an option for him. The economic situation was so bad that he could not even find part-time work and certainly could not think of returning to school. It would have been easy for him to become desperate and rebel against what was expected of him. He could have given up and simply left his sister's house. He could have turned to drugs and crime, as many other young people did.

What cultural values lay behind his decision? Chanda's sense of responsibility for his family in the city and back in the village dictated his decision: he needed cash to support them.

What cultural values were reflected in the reactions of the other people in his life to this decision? The people in his village (and one assumes his sister in the city) think highly of Chanda because he is showing that he is resourceful and dedicated to his clan and capable of carrying out his responsibilities.

Note: Chanda's decisions are rooted in the core traits of the culture. He migrated because his family and the elders thought he should; his choice reflects the vertical culture and its emphasis on respect for elders. It also reflects solidarity, the expectation that a young person would contribute to the family. Deciding to sell cigarettes reflected solidarity and perseverance. Running through all this we also see a sense of belonging: Chanda seems to know who he is and where he belongs in the village. This does not seem to change, even though he has left the village. The reactions of other people to Chanda's decision reflect these same cultural traits.

Changes in Chanda's Life

Consumption

> *Akachepa Kakufwala:* Or, only the piece of clothing one is wearing cannot be shared. One should learn to share everything, even when there is very little.

The opening of the Zambian economy to foreign trade increased the availability of goods and services in the country, but only for people who have money to buy them. In the city Chanda sees new imported products – many at lower prices than before – but because he and his family need his meager income just to survive, he doesn't buy many of them. He also has to buy things that before were freely available to him. In the village, people grew their own food, wore used clothing that was often sent from the city, and entertained themselves with traditional celebration. Now he has to pay for these things.

Chanda is aware of the unwritten rule in the city that everyone has to "keep up with the Joneses" and he sees people going to great lengths to acquire some of the latest consumer goods. This is a new pressure for him. In the village, for example, no one paid attention to what he wore; people often dressed in tatters and old clothes. Chanda has adopted some Western customs, such as wearing blue jeans and tee-shirts. And he wants some of the things that he sees all around him, like movies and new foods, but he can't afford them.

Not being able to wear the new fashions or buy the latest goods makes it hard for Chanda to feel he belongs in his new circle of friends. Moreover, his new sources of entertainment often involve foreign cultures, such as Western movies. Seeing how people in other places live builds even more aspirations in him that he cannot achieve. This further detracts from feeling he is a part of the city. He wants to belong but can't keep up, and this frustrates him.

Production

Uwanigila Mu Mushitu, Tomfwa Nsanswa: Or, when a person enters a thicket, that person does not get afraid and turn back when hearing sticks breaking. Perseverance in difficult times is important.

Ubunag'ani, Tabulisha Kasuma: Or, laziness does not enable one to eat good things. People should work hard in order to lead good lives.

Muchanga boy: A servant, one who serves others by fetching things.

Chanda's work has changed. In the village he studied and helped on the farm. Now he works in the growing service sector in the informal economy in the city. He sells cigarettes, one at a time, in the city streets. He had hoped to get a "good job" in Lusaka, but in the difficult job situation there he didn't have the education or skills to do so.

Back in the village, farming was not considered a job or a business: it was simply how people made ends meet. But Chanda and the people in his village don't consider selling cigarettes on the streets a job, either. It is unpredictable, brings in very little money, and is thought to be a temporary arrangement until something better turns up. A job is something that brings in a reasonable amount of income at the end of the day, such as working in a factory or the mines, or in a government office. Cigarette street vendors are looked down upon.

Still, Chanda is proud that he was chosen to carry out the important task of helping support his family. He works hard, fearing he will be branded by his family and clan back home as a lazy and useless person. Yet he derives very little pride from his work; in fact he often feels he is a "nobody" and is ashamed that he has to do it. He feels trapped in it and wishes he could find another way of making money, but sees no way out.

Migration

> *Akanwa Ka Mwefu Takabepa:* Or, a mouth of an elder cannot mislead. You can never go wrong if you consult an elder.

> *Umukulu Tapusa Kebo, Apusa Akabwe:* Or, an adult can miss a stone but cannot miss a good teaching. Take the teachings of the elders seriously because they rarely get it wrong.

For a long time, young Zambian men have gone to work in the mines or the cities to better themselves and help their families. What is different with Chanda is his age – he was only sixteen when he left the village. He did not receive the preparation that usually precedes migration; he didn't finish school or learn a marketable skill. His migration was premature. Globalization accelerated a trend already at work in the country. For Chanda, it meant that his migration experience was more difficult than it might have been otherwise.

Chanda feels good because he has earned respect from the village for obeying the directive to move to the city, but still he despairs sometimes. He has a low-status job and worries he will never better himself, does not feel he belongs in the city. He feels at times he would have chosen a different path if it had been up to him.

Going back to live at home now is not an option for him. People in the village expect that anyone who returns from the city will come with wealth and bring gifts for everybody. However, in his straitened circumstances, Chanda cannot do this. It would be considered a disgrace to return empty-handed; he would have failed his family. He wishes he could return but feels he cannot.

Social Relations

> *Amaka Yanseba Kwiminina Pamo:* Or, the strength of birds is standing together. The strength of the community is unity.

> *Mayo Mpapa, Na Ine Nkakupapa:* Or, mother carry me, I too will carry you. One should look after the aged in appreciation for the care and nurturing they give the young.

> *Chitenge:* The piece of cloth a young man buys as a gift for his mother with his first job, to thank her for giving him life.

Chanda's social relations have changed since he moved to Lusaka. In the village, people had the same background and everyone knew everyone else. In the city, people come from many varied backgrounds and were, at least initially, strangers to him. In the village, he could draw on the wisdom and experience of the elders and the ancestors, which had been passed down from generation to generation. This history was his key point of reference. His city community, by contrast, is not well defined and has no history for him.

He does have choices in his social relationships in the city that he would not have had back in the village. But the values of the city – a city increasingly exposed to foreign influences – are very different from Chanda's traditional social values. Chanda is now exposed to social relationships, through the foreign media, that contrast sharply with what he knows from the village. At the same time, he does not have the wisdom of the village elders to help guide him in this new situation. He has to decide by himself how to relate to these new people and whom he can trust. On top of that, he also has to navigate – again, by himself – through the foreign elements he encounters in the city. The tension is that he has more choices than he did before in his social relations, but misses the guidance to which he is accustomed.

Working as a street vendor, which takes many hours each day, Chanda has little time to socialize away from his work. This is very different from the more relaxed pace of life in the village, and it causes some tension for him. Chanda finds that he is making new friends with the people who visit him regularly at his stand. This is a positive thing, but it leads to yet more tension, because sometimes relatives and friends from the village also come to visit him. He then is torn between spending time with his business and his new friends or with his family and clan. He doesn't have as much time to drop things and spend time with whoever is there. This is an unresolved issue and when he moves into doing something new – work that is more structured – it will be more of a problem. Right now, he doesn't feel compelled to do anything about it.

Chanda still has a sense of belonging to his family and clan, and this is a great support for him. He is proud because he is recognized in the village for helping his family. Still, he's afraid he isn't doing all that he's expected to do, because of his difficult financial situation. He hasn't even been able yet to buy a *chitenge* for his mother. He misses the village and also feels frustrated because he doesn't feel he belongs in the city and wonders if he ever will.

Political Relations

> *Umunwe Umo Tausala Inda:* Or, one finger cannot pick a louse. One cannot achieve much alone.

> *Akasabi Ukulya Akasabi Kabiye, E Kunona:* Or, a small fish that is getting fat is feeding on another. It is a criticism of exploitative relationships that are discouraged in traditional society.

In the village, Chanda's identity was formed by his clan. In the city, he lives and works with people from other tribes. This expansion in the kinds of people around him has enlarged his identity; it is more a national identity now. But that national identity is not very clear to him, since he sees lifestyles, dreams, and aspirations that are inconsistent with what he considers to be Zambian traditions, regardless of clan. He also is exposed to increased communication, because of the media, and sees widespread corruption in the political system.

In the village there would have been a venue for Chanda to participate in village issues, once he became a breadwinner. In the city, the vertical power structures he knew in the village are ineffective, and there are no elders to offer him guidance. In principle, the multi-party system opens more opportunities for Chanda to participate in the political process in the city. But in practice he does not have access to a political structure where he can participate effectively in local affairs. He perceives the local government authorities as inaccessible and corrupt.

He feels leaderless and angry at the political system. He and his family feel betrayed by the way the national government eliminated agricultural subsidies without consulting the people. They are torn between their tra-

ditional custom of not criticizing authority and their dissatisfaction with
the government. So Chanda does not know where to go with his complaints or to whom he should give political allegiance. For different reasons, he has lost confidence in both traditional and modern political authority, and in his alienation he cuts himself off from all politics. In essence, he has experienced a breakdown in his political power world and
lives in a political vacuum.

Religious Experience and Expression

> *Umulandu Wa Mubiyo, Cibashilo, Ca Mupini:* Or, your friend's
> situation is an occasion to make a handle out of an axe or a hoe.
> A person should help others in trouble, since he too will be in
> trouble some day.

In the village, Chanda's traditional religion was strongly communal.
Religious figures exerted influence on the life of the community. The
whole village took part in the rituals, which focused on the ancestors and
nature and drew few distinctions between the sacred and the profane, between God and nature. In the city, Chanda is influenced by Christian
teachings and has several Christian denominations to choose from, things
he was not exposed to in the village. He already has been a member of
two different Christian groups: a mainline Protestant congregation and an
evangelical group. They are quite different from what he was used to in
the village. Personal piety is stressed; the focus is on the relationship between the individual and God. The community plays a much smaller role.
Nature is not involved at all, and there is a sharp distinction made between the sacred and the profane.

Chanda essentially has a foot in both Christianity and traditional African religion. He is still bound by African religion, especially the beliefs in
ancestors and spirits. But he feels abandoned by them because of the financial situation of his family and the village and he has become critical of
some traditional religious practices. In addition, in the city it is harder for
him to practice the traditional rites. He can't even find the home-made
beer traditionally used to offer sacrifices to the ancestors. He wonders
whether ancestors and spirits are real in the city, where traditional rituals
cannot be performed.

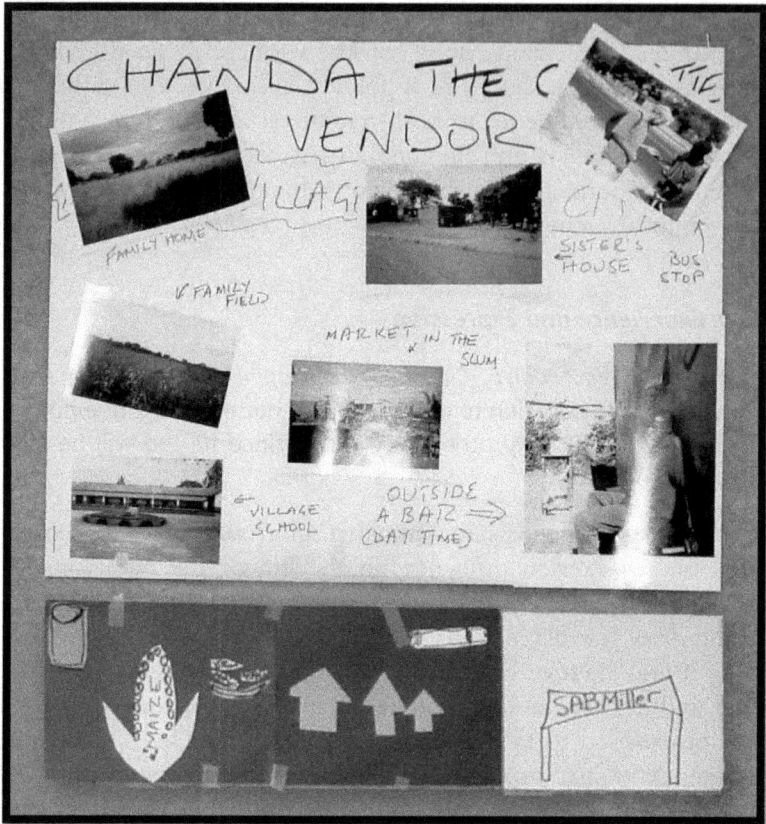

Chanda's mosaic tile, from GEC's Fourth International Consultation

CHANDA'S MEANINGS AND VALUES
AS REFLECTED IN HIS CHOICES

To try to enter into what was going on within Chanda, as an intelligent person and possible agent of change, we focus on two major actions that we observe in the narrative, which can be seen as part of a continuum in time and in Chanda's development:

1. Chanda obeys his parents and village elders and leaves school and the village to go to the city.

2. Chanda, once in the city, becomes a cigarette vendor.

In the first action Chanda's freedom is that of a child who might appear to have a choice to obey or disobey his elders, but who faces very painful consequences associated with disobedience. This action does not constitute a true decision. In the second case, Chanda – ready or not – has become an adult who must decide and act on his own, even though he does not seem to face any desirable alternatives. Because these actions are different in character, therefore, we will discuss below how Chanda sees himself as he proceeds to obey his elders in the first action, but we apply the methodology template (see Chapter 4, p. 78ff., "Research Methodology, Phase II: Finding the Protagonists' Meanings and Values"; the questions template appears on p. 87) in full only to the second action.

Action 1: Chanda obeys his parents and village elders and leaves school and the village to go to the city.

When his parents give him, at age sixteen, the decision that he is to leave the village and go to the city to help support the starving family, Chanda still is a child according to his family and village tradition. He is expected to obey, although now he is being asked to perform a role that normally would be the responsibility of adults: support the family. Up to this point, he has developed while surrounded by the love of his parents and the village. Chanda's values are the same as theirs. They have transmitted to him what they value in the religious, moral, cultural, social, and vital arenas. Chanda's identity at this point is totally tied to his belonging to his family and the clan. He cannot yet conceive of his identity apart from them. Chanda is expected to accept the decisions made by the elders and his parents and to obey without asking any questions. He has not participated at all in the process of making the decision, but he is expected to go to the city nonetheless. Once the elders have decided, Chanda's task is to align his thoughts and feelings with the wisdom of the elders. In principle, he has the choice any child has: to obey or not to obey his parents and elders. But he fully trusts the village elders and his parents – those who have found it fitting that he abandon his education and seek a job in the city.

Surely, he has anxieties as to what will happen to him. The city is an unknown to him and he is not certain he will succeed. He is not sure he can live up to the high expectations the family is placing on him. But, ultimately he knows that obeying the elders' decision is the right thing for him to do. If the elders in the family believe it is good for him to move into the unknown, then it is the right move for him. Although he fears that the wisdom he has learned in the village may not be adequate in the city, he also knows that the city is bigger than the village and holds more opportunities. Chanda begins to think that for the elders to send him to the city means that the city cannot be that bad: elders know better than young people. Besides, to be chosen by the elders to undertake a new and potentially frightening experience indicates the level of maturity the young person has attained. Chanda sees in the elders' decision their determination that he is ready to become a man. He, like all young boys, desires to show to the clan that he is ready to become a man. Working to support his family will prove that he has become a man, an adult. In the back of Chanda's mind also is what he knows about the likely consequences of not obeying the elders – expulsion from the family and/or being cursed by his family. Not being able to conceive his identity outside the clan and family, these consequences are so severe that Chanda cannot consider seriously the possibility of disobeying his parents. So he doesn't have much of a choice. He must obey his parents and the village elders.

Deciding to obey his parents, however, does not mean that Chanda is an automaton, merely following others' decisions. He is very conscious of the economic hardships that he and his family are going through in the village. He is highly motivated by what his clan values and his decision to obey his elders carries a lot of commitment to those values, which he has learnt from them. He just has little freedom to question the elders' decision or to create alternatives other than those that the elders and his family provide. So he drops out of school in the village and moves to the city in search of a "good job."

Action 2: Chanda, once in the city, becomes a cigarette vendor.

A. What can we infer goes on within Chanda as he experiences the new economy and moves on to decide to take this action? What questions may Chanda have been raising and what answers seem consistent with reaching that decision? (Note: This refers to the stages of consciousness, from experiencing to deciding; see Chapter 4, p. 88ff.)

Chanda arrived in the city with the expectation that he would find a "good job" and soon earn money to send back to the family for them to buy food. He first *experiences* the bewilderment of the new things he sees and hears there. He feels attracted to many of them, but his overriding feeling is one of anxiety as he searches for a job in this new environment. He soon is filled with disappointment, unable to find the "good job" that he seeks. He also experiences a new reality. Now, in addition to his village family, his sister's family in the city also has become dependent on him. In the process of looking for a "good job," he hears of the possibilities of earning some income as a *muchanga* boy in "less desirable jobs," such as selling cigarettes on the street or becoming a cook or a garden hand. Does he also hear of illicit ways to make a living in the city, perhaps generating much more money that even a "good job" would do?

He starts asking himself questions, beginning with why he is so unsuccessful in finding a "good job." He tries to figure out how he could go about accomplishing this. He answers himself with what he has been hearing: he does not have sufficient education. He wonders whether he can acquire the needed education, but soon he finds out that it will cost money he does not have. In addition, he is afraid that at his age people would laugh at him for attending secondary school. He asks himself whether he could become a *muchanga* boy, and whether that kind of job, though not considered a proper job, could earn enough income to support the family. He answers affirmatively that he could get such jobs with his limited education. But he also finds out that the *muchanga* jobs generate less income than what he believes he needs to support his two families, let alone buy some of the new things he would like to have. Chanda also feels repelled by these jobs, because they carry a lower social status than the ones to which he earlier aspired. In the process of Chanda asking himself these questions and answering them, he gains a new *understanding* of his economic situation and the job opportunities that he has in front of him – even though this understanding just increases his frustration about the difficulty of achieving the goal for which he came to the city.

Chanda makes further inquiries to test his understanding, to make sure it is correct. He had thought it would be easy to find a good job, but now understands the reality: this is practically impossible with his limited education. Having completed just seventh grade, he does not have the skills and experience required to get the good jobs. So he now has a better understanding of his options, limited as they are. He corroborates the fact that in selling cigarettes he would be his own boss and receive money every day, while in the other jobs he would answer to somebody else and have to wait more than a week to receive his wages. He comes to a conclusion. His *judgment of the facts* indicates that yes, "a good job" is out of his reach because he lacks formal education, but the other, less desirable, jobs are definitely a possibility. Among these other jobs, he judges that the daily income gained from selling cigarettes is more desirable than the arrangement with the other jobs. He needs to send money home as frequently as possible.

Next, he must *decide* what to do. Chanda is torn between his sense of obligation to support his family and the reality of the jobs that he can find. He also thinks of all the things he can buy in the city that were not available in the village. That adds pressure to earn more money. Out of this conflict, Chanda feels tempted to return to the village, but doing so would mark him a failure in front of everybody. Failing to earn money to send home would be an embarrassment in the village, where men are supposed to look after their families. People would laugh at him for having failed and not being man enough. Beyond humiliation, he would be ostracized or banished from his clan because of the shame he would bring on his family. Chanda remembers his family and the elders, whom he trusts. He first came to the city primarily because he did not want to disobey them, but love and trust for family and village energize him as he decides what he believes is the best course of action. Being in solidarity with them is more important to him than his own needs. So he *decides* to become a *muchanga* boy selling cigarettes on the street to support his family. He finds it *worthwhile*, that it is good, for him to do this – despite the work's low status and making less money than what he had first anticipated.

B. What values appear to drive Chanda's decision? What are the good things that he seeks? (Note: This refers to the scale of values; see Chapter 4, p. 95ff.)

Chanda's immediate motivation to sell cigarettes on the street is to generate the money needed to meet his and his family's basic subsistence needs – his *vital values*. He needs enough income to meet these needs. That is why he seeks a good job, a *social value*. But beyond these values is the major driving force that brought Chanda to the city in the first instance: the *religious, moral, and cultural values* that together demand that Chanda carry out the responsibilities of a man in his culture and support his family. He reaches the decision to sell cigarettes on the street in the context of his *ultimate values* of love for his family and respect for the elders. It is also what he believes his ancestors expect from him. These *ultimate values* are the primary force driving his decision. Obeying the elders and the family is the right thing for him to do, his driving *moral value*. And this moral value permeates and is infused by the *cultural values* that establish the proper relationships among family members, and between family and the rest of the village. There is little room for selfishness in Chanda's world without endangering his sense of identity in the village and the clan.

C. How does Chanda's new knowledge and decision change the horizon of meanings in his world?

Once Chanda commits to staying in the city selling cigarettes on the street, something big has happened to him. His horizon has expanded from that of a child who does what he is told, to the horizon of an adult who takes responsibility for his actions. The love of family and trust of elders are still an important source of energy in Chanda, but there is some new personal energy in his life. He has begun to take care of others. And these others now go beyond his family in the village to include his sister's family in the city. His horizon also has expanded even beyond that of an adult in the village. Chanda's decision brings new meanings to his surroundings in the city, where he has found more things to consume, work opportunities different from those in the village, many people with languages and traditions different from the clan back home, and no elders available to guide him. His horizon has expanded well beyond the vertical structures of the village to include the more diverse structures of living in the city.

D. Given Chanda's new horizon of meanings, what can we infer goes on within him as he moves to implement his decision? What questions may he have been trying to answer as he puts his decision into action? What values of Chanda are engaged in this implementation? (Note: This refers to the stages of consciousness, from deciding to acting; see Chapter 4, p. 90ff.)

Chanda has made a decision as an adult, but does he really mean to live with the implications of staying in the city selling cigarettes? Because he is at peace with himself, we know he answers affirmatively. He *judges it worthwhile* to accept the consequences of a life different not only from what he knew in the village, but also different from what he expected to find in the city. As he answers affirmatively, he begins to own his decision and take *responsibility* for it and the changes it implies in his life. Guided by his love of family and village and his village traditions, he begins owning a new point of view. These are the *religious, moral, and cultural values* that drive Chanda. He will, indeed, contribute to support his family, as a man in his culture does. These values and his new point of view now become the foundation for how he sees his life in the city and looks back on the life he left behind in the village.

But there are still questions about his situation that need to be answered. How is he to relate to the people from other clans he meets in the city? He finds it *reasonable* to relate to them, despite their clan origin; they become the people from whom he buys the cigarette boxes and the people to whom he sells the single cigarettes. They even become his friends when they stop to talk with him at his stand. He asks himself, are the village elders of any use in the city? The elders are still a source of respect for the wisdom they have about life in the village, but Chanda finds that their value to him in the city is less.

In answering these questions, Chanda adapts what he considers good, and what gives meaning to his life, in his culture, his *cultural values*. Now his world includes people from other lands and he realizes the limitations in applying the wisdom of the village elders to his city world. As he starts adapting his life to put his decision into practice, he asks himself questions about exactly how he is to go about organizing his job of selling cigarettes on the street. He knew how adults organized their jobs in the rural village; here he has to create something new. He has to figure out the arrangements, first, for how to buy the cigarettes: how much money is needed and how does he find that money? Then he asks himself about the places it might be most advantageous to sell the cigarettes on different days or times of the day. He determines that the street is good during the day, but the pubs are better at night. Chanda also finds out that at the end of the month, when salaries are paid, workers celebrate more at the pub and he can sell them more cigarettes than usual. Then he asks how to send the money back to his family in the village.

As Chanda answers these questions, he uses his intelligence to gain an understanding of his life in the city selling cigarettes. He is adapting what he considers good in how to make a living – a social arrangement and so a *social value*. He has adapted the social standards of what work is in the village to what is in the city. He is changing how he values a good job: he now values selling cigarettes to support himself. It is not the job that he wanted. He has found that farming in the village is not an option any more. He feels ashamed of becoming a *muchanga* boy; but, particularly at the end of the month when more money comes in, it does not appear such a bad job. More important, being a *muchanga* boy allows him to help support his family (his vital and moral values) and earns the respect of the village for being a man who supports his family (his cultural and moral values). It is with this new understanding of his situation in the city that Chanda becomes a cigarette vendor on the street. As he starts selling cigarettes, the *experience* becomes the new lens through which he sees the rest of his life in the city, as well as how he earns a living in the future. Chanda adapts what he values along his whole scale of values. He is frustrated that he cannot do better materially, but he has found ways to adapt in order to pursue what is good, what he values in his life.

E. Do we detect changes in the relative weights Chanda now places on different values within a given level of values and among different levels of values? Does Chanda seem comfortable with his decision and action? (Note: This refers to the tensions within and among the levels of values; see Chapter 4, p. 102ff.)

The life of Chanda changed drastically after he left the village for the city. In the process, he has become an adult and, as such, he has had to put more weight on *social values* – what is good in the job that allows him to support his family. He has adapted his *cultural values* to incorporate the other cultures and traditions he finds in the city. He remains closely attached to the cultural values of the village that give him his identity, but now he is also more open to the traditions of other clans and the ways of the city. But his *moral and religious values* remain the compass of his life, what ultimately guide his decisions. He attends Christian churches, but his traditional religious sensibilities and their ethical implications for taking care of his extended family remain dominant. Chanda is frustrated that, regardless of how hard he tries, he cannot provide for the needs of his family and his own needs in a better fashion. But he seems at peace that he is doing the right thing, the best that he can with the options that he has. His family is better off for his being in the city selling cigarettes on the street.

The new situations Chanda faced in the city caused imbalances at all levels of values on his scale of values. How to get food, how to find work to support his family, how to find meaning in his new environment, how to gain respect and relate to others, how to worship: in all these areas, he faced unsustainable new tensions. These tensions arose from the imbalances between the pull of the tradition on the one hand and the pull of the new environment of the city on the other. But he succeeded in restoring balance between these two poles. His ultimate religious values help him to adapt so he finds dignity as a *muchanga* boy in the city. These moral values, in turn, help him reestablish balance between his previous idea of a good job and the reality of being a *muchanga* boy; this is balance at the social level. He accepts how he must live day to day in the city; this is balance at the vital level. It was his love of family and clan and village traditions that he kept as his guide, and he is at peace.

RESEARCHERS' REFLECTIONS

Zambia's Economic Globalization and Chanda

Chanda's village was unprepared for the elimination of NAM-BOARD. The village livelihood had come to depend on the agricultural subsidies it provided, but the government could not afford them any longer. And the system was abolished between one day and the next, with no warning. Their source of inexpensive fertilizers, technical assistance, and credit disappeared, and they had not even been consulted in the process. The government had indeed implemented market-oriented measures, but there were no institutions in place to make the market function for the village. There was no private financial institution to give the villagers credit to buy agricultural supplies and to tide them over until the harvest. Nor did the villagers have access to any private distribution system that would bring their produce to the market at a reasonable price. Instead, they could only fall prey to speculators. The government could have foreseen these results. In any case, no resources were made available at the time to facilitate a transition to a more viable system in Chanda's village.

In the city, Chanda fends as best he can by selling cigarettes, one at a time. But he is deprived of any hope of finishing his education. He has almost no access to any way of working out of his current economic predicament: living with his sister and her family in a slum of Lusaka. His life has been totally disrupted by the economic measures, but he has been given hardly any tools to manage the transition and have an opportunity in the new economic system.

Zambia's economic situation before the opening of its economy was unsustainable. But the new system has been a failure for people like Chanda and the others in his village. Without appropriate market institutions and necessary provisions for the transition, the new system has had devastating effects for Chanda and his village.

Getting to Know Chanda: Our Journey

When we first met Chanda and listened to his story of how the Zambian economic liberalization measures had inflicted so much economic distress on his village and how this had led to his difficulties in the city, we were moved with pity and compassion. We felt for him. We also felt anger at the injustice meted out to Chanda and his family, who were left without any ready alternative for economic subsistence.

As we engaged in our cultural analysis, and the narrator continued to listen to Chanda's story, our feelings and understanding of Chanda began to evolve. We watched more closely how he dealt with the new challenges. We began to notice a change in our interior reaction towards him. In the words of Leonard Chiti:

> "My initial feelings of pity, compassion and anger began giving way to respect and admiration. I was moved by Chanda's ability to make the decision of his parents his own and the courage and fortitude he displayed in coming to terms with the abrupt change that had taken place in his life. In particular, I was encouraged and strengthened by the manner in which he negotiated the abrupt change from being a dependent to becoming a provider. Such a transition takes many years under ordinary circumstances. The economic, political and cultural changes that accompanied the opening up of the local economy to global forces were unprecedented and this required tremendous courage on the part of Chanda to appreciate his family's concerns that he helps out supporting the family. The love he showed his family won my admiration.
>
> "I watched Chanda deal with the tensions and frustrations engendered by his move to the city. I felt the pain that he felt even as he spoke about things he barely understood such as his immediate insertion into city life and the new things that he saw, heard and experienced. I thought what got him through was his fidelity to the cultural values that he had learned from his elders and also his faith in God. This transformation brought consolation to me."

However, despite the help that the village tradition and love for his family gave Chanda in finding meaning in his life in the city, at the time we thought Chanda might not be integrating the tradition into this life and might not be making a significant adaptation to his new world. His parents found pride in working the land. Young men who migrated before Chanda found respect working in the mines or in the government. But Chanda did not seem to find meaning in his work beyond what it allowed him to do for the family; he certainly derived neither much income nor any pride or respect from it. We wondered whether he was questioning his sense of worth and ultimately his identity.

We could see the frustrations arising from the conflict between Chanda's traditional values and his reality in the city. We were concerned that even though Chanda's community had changed, his social relationships were still dominated by the village structures. He seemed to continue to define himself as a village person, tied only to the clan and his family. Although the elders who sent him to the city know little about the situation there, Chanda seemed caught because he did not think he could question their decisions and he worried that he would disappoint his extended family as he tried to support all of them. He accepted responsibility for caring for the weak and less fortunate in his family and sending money to them was his highest priority. But he also saw the new and attractive things that are available in the city, and he wanted to have them. The village's political structures did not help Chanda to adapt the city or help him feel he belongs there. In the city environment, those village structures have lost significance for him; at the same time, he did not feel he could participate in the city's modern political structures. He seemed in practice disenfranchised and cut off from both political structures.

But we could also see that, despite still longing for the village and feeling he did not belong in the city, he was already different from what he would have been if he had stayed in the village. Chanda was gaining personhood in the context of the city. He was being "urbanized" and "globalized," whether he liked it or not. The question was whether in this process he was maintaining his personal integrity or self-destructing. We saw the key to Chanda's human development to be whether he could bridge the gap between what was happening to him in the city − a city that the greater opening to market forces has exposed to a bigger world − and who he was in the context of his Zambian village, with its tradition of reverence for elders, ancestors, and nature, and a community of solidarity. We were not sure how he was straddling the two worlds.

It is only when we began to see Chanda as a decision-maker in the city, and acknowledge his intelligence and the role of his values in reaching these decisions, that we came to appreciate Chanda's role in creating and shaping his own life and finding meaning in it. Seeing him in this way we can see he has more control over his actions and is not just a victim. He uses his intelligence to understand his possibilities and he makes conscious choices every day about the things he will do and how he will do them. Most of the time, he has few options, but he brings his values to bear in deciding among these options. And as he puts these decisions into actions, he begins to adapt his traditional values to the circumstances that he now finds in the city. He is an actor who helps create his new reality, limited as it is, and that reality has meaning for him.

His tradition guides him, but he also takes responsibility for his decisions as he expands his horizon and adapts his traditional cultural values to reflect his love for family and respect for elders and ancestors within his new surroundings. He has established new social relationships and has created for himself a way of making a living very different from the farming and hunting he knew in the village. He has learned to take care of his basic needs in ways very different from those in the village – and he finds meaning in all these new ways.

Despite Chanda's difficult economic situation, he is not desperate. His love and respect for family, elders, and ancestors shape his personal values and ultimately lead to his decision to sacrifice himself. In this love we can see an expression of his religious values. Even though he is somewhat distanced from the traditional expression of African religion, he still experiences God as a driving force. It is now primarily through the love of his extended family and the support of the village elders – even if ineffectual – whose wisdom he considers to originate from God. His faith helps him find meaning in his life in the city: his hardships and his help to the family are appreciated by the elders in their divine wisdom and will be rewarded by the ancestors. This gives him self-esteem and strength to make all the creative adaptations that he has made in the city.

In the city he sometimes doubts the power of the ancestors because he cannot worship them there in the way he did in the village. So he turns to Christianity to make contact with the transcendent, thus finding a new way, in his new environment, to express his spirituality. His fellow Christians also mediate God's love for him. Chanda now finds meaning in a Christ who shares human suffering and a God who is willing to enter into a personal relationship, in contrast to the more remote God of the African tradition. At the same time, Christian charity and the fourth commandment to honor father and mother reinforce his traditional respect for elders and family and bless his sacrifices to support the family. Somehow, Chanda finds meaning in his balance of Christ and African tradition. Though he probably has not truly integrated these two visions, he seems to be confident that in the end, God will work things out and that things will turn out better for him in the city than in the village.

Delving into what must have been going on within Chanda in terms of his decisions and the values that guided them changed our understanding of him. In the words of Leonard Chiti:

"Chanda's transformation has continued to evolve and [I see] he is now an active subject in the globalization process. To sell cigarettes on the street may not be what he would have chosen under more favorable conditions. Nonetheless, it is something that gives him a sense of value and meaning in his life as well as making it possible for him to contribute in a modest way towards alleviating the suffering of his family. This gives me the confidence to believe that even though in the short term Chanda has suffered due to the adverse impact of globalization, in the long term I believe that if Chanda remains faithful to the values of his clan and his religious beliefs he will emerge as a winner in the globalised environment.

Chanda has succeeded in meeting the expectations of his family to some degree but most importantly he has grown into a man, which is the ultimate goal of any Bemba child."

Chanda for us now is a source of inspiration and hope. In this project's process of getting to know Chanda, we also were transformed and developed a new respect for him.

Development Policy Implications of Knowing Chanda in This New Way

We have gone from knowing Chanda primarily as a victim worthy of pity to knowing him as a creative person worthy of admiration. We have seen how, despite his very difficult economic situation, he is capable of a positive and creative life in pursuit of his aspirations to shape a better future for himself and others. How can we tap into the creativity that we have discovered in Chanda so it can become an engine of development not only for Chanda, but also for others like him in Lusaka?

Focusing first on Chanda, we immediately feel the need to bring him up to the same level of understanding of himself as we now have of him. A friendship has developed between Chanda and the narrator, Leonard Chiti, and we feel a debt of gratitude to him for helping us see his world in a different way. But he does not yet see himself in the way we see him now. We need to help him reflect on the import of the decisions he has made, how his intelligent understanding of the city reality emerged, and how what he values has guided the decisions he has made and shaped his life in the city. He is not yet in touch with this creativity. He does not give himself credit for forging ahead and not giving up hope in spite of major difficulties. To guide him in this reflection, Leonard Chiti plans to build on his friendship with Chanda.

To assist Chanda with improving his economic situation, Leonard Chiti plans to investigate existing development programs in Zambia designed to help the urban poor and then explain them to Chanda. The objective of this conversation, which could take several meetings, would be to help Chanda, first, see that some help might be available to get him out of the single-cigarette vending occupation into something better. Then Leonard Chiti plans to help Chanda understand the nature of these programs and help him decide whether he wants to pursue any of them or, perhaps, come up with another alternative path. The important point, though, is that in our new understanding of Chanda, he is the primary decision-maker and Leonard Chiti is just a facilitator.

But how do we expand this approach to development, based on getting to see the world through the eyes of the poor, to go beyond Chanda? How do we bring our method to scale? As development practitioners, we are concerned with the development of not only Chanda but also the community as a whole. In our approach, the first step has to be to create a community of "Chandas" that can represent the community as a whole. But before the group can be brought together, Leonard Chiti envisions befriending individual candidates. Once they come together, Chanda's story can be the catalyst for them reflecting on their individual stories. This reflection would explore how they have come to understand their reality and how, despite their critical economic condition, they have made a number of decisions that reflect their will to improve themselves and those around them whom they love. They would be able to name their values. The objective of this discussion would be for this community to see themselves as actors in the global story, not just victims; that is, actors that with the appropriate support can create a better economic reality for themselves.

Having built the community group and strengthened the members' self-consciousness, the next task would be for this community to consider development alternatives they would like to explore. The development practitioner's function then becomes to facilitate this exploration. This may include bringing other relevant actors such as government program managers and local businesses to participate in this conversation. Simultaneously, the practitioner may be working with these other actors to see Chanda and his community in the light that we have come to see him.

An alternative approach to building up Chanda's community could be to start with a given development project and then build Chanda's community around the design and implementation of this project. However, the distinctive part of our approach would always be that the community is the decision-maker and the development practitioner a facilitator. And the first step would often be for the members of this community of poor people to get in touch with the capabilities they already have exhibited, as well as the cultural, moral and religious values that guide their lives.

Chapter 8

Núria in Spain:
A Young Cosmopolitan in the
New Catalonia

A protest by students at the University of Barcelona

NARRATOR: JOSEP F. MÀRIA, SJ

Professor, ESADE; member of Cristianisme i Justicia
Barcelona, Catalonia, Spain

Narrative Summary and Economic Background

Núria grew up in a midsized city in the Autonomous Region of Catalonia in Spain; she was a teenager in the late 1990s. During her lifetime, Spain opened itself to the world in every regard. The economic and cultural environment in which she grew up was very different from what her parents had experienced. Núria spoke Catalan, instead of Spanish, because speaking Catalan was not forbidden any more. She had broad access to goods and media from other countries. She could and did travel easily and also studied in other European countries for short periods. She had a great exposure to immigrants from Africa and the rest of Spain and their cultures. In 2003 she was in her third year at the university in Barcelona. She was also active in international issues such as environmental protection and opposition to the U.S. war in Iraq. Núria would like to study or work in other countries after graduation, and she knows she may have to get an advanced degree.

Spain began to open itself to democracy, market forces, and international trade in 1975. That year marked the end of Francisco Franco's military regime, which had ruled since the end of the Spanish Civil War in 1939. Spain joined the European Union (E.U.) and NATO in 1986; this institutionalized the democratic reforms made after the dictatorship ended and opened the country's borders to more trade with the E.U. But an even greater economic opening occurred with liberalization measures that were initiated in 1992. Also in that year, the Olympic Games were held in Barcelona. This event gave worldwide legitimacy to the identity and culture of Catalonia and made Barcelona a recognized international tourist destination.

NARRATIVE

It was a sunny afternoon in Barcelona in the spring of 2003 when Núria met with her former high school tutor, a Jesuit. Núria and some of her friends had been studying in Barcelona at the university now for three years. They talked about their lives since high school and Núria's other friends: Beatriu, who was studying in Prague (Czech Republic), and Carme, who was in Innsbruck (Austria). The two of them were studying under the Erasmus Program, which offers young people scholarships to study at any European university for a semester. Maria was preparing for her Erasmus trip to Denmark and Norway in the fall. Núria did not have immediate plans for an Erasmus trip, but she reacted to Maria's plans with envy. For some time, Núria has been staying in touch with her friends abroad through the Internet.

Núria was born and grew up in a city of 120,000 people in the Autonomous Region of Catalonia in Spain, about one hundred fifty kilometers from Barcelona. As well as Spanish, she speaks Catalan, which she uses with her family and friends. Her father is a manager in a business company and her mother is an economic advisor to small businesses. They too were born in Catalonia. She has one brother, Pere, eleven years younger, who was adopted in an Eastern European country as a baby.

High School

The Jesuit high school where Núria and her friends studied had students from Aragon as well as Catalonia: it was located at the border between the two provinces. But classes were conducted mainly in the Catalan language. Everybody had to study Catalan but the Aragon students didn't get a grade in it, and they could write the exams in their other subjects in Spanish. However, there were no big divisions among the students because of the regional and linguistic differences.

The emphasis on using Catalan in school, as well as everywhere else in Catalonia, had behind it a long history of suppression. Speaking and teaching Catalan had been forbidden during Franco's dictatorship (1939–1975) and also at earlier times during Catalonia's history. So the many migrants from the rest of Spain who came to Catalonia during the 1960s did not learn Catalan in school or through the media. More recently, migrants were coming from other countries as well, further jeopardizing the survival of the Catalan language.

In addition to Catalan and Spanish (Spain's major language), Núria also studied English. She liked languages and at one point had been thinking about translation and interpretation as a possible career. Two summers earlier she had been to England to study English, and there she had met students from all over the world: Japan, East Asia, and of special interest to her, one boy from Hungary. She thought it was fantastic that she had friends in faraway countries. When she came back to her hometown, she started to write letters to her friends. After two years, though, she wrote less often. After English, Núria also studied German and French and thought about applying for an Erasmus Scholarship after high school.

To meet one of her high school requirements, Núria and her schoolmates enrolled in a Social Experience class for one semester. In this class they worked once a week in a social work center. Núria decided to work in a Third Age Center helping and accompanying elderly people. Her friend Ester went to the Catholic Center for Children, where she worked with children with academic problems. Some of them were children of immigrants, both from other regions of Spain and from Central and Northern Africa.

In their third-year religion class, the teacher introduced Núria and her friends to the different religions of the world and compared them to Christianity. Núria belonged to the majority of the students at the school, who were Catholic but did not go to Mass on Sundays. She had her doubts about faith.

In her free time, Núria often listened to popular music: many English-speaking groups, some Spanish-speaking groups, and a few groups singing Catalan rock. She and her girlfriends loved the movie *Titanic* and they used to sing its theme song, "My Heart Will Go On," all the time. They went to a lot of movies, especially movies from the United States and other countries.

Núria's best friend Maria played on a volleyball team, but Núria had a back problem that prevented her from doing certain sports. Her other good friend Beatriu acted in an amateur theater group, while Ester's hobby was the movies! Other cultural activities, like Catalan folkloric groups or special interest school groups, did not interest Núria and her friends, nor did they choose to take part in their school's Christian Life Communities. Núria and her friends supported Barcelona's soccer team (Barça), and followed its games on TV, even though the coach and most of the players were not even from Spain.

Núria and her classmates went on excursions with their teachers within Spain. One year, they traveled to the north of Spain to visit some cities and a nature park. Another year, they went for three days to the south of Catalonia. For two days, they visited castles and churches that reminded them of their common history, and spent an afternoon at the beach. They spent the whole third day in Port Aventura, a big theme park. The park had five thematic areas: the Mediterranean, Mexico, Polynesia, China, and the Far West. Núria and her friends had a very nice day there. They danced in the Mexican restaurant with the *rancheras*, and laughed when the woman in the American saloon invited one of their teachers to act as a cowboy and kill the bad sheriff.

Núria was always quite slim, thanks in part to the gymnastic exercises she had to do to correct her back problem. But Laura, another friend of hers, was very worried about her weight; sometimes she snuck away during lunch, and her teachers had to watch her carefully to make sure she ate enough. Later, Laura left her old group of friends and started spending time with people who dressed very strangely and sometimes smoked marijuana.

Most of Núria's friends were girls, but she did have a male friend, Vicente. Vicente's parents were farmers in a village thirty kilometers away from the school. They were proud of their son and his grades but they worried about the future of their village. Farming was always a hard business, but the recent agricultural integration of Spain into Europe and competition from Third World countries had made it even more difficult. Opportunities in the village were very limited, and most of its young people went to live in the cities when they married. The local elementary school had fewer students every year.

At the University in Barcelona

At the end of high school Núria decided she wanted to study something related to her interest in ecology, and chose biology. She also wanted to go to one of the universities in Barcelona, which were better than the one in her home town (and farther from the family). Her parents wanted her to study law or economics, which they thought would be a more likely path to a good job, and wanted her to stay close to home. But finally, Núria's parents respected her decision and paid for her to study at a university in Barcelona.

During her first year in Barcelona, Núria had problems adjusting and was homesick a lot. She often went home on weekends. But she gradually got to know other students in Barcelona in the same situation, who became a second family for her. This new family was made up of students from all over Catalonia and, over time, from other parts of Spain. One summer, Núria went to Germany for twenty days to participate in an international camp where young people from different countries worked on an ecological project and participated in artistic activities. That gave her an opportunity to form yet another new family, a global one, with the participants in the camp.

The Present

Now in her third year at the university, Núria is happy she went to a different city to study. She has adapted to living in Barcelona and spends much of her free time there. She has continued studying German and now studies guitar as well. Together with other students in her residence, she has gotten involved in protesting the war in Iraq and in projects in support of Palestine. On weekends, she organizes trips for biology students to environmentally protected areas in Catalonia to study birds' behavior.

Her parents, however – particularly her mother – complain about her spending so much time away from home. They tell her that they need her help with Pere, her brother, who is now eight years old and has behavioral problems at school and at home. Núria's parents have even accused her of being selfish, because she doesn't spend more time at home to help with Pere. But Núria and the rest of her family believe that Pere's problem is that her parents are too busy with their professions and do not spend enough time with him.

Núria feels bad about her brother and his problems but is proud of her growing independence from her family. Yet she complains when her mother is not aware of her activities in Barcelona. She says, "Every time I speak with my mother, I have to remind her what particular activities I am doing at the moment."

She is satisfied with her chosen field of study; she is working as a research assistant for some of her biology professors and has the possibility of collaborating with these professors on publishable research in the future. This makes her very happy: she's able to show her parents that she can earn money and that she has a solid professional future in biology, even if she has not studied economics or law.

Looking at the Future

Núria knows she might have a career as a university professor or researcher in a field like biostatistics and physiology. But she doesn't think she wants to follow this path. She has decided to specialize in biochemistry and biotechnology and would like to work in a biotechnology company, perhaps in a foreign country. She also would like to study abroad to get a postgraduate degree, in case she chooses to pursue a career in academics. She sees how her professors feel more and more compelled to get postgraduate degrees.

Núria's parents are now very proud of her, since her professors have taken an interest in her career. They are also glad she is beginning to think about working for a company. But they would be less happy if she went to a foreign country for three or four years to study or to work. Núria is unlikely to rely on her parents to make this decision. But if she decides to study abroad, they will probably accept (and pay for) her decision.

CULTURAL ANALYSIS

Núria's Traditional Culture

The traits below are representative of the culture of Catalonia, an Autonomous Region of Spain. The culture goes back to the Middle Ages, yet it was oppressed for long periods of time, most recently under Franco's rule (1939-1975). In recent years these traits have been modified or weakened by the large number of immigrants and descendants of immigrants, both from the rest of Spain and from other countries.

1. *Strong ethnic identity* of being Catalonian. This strong identity is based to a large extent on the people's own *language* and particular *history*.

2. *Good business sense.* A trait associated with this one is being *tight with money.*

3. *Sense of practicality.* However, Catalonians also are *idealistic.*

4. *Cosmopolitanism.* This is a way of life. Catalonians look more to other European countries than the rest of Spain.

5. *Close-knit family relationships.* This is evidenced in this narrative by the involvement of parents in their children's profession-al and personal decisions, the financial dependence of uni-versity students on their parents, and parents' desire to have their children stay near home.

Núria's Critical Decisions

1. She decided to go to university in Barcelona and study biology.

What were her options? She could have stayed in her hometown and gone to university there. She could have decided not to go to university at all, although that wasn't very likely, given the high val-ue she and her parents place on education as necessary for success. At the university she could have followed her parents' advice to study law or economics.

What cultural values lay behind her decision? At the end of secondary school, Núria wanted to go to another city, Barcelona, for her uni-versity studies. She wanted to be in a bigger, more diverse, city with better universities than at home. She had clear ideas on what she would study: biology.

What cultural values were reflected in the reactions of the other people in her life to this decision? Her parents didn't like her decision. Her moth-er preferred economics or law for her daughter, because they would be more lucrative. Her father thought that biology was not a career leading to a solid professional status. Her parents also wanted Núria to stay closer to home for school.

2. Once at the university, she decided to spend her free time mostly in Barcelona, studying German and guitar, working with her professors, and taking part in political activities. During vaca-tions she traveled in Europe, both for fun and for learning.

What were her options? She could have gone home every weekend and on vacations to visit her family and help take care of her younger brother.

What cultural values lay behind her decision? Núria liked being with the other people in the student residence where she lived, who came from other towns and even other countries. She felt that they were a support for her new life in Barcelona.

What cultural values were reflected in the reactions of the other people in her life to this decision? Núria's parents complained about her spending so much time away from them. They also wanted her to help with her brother, Pere. They have even accused Núria of being selfish for not coming home more often. Núria's friends are doing the same kinds of things that she is, staying in Barcelona and traveling and not visiting home very much.

Note: Núria's decision to go to another city to study, and her decisions about how to spend her free time, are consistent with *cosmopolitanism* and a move away from the *ethnic Catalonian identity.* Those decisions also reflect her desire to break away from the Catalonian *close-knit family* relations. In contrast, her parents' desire to have her stay close by was consistent with that tradition. Their initial negative response to her choice of biology, instead of law or economics, was in keeping with the Catalonian traits of *practicality* and *good business sense,* traits Núria is ignoring in her decisions; she decides more out of *idealism,* which is also part of the culture. In general, we can assume that her friends are motivated by the same values that motivate Núria.

Changes in Núria's Life

For Núria, the opening of Spain to the global economy has meant a much greater exposure to the cultures of the United States and the rest of Europe and a broadening of her horizons, both when she was growing up and as she looks to the future. The improvement in the Spanish economy gave her family the means to support her studying in another city and to be more independent of her parents: in essence, it allowed her to take advantage of the new opportunities.

Consumption

Núria enjoys a higher standard of living than her parents did when they were young. She has more disposable income because of her family's increasing affluence and she is also able to earn some money at the university. Because of Spain's opening to global trade, she can – and does – spend a good portion of this money on the many imports now available. Since at least her high school years, she has had access to foreign movies, television, and music and she is thrilled about it. She reads less than her parents did. She likes going to the new cultural places that have sprung up, such as clubs, shopping malls, and theme parks (similar to Disney World). She uses the Internet, cell phones, and email to stay in touch with people.

Her food, her clothing, the music and movies she likes: all these things are influenced by other cultures, especially American culture. As an adolescent, she and her friends were obsessed with the movie "Titanic" when it came out. From the university and her travels, she knows people from other cultures. She is less exposed to her own Catalonian tradition than her parents, who grew up in a world much more homogeneous, more focused on traditional Catalonian culture. Núria and her friends also spend a great deal of time with the media and with "virtual" activities such as computer games and the Internet – at the expense of interacting with real people, especially people her parents' age or people closer to the traditional Catalonian culture. She is much more subject to the pressure to consume coming from advertising and the media directed at young people.

Production

For a person of Núria's age and economic class, working means going to school. She has had many options for schooling, more than what her parents had, and she had more leeway in choosing a field of study than they had at her age. Her choices after she graduates have been expanded enormously by Spain's integration with the E.U., which gives her access to a much broader labor market. This provides her with a wide range of career opportunities that might not be available within Spain.

However, Núria knows that in the current Spanish labor market, she will face greater job competition than in the past and she worries about it. A bachelor's degree is no longer enough for many positions because so many people have this degree. She's thinking of studying or working for a while in a foreign country to make herself attractive to future employers. The idea of a job abroad is normal for her; it would not have been for her parents. She is excited at the prospect. She believes that a few years of such an experience would offer an employer a double guarantee: that she speaks a particular foreign language very well and that (if necessary) she handles herself in a foreign culture.

On the other hand, her parents' wishes for her are probably the same as they would have been in a previous generation; they have not changed. They still want her to follow a practical and lucrative career and one that will not take her far from home. But after an initial reluctance about her choice of biology, they are happy with it, because they see that it can offer a viable career in academics or, as Núria is now planning, in business.

Migration

Núria's own experience of migration comes from her going to Barcelona to study and, to a lesser extent, from her short trips abroad. She also grew up in a more multicultural environment than her parents did; Catalonia now has immigrants from many other countries and from other regions in Spain. She went to high school with these immigrant children. In university, too, she has gotten to know people from different cultures. She has developed an attitude of acceptance and tolerance towards other cultures because of her experiences.

For her age, Núria has traveled extensively and has friends all over Europe. She is always interested in learning more about foreign cultures and products. She feels that she is part of the whole world. As young people, her parents did not do such things. She also is considering moving in the future, at least temporarily, to another country within the E.U. for work or further study. She feels quite comfortable with the idea of migrating, at least temporarily, and with living in a multicultural society.

Social Relations

The social world Núria lives in is quite different from her parents' when they were young. She already grew up in a family with nontraditional roles for women. Núria's mother is a professional who has two jobs. Also, because Núria grew up among immigrants and because of her travels, Núria's social world is wider, more global, than her parents' was. The media, with its foreign cultural influences, and the new technology such as the Internet have helped shape her social relations as well, exposing her to the ways other people live and relate with each other. These foreign influences are a big part of her world.

Núria gained independence from her parents earlier and to a greater extent than they did from their parents. This is partly because of the greater affluence associated with the country's opening. This money brings a degree of freedom not possible fifteen or twenty years ago. Once she went off to the university, she did not have to obey her parents the way they did their parents. She can choose not to help with her brother. Because she does not live with her immediate family, peers play a more important role in her life than they did for her parents. And the kinds of things she and her friends do together – movies, concerts, theme parks – are the same things other young people around the world do. The more local and traditional institutions that were so important in her parents' lives, such as family, parish, folkloric dances, theater groups, athletic clubs, are much less influential in Núria's life.

Núria likes the freedom of being away at the university and being in charge of her free time. She is proud that she is becoming more independent and resists her family's efforts to pull her back. The various activities where she meets young people from other places build her identity and her self-esteem. She wants to maximize her opportunities and broaden her horizons, and she sees her ties to her hometown as being in direct conflict with this goal.

Political Power Relations

Núria and her parents grew up in different political worlds. They grew up in Franco's dictatorship, where the Catalan language was officially forbidden. She has always lived in a democracy, in which Catalonia has gained some independence from Madrid and Catalan is the official language for the Region. Núria takes these political freedoms for granted; she has no real awareness of the oppression that existed under Franco or the fight to gain political freedom.

She has a sense of global citizenship and her political interests are global; they go beyond Catalonian and Spanish politics. She is active in things like protesting the U.S. policy in Iraq and working for the environment. Her interests tend to focus on the kinds of issues that cross national boundaries and have fluid memberships; she is not drawn to local or national organized structures like political parties or trade unions. She feels a sense of solidarity with people from different countries and feels compelled by her passion to speak out and be active politically.

Núria, unlike her parents, has the freedom to be an activist, to protest. Living in the dictatorship, they did not have that option when they were young. Núria also has a much greater opportunity to express her Catalonian identity than her parents did. But even though she attends a school taught in Catalan – which was not allowed under Franco – she is divided on asserting that identity. If a foreigner asked Núria about her national identity, she would say: "I am Catalan, not Spanish. I want a State for my Nation: I want an Independent Catalonia." She is a supporter of Futbol Club Barcelona (a symbol of the Catalan Nation under Franco's dictatorship); and she was proud to be Catalan in 1992 with the success of the Barcelona Olympic Games. But if she were in Asia or America, she would probably say also that she is a European.

In reality, the Spanish social and political environment is shaping Núria's identity also. But this Spanish "level of identity" is weakening in favor, simultaneously, of a global identity (European) and a "local" one (Catalan).

Religious Experience and Expression

The influence of religion, specifically Catholicism, has waned in Catalonia. Today religion has much less influence there than in the rest of Spain. Although Núria's roots are in the Catholic Church, they are not as deep as her parents'. As young as high school age – and even though it was a Jesuit school – she was not attending Mass regularly. Now she does not follow any formal religious practices or find meaning in her religious tradition. Instead, her spirituality is based on her experience of global solidarity and interest in ecological justice. She feels energized by the meaning she finds in connecting with other people and working for a better world.

NÚRIA'S MEANINGS AND VALUES
AS REFLECTED IN HER CHOICES

To enter into what was going on within Núria, as an intelligent person, we focus on two major actions that we observe in the narrative. These actions took place over time and as part of Núria's development from being an adolescent to becoming a young adult.

1. Núria chooses to go to university in Barcelona instead of Lleida.

2. Núria, after a year or so in Barcelona, spends most of her free time there and does not go back to Lleida often.

The first action takes place when Núria is still an adolescent; in the second action, she is more of a young adult. Because of the difference in Núria's level of responsibility in the two actions, the value-ethics methodology is applied more fully to the second action. (For details on the methodology used to analyze the interior process behind Núria's actions, see Chapter 4, p. 78ff., "Research Methodology – Phase II: Finding the Protagonists' Meanings and Values". The questions template appears on p. 87.)

Action 1. Núria chooses to go to university in Barcelona instead of Lleida.

A. What can we infer goes on within Núria as she experiences the new economy and moves on to decide to take this action? What questions may Núria have been raising and what answers seem consistent with reaching that decision? (Note: This refers to the stages of consciousness, from experiencing to deciding; see Chapter 4, p. 88ff.)

First, during secondary school, Núria *experienced* the global economy through exciting friendships with young people of her age in an English-language course in England. She went on writing letters to her international friends for some months. But during her childhood she had also experienced a positive family life and the fellowship of local friends. When she faced the decision of her university studies, she compared her *understanding* of her life as a university student in Lleida with her life as a university student in Barcelona. In Lleida, she would live in her parents' home, and her schoolmates would be students from the limited region of Lleida. The academic quality would be lower. In Barcelona, she would live far from her family and local friends in a residence with other students from other Catalan or Spanish regions. The academic quality would be higher than in Lleida. Besides, in Barcelona she could choose from among a wider range of careers, and she wanted to study biology (an option that was not available in Lleida). Opportunities for future employment would be greater in Barcelona, and there she could even try to find a temporary job in a foreign country. As she reflected on this understanding, she *judged the facts* of both alternatives: staying in Lleida would keep her nearer her parents, brother, and childhood friends; but on the other hand she felt free and excited to start new relationships and a more global future in Barcelona. Even though she loved her family, she *morally judged and decided* that exploring the broader possibilities of her life and career was a better option than staying in Lleida.

B. What values appear to drive Núria's decision? What are the good things that she seeks? (Note: This refers to the scale of values; see Chapter 4, p. 95ff.)

The values that drove Núria's decision were in conflict. On one side were family love and attachment to her city and friends; on the other side were the attraction of a broader (Catalan, Spanish or European) range of friendships, the possibilities of a better education, and a richer professional life. Emulation and social status might have been also significant values in the decision to leave Lleida: the wealthiest students in her secondary school were going to Barcelona for university studies; the less wealthy usually stayed at home.

C. How does Núria's new knowledge and decision change the horizon of meanings in her world?

As Núria thought of the possibility of studying in Barcelona, she realized that her life could be fuller if she went to Barcelona: new relationships, better possibilities to learn, new possibilities to travel or to work. Her future (profession, job, family) would be chosen from among a wider variety of options if she went to Barcelona.

D. Given Núria's new horizon of meanings, what can we infer goes on within her as she moves to implement her decision? What questions may she have been trying to answer as she puts her decision into action? What values of Núria are engaged in this implementation? (Note: This refers to the stages of consciousness, from deciding to acting; see Chapter 4, p. 90ff.)

As Núria moved to implement her decision, her fear of feeling homesick, or her remorse over leaving her brother, were balanced by the value of freedom. She was aware that she would feel homesick at the beginning, and that her parents and brother would miss her, and would press her to be with them as long as possible. But the intuition of a fuller life –a life with more options – was stronger. And, in any case, she would be able to meet in Barcelona many of her current Lleida friends, who also were going there for the university.

E. Do we detect changes in the relative weights Núria now places on different values within a given level of values and among different levels of values? Does Núria seem comfortable with her decision and action? (Note: This refers to tensions within and among the levels of values; see Chapter 4, p. 102ff.)

The decision to go to Barcelona was driven by Núria placing a heavier weight on *social and cultural values*, not on her trying to better satisfy her basic needs (*vital values*). In fact, if she decided to study business administration in Lleida and work afterwards in her mother's business, she probably would attain a higher income and quality of material life than if she became a biologist in Barcelona. But her intuition was that staying in Lleida would mean settling for attaining a lower level of social and cultural values.

Action 2. Núria, after a year or so in Barcelona, spends most of her free time there and does not go back to Lleida often.

A. What can we infer goes on within Núria as she experiences the new economy and moves on to decide to take this action? What questions may Núria have been raising and what answers seem consistent with reaching that decision? (Note: This refers to the stages of consciousness, from experiencing to deciding; see Chapter 4, p. 88ff.)

Once in Barcelona, Núria felt really homesick during her first year there. Initially, this was her basic *experience* of free time. That's why she used to travel every weekend back home, to visit her family and friends. But slowly she started to make new friends at the residence and at the faculty of biology. She *experienced* positive feelings towards the new environment: spending weekends in Barcelona with the freedom to choose among a wider range of options and with less social control than in Lleida was satisfying for her. She could even meet some of her friends from secondary school who were also studying in Barcelona: they would help her overcome homesickness and reinforce her feeling that she was living a free life – free because it was far from home. Going back to Lleida relatively often was necessary to address her homesickness; but in these visits she would prove that she was more global, more cosmopolitan, than the students who had stayed in Lleida. But in Lleida, she also *experienced* complaints from her parents about her absences and her lack of support in the education of Pere, her brother with behavioral problems.

Núria's experiences broadened her *understanding* of the differences between life in Barcelona and life in Lleida. She realized that Lleida is "a big village" and Barcelona an anonymous capital. She could now understand herself as a more autonomous person (not so dependent on her family and home city), one who had possibilities of living in a larger context than what her childhood offered. She certainly came to understand her position in her family in a new way. She began asking herself if her parents were being fair with her, loading her with the responsibility of taking care of her brother. This was an ongoing question: Núria had not solved it; and it was triggering reflection and new understandings of how to use her free time. She also came to understand the difference in leisure options between Barcelona and Lleida: more options for shopping, for cinema movies, for new relationships... in Barcelona. Reflecting on this new understanding, Núria *judged the facts* of these two options of using free time and arrived at what she believed was true. So she reached a *moral judgment and decided* that it was good to spend some weekends away from family and its social controls, without responsibilities for her brother; and instead she would take advantage of the appealing and increased number of leisure options available in Barcelona, the anonymous capital. However, for any given weekend, she negotiated her weekly leisure agenda. The actual selection depended on the family's requirements, on the specific options of free time in Barcelona ("This weekend, I'll stay in Barcelona to study a little more and to go to the theater with some friends"), on Núria's mood, on her financial situation ("I've run out of money"), on her remorse ("My family needs me"), etc. In developing her *moral judgment*, Núria was addressing different tensions: between a legitimate meaning of freedom (explore wider possibilities or human relationships) and a selfish meaning (away from responsibilities, homesickness); and between the true love of her family and the sentimental blackmail of her parents. Probably Christianity (understood as "the Christian values/ethos learned during secondary school") was playing a role in her fight against selfishness and in favor of responsibility. Christianity was also playing a role in her efforts to fully develop her personality, although in tension with the traditional interpretation of the commandment "You shall love father and mother"... and brother!

B. What values appear to drive Núria's decision? What are the good things that she seeks? (Note: This refers to the scale of values; see Chapter 4, p. 95ff.)

1. *Vital values.* These values did not drive Núria's decision to spend her free time in Barcelona. Her parents always provided for her basic needs generously, but they could be tempted to use the financial restriction to "invite" her home more often.

2. *Social values.* On the one hand, these values were relevant to Núria when she decided to study biology and not business administration. In the last years of her academic career, though, her new interest in working for companies – as opposed to in academics – could be understood as a partial surrender to selfish values. This surrender was paradoxically good news for her parents, who were more "pragmatic" than she. On the other hand, her interest in biology was better served by her activities during her free time in Barcelona than in Lleida. When she participated in an environmental campsite in Germany, she was pursuing social values and affecting her professional future.

3. *Cultural values.* What is "home" for Núria? Where does she feel she really belongs? Consciously or not, by spending more time in Barcelona, Núria is trying to become "more cosmopolitan." Barcelona is a better starting point than Lleida from which to take off towards cosmopolitanism. And Barcelona is still Catalonia for her, which is an advantage because she is a Catalan Separatist who loves her homeland. Núria certainly experiences a tension between a local identity and a global identity – not as alternatives, but as ongoing coexisting tensions within her life.

4. *Moral values. Solidarity.* Núria clearly cares for the environment and for social causes such as opposing the war in Iraq. This solidarity comes partially from her identifying with her group of friends in Barcelona, taking part in the culture of Barcelona students, and partially from her feeling true solidarity with the other, with her neighbor. This feeling of solidarity was rooted in two things: her Catholic education (she had experienced the value of solidarity with specific suffering people in secondary school with the compulsory course in Social Experience) and her environmental values.

5. *Freedom.* Núria's wish to stay in Barcelona – or to travel – in her free time was motivated by the value of freedom, in a *positive* and a *negative* way. Positively, there are more opportunities to develop her personality. Negatively, she wanted to prove to herself that she was capable of living away

from her family, that she could overcome homesickness; and she wanted to have fun away from the social control in Lleida.

C. How does Núria's new knowledge and decision change the horizon of meanings in her world?

Many of her intuitions when she decided to go to Barcelona were being confirmed. First, the career of biology was attractive to her, and it offered an opportunity to travel all over Catalonia in order to discover its birds. Her academic performance also attracted the interest of some professors, who suggested to her collaborating in their department. Second, Barcelona and biology were starting points for international trips. In summary, her group of family/friends and her childhood landscapes were broadened, and this changed her horizon of understanding of life. This was particularly so with her horizon of decision about her own life. She progressively knew that she would be able to work as a biologist (rather than in the family business) and maybe could be able to find a partner and start a family far from Lleida.

D. Given Núria's new horizon of meanings, what can we infer goes on within her as she moves to implement her decision? What questions may she have been trying to answer as she puts her decision into action? What values of Núria are engaged in this implementation? (Note: This refers to the stages of consciousness, from deciding to acting; see Chapter 4, p. 90ff.)

1. Moral judgment. In implementing her decision to spend more time in Barcelona or in travel, Núria became more aware of the costs and benefits of this decision. She experienced it in terms of feelings: on the one hand, emotional distance from her parents and homesickness; but on the other hand, the joy of acting on her own ideals. She became more aware of the actual cost of freedom and the cost of solidarity/ environmental concern. Maybe she even experienced a feeling of remorse in pursuing her own interests in Barcelona and not spending more time with her brother and parents. After balancing these feelings, she decided it is worthwhile to put her decision into action. Although still experiencing conflicting feelings she finds this decision is consistent with her *moral values*. She takes responsibility for her decision.

2. Judgment of facts. Núria's initial homesickness receded after she chose to spend more of her free time in Barcelona. Besides, Internet resources and cell phones probably helped her overcome it. Her blending identity in terms of the tension local-global was displaced towards the global pole after her "integration" in Barcelona, after widening her group of relations towards new friends – some of them foreigners. Probably her attitude toward the traditional value of family bonds was altered. She adapts her traditional *cultural values* that she learned in Lleida to incorporate a more global sense of belonging.

3. Understanding. The changes in Núria's lifestyle caused by her decision to spend more free time in Barcelona were not causing major problems when she came back to Lleida. Her new friends and new activities were accepted by "local" friends and family as part of Núria's new cosmopolitan identity: mainly with admiration, but with a certain fear, because if Núria were to become "too global," she could finally go and actually live abroad. Núria adapts the social values of a student from Lleida to the social values of a student at the university in Barcelona.

4. Experience. Living in the two societies helped Núria experience the more local life in Lleida as limited, but warm; and the more global life in Barcelona as open and less limited but colder.

E. Do we detect changes in the relative weights Núria now places on different values within a given level of values and among different levels of values? Does Núria seem comfortable with her decision and action? (Note: This refers to tensions within and among the levels of values; see Chapter 4, p. 102ff.)

1. *Vital values.* Núria's patterns of consumption changed little with her decision to spend more time in Barcelona. Wider possibilities in shopping (especially in clothing) and in cinema, theater, and concerts were the only difference.

2. *Social values.* In her spending more time in ecological and sociopolitical issues, Núria discovered an alternative way of organizing society. Social movements and NGOs trying to change society and to influence the behavior of companies were more present in Barcelona than in Lleida. Núria also began to see with new eyes her parents' professional activity.

3. *Cultural values.* In Barcelona and in her trips abroad, Núria is widening her world vision. She realizes that societies organize life in different ways and individuals have different cultures, languages, and religions. The planet is bigger than Catalonia and suffers social and environmental problems. This variety bewilders Núria... especially when she asks herself practical questions about her future: where will I live? Where will I work?

4. *Moral values.* Núria is certainly more aware of the global challenges this world is facing. This comprehension sets the foundation for becom-

ing a more responsible adult, and in a way that would have been different (not better: just different, more local, more traditional) if she had stayed in Lleida.

5. *Ultimate values.* Núria's family does not have a religious practice and in Barcelona religion is very much absent from the public space or the public debate. Many Christian youngsters do not say they are Christian, especially at the university. So Núria did not act upon an explicit formulation of ultimate values involved in her decisions. She addresses the tensions between global/local, solidarity/freedom, tradition/modernity, family/independence, according to her temporal feelings and the values inherited (remembered) from childhood. However, her acknowledgement of religious diversity, together with a consciousness of her limitations, has evoked in her an interest in spirituality: not for a specific religion ("Religions are relative to the cultural environment"); but for the care of one's own spirit, for the search of an inner balance.

6. *Changes in relative weights among levels of values.* The immersion in a global culture (Barcelona and overseas) has increased Núria's perplexity about her own values. She is now more aware of tensions between the different levels (vital vs. social, cultural vs. ultimate). This perplexity increases as she asks herself practical questions, which are the ones that finally reveal her true "values." "This world is more complex than I thought; and the decisions I must take – now that I am finishing university – include multiple choices. What are my real options? How will I decide between them?" Núria has more questions than answers.

RESEARCHERS' REFLECTIONS

Spain's Economic Globalization and Núria

By all accounts, Spain's integration into Europe and the economic liberalization that opened it to global market forces have served it well. Most Spaniards are very satisfied their country is more integrated with the rest of Europe. Politically, after the isolation of Franco's regime, they pined for this closer relationship. Economically, the liberalization and integration brought a higher standard of living for most people. Núria's family has shared in this economic wellbeing.

A Spain that was a member of the European Union, and more open to market forces, meant that Núria grew up in a world where local and national boundaries were weakening. Catalonia's prosperity increasingly attracted migrants, and Núria grew up with their children in her city and school. The opening of the border exposed her to an influx of foreign media, movies, and consumer items. She has traveled to other countries and made friends from other cultures. All this has made her much more globally oriented than her parents. As a result, her perspective is much broader than theirs was. It goes beyond Catalonian and Spanish concerns and includes the environment, the war in Iraq, and other international issues.

Getting to Know Núria

As a young person, Núria is moving from her childhood life (with local experiences, a limited understanding of her possibilities, and a limited capability to interact with the world) to an adult's life (with broader experiences and a broader understanding of her possibilities of interacting with the global world), in a context of regional migration for academic reasons. This change throws her childhood values into crisis, and allows the flourishing of other values.

In terms of *vital values*, her future profession is a serious concern for her but she seems to have overcome the dilemma of "Stay in Lleida, study law or economics, and work in the family business" vs. "Go to Barcelona, study biology, and where are you going to work?" In her decisions about her free time in Barcelona or abroad, *vital values* (funding) do not seem to be a problem, since her parents apparently pay and she has a certain financial independence with her part-time work at the university. In *social and cultural values*, the question of freedom (negative freedom as independence from parents and from social control; and positive freedom as a broader range of opportunities to explore her ideals and dreams) is central for Núria.

Combating the feeling of homesickness has certainly been helped by new technologies (Internet and cell phones). They have also helped Núria keep in touch with her friends from secondary school. The wider opportunities have helped Núria consider a new professional horizon and she seems to have opted for this broader horizon. At the end of the narrative, one is not sure if this new horizon will lead her to engage in global causes (environment and development problems), or if she will use her global connections just to become a global manager/consumer without social concerns. Let's hope that the values of solidarity that Núria practiced in her Social Experience course in the secondary school and the *ultimate values* that the Jesuit school conveyed will emerge sooner or later in her life in terms of engagement for development and solidarity.

Implications of Our New Understanding of Núria for Ministry

The implications of Núria's case for the education in values at the university level are the following:

1. In the first years of studies, the student who has moved to a different city very probably faces a crisis of homesickness, combined with pressure to succeed academically. This crisis creates psychological tensions that pull the student on the one hand toward spending his or her free time going back home; and on the other hand, toward activities in the city. These city activities include staying out late at night, drinking, smoking, etc., but also sometimes taking advantage of the broader positive possibilities for leisure available in a big city. In this initial stage, a professor or advisor can only help the student to survive (pass courses, not fall into depression or addictions), by helping her manage these tensions.

2. After the first or the second year at the university, the student often overcomes homesickness and is probably more autonomous. The student is more aware of the opportunities in the city, and is also more ready psychologically to take advantage of these opportunities. This is the time to remind the student that she has a family, and that the family might need her to come to visit more often. This is also the time to offer opportunities to practice values like solidarity (working for NGOs, attending protests in favor of big causes, etc); and to try to connect these values with the student's future professional responsibilities: fostering solidarity not only in weekends, or as a private citizen, but also solidarity as a professional.

3. The process of adjusting to life in the university in a big city has implications for the student in terms of changes in perceptions, in understandings, and in values. These changes can take students toward an integrated, responsible, and free personality, or toward a disintegrated selfish and addictive personality. Therefore, professors should offer – always respecting the individual's freedom – courses, activities, and informal exchanges that give the student spiritual and intellectual tools to get in touch

with his or her own decision-making process, when the student, in the normal course of things, is faced with such decisions. Apart from these spiritual and intellectual tools, the authenticity of the professor is important: if he/she is perceived as "someone who wants to direct my life according to a doctrine," the student will not consult him.

4. This internal development of progressive decision-making – progressive construction of an integrated, responsible, and free personality – is nowadays more complex because of globalization. The professor should accompany the student in understanding her cultural context so she follows traditions because she finds value in them rather than because they are imposed. There are many different traditions available to a youngster and certain elements of each tradition can help her in the development process Professors or other adults can be an inspiration for a student as she tries to find her particular "place in the world" – her particular vocation. This vocation has, necessarily, a global dimension: the student will become – today more than yesterday – a global professional, a global citizen. Therefore, during the university years it is good to offer possibilities for studying abroad (Erasmus Project) and for practicing solidarity abroad (leisure trips or international professional internships). These "experiments" should always be evaluated by the student: how have her values and personality been affected (in positive or in negative terms)? Have they made her a more conscious, more competent, and more compassionate professional or citizen?

Narrator's Personal Reflection

The former reflections arise from the narrator's inquiry into and reflection on Núria's process of integration in Barcelona during her time at the university. They have been contrasted with the narrator's experiences accompanying other students who came from villages or small cities to study in Barcelona: particularly to ESADE Business School, where the narrator is a professor. Some of these students actually came from the same secondary school where Núria studied, in Lleida.

Núria's case has contributed a great deal to the author's understanding of the tension that a student feels between spending leisure time in Barcelona/abroad and spending leisure time back home, with a contribution to the family's welfare. The case has also helped clarify how to build an "integrated" or "non-addictive" personality in a particular context. This is a context where the family is far away, where globalization is changing the cultural references, and where the Church – or in general a Christian community – is not a "reference group": this is the case of Núria, and of many university students today in Barcelona.

As a professor and as a Jesuit in a university, the narrator has discovered the importance of offering university students different opportunities for sharpening their moral values in the context of love for others and for increasing the students' awareness that these values contribute to an integrated personality. Among these occasions are academic courses that incorporate explicit discussions of human moral values, possibilities to go abroad for internships or for further studies, opportunities to volunteer in NGOs, etc. All these activities need a "debriefing," which is an occasion to connect with adults and reflect together on the contribution of that specific action to the students' personal development... in the horizon of a global professional, a global citizen.

Epilogue

In June 2009 the narrator traveled to Lleida and met Maria, a close friend of Núria. They had studied together at the Jesuit Secondary School in Lleida, and also biology at the University of Barcelona. In 2009 they were both working – but, surprise, Núria was working as a researcher at the faculty of medicine in Lleida! She was sharing an apartment with Mariona, a friend from the secondary Jesuit School who is a doctor and works in a local hospital. Maria commented ironically: "In our group, Núria seemed to be the most detached from family and home city, but she was finally the first one to come back to Lleida."

Are these contradictions typical of young people? Certainly.

However, Núria's recent history can be also interpreted in terms of a tension between local culture and global culture, lived during two moments of her youth. In a first moment, Núria tried to fly away from home: fighting homesickness, trying to enjoy freedom from the family and friendship of new friends (including foreigners). She was trying to fly as high as possible. Like Icarus, she was attracted by the sun of a *global* world, far away from the mortal, and limited, *local* earth.

But we have roots and deep feelings attached to childhood landscapes, friends, and relatives. And these roots make flight tiring.

So Núria changed her mind and decided to come back to Lleida, like the prodigal son. Maybe with less remorse: without saying, "Father, I have sinned against Heaven and against you" (Luke 16, 21). And not back to her parents' home, but near it. Now she meets old friends more often. And she works as a biologist at the university, an excellent and responsible job in professional terms.

Has Núria abandoned the global dream, the joy of flying? We do not know. The parable of the prodigal son stops at a certain point: its end is open. Will the older son enter the feast? *Will the younger son leave again?* Maybe *home* is not only a geographical concept. Probably Núria felt at home in Barcelona or travelling abroad during her time as a university student, during her involvement with environmental and social causes. Probably during this long journey, first out of Lleida and then back to Lleida, her understanding of *home* has broadened. And her comprehension of what a professional (a biologist) must do has gained in solidarity.

After all, maybe in 2009 she is only back to her older home for some time. If we want to verify this hypothesis, we will need to ask news from Núria in future years...

Chapter 9

Jorge Enrique in Mexico: Will He Leave His Home? *

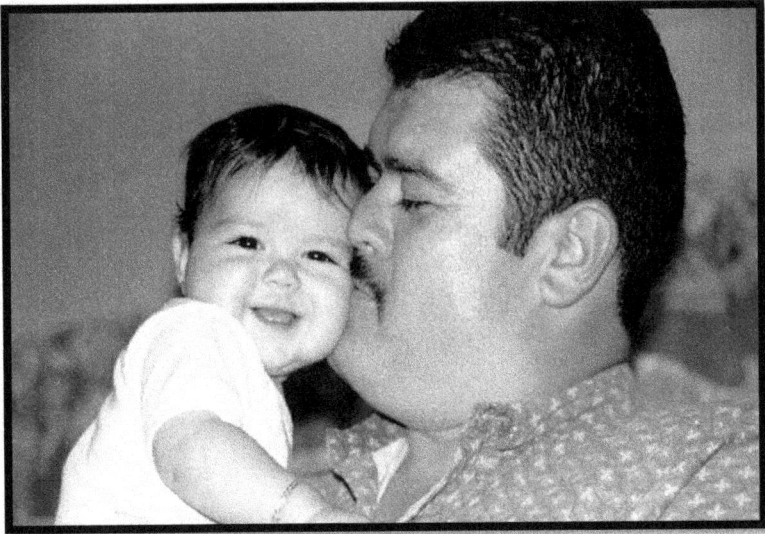

Jorge Enrique with one of his children

NARRATOR: DAVID VELASCO YÁÑEZ, SJ

Professor and Researcher
Instituto Tecnológico y de Estudios Superiores de Occidente (ITESO)
Universidad Jesuita de Guadalajara
Jalisco, México

* A Spanish translation of this chapter is available online at:
woodstock.georgetown.edu/gec

Narrative Summary and Economic Background

Jorge Enrique's life changed dramatically when the tire factory where he worked, Euzkadi, shut down. Located in El Salto, Mexico, the factory was owned by a multinational company and in the past had had a strong labor union. It was a very good job for Jorge Enrique, with better wages and benefits than many other places in Mexico. But in 2001, the owners said that Mexico's new lower import duties allowed cheaper foreign tires to enter the country and they couldn't compete without concessions from labor. Now in his thirties, Jorge Enrique is involved with his union's efforts to force the factory's reopening. He wonders if he should go back to work in the United States, which he did when he was younger. It would be easy for him, because he has a "green card" — a legal entry visa.

The old Mexican economic system crashed in 1982 under the weight of mounting international debt and fiscal deficits. It was a closed economy; domestic production was protected by high import tariffs and major industries were often in government hands. The immediate response to the crisis included severe economic austerity measures backed by loans from the IMF. This was followed by economic restructuring, particularly after 1988, marked by privatizations and liberalization of international trade and investment. Over the next decade, these measures were supported by Mexico's implementing the Uruguay Round of trade negotiations and, in 1996, signing the North American Free Trade Area Agreement (NAFTA) with the U.S. and Canada.

Mexico's economic restructuring affected El Salto. Foreign companies made new investments — Continental Tire of Germany bought Euzkadi — and old plants, like the textile factory where Jorge Enrique's father worked, had to close. In the country as a whole, the already ongoing migration to the U.S. accelerated as agriculture's contribution to the economy fell by nearly two-thirds, down to 4 percent of GDP by 2000.

NARRATIVE

When Jorge Enrique Was Young

Jorge Enrique was born thirty years ago, in San Antonio Juanacaxtle, a little village in the state of Jalisco. He has no siblings, because his mother was sterilized, without her knowledge or consent, shortly after he was born. San Antonio has been there since the end of the nineteenth century. It was named after a large waterfall that used to flow nearby a long time ago, when the river Lerma was huge. The village is close to the large industrial corridor named El Salto. Jorge Enrique and the corridor grew up together. When he was a child, there was already a textile factory near the river where he and his friends used to play. His father worked there for some years. Before that, around the time Jorge Enrique was born, his father had been a *campesino* and then later a bricklayer. When the big factories began to come to El Salto, a lot of people started to work in construction.

One of the first new factories was the tire factory, Euzkadi. Many of Jorge Enrique's uncles and grown-up cousins started working there; he started dreaming about working there, too. Unlike the labor unions connected with the government's party — the Partido Revolucionario Institucional (PRI) — Euzkadi's labor union was independent. It was very good at getting workers' jobs back after they were fired and getting good salaries and benefits for them. It even achieved collective bargaining.

Jorge Enrique was still in school when an economic crisis hit his family. The textile factory where his father was working got into economic difficulties and the government bought it, later transferring it to one of the government labor organizations. The bosses changed and soon the workers went on strike. His father had to look for another way to make a living and support the family. They had saved some money, so they enlarged their house and opened a restaurant. They sold *pozole*, *tostadas*, and hamburgers. It still opens on Sundays when people go to Mass and on Tuesdays, when lots of people come to visit San Antonio.

Going North

Many people in Jorge Enrique's mother's family had gone to the United States to live and work, sometimes for short stays, sometimes for many years. He remembered his uncles and his cousins leaving and coming back with good money. That made it possible for them to afford more things in San Antonio. Jorge Enrique saw this not only in his family but with other people, too. The travelers brought things back from the States, and a lot of people in the village started dressing differently, even talking differently. Cable TV arrived, as well as many new things for the house that people had not seen before. Sometimes Jorge Enrique's relatives would not come back for a long time, but they kept sending money. And when they did return, there would be a huge party. More and more farmers in the area were starting to work in the factories in El Salto or leaving to go to the States.

When Jorge Enrique finished high school, he thought about going north, too. He knew he didn't want to continue his studies and he was not interested in the jobs in El Salto. He had been working in the textile factory in the afternoons and already knew of the dismissals caused by economic difficulties. Jobs in El Salto generally didn't pay well enough, he thought; so at nineteen years old, he went to the U.S. He got all the papers to do it legally; his relatives helped him, since they already had contacts in the U.S. He never thought of going there illegally, nor had anybody in his family. When he went in 1994, Jorge Enrique lived with members of his family in Chicago and worked with them doing landscaping. Although their customs were not the same any more as those in San Antonio, they were similar. He went north with the little English he had learned in school, but once there he learned much more and that helped him meet other people. He continued going to Mass on Sundays. He was young and restless, though, and the first year spent his time enjoying himself.

For several years he would go back and forth. He stayed with his family in San Antonio for four months in the winter, when snow puts a stop to the landscaping work and workers in that field can collect unemployment benefits in the U.S. (a friend arranged it so he could be paid without the periodic interviews in the unemployment office). It was then that Jorge Enrique started thinking more seriously about working at the tire factory. It was very hard to get a job there, however. The union required that one first buy a *pase* and the *pases* were very expensive. When he first considered it, he didn't have the money to buy one. He figured that if he began saving money more carefully while working in the U.S., he soon would have the money.

So he went back north once more, this time to Inglewood near Los Angeles to work with his uncle. He was determined to save the money he needed for the *pase*. After a year, he did. He could have stayed in the States longer, but he missed his parents and family. He also did not like the jobs he found available to him in the U.S. So he returned to San Antonio at the end of 2000.

Union Membership

When Jorge Enrique returned, he had saved enough money to buy the union *pase* to work at Euzkadi, the tire factory, which in the meantime had been taken over by a German company, Continental Tire. He paid the *pase* cost of sixty thousand pesos (about six thousand dollars) and he got a job there, starting in the cleaning area. Little by little he got better jobs, working eventually in the production area. When he first started working, his involvement with the labor union was limited to attending the general assembly to find out what was going on. He liked the job progression he could look forward to and, even more, the fact that he was assigned a specific task to do – not like in his jobs in the U.S., where the boss constantly was changing what he had to do. He felt that that was being a *mi-lusos* (literally, a thousand uses) and found it degrading.

Soon Jorge Enrique got married, to a woman named Isabel from Rancho Nuevo, which is close to San Antonio. Since he was a *tire man* he was attractive to the girls, it being well known that their salaries and benefits were the best in town. They had a little boy, who was the joy of the whole family. They expanded Jorge Enrique's parents' house and they lived there, with enough independence to suit them.

The tire company was working at full capacity and there was a lot of opportunity to work overtime, as much as the equivalent of four extra days a week. Jorge Enrique was interested in saving money and worked as much overtime as he could. Everything seemed to be going smoothly...

Trouble at Euzkadi

One day, in the fall of 2001, Jorge Enrique read in the newspaper: "250 Workers from Euzkadi will be Losing Their Jobs." Then he learned from a priest friend of the family that over the last year, 22,500 jobs had been lost in El Salto. He was upset and worried; he knew the situation could become difficult. He figured that the employees who would be fired would be the ones most recently hired. He thought, "They couldn't fire those of us who've been there for a long time; that wouldn't be fair."

He also had heard that the Goodyear tire factory in Tultitlan, Estado de México, had closed. That worried him, because the struggle there was not any longer about keeping the factory open; now the most they could ask for was a fair compensation. He hoped the same would not happen at Euzkadi, where the labor union was trying to negotiate a freeze on firing in exchange for workers increasing production and reducing absenteeism. The latter was a big source of complaint from management, who said that workers didn't mind skipping one or two days of work a week, because their wages were so high that the lost income didn't affect them much.

Jorge Enrique waited to see what things the union had been able to negotiate. He didn't want to be included in the dismissal list and he was anxious. He now was married and had a child. He was confident he would be staying in the factory, but nothing was certain. He remembered well when his father had lost his job under similar circumstances. He started thinking about going to the U.S. again, to save money and send it to his family. But with a wife and son, it was even more difficult than before to think about being far away from the family.

The Closing and Afterwards

The management of Euzkadi alleged that new competition from imported Korean tires, resulting from Mexico's lowered import tariffs, made it impossible for them to compete any longer under the company's current labor costs. An agreement could not be reached. The factory did not dismiss any employees; instead, it closed on December 16, 2001. Jorge Enrique believes it closed illegally. By this time, he had decided to stay in Mexico for the time being, so he became fully involved with the union. His job with the union was to keep watch outside the plant, to make sure Continental − the factory's current owners − did not remove the machinery from the plant. He also spent a lot of time with other union members in assemblies and meetings.

The workers' protest − which they called a *huelga*, a strike − erupted on January 22, 2002. There were demonstrations and attempts to meet with political leaders. At one point, the union leadership went to Europe, to go directly to Continental's headquarters in Germany. Many international human rights organizations also began to pay attention. In June,

Continental tried to formally shut down the plant in El Salto, but the union guards held firm. At the end of August, the union decided to end the protest, although they would continue to keep management out of the factory while they pursued the legal process. After almost a year of striking, on December 16, 2002, 250 workers formerly in the union opted for the liquidation the company was offering, which Jorge Enrique thought was a pittance. One hundred fifty of them have already gone to the United States.

Continental tried several ways and on several occasions to oust the union guards and remove the equipment, but could not. The workers who were guarding the factory were under a lot of pressure to accept the liquidation but they never gave up. Then, in 2004, two years after the strike began, the Junta de Conciliacion y Arbitraje (a labor arbitration board) declared the strike to be "existent" — legal. It was a huge victory for the workers who were determined to hold out for a fair resolution to the conflict.

The Present: Fall 2004

The plant is still closed but Jorge Enrique keeps busy. He continues volunteering with the union as it tries to force the company to either reopen (his first choice) or to offer a better settlement. He has been involved in supervising local elections. He works with his wife selling leather goods in the store she runs and helps her take care of the children while she works there. The store does not make much money, but it earns enough for them to eat. He also works in the restaurant with his parents.

He is starting to think about going to the States again, because he needs to earn more money. What stops him is his family, and not because they say anything about his current situation. He doesn't want to leave them. Being with them, watching his children (they have two now) grow up is the most important thing for him. He actually thanks God for the additional time he can spend with the children and the rest of the family now that the plant is closed. His religion gives him much support, especially the sacraments. The church is close by and he and his family go regularly to Mass and receive communion. In 2004 he had his second child baptized. His faith helps him to put his trust in God.

Jorge Enrique and his family, at the baptism of one of his children

He thinks about the future a lot, trying to figure out what management might do, what the union and the politicians might do. He realizes that it is very unlikely the plant will just reopen. Some workers think that the best outcome would be to reopen the factory as a cooperative and put its management in the workers' hands, but that too is unlikely. He feels lucky in not having pressure from his wife to accept the liquidation compensation, which he thinks unfairly low. Many workers who took the liquidation have already spent it, and have had to look for other jobs. There are many more *taquerias* and taxi drivers around as a result. That would be his future if he accepted the money and stayed. Of course, if there is an emergency, he might have to accept the liquidation money.

Jorge Enrique also has his eye on some property that the company owns, and he knows that the proceeds from its sale would be distributed only among the remaining union members, the ones who have not accepted the earlier settlement. He knows there is a risk in holding out like this; if the union is unsuccessful then he will be forced to take whatever the company offers, and it may well be very little. Not everyone in the village approves of the union's efforts to force the plant to reopen, and these people are critical of this decision. But he has thrown in his lot with the union and he has support from the other people who have joined in this struggle. So he thinks and he works and waits for the future to happen.

CULTURAL ANALYSIS

Jorge Enrique's Traditional Culture

Jorge Enrique's roots lie in the traditional rural culture of Mexico, the culture in which his parents grew up. However, this culture has been affected by the industrialization and modernization that have occurred in nearby El Salto over the last thirty or so years. Many of the traits below are not as strong now as they used to be. Moreover, all of them may not be dominant elements in Jorge Enrique's life; however they are all there in the background and play a role in his world.

1. *Strong Family Bonds.* Family is so important that preference given to family members in business and politics is not considered corruption. The relationship between parents and godparents − *compadrazgo* − is especially important.

2. *Sense of Community.* There is a tradition of community organization and working together on projects, particularly church-related ones.

3. *Religion.* The Catholic faith occupies a central place in people's lives, with Sunday Mass an important observance.

4. *Machismo.* Men are dominant in the culture, with the result that women have a distinctly inferior status.

5. *Fatalism.* A common expression is *Si Dios quiere* − if God wants.

6. *Focus on a Leader.* Communities often function around a leader, who is called *el responsable.*

Jorge Enrique's Critical Decisions

1. He decided to migrate to the United States to work, after he had finished secondary school.

What were his options? He says he had no other option. His father wanted him to keep studying and prepare for a career. But Jorge Enrique did not like this idea. He had already worked for a while in a textile factory until they had downsized and didn't care much for that, either.

What cultural values lay behind his decision? He says he was young and he wanted to do something different. He wanted excitement and he wanted to travel. He also wanted to make money. He knew from his relatives who lived there that he could do this and knowing that they were there influenced him as well.

What cultural values were reflected in the reactions of the other people in his life to this decision? His parents were sad, because he is their only child and they didn't want him to go away and maybe even stay in the U.S. As for everyone else, Jorge Enrique says that one *norteño* more or less made no difference to them.

2. He decided to work at the Euzkadi factory, several years later.

What were his options? Jorge Enrique was legally in the United States making good money at the time, and he could have stayed. He says now that that might have been better, but who could have foreseen that the factory would close?

What cultural values lay behind his decision? Money, he says; no other reason. When the factory was at full production, people could earn whatever they wanted with all the overtime available.

What cultural values were reflected in the reactions of the other people in his life to this decision? Other than a few of his close friends, Jorge Enrique says many people were jealous of his new job because they're not used to seeing people better themselves.

3. He decided to refuse to accept management's liquidation offer and instead stayed active with the union after Euzkadi closed.

What were his options? He says he worked hard and saved his money while he worked at the factory, and so he has options open to him now. He does not have to take the liquidation settlement, which he considers unfair. Also, his wife has a retail business that brings in some money. However, his main option was – and still is – to go back to the United States. His uncle Chava tells him there is a lot of work available there.

What cultural values lay behind his decision? Jorge Enrique says that the company's liquidation offer to its workers is not fair. His goal is to get the factory reopened and if not, for it to give a good liquidation settlement to the workers.

What cultural values were reflected in the reactions of the other people in his life to this decision? The people involved in the workers' actions – the workers and their families – support this action. But those not involved are critical of it.

Note: For all three of Jorge Enrique's decisions, *money* was an important factor. However, his *strong family ties* were the stronger motivation for the last two decisions. These two factors come together in the last decision: it was money, but it was not only for himself but for his family as well. Family ties also lay behind his parents' reaction to his original decision to go to the United States. The reaction of other people in town to his leaving – indifference – shows how much the traditional value of *community* has eroded in recent years. Their jealous response when he got the job at Euzkadi shows this as well.

Changes in Jorge Enrique's Life

In a certain sense, globalization has always been part of Jorge Enrique's life, through the long-standing and ongoing migration between Mexico and the United States. It is not a new phenomenon. Industrialization also brought economic changes, and it came to Jorge Enrique's world before he was born, when factories began to be built in El Salto. But industrialization is different from globalization. In fact, industrialization in

Mexico up to the 1980s took place behind high import barriers that protected it against global forces. But Mexico's opening to global economic forces accelerated in the 1990s, and Jorge Enrique has lived most of his adult life being affected by the changes it brought. Globalization most dramatically affected him when he lost his job at Euzkadi.

Consumption

A cada capillita le llega su fiestecita: **Even a small chapel has a feast day. Even the poor can get to enjoy some little things.**

Jorge Enrique has access to a larger variety of consumer goods and services because of the opening of the Mexican economy. Many new items are available in the stores, though not everyone can afford to buy them.

This is not a totally new phenomenon, however. Jorge Enrique could buy consumer goods like blue jeans and modern music in the village some time ago, when the industrial zone in El Salto was first established. Access to radio and television exposed him, and everybody in the village, to the wider world and to different ways of living. This exposure to modern consumption has been somewhat gradual, beginning with industrialization and speeded up by globalization.

More important, perhaps, Jorge Enrique has lived in the United States and is surrounded by friends and relatives traveling back and forth to the United States who expose him to many new consumer items. When he was working at Euzkadi, he had a good salary and was able to provide many of these new goods and services for his family. They enjoyed a way of life with many little luxuries, more than his father could have provided as a young man. Now that he is not working at Euzkadi, he and his family cannot live the same way. So his consumption was first broadened, and then lessened, by globalization.

What Jorge Enrique and his family consume today is different from life years ago in another way as well. People today make fewer things at home than they used to, preferring instead to buy them ready-made. For example, traditionally women made tortillas from scratch, starting with grinding the corn to make the flour. Today, Jorge Enrique's wife and many other women don't even buy flour to make tortillas but buy the tortillas already made from the store. With many of the women working outside the home, this is not surprising.

Production

Al que madruga Dios lo ayuda: **God helps the industrious ones, who start early.**

Factories began to be built in El Salto about thirty years ago and it quickly became an industrial zone. Many people in the area abandoned farming to take jobs at one of the factories; Jorge Enrique's father took one at a textile plant. Industrialization meant that people now had more choices than they did before in how they made a living.

Globalization really entered Mexico beginning in the 1980s, when it opened its economy much more broadly to international trade and other global forces. Among other things, the opening made possible foreign ownership of factories and the Euzkadi factory was bought by a German company. All this touched Jorge Enrique's life, but it was in the background; he was not aware of it.

It was when Jorge Enrique lost his job at Euzkadi that he felt globalization really affecting him. By 2001, the economic opening was lowering import duties and allowing more tire imports into the country. Continental Tire, the German company that owned Euzkadi, responded to the new competition first by trying to reduce its labor costs and, when that didn't succeed, then by shutting down the factory and dismissing all the workers. Industrialization had brought Jorge Enrique the option of working at the tire factory, but globalization made his job vulnerable to international forces.

Now, Jorge Enrique is a union activist volunteering to help guard the factory; he also works in the family restaurant and helps his wife in her business. He's gone from manufacturing to the service industry — at least temporarily and somewhat reluctantly.

Migration

El mono, the monkey: **One who swings nimbly among branches.**

For Jorge Enrique's village, the current migration has been an intensification of a phenomenon that already existed. Mexicans have been going to the U.S. to work for years; the north has always offered better economic opportunities. Sometimes they go back and forth between the countries; sometimes they settle in the north. In Jorge Enrique's family some of his mother's brothers migrated north years ago. But in recent years, globalization has made this migration somewhat of a greater necessity; for the people in Mexico who have lost jobs, the incentive to migrate has increased. So the process has been accelerating.

For Jorge Enrique, the option to migrate to the U.S. is an accepted part of life. It was one of the first solutions that came to his mind when he was young and searching for a way to make money, and it's an option that's always been there since the strike. Migrating to the U.S. is one of several possible choices he sees for his future. In addition, for him, the migration process is both legal and easy because he has a "green card," a permanent resident visa for the U.S. This contrasts greatly with the large number of Mexicans who have gone north illegally.

Migration to the U.S. today is different, but it is a difference not in kind but in degree. The lure of working in the United States seems to have increased. In fact, the number of Mexican-born people living in the United States has grown tenfold from the 1970s to the 2000s.

Social Relations

> *La raza,* the race: For Mexicans it means a group of people with whom one is very close, even if they're not blood related: my people.

The economic opening and the ongoing migration to the U.S. have changed many social relationships in Jorge Enrique's village. He learns about new attitudes and customs from the media. He sees and hears for himself that there are other ways of doing things, different ways of living. Also, like many other people in his village, he has gone to the U.S. and returned, bringing new attitudes and customs back with him.

One big change has been in the external manifestations of the traditional *machismo.* In the past, women's lives revolved solely around their homes and families. But today, many women work in the factories in the industrial area. When Jorge Enrique was growing up, he already saw women working outside the home, especially before marriage. Now, his wife Isabel owns and manages her own small retail business, and Jorge Enrique not only accepts this, he is happy about it. He is also very involved in caring for their children now that the union strike allows him more time to do so, and he enjoys this. His attitude would not have been common a generation ago (and indeed is not so common even today).

Jorge Enrique has always felt rooted in the community of San Antonio, where he grew up. But because of migration, his community actually reaches beyond San Antonio; members of his extended family live in the United States. He lived with these relatives during his stay in the north and still feels connected to them.

Globalization has changed his social relations as well. Since he was fired from the factory, he has formed stronger relationships with the other men in the union, in particular with the ones who, like him, are holding out for a better settlement from the company. The union's task is to guard the doors of the plant to ensure that it stays closed and nothing is removed while negotiations go on. Jorge Enrique and a small group of men are in charge of this. But it does not involve much effort, and leaves a great deal of time for socializing. These men have become an important part of Jorge Enrique's life.

Political Relations

Ay, reata, no te revientes que es el último jalón: Rope, please, do not break; we have only one more tug left to do. Hang on, we're almost done.

Because of his involvement in the union's struggles, Jorge Enrique has had greater exposure to the Mexican political system and how it works than he would have otherwise. He has become familiar with the local judicial process – and he has seen how unjust, and even corrupt, it can be. One might look askance at Jorge Enrique's union charging a steep fee for a worker to join the union; however, he does not seem to consider this practice inappropriate. He did see inequity in the political system's response to the union's efforts to obtain a favorable outcome of its dispute with the tire company. He perceived that the judiciary system showed partiality to the company and that there was no due process. Jorge Enrique did not hesitate to label it corruption: his eyes have been opened to many things. Moreover, his political awareness is actually global now. He has been exposed to politics at the international level, not just the local or national level. He has learned about the German company that owns Euzkadi and his own union's German counterpart.

But it is not only Jorge Enrique's political awareness that has grown because of globalization; his political options and involvement have as well. When his father was young, the only real union was the one associated with the government. People could not become actively involved in an independent union that took part in the political system and use it to accomplish things, as Jorge Enrique's union is doing. Also new is the relationship between Jorge Enrique's union and the one in Germany. In addition, Jorge Enrique has been involved in monitoring local government elections; this was not unknown in the past, but it was much less common. Overall, we can say that the new political realities have offered opportunities for his greater involvement and have allowed Jorge Enrique some growth in his political awareness.

Part of the reason for his greater political involvement is the growth of the media in recent years, which was mentioned above. More media means more information, and information is crucial for political opening and involvement. Not only can Jorge Enrique and the other people in San Antonio now follow their favorite sports teams and the teams of other countries on the TV and radio, but they can also learn about political events in other parts of Mexico and all over the world in a way unimaginable not that long ago.

Religious Experience and Expression

> *La Virgen de Guadalupe:* Our Lady of Guadalupe, patron saint of the Americas. Devotion to her is deeply rooted in Mexican culture.

The forces of migration and the widespread access to media have exposed the people in Jorge Enrique's village to new ideas and new ways of doing things in religious matters. Having noted this, in practice not much has changed in religious expression for him and the other people in San Antonio — nothing beyond the changes in the role of the laity that came as a result of the Second Vatican Council.

It is true that the laity have a greater role in the church than they did in the past. Jorge Enrique now sees lay people taking communion to the sick, something that only priests did before. It seems, too, that the church's authority in general is not as strong as it used to be; the lay people are more independent. They are certainly more knowledgeable; through the media they can now find out about the church in other parts of the world. However, despite these changes, which have been led by the institutional church, many of the area's religious traditions remain practically intact. Jorge Enrique and his family still go to Mass every Sunday.

The sacramental milestones — baptism, confirmation, weddings — still occupy a central place in his life and culture. In general, Jorge Enrique's religious expression has stayed practically the same, as it has for the rest of the village.

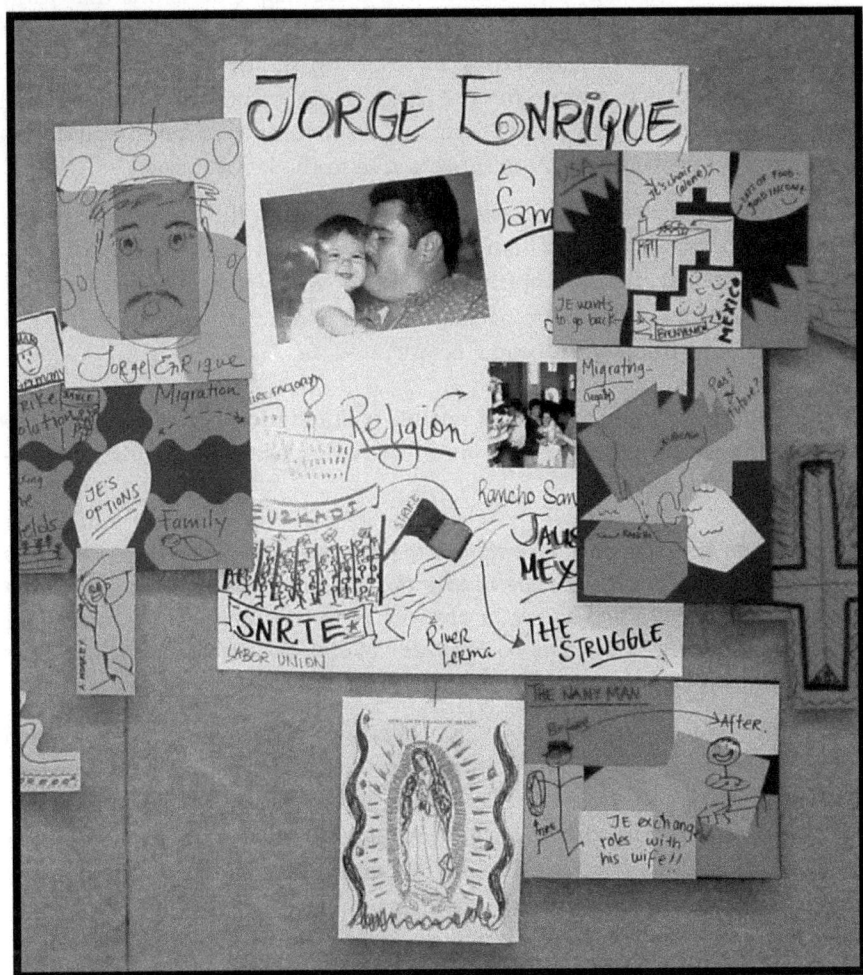

Jorge Enrique's mosaic tile from GEC's Fourth International Consultation

Jorge Enrique's Meanings and Values as Reflected in His Choices

In the cultural analysis, we identified three major decisions that Jorge Enrique took throughout his life and which the narrator discussed with him. Of these decisions, we chose to focus on the most recent one. This decision best reflects a more mature Jorge Enrique and more recent global economic forces acting on his life: it was his refusal to accept a liquidation payment and instead becoming more active in the labor union.

Below we analyze this decision and action using the methodology and template we presented in Chapter 4, p. 78ff., "Research Methodology – Phase II: Finding the Protagonists' Meanings and Values." (The questions template appears on p. 87.) Our analysis was reviewed by the narrator, but could not be verified with Jorge Enrique.

Action: Jorge Enrique refuses to accept a liquidation settlement and increases his participation in the union activities when Euzkadi's management closes the factory.

A. What can we infer goes on within Jorge Enrique as he experiences the new economy and moves on to decide to take this action? What questions may Jorge Enrique have been raising and what answers seem consistent with reaching that decision? What feelings might be involved? (Note: This refers to the stages of consciousness, from experiencing to deciding; see Chapter 4, p. 88ff.)

Jorge Enrique first *experiences* apprehension about losing his job when he reads the newspapers' report that jobs will be lost at Euzkadi and when he learns that the Goodyear plant in another state has been closed. He also hears the reports from the union negotiators who work to prevent the loss of jobs at Euzkadi. Finally, the apprehension becomes a reality when he hears directly: management announces that the factory will be closed for lack of an agreement with the labor union. His initial apprehension develops into fear, anger, and anxiety about how he would make a living with the closing of the factory. Memories of his father losing his job with a plant that never reopened are still fresh in his mind. He feels some comfort in the fact that he has an entry visa to work in the U.S.

Jorge Enrique had advance warning about the plant closing, but he is still shocked and needs to figure out what is happening. Why would management do this? Is it just greed? Or do they have some grounds? Can they get away with causing so many people to lose their jobs? Can the union still do something? Is there a legal recourse available? Can he and his family subsist on his small savings and his wife's income from the little retail store? Would another good job be available in El Salto? Would he find work if he went back to the U.S.? What are other workers doing? In answering these questions himself, he develops an *understanding* of his employment predicament.

After much pondering of these questions and similar ones, Jorge Enrique reaches some conclusions. He is angry as he *judges the facts,* as he knows them, and concludes that the primary responsibility for him losing his job lies with management and that the liquidation settlement they are offering is grossly inadequate. He concedes that management's allegations about employees' poor performance might be true with some employees who possibly need disciplinary action. But the magnitude of the problem does not justify closing the plant. That, he thinks, is totally unfair. He believes it so unfair that it makes sense to him when the union says that there is legal recourse for them to follow. Finding another good job in El Salto is out of the question. Euzkadi was the best. After checking his finances, he also concludes that he and his family can get by, at least for a while, with his savings and his wife's little store. A call to his uncle in Los Angeles also provides another safety net with the report of a lot of work available there.

He now has conflicting feelings about how to reach the best decision. He could forget the whole thing, accept the liquidation payment, and go to work in the U.S. That path would produce the most money, but it would mean a separation from the family, doing a type of work he does not like, and letting the Euzkadi management win the day. He could accept the liquidation money and stay in El Salto, but it would be hard to find another job that paid much money. Also, it would let management get away with closing the factory. Finally, he could refuse the liquidation, become more active with the union, and make do with his savings and his wife's store revenues. Financially this choice would be difficult, but it would keep the family together. This path also would make it possible to stand by in case the factory reopened – which would be the fair thing for management to do, in Jorge Enrique's view. Justice for him and the other workers would be done if this happened, or if at least a higher liquidation compensation could be gained.

He hears conflicting views from the people close to him. His family in Mexico wants him to stay with them and is willing to put up with the financial sacrifices that might be necessary. But his relatives in Los Angeles and San Antonio believe that the smart thing to do is migrate to the U.S. to work there. Other Euzkadi employees who have already accepted the liquidation settlement believe that holding out for a better settlement is not worth it. Many people in town agree with them. Perhaps they believe that confronting Euzkadi's management would only result in severe retaliation from management at Euzkadi and other companies in El Salto.

Jorge Enrique is still angry but, after much deliberation, his love for his family, supported by his religious and sacramental life, tip the scale on which he weighs his alternatives: he makes a *judgment of value*. He *judges* that the most worthwhile (valuable) course of action is to keep the family together; going to work to the U.S. would be too painful for him and his family. He also feels that the unfairness of the plant closing needs to be addressed. He *decides* to stay in Mexico and stand firm and collaborate with the labor union to help confront management and get his job back or a better liquidation deal. He is aware he might have to revisit the choice of going to work in the U.S. if the union fails; however, if the union is successful the current income sacrifice might well be worth it economically.

B. What values appear to drive Jorge Enrique's decision? What are the good things that he seeks? (Note: This refers to the scale of values; see Chapter 4, p. 95ff.)

A very important force driving Jorge Enrique's decision to try to preserve his old job is his desire to secure this source of livelihood for himself and his family, his *vital values* – his need for food, shelter, etc. But he does not want just any job; he wants a good job. The value that he places on his job is a *social value* that helps him generate income to support his and his family's basic needs. Jorge Enrique's factory job also provides meaning, defining what he is: a worker in his village, a *cultural value*. Working at the company that pays the best, being "a tire man," confers a higher status than other jobs available to him. His job at the tire plant is a source of dignity as a Mexican worker. This dignity, together with the unfairness he perceives in management's decision to close the plant, are important *moral values* that guide his decision. (As time working with the union passes, he will become concerned as well with justice not only for himself but also for the other union members.) Because of the importance of these moral values to him, he is willing to challenge the order of society, *social and cultural values*, and protest management's actions. But on top of all these values reigns Jorge Enrique's love for his family and his religious faith. Family and religion are major sources of meaning in his life (*cultural values*); but beyond providing meaning, love for his family and a sense of reliance on God guide him. This is the *ultimate value* and context in which he reaches his decision to refuse the liquidation settlement and, instead, increases his participation in union activities.

C. How does Jorge Enrique's new knowledge and decision change the horizon of meanings in his world?

Once Jorge Enrique decides to become a union activist, there is a big change in the way he views his world; i.e., his stance – his horizon. Although he still goes to the plant every day, his world has changed. He has decided to throw his economic lot in with the union. He begins to see management and the union in a new way. Management is no longer a benign source of employment, and the union begins to be much more than a useful tool to get a good salary. Now management is to be opposed, and the union starts to be a group of men with whom he is in solidarity. He is now willing to rely on the political power of the union to confront the power structures of business and government in his society. He has also tested how important it is to him to be close to the family that he loves. The family-separation hurdle to migrate is much higher now than it was a few years earlier.

D. Given Jorge Enrique's new horizon of meanings, what can we infer goes on within him as he moves to implement his decision? What questions may he have been trying to answer as he puts his decision into action? What values of Jorge Enrique are engaged in this implementation? (Note: This refers to the stages of consciousness, from deciding to acting; see Chapter 4, p. 90ff.)

His new point of view, or horizon, and the values that shaped it, will guide him as he implements the decision and adapts his world. Having decided to refuse the liquidation settlement and instead become more active with the union, Jorge Enrique first must confront the realities associated with his decision. Does he really want to implement it? Can he truly see himself as a labor union activist? Can he accept making ends meet without a regular income for his work? Is he prepared to risk not ever being offered another job in El Salto because of his union activism? He is still angry with management and apprehensive about the consequences of his decision. Nonetheless, his actions indicate that his ultimate values lead him to answer in the affirmative. In fact, he judges it *worthwhile* to put his decision into action and he takes responsibility for the consequences.

He seems to be at peace with his decision; it is consistent with his *ultimate values* of love for his family and his *moral values* of dignity and justice.

Jorge Enrique indeed wants to be a union activist, at least until there is a resolution to the Euzkadi situation. But he feels the stress caused by the fact that being a union activist has a different meaning in the village than holding a regular job does. Being a union activist is less valued. Does he really want to be associated with this way of being in the village? Does this mean that he is prepared for this bigger involvement with the union? His actions indicate that he answers positively and he appears to have found these adjustments *meaningful* to his way of life. This implies adjustments in his *cultural values*. As a union activist, his "work" at the plant, although not as an employee, will involve much more interaction than before in meetings and joint decision-making with the other union members. Is he prepared to change these relationships? In addition, Jorge Enrique will be depending on his wife's store (and his parents' restaurant) for the family's income, and he will find himself with more free time at home when the children are around. These are nontraditional roles for men in his society, dominated as it is by *machismo*. How will he handle this situation? Is it OK to help in the store and with the children? This requires adjustments in both his *cultural and social values*. The values guiding his decision now lead to a new, very different, *understanding* of his work environment and the traditional economic relationship between man and wife in Mexico. As Jorge Enrique begins to *act* as a union activist, he *experiences* his world in a new way. The meanings and values of his world have been changed as he has changed the activities and experiences of his day. Family, village, management, and union mean new relationships; in the process he has also altered what he considers good in these relationships.

E. Do we detect changes in the relative weights Jorge Enrique now places on different values within a given level of values and among different levels of values? Does Jorge Enrique seem comfortable with his decision and action? (Note: This refers to the tensions within and among the levels of values; see Chapter 4, p. 102ff.)

We can see the shifts in the weight that Jorge Enrique places among different levels of values more clearly by comparing his decision to become a union activist with earlier decisions of his. We can compare the current decision with the decisions to migrate to the U.S., the first time for the adventure and the money, and later on to save money in order to buy a *pase* to the labor union. His private interests and economic goals heavily drove the earlier decisions: it was the income he expected to generate in the U.S. In contrast, in the current decision his religious values and his love for his family carry a heavier weight. His *ultimate values* inform his *moral values* and prevail over the *social value* associated with the income consequences of deciding to become a union activist. His sacrifice of income also implies a lower weight for his *vital values,* which are supported by that income. It is true that if the union protest is successful this decision may also provide high income if the plant reopens or there is a much larger settlement. But there is high uncertainty as to whether that would be the final outcome. Jorge Enrique is placing more weight on his *religious and moral values than on his social and vital values.* He is doing what is right for the family he loves. His *social and vital values* will have to suffer as his income is reduced, at least for the time being. He is also putting less weight on the *cultural values* of what his village considers to be the best job for him and for his proper role as a man in his society. Not having the tire company job, it would be preferable, culturally, to go to the U.S. to work, as many others – including Jorge Enrique – have done in the past. Instead, he chose to become a union activist and a homemaker.

The changes in the relative weights given to different levels of values also demand adjustments in Jorge Enrique's values within each level. *Within moral values,* there is an adjustment, as these values now include not only what is right for him and his family but also extend to justice for other employees. In Jorge Enrique's anger there is a sense of the injustice of closing the factory and offering only a meager compensation. In rejecting management's actions, and joining forces with the activist union, Jorge Enrique develops a better understanding of the needs of others in the union who are in a similar situation. He adds justice for others, and care for the wellbeing of the group, to his concern for his family. *Within cultural values,* there is greater significance in the meaning the labor union has for him. In the past, the union and its leaders were primarily a mechanism for Jorge Enrique to address his economic needs. Now it is a social institution in which he is proud to participate to achieve common goals. In the domestic area, Jorge Enrique now also places less importance on the traditional machismo, as he spends more time helping with domestic chores and has increased financial dependence on his wife. *Within his social values* there is a shift in how he values the labor union and management as mechanisms to earn a living. He is now willing to work with the union, not just call on them for assistance. In the process, he has also assumed a more antagonistic position towards management. Finally, *within vital values,* there must be a rearrangement of what he considers good to satisfy his own and his family's needs with a reduced income. Jorge Enrique seems comfortable with his decision and action. He wishes life were as it was before when he was working at the tire company, but he believes he is doing the right thing and he acts in relative freedom.

RESEARCHERS' REFLECTIONS

Mexico's Economic Globalization and Jorge Enrique

Jorge Enrique experiences the impact of trade liberalization most directly when he loses his job. The plant where he worked is closed, alleging it cannot compete with the now cheaper imports from Korea. Trade liberalization has had both positive and negative effects on Jorge Enrique and El Salto. They benefited when new plants financed with foreign money invested in the area, as when Continental Tire bought Euzkadi. But they suffered when local factories had to close because they weren't competitive with imports and people lost their jobs. This happened with the textile plant where Jorge Enrique's father worked, as well as with Euzkadi.

In the case of Euzkadi there is litigation underway and we do not know what concessions management asked labor to make, or what the union was prepared to agree to. Nor do we know what other inefficiencies, besides the alleged high labor cost, exist there that management is not addressing. However, we do know that Continental Tire has another tire factory in Mexico that still is working. Is the Euzkadi union a bit too intransigent? Is management too callous about the effects on employees of shutting down the plant? We do not know the answers to any of these questions. But taking management's allegations at face value, here is one of the realities of liberalizing trade: more foreign competition will ensue and some domestic plants will not be able to survive. This might well be the case with Euzkadi!

International competition improves the efficiency of local production by shifting it to what it can do best and importing what other countries do best. But what about Jorge Enrique and the other workers at Euzkadi? What provisions are made for these people − just the hope that they find another job, probably at lower wages and benefits? The job at Euzkadi was the highest-paid job Jorge Enrique ever had and he does not have any special trade skill. That might be the cruel reality. But does it have to be that way? Jorge Enrique and the other union members have thought of the possibility that the company might abandon the plant and let the union run it for its own benefit. But who is going to teach these workers how to manage a tire production factory?

In the case of Jorge Enrique, from a purely economic point of view there is an alternative open to him for finding a job relatively easily: he possesses an entry visa to the U.S. But he never liked the jobs that he could find there – even when they paid well. In addition, migration, even in his circumstances, has a very high cost in terms of broken family ties and separation from the familiar culture.

Getting to Know Jorge Enrique: Our Journey

The development of the narrative and its cultural analysis led us to experience Jorge Enrique in two contrasting modes. On the one hand, we could see him as the victim of global economic forces (and perhaps callous management) that have closed the tire factory where he used to work. Working there was a dream. Now that dream had been broken and his economic future was in doubt. On the other hand, we could also see Jorge Enrique as a decisive person who does not exhibit the passivity of a victim. He repeatedly assesses his options, reaches new decisions, and acts – even if only with the sophistication of somebody who can act merely to keep his options open. As a decisive person, we thought that Jorge Enrique's primary driving force was having what he considers "a good job," with the associated income, working conditions, and material life. However, we also recognized that this drive was qualified by his love and desire to be with his family – factors in his decision not to migrate to the U.S., at least not yet.

As we looked closer into Jorge Enrique's decision-making process and motivations, we learned more about what he considers to be "a good job." We came to understand that "a good job" to him is determined not only by the nature of the job and what it pays – social and vital values – but also by what his Mexican culture as lived in the village values. Being a "tire man" is considered to have a higher social status, has more dignity, than being a union man or a *milusos* in the U.S. It is not just money and working hours that define a good job for Jorge Enrique. Cultural and moral values are also important, maybe even more so.

The exercise of looking at the world through Jorge Enrique's eyes, within the context of his scale of values, threw new light especially on the importance to him of his religion and associated values. The narrator had stressed the importance of religion to Jorge Enrique, but we had not connected this point with Jorge Enrique as a decision maker. We had seen the expression of religious values manifested in the culture of Sunday Masses, baptisms, marriages, and other religious celebrations. But we tended to see these expressions primarily at a cultural level – as what everybody does in the village. Now we could see that Jorge Enrique's faith in a paternal and loving God shapes everything for him. And if religious faith is the bedrock of his life, the love he feels for his family and the strong bonds he has with them are its best manifestation. This love is a strong force behind his decisions. The traditional Mexican family remains strong in Jorge Enrique's life. At the point of deciding, Jorge Enrique might have chosen to think only of himself, but he doesn't. In his most recent decisions, if not when he was younger and first came to the U.S., he chooses what is best for the family. What Jorge Enrique finds valuable is grounded in his strong religious faith and his love of family. These are the ultimate values that provide the horizon that guides his decisions. These values help him reach judgments in his new world and help him understand and experience his new reality as he becomes a union activist and waits for a better solution to his situation.

By identifying the primacy of Jorge Enrique's religious and moral values, we came to a better understanding of how he has expanded his concept of justice and adapted his cultural values. Originally, as he refuses management's settlement offer and appeals to the union, he seeks justice for himself. But as he implements his decision this justice is now broadened to include the other activists remaining in the union. In the broadening of his community, Jorge Enrique's righteous anger has also broadened. The frustration of dealing with a powerful multinational company and a political system that appears to be partial to business has created a real anger and desire for justice in Jorge Enrique. His moral/personal values lead him to channel this anger into the union's confrontation with the company's management. He now extends the love of God he perceives in his religious values to a broader group of people: his union co-participants. We began to see that his trust in God also helps him find what is good in his new predicament, as in his new social relationships within the union and the greater amount of time he can spend with his children. In the process, he adapts how he lives his values within his culture and social relationships. The traditional *machismo* seems to have a lesser hold on him and he becomes more active in asserting his worker's rights instead of just relying on the union, *el responsable*.

In our new understanding of Jorge Enrique, we recognize him as able to go beyond his traditional Mexican culture – the culture as lived in *el rancho* of San Antonio with its exposure to the nearby industrial zone and the migratory experiences of the many people who move between Mexico and the U.S. Guided by his values, he blends elements from *el rancho* culture with the new elements of his changing, globalized world. He is capable of judging the values of both cultures, distinguishing among them, and deciding what seems to him to be the best course of action. He adapts his world to conform to his new understanding of his world. He becomes an active participant in how he shapes his new world. He takes responsibility for his decisions as he puts them into action. His values create something new that is good because he becomes a more responsible agent of development, even as his external circumstances deteriorate.

Jorge Enrique's personal development, however, is fraught with underlying tensions whose resolution he seems to leave in God's hands. He knows he can always go to the U.S. to work and make more money than he could at home – but it would entail leaving his family. As he volunteers with the union and waits for the tire company's fate to be decided, he keeps his options open. It could be said that this decision puts his life in abeyance. But his decision can also be seen as his way of living out his faith, his complete trust in God. He is open to either migrating to the U.S. or staying: "What God may decide." He has a spontaneous hope in God and he is not worried. He searches for what is good and this imparts a new meaning to his life as he confronts the negative impact of the forces of the global economy on his own life.

Chapter 10

Joseph in China:
Rural Tradition and City Prosperity

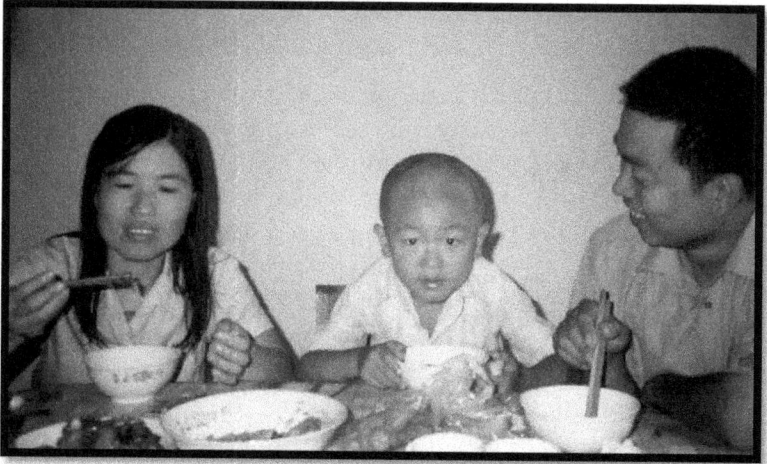

Joseph with his wife and son, enjoying dinner at home

NARRATOR: REV. TIANZHI PETER CHEN

Priest of Qingdao Diocese
Qingdao, China

Narrative Summary and Economic Background

Joseph, now in his thirties, was born in a small village in rural northern China, in the central eastern part of Shandong Province. He was one of seven children and his family was Catholic. In 1991 he migrated to the city of Qingdao. Chinese economic reforms had led to less demand for farm labor in the village and greater opportunities in the cities. In Qingdao, Joseph and his wife live with their one son and work very long hours, he in an electronics factory and she in a Korean-owned clothing factory. Their lifestyle is very different from the one they left behind in their respective villages. Their combined income allows them to maintain a relatively high standard of living compared to what they had before. It also allows Joseph to send money home and thus fulfill a Chinese son's traditional duty to provide support for his parents.

China still maintains the communist political system it adopted in the 1940s. But in the early 1980s, it embarked on a new economic program of ever-increasing reliance on market forces – including an opening to international trade and foreign investment. China finally joined the World Trade Organization in 2001, accepting the organization's requirements to maintain free trade. As part of its liberalization program, in 1982 it abolished its former system of agricultural communes. This change had a great impact on rural villages, like the one where Joseph was born. The old production teams there, composed of several families, were dissolved and individual families began to work for themselves, renting from the government the land they worked. Agriculture became more mechanized and there was less and less demand for farm labor. At the same time, the economic growth produced by the market-driven policies generated more opportunities to earn money outside farming, especially in the cities. For example, one of Joseph's brothers and his brothers-in-law found jobs in carpentry and construction. In the years before 1984, agriculture's average share of the economy was 32 percent; in the years after, it decreased to an average of 22 percent. In its place, the service sector grew. Since the 1980s, China's economic liberalization policies have produced some of the highest rates of per capita income growth in the world.

NARRATIVE

Joseph's Childhood

The soft voices could be heard easily throughout the house. Although they had scattered after dinner, the Chen children came quickly when they heard their parents call. The eldest son, Anthony, shut the doors and John quietly slid the thin windows closed. Joseph, the youngest brother, pulled down the shades to block the moonlight. The boys joined their four sisters and sat obediently in a small, dimly lit room as their father began the family's nightly prayers.

Joseph listened as his mother retold the story of her ancestor's conversion to Catholicism. The story of this person's powerful journey of faith more than two hundred years ago filled Joseph's heart and imagination against the backdrop of the quiet words of the Hail Mary and the Our Father. After the prayers and some lessons from the catechism, Joseph quickly fell asleep, alongside his brothers and sisters.

The next morning, before they left for school, their father reminded the children not to tell anyone about their prayers and lessons. Joseph knew this, because his parents told him every morning, but he did not understand why. Then he set out for school with Anthony and John, still hungry after their small breakfast. Walking past the fields, they saw a lot of their friends' parents farming together. Even though few other children his age lived nearby, Joseph had made many friends and the Chens were close to their neighbors. The houses they passed resembled their own, weathered from years of exposure to the elements. Between the houses, Joseph saw clear sky over the deep, flat plains of beans, wheat, and corn.

Made up of about two hundred fifty families, their village stood in the central eastern part of China's Shandong Province. It was like many others in northern China in the 1970s. Well before Joseph was born, Mao Tse-Tung's Communist Party had taken the land formerly owned by landlords and allocated it to groups of families. Joseph's family worked as one of fifty families in a production team, a *Sheng Chan Dui*. On their land they cultivated crops that would feed the entire community. As the crops were harvested, each family received a share. Any produce left over was sold for money, which was then divided among the team families. Joseph knew his family grew more food than most of his friends' families because he had more brothers and sisters. However, he also knew that because his father's health did not allow him to work as much as other men, his family received less money from selling the extra crops.

Joseph always had enough to eat, but never more than enough. His diet was plain. He rarely had anything other than grain, corn, sweet potatoes, and other vegetables, and there was only enough to get him and his family through the day. Once a year, around the New Year, Joseph enjoyed eating the meat of whatever animal, usually one close to death, the village killed for celebration. Usually it was donkey meat, but sometimes they had beef. Months had passed since he had tasted meat.

Joseph was not exposed to the world outside his home and village. His life was simple: his parents worked just to live. Indeed, they had only what they needed to get by and nothing more. If the harvest was poor, they had even less. Yet Joseph drew comfort from his family, his faith, and the work on the land.

The Beginnings of Change

In the early 1980s, when Joseph was a child, the Chinese government began to loosen its centralized agricultural policies. These changes reshaped much of the village life he knew.

His family continued to live in the same house in the village, but the government no longer allocated the land or dictated what they had to grow or how much they could keep. The government still owned the land, but families could now lease their fields and keep the proceeds from selling their products. Families that used to work with each other now competed to produce and sell their crops.

Joseph's family joined with his uncle's family to lease a larger plot of land. Though they still lived and farmed in the village, the Chens changed how they planted. The family began growing cotton and raising cattle for cash. On the day Joseph's father brought home the family's first bull to help with farming, the children beamed with excitement. The concept of investing in a bull in order to make more money was something unfamiliar to Joseph and his siblings, and so the children enjoyed the bull more as a pet than as a moneymaker.

Joseph's parents were concerned about the changes taking place in their community and the local economy. But the added income allayed their misgivings. Joseph's father had farmed his whole life, expecting no more from it than the basic necessities. Now he saw his new income as a way to improve the family's well-being. During the first few years after the changes in the farming system, their income increased and they could buy more things. Soon their new financial security allowed them to tear down their old house and build a new one. Joseph was even able to call his friends after his parents bought a telephone.

New technology began to transform farming and make it much easier, even though in some ways it was more expensive. Before, a large number of men and women were needed to plant and work the fields; now, oil-powered machines like tractors did the same job faster and required many fewer people to do the same work. Even harvesting now required fewer hands. This innovation changed the pace and dynamic of farming in the village. It also made it necessary, and possible, for more people to work in non-farming jobs. Soon the number of laborers in the village looking for work was greater than the work available. Not surprisingly, other villages and farmlands were experiencing the same thing.

Now almost old enough to get a job, Joseph began thinking about how this might affect his future. He considered the alternatives. In the village, he could farm like his parents, or he could work at a trade: he could become a carpenter, like his brothers-in-law, or work in construction, like his brother Anthony. But he concluded that in the village there were more able hands looking for jobs than there was work to do. Many young people, including a lot of Joseph's friends, were moving to the city. They found work easily there and made a lot more money than in the village. Joseph thought he might follow them. However, the thought of moving away from his family was disheartening; the decision to move to the city would not be easy. And Joseph felt an obligation to stay close to the family and help care for his parents.

Had he been the oldest son in the family, or if he had not had any brothers, Joseph would never have considered leaving his village. But since his oldest brother, Anthony, was living nearby and helping support their parents, this made it possible for Joseph and John to work and live elsewhere. Joseph decided to move to the city and look for a job where he could make enough money to provide for his parents financially. It was a new way to satisfy the traditional Chinese responsibility of a son to support his parents. Joseph left home in 1991 and went to live in the city of Qingdao.

Life in the City

Joseph knew very little about Qingdao. Nothing in the village could have prepared him for, or made him fully understand, life in the city. Filled with foreign influences, Qingdao introduced Joseph to technological, cultural, social, and economic change. Everywhere he walked, drove, or looked, he encountered a culture in transition, filled with new sights, sounds, tastes, and smells.

The city's buildings were unlike any in his village. In just a few minutes he saw more people walking in its streets than he usually saw all day long back home, and after walking ten blocks, he still did not see anyone he knew. The people Joseph did meet spoke, dressed, and ate differently than any of his family and friends. He could not find a patch of grass large enough to grow even a few stalks of corn. But the cars were fabulous – Joseph especially liked the speed and roar of the motorcycles. The city's lights were captivating, the clothes stylish, and the dinner options exotic. Unfortunately, Joseph could not afford any of these things. Still, he could not help dreaming of buying one of those motorcycles.

Soon he began working in an electronics factory. Even though he thought about taking jobs that he might have enjoyed more, he liked the fact that this job paid more than any others he knew. His paycheck paid for an apartment and food, and had enough left over to send some home and save some for the future. During his first few years in the city, Joseph, like most other young people, became accustomed to this new Western lifestyle. He continued to care for his parents and appreciated the traditional Chinese values, but came to prefer the Western city way of life to the way of life in the village.

The factory where Joseph worked was privately owned by a Chinese family. Because it was small, Joseph came to know the owners. He learned from them that the owner started building the factory in 1982, around the time that Joseph's father had bought the bull. He also discovered that the total sales of the factory were nearly ¥100 million (U.S. $12 million) a year. Joseph remembered when his family received only ¥100 (about U.S. $12) a year from the village, and sometimes lived without any annual income at all! Now, after ten years working at the factory, Joseph was making about ¥1,000 (about U.S. $120) every month – a very good wage for an ordinary worker in Mainland China. That allowed him to send several hundred Yuan to his parents every year.

Joseph got married in 1997, to a woman whose family also lived in a village, though not the one where Joseph grew up. He continued to work at the factory and his wife made clothing in one of the many Korean-owned companies in Qingdao that produces for the export market. The two of them worked ten and fourteen hours a day and had little time together. There was no option to work fewer hours because the factories often required it. Still, they both appreciated the opportunity to make a solid and steady income. In fact, Joseph's wife made more money than he did because she worked four more hours a day and an extra day every week. Joseph also knew the hours could be worse: his brother Anthony in the village worked from sunrise to sunset, seven days a week.

Joseph and his wife sent their son to be raised by his grandparents in their village, until he was old enough to return to Qingdao and enter kindergarten

Joseph's wife gave birth to a baby boy and they felt they had to send him to Joseph's parents to live. The baby later stayed with his other grandparents in their village. Joseph and his wife wished that they could care for their son themselves. But as much as they loved him, they knew they could not afford for one of them to stay home. Nor did they want him to go to one of the state-sponsored day-care centers. They also wanted to be able to support their son later on by sending him to a good school, and so they kept working long hours to save more money; they viewed their son's future education as an important investment. When the son became old enough to go to kindergarten, he came back to live with them in Qingdao.

Joseph's Day

As a family man in the city, Joseph's day is very different from that of his father and the other men in his village. The sounds of pre-rush hour sirens wake him just before his alarm clock startles his wife. Stepping out of their low bed, Joseph slowly shuffles to his dresser, which holds a few shirts and pants — they look more like those portrayed on Qingdao's billboards than his old farming clothes. Putting on his company shirt and name tag, Joseph looks over at his sleepy-eyed wife, who is recovering after another long day and short night.

He opens a window that faces some apartment buildings and the street, and the sounds of morning traffic rush in and fill the room. Beyond the hall, Joseph hears the banging noises of early-morning cartoons and the opening of the refrigerator. His son is already watching TV. He takes a few minutes before grabbing his breakfast to enjoy sitting with his son. As he looks at the boy's open backpack, Joseph experiences the familiar worry of school tuition, a worry even more intense since they have begun to think about buying their first house. They know that tuition will only increase in the higher grades. Even with their two jobs, their income does not seem enough for all they need and desire. Sometimes he still thinks about that motorcycle, but only in passing.

That evening, back home after his day at the factory, Joseph prepares dinner and takes a few moments to clean and straighten up the apartment. He does not feel as strange anymore doing a lot of the things his mother used to do for his family. He gives his son a snack before he watches the evening news, both of them waiting patiently to eat. Finally, Joseph's wife comes through the door around 10:30. After a short meal, Joseph tucks his son into bed. He is glad to have him back home. Then he and his wife enjoy a few quiet moments together.

The last thing Joseph and his wife do before going to sleep is kneel in front of the icons in their room and pray the rosary. Tonight they thank the Lord for the recovery of Joseph's father, whose illness had worsened enough for Joseph to leave his factory job to go spend a couple of weeks with him. Joseph prays every night and it gives him strength. He wishes they had time to go to Mass, but it is too hard. The nearest church is about ten miles away from where they live. But to get there, they have to change buses twice and it takes one and a half hours. The bus fare is a large amount of money for them and there is also only one Mass, at 7:00 a.m. So they go to Mass when they can, about once a month. He knows that this bothers his parents and this saddens him.

Many hours away from his parents, the village, and the fields, Joseph finds comfort in his faith and in the closeness of his wife and son.

Images from Joseph's life in the city and the village

CULTURAL ANALYSIS

Joseph's Traditional Culture

These are traditional Chinese cultural traits that go back many centuries. Some are important in Joseph's life; others are less so. Some contradict the values that were taught by the Communist Party in China, at least until very recently. Joseph also grew up in a Catholic family, which taught him yet another set of values.

1. *Strong Sense of the Spiritual.* Chinese traditional religion permeates everyday life. Ancestors are very important; they are seen as the source of life. People often visit shrines to pray and ask for favors. Chinese who are Catholic manifest this spirituality in a different way.

2. *Close-knit Family.* This includes the responsibility of grown children, particularly sons, to help support their parents.

3. *Relationships are Important.* Family, friends, and community give people a sense of belonging. There is a Confucian notion that *harmony* is central in social life.

4. *"Going with the Flow."* This idea from Taoism permeates the culture. If a harvest is bad, for example, farmers do not complain or blame God but simply accept it and move on.

5. *Importance of Education (Civil and Religious).* Parents want this for their children because it can lead to a better job and higher status. There is also a strong respect for intellectual achievement.

6. *Belief in a Strong Role for Government, as a Necessary Evil.* This value has been part of Chinese culture and identity since 200 BC. The current communist government fits into this historical context.

7. *Industriousness and Frugality.* This has long been a part of Chinese culture.

Joseph's Critical Decisions

1. He decided to go to the city to work when he was old enough to get a job.

What were his options? He could have stayed in the village and worked either on the farm or in a trade like construction or carpentry, which would have taken him traveling outside the village.

What cultural values lay behind his decision? Joseph wanted to work and make money, but there were more workers than jobs in the village and the jobs that were there didn't pay as well as city jobs did. By getting a good job in the city, he also could fulfill his traditional responsibility to support his parents.

What cultural values were reflected in the reactions of the other people in his life to this decision? His family participated in Joseph's decision, which was usual in their closely knit family. Also, in the village many other young people were migrating to the city looking for work and money, as Joseph was. There were not many reactions from the other people in the village, although if he were getting very rich, they would be jealous. In the city, Joseph doesn't really know his neighbors, so there is no reaction from them.

2. He and his wife decided to send their son to Joseph's parents in the village so they could take care of him while he was a baby.

What were his options? Joseph and his wife could have sent the baby to one of the state-sponsored day care centers but they did not want to do that. And they could not afford for one of them to stay home to take care of him, so that was not an option.

What cultural values lay behind his decision? Joseph needed to work long hours to make more money. He wanted to be able to support his family in a better lifestyle, pay for his son's schooling, and save for the future. He viewed his son's future education as an important investment. He also wanted his son to be raised in the Catholic environment his parents could provide, rather than in the state-run nursery.

What cultural values were reflected in the reactions of the other people in his life to this decision? His parents agreed to help him with his son out of love for the family and their Catholic faith. It also was common in the village for people to take care of their grandchildren.

Note: The main cultural values guiding Joseph's decisions were strong *family ties*, maintaining *harmony* in his relationships with parents, *industriousness*, and *frugality*. "*Going with the flow*" influenced his decision to go to Qingdao, because other young people were doing the same thing; he was not rebelling in leaving the village. The value of *education* influenced him to send his son to his parents so he and his wife could keep working, which was partly to save money for his schooling. His parents and siblings supported his decision to move to the city, acting out of their sense of *family*. The other young people who left the village had values similar to Joseph's.

Changes in Joseph's Life

China's economic opening led to dramatic growth, and also caused changes in many areas of Joseph's life.

Consumption

In the city, Joseph finds a great variety of consumer goods in the stores, many of which are imported. There was much less available in the village. The prices of these goods are higher than village goods were, but his income has gone up as well. Joseph and his wife have more money than they did when they lived in their villages and now own items unimaginable in their childhoods. They have a television, a telephone, and a refrigerator and are saving to buy cable TV, a motorcycle, and a house.

Like many others in the city, Joseph and his wife have adopted a Western style of consumption. They wear Western clothing, eat some Western foods, and so on. Their lifestyle is changing as their society changes. They also are able to consume a few things for the sake of enjoyment: a television, for example. They do not have much time for them, because of their long hours, but they enjoy these Western luxuries when they can. Things were different back in the village, where they had only just enough to live. For a while, the changes Joseph and his wife made led to some tensions with the elderly in the village, but this has lessened in recent years. Joseph does not feel any tensions with these changes, and believes his lifestyle is better than it was in the village. He enjoys the freedom that comes with all these new choices and is at peace.

Production

Da Gong Zai: The boy leaves home for the city to work.

Joseph's work has changed: from farming in the village to working in a factory in the city. He went from doing farming work and following the agricultural cycles to working as an employee in an electronics factory. He also went from working with his family and sharing the harvest to working as an individual for a salary.

He has rejected the option of working in the government, because he would not join the Communist Party, which is required for those jobs. In the factory, he works long hours — from 7:00 a.m. to 5:00 p.m. six days a week – and his wife works even longer hours than he does. Yet he feels this is less demanding than when he worked in the fields. His brother Anthony, who still does farm work, works all day, seven days a week, and never gets time off.

Joseph's concept of work has changed with his move to the city. When he farmed, he worked to survive and ate from what he produced. Very little cash was involved. Now he works both to survive and to provide a better life for his family now and in the future, and his work decisions are driven by monetary income. He defines a good job by how much money it brings in; more money is better than less money. The kind of job he has (within legal limits) does not matter to him. Even his concern for his son's education is driven by his desire for his son to have a better job with more income. Higher-paying jobs also confer more social status. He is satisfied with his factory job, despite its long hours, because it brings in a good income.

Migration

Ming Gong: A peasant worker comes to the city.

With China's economic opening came increased technology and a resulting decreased need for farm labor. Along with many other young people, Joseph realized that better jobs were to be found in the city factories. So he left behind his family and his traditional village life for the chance to work hard and make more money. He left his familiar world for a completely new environment. In the city, he lives near his job and does not even try to find other people from his village.

But he and his wife enjoy their new living situation. What is important to them is that their neighborhood is secure and that it is convenient to where they work. They also like the freedom and excitement that comes with city life, as well as the opportunities. Joseph doesn't want to return to the village. At the same time, he still maintains strong ties with his family there.

Social Relations

Qing Jian Zhi Jia: Building up the family with hard work, industry, and thrift.

In the village where Joseph grew up, everyone knew everyone else and socialized together. Families worked together on their land, and neighbors worked together as well. Work was a permanent way of life. Now that he lives in the city, his life is very different.

In the city, Joseph finds that his neighbors and his coworkers are different groups of people. Joseph hardly knows his neighbors. He knows his coworkers in the factory but realizes that he is there only as long as the company is willing to keep him; it is not permanent. It is also more competitive, and with everyone working such long hours the possibility of socializing outside work does not exist. So his job does not provide a sense of community, either. He feels connected to his parents — he supports them financially and visits when he can — but he is not present on a daily basis. Because he and his wife work so many hours, they also cannot spend much time with their son and with one another.

His wife works more hours than he does, and this is a big change for both of them. It means that she cannot do all the child care and housework, which was the traditional pattern. Joseph now helps her with these things. This is a role reversal for both of them. There is some sadness about it, but it is a common practice in the city and they are at peace with it.

Political Power Relations

When Joseph was a child in the village, his family was not involved in politics at all and never had much influence on the political structure. Their Catholic religion meant not only that they didn't have access to the benefits of belonging to the Communist Party but were also subject to active discrimination. Joseph grew up in this environment. Later, China's shift to a more market-based economy resulted in a certain openness in the religious and political areas. This opening also increased the influence of Western values, especially the Western concepts of individualism and human rights. With it came a greater presence of NGOs and more freedom in civil society. However, the role of the government remained strong. Joseph and his wife pay little attention to these changes. Though they have more opportunities to participate, they have less time.

However, these changes did improve life for Catholics in many ways, particularly in the cities; Joseph and his wife face less discrimination for being overtly Catholic. For perhaps the first time in China's history, its small Catholic population has an easier time practicing their faith.

Religious Experience and Expression

Ting Tian You Ming: Obey the heavens and follow the fate.

The traditional Chinese sense of the spiritual found a different manifestation in Joseph's family, with its 200 years of Catholic practice. Their Catholic faith contrasts sharply in some ways with Chinese tradition. In the tradition, religion is not considered very important and was even looked down upon. This attitude became worse under the communist state. But for practicing Catholics like Joseph's family, religion is central. In the tradition, God is not necessarily the creator and while this God has a personality it is not very clear. For Catholics, though, God is the creator and sustainer. Ancestors are very important in the Chinese tradition, unlike in Catholicism. Finally, the tradition does not have the concept of good and evil spirits, whereas good and evil are very much part of Catholicism.

When Joseph was growing up, his family faced a great deal of discrimination because they were Catholic. As a consequence, they practiced their faith in secret. With China's greater acceptance of religious freedom, now, in the city, Joseph can freely attend Mass and the Catholic church he goes to attracts thousands of worshippers. However, he and his wife are less able to worship in community now, because of time and financial constraints. Not only do they work long hours, but it is expensive and difficult for them to get to Mass. So Joseph's faith is more private now – and he is not at peace with this situation.

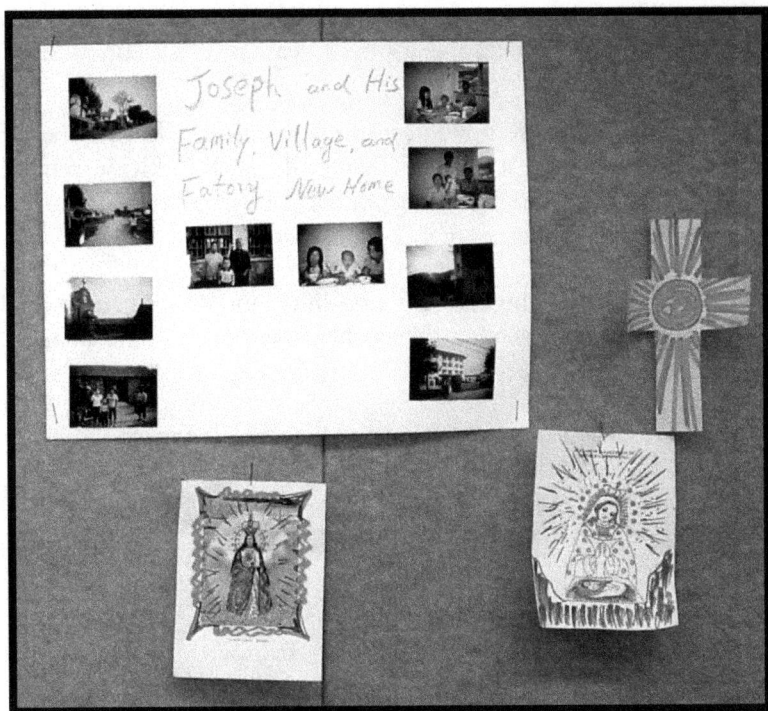

Joseph's mosaic tile from GEC's Fourth International Consultation

JOSEPH'S MEANINGS AND VALUES
AS REFLECTED IN HIS CHOICES

To enter into what goes on within Joseph, as he deals with his life in a China more exposed to global forces, we focus on one particular action of Joseph:

> Having lived in Qingdao for some time, and despite some doubts, Joseph remains working there and does not return to live in the village.

In the Cultural Analysis section, we studied his decisions, first to move to work in the city and then to send his son to stay with his parents until the child could start school. Both these decisions can be seen as submerged in the decision and action that we have selected. The decision to stay in the city builds on his earlier decision to come to the city, but involves a better-informed understanding of life in the city after living there for a while. Given Joseph's Catholic values, sending his son to be raised by his grandparents during his early years is also a function of Joseph's staying in the city.

Below we analyze this above decision and action following the methodology and template presented in Chapter 4, p. 78ff., "Research Methodology – Phase II: Finding the Protagonists' Meanings and Values". (The questions template appears on p. 87.)

Action: Having lived in Qingdao for some time, and despite some doubts, Joseph remains working there and does not return to live in the village.

A. What can we infer goes on within Joseph as he experiences the new economy and moves on to decide to take this action? What questions may Joseph have been raising and what answers seem consistent with reaching that decision? (Note: This refers to the stages of consciousness, from experiencing to deciding; see Chapter 4, p. 88ff.)

When Joseph contemplates whether to stay in Qingdao, he has been living there for some time. He has been *experiencing* the city personally. Back in the village, his experience of the city had been only through what he had heard and seen from other young people in the village who had migrated to work in different cities earlier. Joseph had heard their stories and talked with them when they came back home to visit during the Lunar New Year holiday. He also had seen the gifts they brought to their families and the money they were able to send to them on a regular basis. That was his experience of the city then. But by the time he faces the decision of whether to stay in Qingdao he has been living in the city and working in the factory introduced to him by two village friends who had migrated to Qingdao a year earlier. He now experiences the pride of having learned to be an electrician – a job with a good wage. He also has made some new friends among the other people working in the factory. He feels grateful for these friendships. He recalls his parents teaching him the ancient expression: "At home, rely on parents; in foreign lands, rely on friends." He is very pleased that the hope he had of making more money in the city has turned out to be true. He is pleased that he can send money to his family and, because of Qingdao's proximity to the village (a hundred miles), he can visit the family not only on holidays but on other occasions as well. And because of the money he earns, he can eat, dress and live better – he feels he is living a better life in the city than he could have had in the village.

But Joseph also experiences things that were quite new to him. Working in a factory with strangers is very different from working back on the farm, when the whole family worked together and consumed what they produced. He misses his family. Housing is very different also, much more crowded, and he has less space to live. He is amazed at the many tall buildings with thirty or forty floors, or even higher. He had seen hardly any cars before; now he has seen many kinds of cars, trucks, buses, traffic jams. And then there is the large number of people walking on the streets. He feels overwhelmed, lost, in the ocean of buildings, cars, and people. He also has found that people in the city are much more diverse than what he had known before. At work he meets people from southern China, Western China, and Manchuria. He can hear their dialects, but is dismayed he can't understand a word of what they say. The way they interact with others and the food they eat is also very different from what he knew and he doesn't always like it. And then there are the foreigners with "yellow hair, blue eyes, and big nose," who speak even more differently. He thinks their speech sounds like birds. Joseph is fascinated by this diversity of people but not always pleased. At work, some of his colleagues sometimes give him a hard time and he feels hurt. He also has realized that crowds can be dangerous, as when his wallet was stolen in a crowd, or when the police broke a street fight by force and proceeded to make arrests. The city could be dangerous. He remembers the simplicity of life in the village and longs for it. He experiences life in the city as a struggle and a fight in order to survive. He feels an anxiety he had never experienced in the village.

He wonders if maybe he should leave the city and return to the village to work on the farm. He asks himself questions to compare his experience of life in the city and what it would be back in the village. How does life in the two places compare in terms of what seems important to him: how much money could he make for himself and his family? How could he meet his obligations to his parents and now his wife and son? What about the quality of life? How hard is the work? How stable and predictable is life? How does one find friends and relate to them? How accessible is worship? How much personal security is offered? How does he feel about the answers to these questions? Joseph examines his experiences in the city as well as in the village in order to answer these questions. In the process, he develops an *understanding* of the strengths and weaknesses of living in each of these places.

Finally, he comes to a conclusion – a *judgment of the facts* – that it is true that in the city he can earn much more money than he ever could in the village. Therefore, working in the city makes it possible to support his parents and his wife at a higher level of physical comfort: he and his family can have a better way of life in terms of material things. On the other hand, the city is a much more difficult place in which to make a living. Both the city and the farm entail hard work, but it is much more unpredictable in the city. The city is also much more complex and dangerous. In the city one cannot know everybody, as in the village, and even friends cannot always be trusted. The city is a struggle well beyond the predictable lifestyle of the village, with "a wife, children, and a warm bed," a place where one "goes out to work as the sun rises and goes home and rests as the sun goes down." So Joseph's question to himself becomes: do I want to stay in the city earning the income that makes possible a better living standard and a future, but represents a life of struggle and even danger? Or do I want to go back to the village, where the living standard is much lower but it is an easier and simpler life?

For a long time, he weighs the pros and cons of each choice. Progressively, it becomes clear to him that he values achieving a better living standard in the city more than the predictability and security that the village can offer. That better living standard does not only mean a more comfortable life, it also means success for him, because he can afford more support for his family and so be a better son, a better father, and a better husband – a *moral judgment* based on his *moral and ultimate values*. So he *decides* that the better course of action is to stay in the city, thus accepting responsibility for a life that is harder than back in the village.

B. What values appear to drive Joseph's decision? What are the good things that he seeks? (Note: This refers to the scale of values; see Chapter 4, p. 95ff.)

Joseph is seeking to satisfy the basic needs for food, shelter, and clothing of his family and himself in a satisfactory way, providing a life with some comforts – his *vital values*. To do this, he needs the income from a good job, which he finds working as an electrician in a factory in the city – his *social values*. But the major force driving him is the value that his culture places in taking care of aging parents. That, he believes, is the highest value and responsibility of any individual. His parents are in good health but have no income, so Joseph sees it as his and the siblings' responsibility to provide the money necessary for their parents' food, housing, medical care, etc. This is both a *cultural and a moral value*. It becomes a clear *moral value* when Joseph weighs the simpler life of the village that he misses against the struggles and dangers of the city that generates the income necessary to support his parents. He chooses what he believes to be the right course of action, to provide as much as he can for his parents and his wife and son. Beyond what he values morally are the religious roots of Joseph's Catholic upbringing, where he learned of love of God and family. Love of God, parents, and family are his *ultimate values.* They are the primary guide in his decision and these values are not only consistent, but they also enhance the way in which Joseph pursues what is good according to his culture and his conscience.

C. How does Joseph's new knowledge and decision change the horizon of meanings in his world?

Joseph first came to Qingdao looking for a better life. In the process he discovered the many good things that the city has to offer, as well as the struggles and dangers that life there entails. Life in Qingdao now has a new meaning for him, different from when he first arrived. But having made the decision to stay, the horizon of this meaning is expanded further. In accepting the struggles of the city, he gives them new meaning, in relation to the good that he seeks. They form the price that he is willing to pay to pursue what he believes to be the loving thing to do for his family, and the fulfillment of the responsibility to parents in his culture. After making the decision to stay in Qingdao, Joseph still goes to work in the same factory with people very different from him who sometimes hurt him, he still has to fight the crowds and the traffic in the city: but these things now have a new meaning for him. Being a Chinese son has a new meaning for Joseph in a China more open to global forces.

D. Given Joseph's new horizon of meanings, what can we infer goes on within him as he moves to implement his decision? What questions may he have been trying to answer as he puts his decision into action? What values of Joseph are engaged in this implementation? (Note: This refers to the stages of consciousness, from deciding to acting; see Chapter 4, p. 90ff.)

After reaching his decision to stay in Qingdao, life in the city takes on a new meaning, but Joseph still has to go ahead and implement the decision. Very soon after reaching the decision, he asks himself: is this really what I want to do? Can I really stay living and working in Qingdao? We know he answers these questions in the affirmative. In doing so, he reaffirms his *judgment that it is worthwhile* to remain living in the city, despite its difficulty. In other words, he truly assumes *responsibility* for his decision and the adaptations that he has to make in his way of life. He begins to see himself permanently living in Qingdao. His conscience is at peace; it is the right thing to do. His decision indeed is consistent with his moral values. He also begins to pray to God more regularly. He feels that in the city he needs God's protection even more and that he needs to rely on God much more than he did before. His *religious values* seem to deepen as he becomes more pious. He also begins to realize that now he would want his son to become a "city person." To have legal Chinese city citizenship would enable him to remain in the city indefinitely, in contrast to having a rural citizenship, which requires a permit to live in the city. This would be the right thing to do for his son. So what he *values morally* expands – but without detracting from what he had already valued as the right thing to do for his parents. Those central *cultural values* of the village regarding parents and family have been a strong guide in Joseph's decision and continue to be central to what he values. He grew up in a large family, with several brothers and sisters, but he and his wife have only one child; so now he needs to think of family in a different way. Family in the village was a working unit, but he and his wife work in different places. He must accept the fact that he cannot see his parents every day. Joseph realizes he also needs to deal with his feelings of alienation in the city, where he hardly knows his neighbors and does not know the many people he sees on the street. He is torn by some of these feelings, but reasons that it is important for him to adapt himself to his life in the city. He finds the necessary adaptation *reasonable*. He begins to see the good in the social arrangements of his job in the factory and the housework he has to do at home. He sees them in a new light. He comes to accept the new social structures on which he relies to live in the city and he adapts his *social values*. The informal groups in the factory may not always be trusted, and the house chores he has to perform may not be to his liking, but he values them now. They are part of his life in the city, which makes it possible to earn the money he needs to satisfy not only his vital values but also his higher values – cultural, moral, and religious.

As Joseph *acts* on his decision to stay in the city, going to work and the rest of his life in the city become a *new experience* as he adapts what he values along the whole scale of what he seeks as good. There is a renewed purpose to his values. He has confirmed that, despite the struggles of the city, supporting his own family and his aging parents in the best possible manner is his ultimate value. This is what he does out of love and this love guides the adaptation of the other values as he remains in the city.

E. Do we detect changes in the relative weights Joseph now places on different values within a given level of values and among different levels of values? Does Joseph seem comfortable with his decision and action? (Note: This refers to the tensions within and among the levels of values; see Chapter 4, p. 102ff.)

One can see changes in the composition of what Joseph considers to be good among his vital, social, and cultural values. In terms of his basic needs, his *vital values*, he finds new types of food and clothing in the city that now he appreciates as good. He discovers and values new electronic products, such as his cell phone. His *social values* now include new formal and informal arrangements that support how he makes his living, such as the factory job and the informal groups within the factory. They also include other new structures, such as the police, which keep order and which sometimes he fears, and the transportation system that helps him move around and go to Mass on Sundays. Among his *cultural values* there is now a new sense of belonging in the city as well as in the village. But these changes in vital, social, and cultural values do not seem to come at the expense of placing a lesser weight on *moral and ultimate values*. To the contrary, Joseph's decision to stay in Qingdao seems to have deepened these values in him. His value of taking care of his parents, wife, and son in as good a manner as he can has been tested. To achieve this good, he is now prepared to pay a price in terms of the struggles and danger of living in the city – he places a heavier weight on moral values. He also seems to put more weight on his religious or ultimate value of love of God, as he develops a more trusting reliance on the God who protects him in the midst of the problems of the city. Furthermore, one can say that the heavier weight that Joseph now places on his *religious, moral, and cultural values* helps him to see the good in city things. He sees them in a different way than when he first came to the city, a less materialistic way. That might not be the case for other Chinese people who migrate to the city. But in Joseph's case, his religious and moral values make a difference in how he adapts to live in Qingdao, away from the village and his parents.

RESEARCHERS' REFLECTIONS

China's Economic Globalization and Joseph

China's modernization and economic liberalization have led to great economic achievements. In the mid-1980s, it had an income per capita like that of the poorest countries in the world; that income more than tripled in less than a decade. One must also note that China is still a communist country and its economic liberalization started from a place of extreme government intervention in every aspect of people's lives. So it is not surprising that in liberalizing the economy, China took a much more directed and deliberate approach than many other countries joining the global economy at the time.

Massive privatizations never took place and much of the country's production and financial sector remains in government hands. In fact, though China tried to join the WTO, they were not able to do so until 2001, more than twenty years after the new program was announced. For many years the rest of the world did not think that China, with its government's large involvement in the country's economy, could be reliable as a full participant in the WTO. Foreign investment in infrastructure and significant industries often requires a joint venture with the government. Globalization in China continues to take place under heavy controls by the state.

Joseph was able to capitalize on the country's increase in income per capita when he left the village to work in the city. His income is many times larger than what people earn on the village farm, even after modernization. He has to work very long hours in the factory — much longer than standards in the Western world — but those long hours do not seem particularly longer than his brother's work on the farm. He enjoys the higher living standard that his higher income can buy, including the new imports. He has higher economic aspirations for himself and, particularly, for his son. In some sense, Joseph's village-to-city change is similar to people's experience in other countries when agriculture is modernized. But the starting point for China was very different. Communism meant that agriculture was communal and both work and harvest were shared. For Joseph and other migrants in China, moving to the city required an even greater adjustment to change.

Getting to Know Joseph: Our Journey

Our experience of Joseph, from reading the narrative and exploring the cultural analysis, is that of a young man who responds to the incentives that the Chinese economic liberalization offers in the city. There is the allure of a job that pays much better than anything available in the village and the attraction of a better way of life that goes with that income

– better food, clothing, medical care, and the new products now available in the city. From a certain point of view, it is the traditional and well-known story of migration from the rural area to the city. It is a story repeated millions of times for centuries around the world, except for the fact that in China it is happening while the whole economy is also being transformed. But when we study Joseph's meanings and values we see there are higher values involved in his decisions. Joseph's decisions, first to migrate and then to remain living in the city, are driven by cultural, moral, and ultimate values as well. The strong tradition in which sons are expected to be responsible for the physical and financial support of their aging parents is critical to understanding him. Joseph finds that the best way for him to support his parents is by working in the city and sending money home – providing much more money than what he could have done if he stayed in the village. In addition, he visits his family as frequently as he can, especially during the Chinese holidays.

When we focus on Joseph's whole scale of values, new dimensions appear. His moral values now show his capacity for self-sacrifice. The city does offer the possibilities of good material things. But it also involves struggle, hardships and even danger. Joseph actually is tempted to go back to the village, but he decides in favor of the better thing to do for his family: to stay in the city, despite the difficulties. In the words of the narrator, understanding Joseph in this way shows him as "brave, wise and persistent [on his higher values]": survival in the city has not been easy for him, but Joseph still tries to do his best to take care of his family. He is a good son, a good husband and a good father, willing to sacrifice himself to give all of them a better way of life. And he does this in the context of the increasing love that he has for God. Joseph finds God's love in his family and in the protection he feels God provides him. This love allows him to transcend himself, to be for others instead of only for himself as he adapts to the ways of the city.

Development Policy Implications of Knowing Joseph in This New Way

We will take the pastoral ministry point of view to address the implications of what we have learned from Joseph about human development for migrants to the city like him. The country's economic development has provided an improvement on the good Joseph can achieve in terms of his vital values and, as a consequence, his ability to meet his moral and cultural duty to support his aging parents and his family. But we learn from his story that there are big gaps in what he values in terms of social structures and a sense of belonging to the city culture. There are no social structures in the city comparable to what the village offered.

Joseph feels that he probably would stay in the city for the rest of his life, and so will his son, but the government still does not consider him a "city person" but a "rural person." On his identity card, the residence address is still the address of his village. Not even legally can he feel "at home" in the city. This fact has consequences for his way of life as he has to pay more for medical care and the education of his son than if he were a "city person." He does not have any of the benefits that city people enjoy. Joseph sometimes feels torn. (The government actually began discussing the issue of changing this census registration system, which was established in mid-1950s, but there are many political and practical obstacles to this reform. At this point, it is still hard to see when this system would be changed.)

Providing a forum for people like Joseph to share their issues – such as their rural citizenship – could be a contribution they would value. Joseph's culture values relationships, and for Joseph there are very few relationships in the city outside his family. Would it make sense for a facilitator to try to establish groups from the same village or region, so the members have a similar cultural background? The goal would be to create a social infrastructure that would provide a sense of belonging and security in the midst of the huge and anonymous city. It would be a place to address on their own the problems they have in common in the city, as well as back in the village – a place to build trust and community. It would be a place where they can be at the center of their own development.

PART III

NARRATIVES TO WHICH ONLY PHASE I METHODOLOGY WAS APPLIED

In Chapters 5-10, Part II of the book presented five narratives that were examined using both the Phase I and the Phase II methodologies.

Part III includes the six narratives to which the project researchers, because of limited resources, applied only the Phase I methodological tools. These are: Telma and Pedro in Brazil (Chapter 11), Venkaiah in India (Chapter 12), Tine Ljubić in Slovenia (Chapter 13), Mee-rah in South Korea (Chapter 14), Maurice in the United States (Chapter 15), and Marie in Cameroon (Chapter 16).

Chapter 16, Marie in Cameroon, was also the subject of an experiment in applying the Phase II methodology. That experiment is presented as an Appendix to the final chapter of the book, Chapter 17. The title of that experiment is "A New Way of Seeing Marie – A Controlled Experiment in Applying Phase II Methodology."

Chapter 11

Telma and Pedro in Brazil:
Fiesta and Struggles in the Pastoral Obrera

Telma and Pedro: two generations of leaders in the Pastoral Obrera

NARRATOR: BERNARD LESTIENNE, SJ

Brazilian Institute for Development, Brazilian National Bishops' Conference
Social Center of the Brazilian Center-East Jesuit Province in Brasilia
Brazil

Narrative Summary and Economic Background

Telma and Pedro are leaders in the Brazilian Pastoral Obrera (PO, or Workers Pastoral), a Catholic Church-affiliated labor group. They witnessed the enormous transformation in the Brazilian labor market that began in the 1970s and accelerated in the 1980s and 1990s, as the country opened its economy to the global market. Now, in the early years of the twenty-first century, Pedro is a factory metal worker in his seventies and was a PO leader in the early 1970s, when it was established. Telma, now in her forties, is one of the PO's current leaders. They embody the two philosophies that have driven the organization over the years. Pedro remains the typical leader of the 1970s: militant, confrontational, and focused on factory workers. Telma reflects the PO today, an organization that emphasizes collaboration and negotiation. The contemporary PO also focuses on a wider group of people – women, youth, unemployed, immigrants, street vendors – and addresses a wider range of workers' issues, which go beyond just employment. In terms of church support, the PO in the 1980s was present in 50 percent of the Brazilian dioceses; currently, it is active in only 25 percent of them.

The PO began during Brazil's military dictatorship, which lasted from 1964 to 1985. Industrialization and economic growth were strong in this period of broad government control of the economy. Many important industries were in the hands of the government and production took place under the protection of high import tariffs. This came to a halt in early 1983, with unsustainable fiscal deficits that led to hyper-inflation and a mounting foreign debt, which Brazil defaulted. In response to the crisis, and following IMF guidance, Brazil imposed drastic austerity measures and abandoned its earlier economic model in favor of more market-oriented policies. However, the economic opening did not begin in earnest until the 1990's. The liberalization's impact on the economic structure was large. The manufacturing and agriculture shares of the economy declined while the service sector's increased. For workers previously employed in the declining sectors, the repercussions were enormous.

NARRATIVE

Pedro: Trade Union Leader and Founder of the Pastoral Obrera

Pedro, now in his early seventies, grew up in a small village in the interior of Brazil. He was an active member of the Brazilian JOC (Catholic movement of young workers), where he received both strong Christian values and a social formation. When he was twenty-two, he left his village and moved to São Paulo to be the JOC coordinator for several Brazilian states. He also began to work in a metallurgic factory, and worked as a metal worker throughout the 1960s and 1970s. In the city he started doing pastoral work among workers, focusing on how to find Christian values in work and in class struggle.

Pedro married in 1964, at the beginning of the military dictatorship. The dictatorship lasted until 1985, and the workers' movement was oppressed and silenced during that time. Pedro and his wife began working together in their *barrio*, the poor district in the town, establishing *comunidades de base*. They discussed the problems the workers faced in their factories, in the union struggles, and in their families. This first group that Pedro and his wife initiated became a kind of inspiration for the PO, which began to emerge in São Paulo in 1970.

During the dictatorship, the Catholic Church was the only arena in which people could work for human rights and democracy. People from many different political perspectives came to the church for this reason. In 1972 São Paulo Cardinal Dom Paulo Evaristo Arns – who was strongly opposed to the dictatorship – called on the PO to denounce the rampant labor exploitation in the country. That same year, the Cardinal asked Pedro to become a member of the archdiocesan Commission for Peace and Justice, which worked on defending human rights.

In 1976, Pedro took part in the formal creation of the national PO. He was the first person to become *liberado* (that is, elected and employed full time) for the PO. At that time, Brazil's economic growth was very good. But the unions were controlled by the government and employers, and the workers received very little benefit from the unions or from the country's growth. In 1978, strikes erupted in São Paulo and soon spread throughout the country and the PO participated in them. The PO was helping build an alternative – and authentic – trade unionism. But these efforts required sacrifice. In October 30, 1979, Santo Dias, Pedro's great friend, labor leader, and one of the founders of the PO, was murdered during a strike. Santo Dias then became an iconic hero in the PO.

The PO at this time was highly regarded both in the trade union movement and in the church, where it influenced other social pastorals. In 1975, the archdiocese of São Paulo placed the PO among its four pastoral priorities; many other dioceses followed this lead. When John Paul II visited Brazil in 1979, Pedro was chosen to make a speech on behalf of all the workers in a stadium filled with more than 150,000 workers.

Pedro has taken part in many struggles: in the trade union movement, the Brazilian Workers Party, and the church. He has spent his whole life fighting and he has been imprisoned and tortured. His community is first the *barrio*, the neighborhood community. It is also the Christian community, from the diocese to the national church. Pedro's involvement with the PO grew out of his faith, which led him to fight for justice. He was fired nineteen times in twenty years because of his activism. At the end, he could not find any factory work, so he had to be employed by the trade union or the church. Pedro is satisfied by all he has done.

Changes in the Country and in the Pastoral Obrera

Towards the end of the 1970s and all through the1980s, the PO grew very rapidly, becoming active in more than a hundred dioceses. It joined with combative trade unions and popular social movements in the fight against unemployment and the high cost of living, and in favor of human rights and democracy. Members of the PO, including Pedro, participated actively in the establishment of the Workers Party in 1980 and a national trade union organization in 1983. But by then, the Brazilian economy was breaking down into hyperinflation and a major financial crisis that led to the country defaulting on its foreign debt.

Economic austerity measures were taken in response to the debt crisis and, especially after 1989, were followed by market-driven policies. These actions increased unemployment and decreased the purchasing power of most poor people. These policies also led to profound changes in the organization of labor. The trade union structure was badly shaken and, in a defensive move, intensified its efforts to defend the labor rights of workers still working in the factories, leaving behind a growing number of the unemployed and the poor working in the informal economy.

The PO leadership in the meantime was struggling to keep up with the changes taking place in Brazil's labor market and social life. By the end of the 1980s, members were beginning to question why the PO was still exclusively centered on trade unionism. Until 1989, its members were mainly male factory workers (metallurgists, electricians, chemists, etc.). But now the labor market included more workers in the service industries and the informal economy and many of these were women. Losing influence, the PO began to search for alternatives.

Telma: The Face of a Changing Pastoral Obrera

Telma is younger than Pedro, in her early forties. She was born in Fortaleza, a town in the northeast of Brazil; her mother still lives there. Telma reflects the festive, hard-working, and struggling culture of that region. Like Pedro, she grew up in the Catholic faith. She worked and fought in *el barrio*. At the end of the 1980s she joined the PO to devote herself to the trade union movement. It was a new world for her: the factories, where she never worked, the trade unions, and political struggle. It was an important and rich change.

Telma was a student at the time, but her PO companions considered her a worker, not a student. There was a certain bias against students in the PO in those days, when formation in the PO was only through militancy, activism, and continuous mobilization. Telma wanted to study, but this was not valued and was even regarded with suspicion. So she gave up her studies for a time. However, she felt that something was missing in the PO: her identity as a woman and her past, which was more popular than trade unionist, were still being ignored. But the PO was beginning to change.

In 1991, the PO celebrated *Rerum Novarum*'s one hundredth anniversary. The Fraternity Campaign, which takes place every Lent in Brazil, chose the theme "Solidarity and Dignity in Labor." That same year, the first Brazilian Social Week, which dealt with the world of labor, took place. Hundreds of seminars were offered by the PO all over the country to prepare and carry out these two events. All these events tackled the question of how the PO should respond to the changed conditions of Brazilian workers.

In 1994, a symbolic event in the PO's evolution occurred: Telma and her friend Darli were chosen as its national *liberadas*. It was the first time two women filled that role. Telma moved to São Paulo to do this; she was thirty-three years old. Soon she became involved with changing the character of the PO.

Telma went back to her studies, eventually earning a master's degree on the culture of migrants in São Paulo. She is happy about this and enjoys teaching classes. She likes her mother and goes to Fortaleza regularly to visit her. She likes São Paulo – the political, economic, and cultural life – but she always talks about going back to Fortaleza. She had a romantic relationship with another PO member for a long time, ten years, but it ended and that was very hard for her. Even though she would like to get married, this has not happened yet.

The New Pastoral Obrera

In 1995 the PO, with other social pastorals, assumed the leadership of organizing the "Cry of the Excluded" (*Grito dos excluidos*), which is now celebrated every year on September 7, Independence Day. When the PO leadership took this initiative, it created a crisis within the organization. Many of the early members were not ready for it. The "Cry of the Excluded" meant a different perception of the workers, beyond the "true" factory workers. The PO was no longer limiting itself to the working class in the traditional, restricted sense. In addition, the PO wanted to address the identity of the worker in an integrated fashion by considering other dimensions, such as being father of a family, husband, living in *el barrio*, religious believer, even a soccer team supporter, etc. It was a new and different, and broader, way to define workers.

Slowly the PO, still linked with the working class, assumed a commitment to the unemployed. In almost all the dioceses where it was present, the PO began to develop initiatives for an alternative economy, based on solidarity rather than profit. It established cooperatives, groups, and associations that organized the members of the community to work together to produce the goods and organize the services they needed.

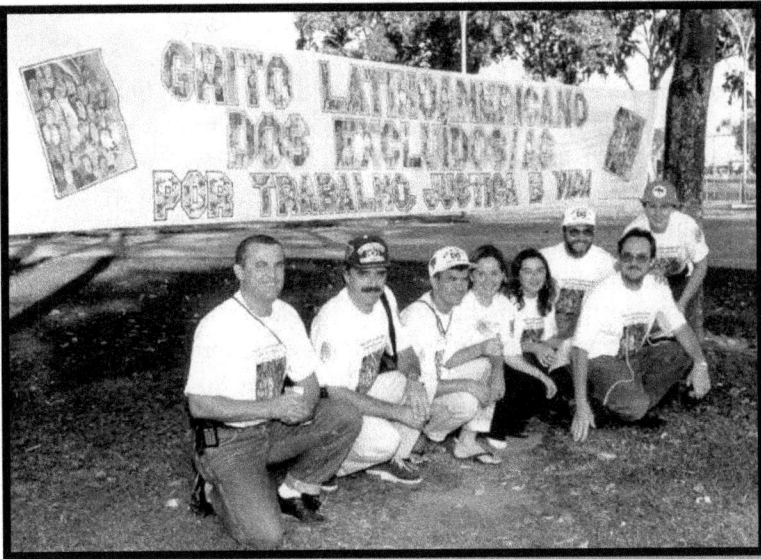

*In 1995, the PO took on a role in organizing the annual
'Grito dos excluidos' ('Cry of the Excluded') event*

The PO was responding to the new concept of work and the working
class that was emerging, even among factory workers. Today's workers in
large factories might belong to a trade union, but not to a politicized culture of class confrontation. Their main interests are in having a house,
education for their children, vacations on the seaside, and a good health
plan. The labor culture has changed a lot and the old trade union culture
of class confrontation is not predominant anymore. In addition, the concept of work in a factory has also changed. While some workers still work
with the traditional tools of the past, others are starting to operate highly
technical electronic machines. Workers learn how to operate these modern machines in about two weeks, as opposed to the old days, when it
took a lifetime to become a skilled tradesman. As a result, the sense of
pride in the product of a skill gained over years of practice is diminishing.

Pedro and Telma and the New PO

Pedro has increasingly accepted the changes in the PO, though having
some reservations. He is more familiar with the factory workers than with

service employees. For him, the PO has to keep roots in the factory workers.

Pedro was very happy with the church of the 1970s, but in his view it has changed a lot since then. In the 1990s, little by little, it stopped issuing social pastorals and pulled back from officially supporting the PO. For him, the new church in Brazil is more Romanized, more turned inward, and less politically and socially involved. This disappoints him.

Pedro's strong personality, his way of analyzing reality, his radical generosity, his suffering in the union struggle, at first intimidates those who meet him. Even though his militant core predominates, Pedro is also very sensitive and has many friends. He is close to his family and that makes him happy. He was surprised and pleased when many of his friends came to visit him after he had surgery in 2000. He is happy, too, that he hasn't changed with the times too much and that he's been able to pass on his values to his children.

Telma is a militant and an activist, too. She fought for autonomy for herself – the freedom to be a worker and the freedom to study. Studying is important to her. Like Pedro, she fought alongside the workers for their rights. And she continues the struggle as a Christian and as a woman.

She is committed to defending life: the excluded, the poor, working women, migrants. She believes that better jobs and housing and access to studies are rights for everyone and that different people and cultures can work side by side for these goals. She is confident in the possibilities and resources of people who have too often been left out.

Telma is friendly and easygoing. She freely expresses herself: animation, doubt, happiness, sadness. She is not only a leader but also a friend and companion. These characteristics of hers played out in the evolution of the PO. Together with her friends, she is working to build the new relationships that the new society requires. She sees a lot of good in the new world.

She thinks that women adapt to new things with more flexibility. They learn how to juggle difficult circumstances and among women there is more dialogue and sharing of experience. Her sense of the sacred has evolved. "I value what I learned in my childhood about the holy even more today, but I express it differently now: in faithfulness, in dialogue, in solidarity. I like celebrations of life with real symbols of our lives and participation from everybody. I don't go anymore to Masses that are dramatically sad and empty."

As for the future, Telma describes her vision of the PO: "We believe in companionship, in the collective dimension of any effort, in social commitment, in solidarity, and in a life struggling for freedom. In order to reach all this, we enlarged the field covered by the PO. Nowadays the PO takes into consideration issues of importance to women, indigenous people, African-origin people, young people, and even homosexuals. As a result of all this, the PO better expresses the pleasure of friendship and life as a *fiesta*. Yes, we have many more festive celebrations with music, songs, flowers, nice clothes, flags, symbols and all other forms of expressing the Brazilian culture with joy and hope."

CULTURAL ANALYSIS

Pedro and Telma's Traditional Culture

Traditional cultural values in Brazil come from its rural areas, even though, over the last fifty years or so, the proportion of the population living outside the cities has shrunk dramatically. Yet this urbanization is relatively recent and many of the traditional rural values prevail. The traits below are important to Pedro and Telma, but they are in the process of being transformed, acquiring other forms of expression in the life of the city. They have been influenced by the inroads of modernity: materialism, secularism, and individualism.

1. *Conviviality and sociability.* Social interaction forms a large part of people's lives, and *celebrations* are very important. There is a great sense of *fiesta,* and celebrations and sports help people cope with life's difficulties.

2. *Religious sense of life* and *widespread syncretism.* People see life as governed by religious laws and they have a personal relationship with the sacred. Their faith is often a fusion of Brazil's different religious traditions: the African, Amerindian, and Catholicism. It also includes a sense of *fatalism;* people tend to rely on providence and good luck instead of pursuing consistent actions.

3. *Relative solidarity.* There is a capacity for working together in activities such as the carnival, patron saints' festivals, or soccer matches, but in "serious things," people become more individualistic.

4. *Subtle, even cordial, authoritarianism, machismo, and racism.* It is done in a sympathetic way, as long as the subordinate, the woman, or the black person "knows and remains in his or her place." In a contractual agreement, power derives from the authority behind it, not the agreement itself.

5. *Skepticism about politics.* People doubt politics can change anything. It is perceived as a way for politicians to derive personal gain.

6. *Avoidance of confrontation.* People dislike making choices among clear extremes, and distrust consistent and coherent positions. Because rigid adherence to any plan can lead to exclusion and confrontation, plans are seen as things to be adapted and improvised on later.

Pedro and Telma's Critical Decisions

1. Despite some difficulties, Pedro decided to go along with the changes in the PO when Brazil's labor force was changing with the opening of the economy. He has been a bit reluctant to accept the new PO.

What were his options? He could have adjusted to the direction the PO was taking in response to the changes in the labor force, or even embraced them, as Telma did. However, he could not consider leaving the PO, which is part of his social and Christian identity.

What cultural values lay behind his decision? Pedro sees reality as a power struggle. He has always been grounded in confrontational trade unionism; over the years, he invested a great deal in forming combative unions.

What cultural values were reflected in the reactions of the other actors in his life to this decision? See this question in number 2 below.

2. Telma decided to work to expand the scope of the PO to include the marginally employed and the unemployed in addition to factory workers, and to look at workers in a holistic way.

What were her options? She could have worked within the PO as it was originally structured, rather than trying to change its direction. She could have quit it entirely and worked for another labor organization, or she could have worked for herself.

What cultural values lay behind her decision? Telma has a strong sense of herself as a woman, as a person of the people, and as a fighter. Her faith is a source of both joy and guidance for her: "Religion expresses itself in *fiesta*. I want *fiesta* for everyone. The sacred expresses itself in dance, in the *fiesta*." She feels connected to everyone and reaches out to everyone; she values tolerance, dialogue, and openness: "There's a feeling of connection with the lost, with victims of injustice, with women who are exploited ... The PO defends workers as whole people, as workers but also as parents, as family members, as consumers ... We are affirmed in our differences, not in uniformity, and it's important to keep up dialogue, to be open to other ways of living and other traditions."

What cultural values were reflected in the reactions of the other actors in her life to this decision? The Catholic Church "lost interest" in the PO by the time the PO began to change. The church focuses now more on internal church issues – catechesis, family, vocations, liturgy, ecumenism – rather than the social justice issues that engage the PO. Most of the combative unions continue to stay in contact with the PO. Many of them realize that they don't know how to maintain contact with the entire range of working people, as the PO has managed to do. But they have not changed their way of operating and still rely on vertical structures.

Note: Both Pedro's and Telma's decisions are motivated by their *faith*, though Telma has less attachment to the institutional church than he does, and by the value of *solidarity*. However, Telma's is a broader, more far-reaching solidarity than Pedro's. Telma resonates with the Brazilian value of *avoiding confrontation*. She also is influenced by the values of *celebration, conviviality, and sociability*. The Catholic Church was perhaps turning back to *authoritarianism* when it distanced itself from liberation theology.

Changes in Pedro and Telma's Lives

Through their close affiliation with the workers and the PO, Pedro and Telma have been confronted with profound changes in the labor market in Brazil. Many of these changes are associated with Brazil's economic opening.

Consumption

> *Quanto mais alto o vôo, maior o tombo:* The higher you climb, the bigger the fall.

> *Dinheiro na mão é vendaval:* Having money in the hand is like being swept by high winds.

Brazil's economy has grown and its market liberalization has made foreign goods and media more available in the country. Brazilians have many more consumer choices than before; they can access the Internet, and buy cable TV and imported clothing, shoes, electronics, and the new designer labels. However, at the same time, the real income (income adjusted for inflation) of PO members has declined. So the choices are greater, but the power to buy them for the typical PO member is much less.

Telma and Pedro are able to use some of these new consumer items. Telma especially enjoys the new technology – such as cable TV and the Internet – that gives her access to other communities in the world. She takes advantage of things that help her in her work and keep her in touch with others and with the world. But her other consumption remains frugal out of choice, as does Pedro's. They are both aware that many PO members cannot afford most of these goods, so they refrain from buying much, to be in solidarity with them. Both Pedro and Telma are not influenced by the pressure to consume and are at peace with their consumption choices.

Pedro and Telma also know, however, that for many members of the PO there is an unfulfilled desire and craving to consume all these new things. They feel anger at the waste of money implied by the consumption of many of these goods that they consider unnecessary and superfluous luxuries. They also are aware of the enormous pressure to consume created by the increased availability of goods and the media. Telma sees this pent-up consumerism as an indication of selfishness and an increase in destructive individualism. So while the new consumer goods are a source of life for Pedro and Telma, for those who cannot afford them they are a source of alienation and a threat to the traditional conviviality and solidarity.

In one aspect of consumer spending – education – a change has taken place within the PO. In Pedro's time, the PO looked down on education for the workers. Telma, on the other hand, has educated herself. She sees education as a way to address the tensions created by the changes in working conditions. Her attitude towards education permeates the PO today and facilitates adaptation to the new more competitive working conditions.

Production

> *Sonho que se sonha só é só um sonho; sonho que se sonha juntos é sinal de resolução:* To dream alone is only a dream; to dream together is a sign of resolve.

> *A união faz a força:* In union there is strength.

> *Palito sozinho é fácil quebrar; feixe não quebra:* It is easy to break one stick but not easy to break a bunch.

> *Uma andorinha não faz verão:* One swallow does not a summer make.

> *Um mais um é sempre mais que dois:* One plus one (people) always adds up to more than two.

> *Quem menos anda, voa:* Who reflects will do it quicker.

> *Beleza não põe mesa:* Beauty does not put food on the table.

The Pastoral Obrera supports workers: this is what it produces. The early PO that Pedro helped to establish – and which he still considers the ideal – was of mobilization and struggle. It worked to change society by organizing workers into labor unions that confronted business on the industrial front, even when it was government-owned. It was focused on male factory workers and grounded in class confrontation. This PO enjoyed great support from the Brazilian Catholic Church hierarchy at the time and was political; it was instrumental in fighting and helping bring down the military dictatorship.

The opening of the economy, which accelerated in the late 1980s, was accompanied by privatizations and new technologies that lowered demand for factory workers. These economic changes, together with an increased migration from rural to urban areas, caused a higher overall level of unemployment. Factory workers and others employed in the formal economy now represent only 40 percent of the labor force; the rest work in the informal economy or are totally unemployed. For those in the formal economy, jobs are insecure and the competition for them is fierce. The unemployment has been associated with low wages and poor working conditions.

Telma's contemporary PO evolved out of years of discussion within the PO about the new working environment. The higher competition for jobs makes it difficult to organize the workers and threatens the traditional solidarity of the PO. Nonetheless, the new PO includes all workers, whether employed in the formal or the informal economy, or unemployed. It also has fewer members, is politically weaker than the old PO, and is not confrontational. It has a more holistic approach to the life of the workers it serves, being concerned with issues that go well beyond those directly associated with employment. It also is more egalitarian in how it functions, with responsibility more shared. Finally, the Catholic Church hierarchy does not provide as much support to the PO now as it did in its origins.

These changes in the Brazilian labor market and in the PO itself have affected the inner workings of the PO. There is tension between those who have jobs in the formal economy and those who don't. In Brazilian society, there is a tendency to consider the unemployed to be in that state through their own fault. There is disdain for them. *"Os empregos faltam, mas o trabalho não falta."* (There are no jobs, but there is no lack of work to do.) Even though the new PO includes the unemployed among its members, there is still a certain division in it between wage earners and the unemployed. In addition, the more active role of women creates friction as it conflicts with traditional gender relations. Finally, the larger diversity of members and issues makes it harder for the PO to identify an enemy and focus on the new structural labor conflicts. This inability in turn makes it difficult to rally labor forces and recruit new members.

However, overall the PO continues to be a source of identity and belonging for its members. The new PO extends this sense to a wide range of people, more than the earlier PO did. Its more horizontal structures encourage communication and community building, which enable PO members to build bridges to the new situations. The PO provides for its members a sense of belonging that affirms values and goals for the group. Belonging to the current PO provides a collective approach to adapting to the new global economy, and simultaneously helps people find self-recognition and affirmation for their individuality, as Telma exemplifies.

Migration

Estou contigo e não abro: I am with you and won't abandon you.

Sonhar em mutirão: To dream together.

Brazil has experienced in recent decades – since the 1950s – a massive migration of people from rural to urban areas in search of work. The rural population, which in the 1970s represented 70 percent of the population, had been reduced to 50 percent in the 1980s. With the economic problems of the 1980s and the beginning of the implementation of the new economic measures, the percentage of the population remaining in the rural areas was less than 20 percent by 2000. The changes in the Brazilian labor market and the character of the Pastoral Obrera are closely connected with this migration.

These migrants now tend to live in huge, poverty-stricken and crime-ridden suburbs – actually shanty towns – that surround Brazil's cities. They are called *favelas;* they have grown enormously in recent years and have changed the picture of labor in the country. Thirty or forty years ago, Pedro's PO was made up of a homogeneous group of factory workers who identified themselves with a particular factory owned and managed by specific entities. Today, Telma's PO has expanded to include a vast number of unemployed and underemployed people of all backgrounds who live in the ever-growing slums of the cities.

Pedro and Telma are both migrants. Pedro migrated to São Paulo from the interior of Brazil and Telma from Fortaleza, in the Northeast. Although they did not settle in *favelas,* they both experienced an intense culture shock between the rural values they grew up with and the urban values that sprang from the harsh conditions of the city – a conflict felt by everyone who migrates.

In their personal lives, Pedro and Telma have both been able to maintain traditional values of family and religion despite the pressures of the urban environment. They are at peace with their own migration and feel that in general migration from the rural areas represents progress and greater opportunities in the city. However, they also feel that Sao Paulo is too big, inhuman, and violent, and they dream about their roots in the rural areas. But for them, like for most other migrants, going back to the village is not a realistic option.

Social Relations

Boa arrumação faz quem na sua casa está em paz: Having order at home, you will live in peace.

Não há cabelo que não chegue no pente (não dá para fugir dos problemas): There is no hair that the comb won't reach.

Na casa, a última palavra é minha: At home, the last word is mine.

Uma mão lava a outra (ajuda mútua): One hand washes the other.

Pimenta no olho do outro é refresco (não é você quem sofre mais): Pepper in the eye of the other is cool for you.

Cada um com o seu santo e com sua leitura da Escritura: Everyone with his own saint and with his own reading of the Scriptures.

Santo de casa não faz milagre: A saint is not recognized in his own country.

The changes associated with Brazil's migration to the cities, as well as the economic opening, have caused tensions in social relations. Severe unemployment and rapid technological change have put stress on families. Mothers and even children working outside the home add to these pressures. In the city, especially in the *favelas*, it is difficult to maintain the traditional religious and familial values. There is greater access to TV and radio, and family and other social relationships have found new models in the *telenovelas* (soap operas) and in the new values – money, economic success, consumerism, etc. – portrayed in the media.

Gender relationships have changed, primarily because of more women in the labor force. The PO has increased the representation of women in its membership and leadership. Since 1995 at least one of the two national leaders has been a woman and the overt machismo of Pedro's generation is under siege.

Pedro is satisfied with his family relationships, but in the PO and the trade union movement he is really fighting himself and with his companions. He feels frustrated at how his influence within the PO and traditional society has been undermined. The adaptation from a vertical to a more horizontal structure has not been easy.

Telma, on the other hand, is happy that she can confront the traditional machismo and other organizational structures that exist in her society. She is at peace with the new gender relationships that she is forging within the PO. Telma believes her adaptation to the new social situation has been facilitated by her being a woman. She believes that women have a greater ability to adapt to the changes brought about by globalization. In her personal life, though, her inability to form a traditional family remains a source of disquiet.

Political Power Relations

Quando não pode com o inimigo, se alia: When the enemy is stronger than you are, find an ally.

Quanto mais tem, mais quer (Crítica aos politicos): The more you have, the more you want.

Entrar de gaiato no navio (entremetido): To enter without being asked is not welcomed.

Devagar e sempre: Slowly and always.

Quem não chora não mama: Who does not cry does not suck.

Estar de barba no molho: To soak one's own beard in water (when there is a possibility of fire): To be cautious.

O brasileiro só fecha a porta depois que o ladrão entrou: Brazilian people close the door after the thief entered.

When the PO was officially established in 1976, it promoted class struggle. It was also heavily involved in national politics. Pedro and the PO were instrumental in organizing a labor movement that generated a series of labor strikes in the late 1970s and eventually contributed to the end of the dictatorship in 1985. In the early 1980s the PO also helped establish a national labor union and the Workers Party. In 2002, the Workers Party candidate, Luiz Inácio Lula da Silva, finally won the presidential election after three earlier failed attempts.

Telma with then presidential-candidate Lula da Silva during the 2002 campaign

The environment in which the PO currently operates has been shaped by the political opening associated with the end of the dictatorship. The opening led to the emergence of a large number of NGOs and independent social movements in defense of human rights. As the political floor opened to independent NGOs and popular movements that formerly could find a voice only through the PO, the political influence of the PO has diminished. At the same time, in the population at large, there is a greater visibility and understanding of issues relating to women, minorities, and the environment. Part of this is connected with the growth of the media, which increases the availability of information and understanding of these issues, as well as other issues in the rest of the world.

The institutional church was the force behind the creation of the PO. The ecclesial *communidades de base* were the training ground for many members of the PO and now for the leadership of many of the new popular movements. However, the role of the institutional church in the PO has changed from one of providing leadership and supporting their involvement in the labor movement, to one in which the PO is only one among many other pastoral interests of the church.

Pedro and Telma have different types of political identities. Pedro has a strong class identity, but centered on factory workers. Telma has a more diverse identity, conscious of all people, not just workers: women, farmers, the unemployed. It is actually more a cultural than a political identity. Pedro views political power as a force to be conquered in order to rule; Telma envisions power through participation and inclusion of the people.

Both Pedro and Telma are happy about the political opening brought about by the end of the dictatorship, though they are frustrated by how slowly political change is trickling down. They hope to be included in the political process of a greater democracy, but are keenly aware that poor people still do not get justice from their government. They struggle in an economy in which there is even more income inequality than during the dictatorship and in which foreign voices, in the form of multilateral organizations, have so much influence.

Religious Experience and Expression

> *Deus ajuda quem madruga; mas dormir não é pecado:* God helps those who get up early, but to sleep late is not a sin.
>
> *Se Deus quiser:* God willing (heard often in conversation).
>
> *Deus escreve direito por caminhos tortos:* God writes straight with crooked lines.

Brazil's economic opening introduced the country to the effects of modernity and post-modernity, and this has touched religious life. Along with the popular Catholic religious traditions and devotions and the Afro-Brazilian practices that predominated before, there now exists a wide array of religious choices: the Pentecostal churches, the Catholic charismatic movements, and even what appear to be non-religious choices, such as indifference and skepticism. Many of these new religions are private and individualistic, unlike the more communal nature of traditional Brazilian Catholicism. They also tend to be less tolerant of the Afro-Brazilian practices. Both Pedro and Telma are upset at these expressions of faith that are personal and inward looking, instead of outward looking in the search for justice.

The Catholic Church in Brazil in the 1960s and 1970s was a major spiritual force in people's lives. Religion and the Catholic formation of Pedro and Telma are very much the source of strength that moves their lives, but today the church is responding much less to their needs. Both of them link their Catholicism with a mandate to work for justice for workers, and they are both upset because they perceive the current church is not fulfilling this mandate. Pedro is dissatisfied because he sees the church hierarchy pulling away from its former central role in the workers' movement. Telma, on the other hand, tends to see the church these days as a global community of solidarity that is not living up to its mandate. In particular, she resents what she sees as the church's increasing institutionalization and continued exclusion of women in church decision-making. Telma has a post-Vatican II view of church; however, one senses that her faith might be wavering.

Telma's experience and expression of the holy has changed. In her childhood she expressed her faith in traditional Catholic practices. Now she sees the sacred in her solidarity with others, particularly the poor. She expresses her faith in celebration with these people, not in the Mass but in *fiesta*. In the *fiesta*, people's lives and traditions are shared and the alienation and loneliness of the city are overcome: for her, it is the banquet of the Kingdom. This contrasts with Pedro, whose religious expression remains very much tied to the sacramental tradition of the church.

INTERPRETATION

Brazil's Economic Globalization and the PO

The Brazilian inward-looking economic system of the 1970s, with its high inflation and fiscal deficits and an ever-increasing foreign debt, was unsustainable. But for Pedro and the PO the high economic growth of that period was progress, even if it required confrontation with management in the often government-owned companies. The new economic system has been very hard on the Brazilian labor force, particularly those represented by the PO. These are trade union factory workers in companies now privatized, those who can now find work only in the informal economy (such as street vendors), and the much larger number — absolutely and relatively – of outright unemployed or severely under-employed people. Much production that before had been made possible behind high import protection was not viable anymore when competing with foreign imports. Privatized companies required fewer workers. New investment most often did not use the old technologies and required a different set of labor skills and even fewer workers. The economic system that produced the high growth rates of the 1970s absorbed the growing labor force, but it proved to be unsustainable. The new economic system, more open to global market forces and promising higher growth, has proven to be financially viable, but it has produced high unemployment and enormous dislocations in the labor market – particularly among the poorer parts of that market represented by the PO.

Whatever economic growth has taken place since the liberalization of the Brazilian economy is not reaching many of the PO members. Those with education, like Telma, are not doing badly. But the rest, who did not have the skills now needed or the opportunity to get those skills, have yet to reap the benefits of the new system. For the uneducated poor person, the opportunities – now that the agricultural and industrial sectors have shrunk in relative terms – are even more limited than before. The new economic system has helped to increase productivity and economic stability. But for most people who lost their previous jobs, and for all those unable to find a job in the formal economy, that economic improvement is of little use.

Pedro and Telma as Persons

In telling the story of Pedro and Telma, it is possible to tell the story of the Pastoral Obrera and the Brazilian labor market at two different points of time: before and after the opening of the Brazilian economy that happened around 1990. Pedro was one of the founders of the PO in the 1970s and is still greatly respected, though seen as a bit old-fashioned. He reflects the PO as it was originally, and still exists. Telma, who is younger, got involved at the end of the 1980s and reflects the new PO. They respond to the changes brought about by Brazil's opening in very different ways, even though they come from the same culture, because each draws on different aspects of that culture as they face the new environment in which they live. Pedro continues to rely more on the vertical structures characteristic of the traditional culture. Telma opposes these vertical structures, while drawing on the traditional conviviality and sociability, as well as avoidance of confrontation. She is able to build new alternatives in the new environment.

Despite their differences, Pedro and Telma do share some core characteristics in how they approach life in the more globalized Brazilian economy. Religion forms the bedrock of both their lives; they have integrated faith and life. They see their efforts to support workers as living out their Catholic faith, carrying out its call for social justice, even though they perceive that the institutional church has decreased its support of the PO. Their values of social justice and a preferential option for the poor lead to a faith of solidarity with the working class. This is different from most Brazilians, for whom solidarity means coming together for social activities. For Pedro and Telma, this trait takes a more serious form and impels their political efforts to improve the lives of workers.

Perhaps because of their faith, Pedro and Telma both have an optimistic attitude toward life, a sense that change is possible. This attitude differs from that of many Brazilians, who are hampered by the traditional fatalism they associate with religion, seen in expressions such as *Dios quisieira or Deus permita*. This fatalism also may affect the work of the PO. For some members, it leads to a resignation when facing injustice; God is seen as perhaps condoning the situation. It also leads to a lack of political consciousness and makes it hard to organize politically. But Pedro and Telma both reject fatalism, as well as a related trait: skepticism about politics. A cynical assessment of politics hinders many Brazilians from getting involved and working for change. But for Pedro and Telma, their sense of solidarity with the workers overcomes skepticism. They have faith that with hard work and patience, sociopolitical conditions can be transformed. They have accomplished a great deal and are willing to be engaged in the political process.

Solidarity also leads Pedro and Telma to react similarly to the many consumer items that are part of the new world. They accept the diversity associated with globalization and are open to seeing the value of goods that they can purchase now; but they exercise their individuality in making moral choices. They both moderate what they buy, refraining from acquiring superfluous things because they know that most PO members cannot afford them. They are open to consuming the new goods, but for them goods are not just something to be consumed; goods are things to be enjoyed, in balance with the good of the group. They are a source of life. But they make distinctions among them. Some they see as unnecessary and frivolous; others they would like to have but don't out of solidarity with other workers. Still others they appreciate and consider necessities in the modern world. Telma in particular is not afraid to be part of this modern world. She takes advantage of things like the Internet and new communication technology to reach out to others around the world in solidarity with those who are victimized by injustice. Global consumption opens new possibilities for both Pedro and Telma. The greater availability of goods in an open economy multiplies the possibility of choices. This "freedom" can lead either to life or death: it can lead to sharing with others, or just to having more for the sake of having more. Pedro and Telma accept this freedom and see it as a link with the tradition of solidarity and responsibility of the old culture and the PO community.

But despite these similarities, Pedro and Telma differ markedly in how they perceive and react to the new world. For example, Pedro sees a devaluing of some traditional Brazilian values, such as family, conviviality, and celebration, in today's cities. However, Telma thinks that for the most part those values are still there; they just manifest themselves in a different form. She believes that they support people's adaptation to the urban world. She sees that many migrants who come from the same region tend to gather together and share their experiences in the city. For her, the traditions of mutual help and respect for the family, and the importance of relating with others, help to give cohesiveness to migrants' new life in the city.

They both see the great flow of migration from the countryside to the cities, and realize that it increases the supply of workers in the city and therefore creates more difficulty in finding jobs and organizing labor under the PO. But they respond differently to this perception. Pedro sees these things more as a call to continue in the PO that he helped to establish. Telma, on the other hand, is idealistic. She sees migration as the signal for the PO to evolve from its past. Her reaction to the changes in the urban labor market is to include all the new types of workers – not only the traditional factory worker – and to address all their needs. She feels solidarity with a broader group of workers than Pedro. She is open to the change and relishes the differences among the origins, needs, and lifestyles of all the workers. She finds in these differences a manifestation of the tradition and of real human values, and welcomes the cultural differences in a global economy.

This is the core difference that separates Pedro and Telma: She is more open to a new world that she sees as positive and he is reluctant to adapt to it. Pedro has some difficulty integrating solidarity with the new dimensions of work. Telma is more adaptable and is able to order the new world more positively. She questions both the old and the new worlds and is able to redefine her work in the PO as producing jobs for more people in a more integral fashion.

Their differences affect their approach to the PO. Pedro's leadership in the original PO was based mainly on a confrontation of classes. The relationships tended to be vertical and stable. Telma is more collaborative and the PO of today is more inclusive and horizontal. She reflects instead the Brazilian traits of conviviality, sociability, and avoidance of confrontation. She is converting old structures, such as gender discrimination, and helping the PO adapt to the new world. She has judged the new order and goes with it, carving a role for herself within the expanded PO community. Pedro, on the other hand, finds it more difficult to adapt to this new horizontal structure. He finds it hard to accept the new values. In contrast, the new environment gives Telma a sense of independence and helps her deal with traditional gender roles. She is convinced that being a woman helps her in adapting.

The contrast between how Pedro and Telma draw on their culture appears sharply in their social relations, within the PO and elsewhere. They are both being confronted with new meanings in those relations. Pedro's, to a large extent, have been defined by the church, the force behind the old PO and the core of his faith and family life. His social relations developed from within the groups to which he belonged: church, factory workers, PO. His views on these sets of relationships have not changed much, although the social world around him has changed as globalization has tended to break these traditional groups.

Telma, on the other hand, has moved from the social relations she learned in her earlier groups – family, *el barrio*, the original PO – to selecting her associations to include a much broader community. Her social relations denote her active presence in a much bigger world. The new PO's meaning comes much more from the bottom, instead of from the church, and is more horizontal and inclusive than vertical and exclusive. For Telma, a wider world is emerging. Her job is to integrate the needs of a broad range of people with what the PO can provide. Her PO social relations function within a much wider community than Pedro's old community of church and factory workers.

Pedro maintains his traditional social relations; Telma confronts that mentality, which is associated with verticality in a society. She accepts the new social relations and enters confidently into the process of identifying herself and being in solidarity with the people. She is willing to enter into horizontal relationships and suffer with the people. Pedro is slowly accommodating with the changes in the PO; Telma is for them. For her, the changes in the PO have produced a broader community that includes all the marginalized people. For Telma, the PO is a "social movement"; for Pedro, it is a bat to go collecting what is due to the workers.

On a deeper level, while both Pedro and Telma find meaning in the political arena and it helps them order their lives, they have distinct views of political power. For Pedro, the meaning of political structures relies on a political party and the party must gain political power to begin transforming society. Change is the result of exercising this power. For Telma, traditional political structures are less important. Power is inclusive and comes from below: better decisions are made if everybody participates. For her, the important political structures are those like women's groups and informal economy workers' organizations.

While faith is central for both Pedro and Telma, they differ in how they express it. Pedro's religious expression maintains old religious values. Telma expresses her faith in celebration with poor people; not in the Mass, but in *fiesta*. For both of them, faith is tied to work. For Pedro work needs liberation, while for Telma works brings pleasure and a joy and includes the broader aspects of life. Pedro deals with the formal labor market; Telma talks about building a "third sector" that includes the informal labor market and the unemployed. His is a faith of sacrifice that leads to confronting the capitalistic exploitation of workers in order to humanize the labor of workers. Telma's is a faith of solidarity that leads her to see work as a better expression of self. She has, in essence, expanded hers and the PO's scope of solidarity.

This difference affects how the two of them see the institutional church. Pedro and Telma both hold traditional Christian values, yet express them in different ways. Pedro's faith is rooted in the traditional institutional church. For him, religious values are shared in a struggle for justice, even through class conflict. Pedro identifies strongly with the basic church of small communities. For him, the church is very much part of the meaning of political power – and this is why he is frustrated because the church does not now appear to be assuming a leadership role in the workers' struggle.

Telma brings the personal side, in contrast to the institutional side, to religion. She embodies the concept of a community of solidarity: you have to involve everybody to find a solution. Her faith is closely linked to solidarity with the workers, broadly defined. She sees the church as a global community of solidarity, in which we all ought to pull together to make a difference – not exactly what she perceives is happening. For different reasons, they both perceive that the church is responding much less to their needs today.

Both Telma and Pedro experience God's love in the dignity of work. But then they diverge. He experiences God in the struggle for justice for workers; she in her solidarity with others, particularly poor people. He finds God in the community; she in the *fiesta*, where people's lives and traditions are shared and the alienation and loneliness of the city are overcome.

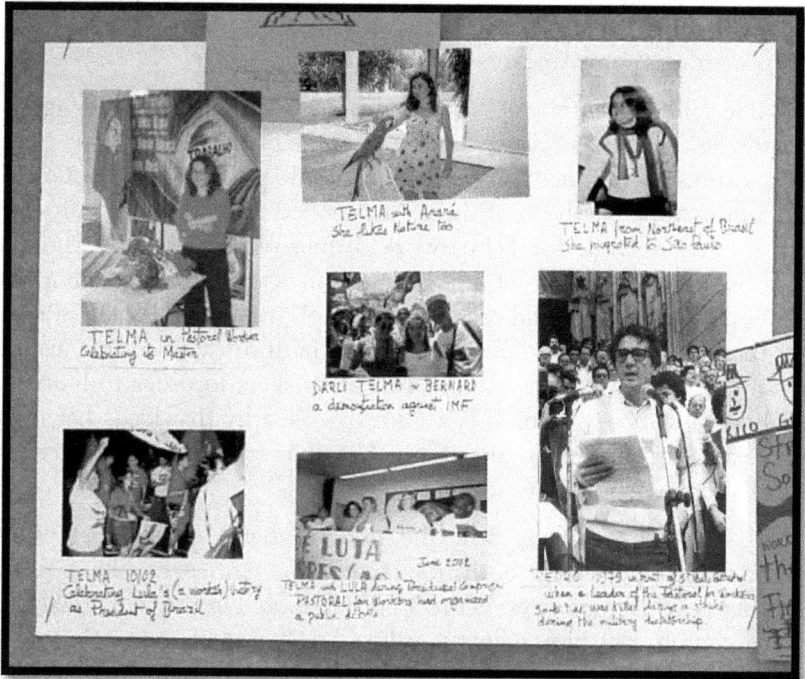

Telma and Pedro's mosaic tile from GEC's Fourth International Consultation

Chapter 12

Venkaiah in India:
Caste and New Chili Seeds

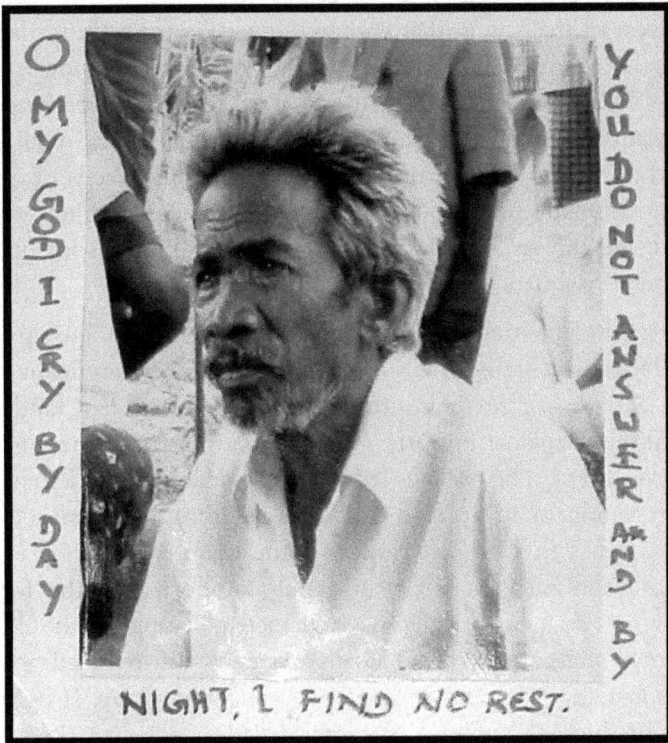

*An excerpt of Venkaiah's mosaic tile
from GEC's Fourth International Consultation*

NARRATOR: AXJ. BOSCO, SJ

Director, CITRA, Jesuit Social Centre
Secunderabad, India

Narrative Summary and Economic Background

Venkaiah was thirty years old and living in a village in the state of Andhra Pradesh in India. He struggled to make a living for himself and his family in the face of poverty and the obstacles created by the caste system. He and his family were Dalits, untouchables, the lowest of the low in that system. Unusually for a Dalit, though, Venkaiah did own two acres of land, on which he grew chilies. Then globalization entered his life in 1998 through something that was small but had a great impact: a new kind of hybrid chili seed, offered to him by a multinational corporation. The seeds promised a bumper crop, but required Venkaiah to change the way he farmed. He did realize the bumper crop the first season, but the eventual consequences were disastrous for him.

After independence in 1947, India's economic growth was characterized by state-driven economic policies, a significant share of the economy directly controlled by the government, and high protectionism against imports – including stringent barriers to foreign investment. The policies led to unsustainable fiscal deficits and total depletion of its foreign exchange reserves and climaxed in a financial crisis in 1991. In response, the country launched a program of economic liberalization, highly supported by the foreign aid donors that historically have helped to support the Indian economy. The country devalued its currency and reduced government subsidies in various sectors, including agriculture. It began to dismantle the social policies of earlier decades and let market forces play a larger role. The liberalization opened the door to greater investment by foreign companies – one of which affected Venkaiah directly. In 1995, with the implementation of the Uruguay Round Trade Agreement, India reduced its import tariffs and further opened the country to foreign investment.

NARRATIVE

The Way It Was

When the sun rose on the horizon, Venkaiah and his family had already been outside working for more than an hour. Standing with his back to the sun, Venkaiah threw a handful of leftover food into the manure pit in the back of the house and began turning the pile over to air it. Looking over his shoulder, he saw his son preparing the seeds with one of the coolie workers. Venkaiah's wife caught his eye as she returned from gathering dried leaves from the nearby fields. She set her armful of leaves by the oven and started a fire, and smiled at her husband as he stopped his work to acknowledge her.

For many years, Venkaiah had savored the pleasure of working alongside the wife and son he loved, enjoying the satisfaction of watching his crops come to harvest. But now, at the start of another season, he still had fresh in his mind how little money the last crop had brought in. Maybe this time it would be different. If not, it would be another season of just scraping by ...

Most of the time, Venkaiah and his family could make ends meet growing chilies, but it wasn't easy. They were Dalits, part of India's untouchables, so they were among the last in the village to get the things they needed for their crops. They had been last in line to get water for their field and had only a handful of coolie workers to choose from, after the bigger farmers in the higher castes had hired the ones they wanted. All his life, Venkaiah had felt that he was treated as a mere afterthought. Still, he was part of a minority of Dalits who owned some land. It surely was something extraordinary that he owned two acres of land, because almost every other Dalit was landless.

Venkaiah, like all Dalits, faced broad discrimination from higher-caste people in every part of his life. As untouchables, neither he nor any of his relatives had ever been allowed to enter the village temple. He was not even considered worthy to offer humble adoration or worship to the higher gods; he could serve only the lower gods of Hinduism. This only furthered Venkaiah's sense of his bad karma, which he accepted with the resignation typical of Hinduism. But religion is so much in the Indian blood that Venkaiah and the other Dalit farmers continued to celebrate the festivals in the way they could, in the Dalit settlements. On these occasions, like at the harvest worship, they duly performed the rites in order not to incur the wrath of their gods. These were also rare moments of joy for them.

In the village, there were separate aluminum tumblers just for Dalits. While they stood outside the tea shop, the tea was poured into the tumblers by the shopkeeper; afterwards, the Dalits would wash their tumblers and keep them in a place assigned to them. It was one more degrading thing among the many endured by the untouchables.

Though tradition and culture insisted that he accept his fate as an unclean, inferior member of the world, Venkaiah secretly longed to taste freedom and dignity. He was tired of fighting for the scraps and leftovers of the community in order to survive. He wished there were a way he wouldn't have to stand idly by and accept the destiny his society and religion had assigned to him.

Changes and an Opportunity

Meanwhile, the world beyond Venkaiah's village had begun to change. Ever since independence, India had tried to follow a "mixed economy" model that blended socialist and capitalist principles. But by 1991, the country's economic policies had led it to near bankruptcy and the government was compelled to initiate alternative economic policies in the so-called New Economic Policy (NEP). At first, Venkaiah and his family were essentially unaffected by these changes, which reduced many government subsidies and opened the economy to more global competition, including more investment in India by foreign companies.

Venkaiah continued to farm the same way he always had for about seven years. Then, right before the 1998 planting season, he heard an agriculture program on television talk about a new type of chili seed sold by a foreign company. Venkaiah had grown up in a farm family and made his living as a farmer, so he had experienced the intimidation of the big landlord farmers. But he had never heard of big foreign companies like the ones he saw advertising on television.

One morning, not long after he had seen the advertisement for the hybrid chili seeds, a salesman came to Venkaiah's door. Venkaiah demonstrated the traditional Indian hospitality and invited the man into his home. He was not used to having such well-dressed and important-looking people show any concern and respect for him, so he was interest-

ed in hearing what this man had to say. The young man introduced himself as a representative of a multinational corporation. Venkaiah was familiar with businesses as big as those of the local landlords, who owned
several farms, but the company this man spoke of seemed much larger
than even those.

The salesman's enthusiasm grew as he presented the idea of supplying
Venkaiah with a new type of seed. Venkaiah was fascinated by what he
heard. Newly engineered seeds had been developed in America that apparently yielded three and even four times as much as the local varieties
and produced longer and bigger chilies. With bigger, better crops, Venkaiah knew he could make more money. More money meant a lot to him. It
meant he could provide his family with more than subsistence food and
shelter. His heart raced as the thought of financial freedom gave hope to
his desire to break his social bondage.

With what would ultimately seal the deal for Venkaiah, the salesman
finally revealed the irresistible offer. The company would give Venkaiah
its hybrid seeds for free. Not only were the possibilities of these high-
yielding chili seeds amazing, Venkaiah thought, but they would cost nothing! Before allowing his customer to get too excited, though, the salesman
explained that there would be one simple condition. Venkaiah would receive a gross of seeds, as long as he bought fertilizer and pesticides from
the company. His family had always used their own homemade fertilizer
and almost never used pesticides, but the deal seemed too good to pass
up. If the seeds really did produce as large a crop as the company promised, the cost and use of the chemicals did not worry him. He agreed and
received the new magic seeds shortly afterwards.

The Opportunity's Outcome

Filled with hope and anticipation, Venkaiah sowed the seeds, with the
help of his wife, son, and some coolie workers, across his two acres of
land. The fertilizer and pesticides primed the soil, and they all nurtured
the crop. As the season progressed, Venkaiah waited patiently to see how
his gamble would pay off. Sure enough, and to Venkaiah's great relief and
excitement, the plants looked bigger and taller than any crop his family
had grown before. After harvesting, drying, and counting the chilies, Venkaiah marveled at the number. The yield was at least three times higher
than the previous crop cycle. Venkaiah's mind filled with how much profit the big harvest would bring and what he might do with the money.

Venkaiah took some of the money he made from early sales of the chilies and went to the city. He was excited about having money to buy more things than he normally could and experienced some freedom from the oppression and limitations of being a Dalit. He sat and took tea with other people as an equal, something he couldn't do in the village. He saw a vast array of technological products, clothes, cosmetics, and other merchandise that he now thought he might be able to afford. He returned to the village with pride, bringing a nice sari and some face powder for his wife and a transistor radio for his son. Venkaiah looked forward to continued happiness and wished he could have bought even more of what he saw in the stores.

But to his confusion and dismay, the price of chilies began to go down considerably. When Venkaiah went to sell the rest of the impressive chilies he had so proudly harvested, he could not sell them at a price high enough to cover his cost for fertilizer and pesticide. He was left with far more chilies than he could store. Apparently, the salesman had convinced many other small farmers to use the high-yielding seeds and there were simply too many chilies now in the market. Venkaiah's earlier hope and trust began to turn into despair and disappointment.

Instead of figuring out how to spend the money he expected from the chilies, Venkaiah had to look for ways to cut his losses and prepare for the next season's harvest. An immediate problem was salvaging his unsold chilies. Unfortunately, he did not own any storage facilities and now could not afford to rent storage. The big landlords had access to government subsidies for cold storage, so the year's crop would not go to waste for them. But being a poor, small farmer, and a Dalit, Venkaiah was not eligible to receive that aid.

Venkaiah wondered if small farmers could unite, but there did not seem to be enough motivation among them to unite as a cooperative group and compete with the landlords. They simply felt abandoned. Feeling betrayed by the man who sold him the seeds, Venkaiah contented himself with saving some chilies for seeds for the next sowing. He longed to have revenge on the big farmers who profited from his loss and manipulation.

The next, and more frightening, problem was Venkaiah's debt. He had taken out a loan to buy the company's fertilizer and pesticide, expecting to pay back the loan and interest with profits made from the high harvest yield. Since prices had plummeted, Venkaiah had lost money and could not repay the loan. He had to find money to help his family survive and make it through the next harvest and maybe get back on track financially. Still in debt from the first loan, he borrowed money from a big landlord – at an interest rate of 120 percent a year! His hope now lay in sowing the seeds from the new chilies, along with the local seeds, and gradually paying back the loans.

The next harvest brought the greatest devastation yet. The seeds Venkaiah had saved from the new chilies never sprouted. The only way for those large chilies to grow was to buy new seeds directly from the company. The local seeds, which had been cultivated on his family's field for generations, had a much lower yield than they had ever had before. It turned out that the company's fertilizers and pesticides had polluted Venkaiah's soil with chemicals harmful to the traditional seeds. He could not return to his old farming system. Stuck in debt and trying to work infertile land, Venkaiah's spirit began to feel sterile as well.

Local farmers and residents in Venkaiah's village look anxiously to the future

Venkaiah found himself caught in a cycle of dependence and debt. There had been some experiments by a nongovernmental organization to produce an organic fertilizer and soil that might allow farmers to go back to the old way of farming. But Venkaiah still could not grow local varieties and so was trapped into using only the company seeds and products. And, in order to afford the seeds and fertilizers, so he might eventually make enough money to pay back his debt, he had to take out still more loans. The interest on these loans from the big landlords increased and efforts to pay them back became even more futile. After a few cycles, Venkaiah confronted the fatal reality of his situation.

Venkaiah was now drowning in debt and unable to provide for his family. He felt totally ashamed as a husband, as a father, and as a man. Facing his shame, he fought the temptation to end his humiliation by killing himself, like many other small farmers were doing. But Venkaiah found strength in his family's love and clung to a fading hope. Any way out required him first to sell his precious two acres of land to pay off the loans to the landlord who had lent the money to him. This was his last resort. Venkaiah wrestled with feelings of shame, anger, disappointment, betrayal, and worry as he transferred the title to his land to the big landlord. But he was determined to sustain his life and family amidst such despair. Now he faced two alternatives: he and his family could continue working on the farm as coolie workers or they could move to the city to find jobs there.

He would have liked to stay on his land, but he was angry at the situation there. He refused to be bonded to his landlord for labor and subject his family to further degradation. Besides, there seemed to be new kinds of work available in the city, and the stigma of being a Dalit would be lessened in the common suffering of all the people there. The anonymity of the city appealed to Venkaiah much more than the unsanitary slums deterred him. So he and his family left the village. His resilience in the city would come from being a Dalit, somebody who knew suffering and degradation well, and from a family he loved.

Small farmers in Venkaiah's village discuss their situation with a friend

Life in the City

The present is grim. In the city, Venkaiah and his family disappeared into slums filled with two million other distraught people. It is difficult to know exactly what they are doing now, but survival in the slums would certainly require perseverance and resilience…

Venkaiah and his son probably get up early to work, on a construction site or perhaps pulling rickshaws. His son may resort to stealing or joining a gang. Venkaiah's wife might be a coolie worker or a domestic worker; it is hoped she avoids the perilous and degrading life of a prostitute.

Venkaiah probably sees all the billboards on the streets advertising movies, cell phones, and other foreign merchandise. After that fatal chili harvest, he had dreamed of coming back to the city as a successful farmer and spending money on these things. Now he can no longer even save enough to buy a small gift for his wife.

Venkaiah and his family probably know other Dalits who have migrated to the city. But social life in the city is very different from what it was in the village, because there is more freedom to interact with people. People do not know each other's identities and caste distinctions are less important. As a worker in the city, Venkaiah is not discriminated against as much because of his Dalit identity. But there are not many opportunities there, either.

Working in construction or pulling rickshaws, waiting to be hired for the day as a coolie or fending off assailants and disease as a prostitute, working the streets in a slum gang or driving a taxi, Venkaiah, his wife, and his son no longer work side by side. But they choose to live – or simply to survive – together. Venkaiah might persevere one day at a time, drawing on the inner hope and strength that first brought him to the city streets.

CULTURAL ANALYSIS

Venkaiah's Traditional Culture

Venkaiah lives in the traditional Hindu culture of India, a culture thousands of years old. Its main elements are below.

1. *Caste system.* Everyone's basic identity is rooted in this system. Each person belongs to a specific caste within the system, and each caste is defined and given a particular status. The individuals in the system internalize and accept the identity assigned to them and to others. The Dalits, the untouchables, are actually outside the system, below all of the castes. They do jobs considered unclean by the system.

2. *Sense of community.* There is a focus on sharing and mutual support. The community provides support for people when they cannot function alone. At the same time there is no real feeling of individuality in the Western sense of the word. There is also a tradition of hospitality and helpfulness to guests and to strangers.

3. *Strong family bonds.* There is a clearly delineated network of kin, including extended family, and a sense of loyalty to it in the face of outside threats. Roles are spelled out very specifically. Marital relationships are seen as long-lasting and elders are respected.

4. *Patriarchal social order.* Women are assigned a subordinate role and are expected to be submissive to men.

5. *Spiritual outlook on life.* There is a sense of the divine in nature. Religion is the lens through which people see life, as opposed to, for example, the lens of reason or science. This does not mean that people are more spiritual, but that religion is the common idiom, much as it was in medieval Europe. This trait serves as a real anchor for people and gives meaning to their lives, even when in very difficult circumstances. "God has given me birth, so he will look after me" is often heard.

6. *Fatalistic and stoic outlook on life.* There is an easy resignation to what is seen as destiny. This is not a religious belief in divine control, but helplessness in the face of overwhelming situations. Patriarchy and the caste system are seen as just the way things are. Related to this trait is a tendency to look up to a king figure, to someone seen as superior, to take charge and rule and solve all problems.

7. *Openness to the new.* Ability to assimilate different traditions, cultures, religions, etc. Instead of an attitude of "either/or," there is a tendency to think in terms of "both/and."

8. *Simplicity and resilience.* The people work hard, make little, and can survive with very little in the way of material things. Hard times and devastating events are accepted as the way life is and people do what they must to carry on.

Venkaiah's Critical Decisions

1. He decided to accept the hybrid chili seeds freely offered to him.

What were his options? He could have refused to accept the new variety of seed and thus change his way of farming; there was nothing that compelled him to do it, beyond the expectation of a higher crop yield. He could have continued planting the kind of seed he had used in the past.

What cultural values lay behind his decision? Venkaiah was willing to take the seeds and try something new, even though he had spent his life farming in the old way. He was hoping to improve his family's financial situation and maybe find a way out of the caste system.

What cultural values were reflected in the reactions of the other people in his life to this decision? We have no information about this.

2. He decided to keep living when he realized that he was ruined financially and had to sell his farm.

What were his options? He could have committed suicide. Many small farmers in India in his situation – facing economic ruin and filled with shame – make that choice every year.

What cultural values lay behind his decision? His love for his family gave him the strength to carry on.

What cultural values were reflected in the reactions of the other people in his life to this decision? Many other small farmers in a similar situation confronted this same choice. In spite of a large number of suicides, most of them, like Venkaiah, chose to live.

3. He decided to go to the city with his wife and son after he sold his farm.

What were his options? He could have stayed in his village and worked what used to be his land – or someone else's land – as a daily paid laborer, a coolie.

What cultural values lay behind his decision? He wanted to make a new life for himself and his family in a place that allowed greater freedom from the caste system.

What cultural values were reflected in the reactions of the other people in his life to this decision? Many other Dalits also were ruined and went to the city. It is possible that they, like Venkaiah, also wanted a new life.

Note: The main trait at work in Venkaiah is his strong sense of *family*. It influenced him to try the new seeds, to keep on living after he was ruined, and to move to the city. *Caste* plays a large part as well, but in a negative sense; two of his decisions were impelled by his hope that he and his family could escape its confines. Other traits also influenced him. He is *open to new things*, such as the hybrid seeds, even though it means changing his traditional way of farming. He feels responsible for his wife and son, something that arises out of *patriarchy*. He has a deep-rooted *spiritual outlook* on life, which strengthens him against the traditional cultural *fatalism* that might have led him to kill himself. Finally, he was not alone in his decisions; he was one of many in the *community* of Dalits going through the same experiences and facing the same choices.

Changes in Venkaiah's Life

The changes in Venkaiah's life stemmed from one thing: his decision to plant the hybrid chili seeds that a foreign multinational company offered to him, on the condition that he buy their fertilizer and herbicide. Everything that happened to him after that – going into debt, having to sell his farm, leaving his village – is linked to that one action.

Consumption

In his early life, Venkaiah couldn't afford many consumer goods. There was a common TV for everyone in the village, which aired agricultural and health programs. It was from one of those programs that he first heard about the hybrid seeds. After his first bumper crop of chilies, Venkaiah's income increased. He was able to travel to the city and he bought some things for his family, little luxuries like a new sari and face powder for his wife and a transistor radio for his son. He was happy he could do this. For him, the extra money meant freedom: the freedom to go to the city to escape the oppression that he, a Dalit, experienced in the village, and the freedom that came with more consumer choices.

But when the market was flooded with chilies, his income went down and this brief period of extra money and freedom ended. He was left with fewer options. In fact, he was worse off than before, because now he was in debt and – as he would discover later – could not get out of it. Not only that, his trip to the city exposed him to advertising and new products, so he was more aware now of all the things that he could not afford than he had been earlier. He was angry and disillusioned.

Again, the changes in Venkaiah's consumption followed the pattern of first an upswing and then a dramatic fall.

Production

Venkaiah was a chili farmer his whole life, growing a local variety of chilies. Every year he sold them in the market and extracted seeds from them, which he then planted to grow the next crop. These chilies did not produce great yields, but on the other hand they also required little investment. He was able to survive.

But all this changed when he decided to use the hybrid seeds. Willing to try new things, he went from traditional agriculture to modern agriculture involving chemicals and technology. He was hopeful at the possibilities it offered for more money and more freedom. But Venkaiah did not have access to the other parts of modern agriculture, like marketing and working capital finance. The chili prices dropped, and he fell into debt, causing worry and fear. Then things became worse: he tried to use his old seeds and was shocked to discover that they would no longer grow well in the field contaminated with the new chemicals. He was unable to repay his debt and eventually had to sell his farm, leaving him angry and full of despair. Looking for another source of income, he and his family moved to the city.

So Venkaiah moved from agriculture as a way of making a living into, we assume, menial work in the city, such as cleaning streets or running errands or doing construction. His options for work became more precarious. For him, the new chili seeds meant an initial upward movement in his source of livelihood as the first bumper crop was realized, with the hope of improving his life, and then a sharp downward turn that left him worse off than before.

Migration

Moving around – even leaving his village – was not something Venkaiah often did in the past. For most people in his village, migrating had not been very common, although the opening of the Indian economy led to a greater movement from rural areas to the cities, as people looked for work and for a better life. This probably influenced Venkaiah's decision to go to the city; others were also doing it.

Venkaiah migrated to the city under duress, after he lost his house and his farm. He also left behind his village habits and customs and the security they provided. He went empty-handed to the city, where conditions are not good in many ways. One can expect that in the city he experiences uncertainty and fear, but also excitement. The city gives him hope for the freedom that comes with not being so easily identified as a Dalit and perhaps the chance to make a new life for himself and his family.

Social Relations

The caste system undergirds every aspect of Venkaiah's life. In the village he was allowed to relate as an equal only to other Dalits, was shunned by everyone else, and was allowed to worship only lesser gods. Even basic freedoms such as access to water for irrigation were severely limited for him. The system shaped his identity, and a Dalit is a negative identity. He felt excluded and rejected; treated as inferior by the other castes, he felt inferior. He was oppressed and had no real freedom in the village. This gave him a deep-rooted anger and hopelessness. His decision to try the hybrid seeds, and later his new consumption, were motivated at least in part by his desire to escape the caste system.

In the city he found a place where he was not known as a Dalit, where he experienced at least a degree of freedom from the caste system that bound him so tightly in the village. There he was known and recognized; in the city he was unknown and anonymous. Perhaps it is the freedom he felt there that gave him an incentive to return to the city a second time, after he lost his farm and was looking for a new life.

As his efforts with the new seeds turned into a disaster, Venkaiah became more and more aware of the system's injustice. He felt a great deal of anger towards the people who benefited from the chili seeds. He was angry at the large farmers whose profits have increased due to greater yields. He was angry at the government that does not make subsidies available to small farmers. He was angry at the company that originally offered the seeds and profited from them. His whole ability to trust within the village community was eroded by his experiences. His treatment by the higher castes had never inspired trust in him; later, he trusted the people who sold him the seeds but that trust was betrayed. Outside his family and the Dalit community, Venkaiah had little reason to trust anybody.

As the man in the family, Venkaiah was always responsible for providing for his family and making all the decisions. Now, the consequences of those decisions include life or death. Many farmers in his situation – bankrupt and ashamed – have chosen suicide. He does have a great feeling of shame at not being able to repay his debts, but he did not choose to kill himself. There was little he could offer his family, but he chose to offer life and the hope that in the city things will be different. Perhaps they will connect with other Dalits there.

Political Power Relations

For Venkaiah the meaning of political power has always been rooted in the caste system and his local community. In the past, he was aware of the local government in his village and the large farmers, but they were basically out of reach for him. They were simply there, reminders of the system in which he lived, where he occupied the lowest rung.

With the economic opening of India, other actors entered Venkaiah's world and affected him, some directly and some indirectly. Among other things, this opening allowed for an expanded role for multinational corporations in India. It was one of these corporations that gave Venkaiah the hybrid seeds. The national government also introduced new policies that reduced many subsidies, such as agricultural ones, that had previously benefited people like Venkaiah. The banks and the big farmers took on larger roles in Venkaiah's life more recently. He had to watch as the banks granted loans at reasonable interest rates to the more prosperous farmers, while only informal lenders would lend to him and only at extremely high rates, 20 percent a month or more.

The Indian central government made an agreement with multinational corporations to protect the farmers, but the remedial measures took a long time to take effect. Laws and provisions for enforcing them are on the books, but with delays and corruption Venkaiah was not able to take advantage of them. A nongovernmental organization (NGO) tried to help small farmers use the old seeds, but their efforts did not work for Venkaiah because the soil was too contaminated. The NGOs also tried to form cooperatives for these farmers but they were unsuccessful, with the exception of a milk cooperative.

All the old actors, and some new ones, now affect his life more, but he is just as powerless to influence them or benefit from them. For example, he couldn't get government subsidies to build storage facilities for his excess chilies but the bigger farmers could. This kind of unfairness in the political arena is nothing new to Venkaiah; he has lived with it his whole life. But with the new global actors in the scene, the consequences to him are worse. He is aware of the injustice, and is left feeling angry and powerless.

Religious Experience and Expression

The changes in Venkaiah's life include some changes in how he experiences God. In the village, he worshipped the lesser gods that the caste system allowed him to worship, and found some joy in celebrating festivals and rituals. He drew energy from them and from his Dalit community. He believed that the gods took care of him and his family, and provided the fruit of his hard work. At the same time, he also believed that the gods were partial, working against him and condoning the discrimination of the caste system. But whatever happened to him was his karma, his fate.

Then he lost everything he owned. The gods were not taking care of him any more; instead they were taking away the fruit of all his work. He didn't have enough to survive. He felt that the gods were not only partial but unresponsive; he felt alienated from them, from religion, and from other human beings. However, in the anonymity of the city, where caste does not have so strong a hold, he may be able to look at religion with new eyes. He may begin to sense that liberation comes from throwing out the old form of religion and becoming a Buddhist or a Christian, as other Dalits have done, because God cannot be unjust.

INTERPRETATION

India's Economic Globalization and Venkaiah

India's inward-looking economy, with its large trade and fiscal deficits, became unsustainable by the end of the 1980s. A financial crisis in 1991 just sealed its fate. A more open economy, with a lesser role for the state and a greater exposure to international forces, was the alternative. Nothing short of that would have been acceptable to the international financial community of donor countries and multilateral agencies on which India depended.

The foreign investment to which India opened its doors more widely is how the global economy entered Venkaiah's life. The chili seeds from the multinational company offer Venkaiah participation in new technology that will increase the productivity of his farm and, therefore, his income and living standard – the usual benefits anticipated by foreign investment in a country. What goes wrong in Venkaiah's case? The seeds indeed deliver the promised bumper crop for him. But, unfortunately, they also deliver bumper crops for all the other farmers who adopted the new seeds. Nobody anticipated what would happen when everybody's bumper crops came to the market! The big farmers from the upper castes manage, because they have access to subsidized cold storage. However, Venkaiah is a Dalit and does not have this opportunity. The only opportunity he can see is to abandon the new and go back to his old seeds and farming methods. Unfortunately, again, it is too late for him. In the process of adopting the new seeds, he had to give up his traditional way of farming, in which he used manure for fertilizer and no chemicals for herbicides and pesticides. But chemicals came attached to the new hybrid seeds – another technological innovation! Now the new technologies have contaminated his soil and do not allow him to return to the old farming methods. He has become dependent on the new seeds, which have a terminator gene – meaning they are sterile and do not germinate when replanted – and the accompanying chemicals. With mounting debt, Venkaiah cannot afford this dependency and is trapped. As a result, he loses his precious two acres in bankruptcy.

The new seeds might have worked for Venkaiah if he had had access to cold storage and credit at a reasonable interest rate. Also, there was a need to find a new market for all the additional chilies being produced in aggregate. The new seeds work in many developed countries. Ultimately, the bumper crops could have made it possible not only for Venkaiah to be better off economically, but also for chili consumers in India and elsewhere to be able to buy better and bigger chilies at a lower price. But in Venkaiah's situation, one could have predicted that was not going to happen. The market structures to support such an outcome for him – credit, warehousing capabilities, and market research and development – were underdeveloped. The caste system added another impediment that would not let it work for Venkaiah.

Venkaiah's economic bankruptcy is not a good business outcome for the multinational companies, either. They do not want people to use their products for one or two crop cycles; they would rather have Venkaiah be a buyer of both seeds and the accompanying chemicals into the indefinite future. However, for the multinational company, recovering from this bad decision might be at most a blip in their quarterly earnings. For Venkaiah, it is economic devastation.

Venkaiah as a Person

At the start of this narrative, Venkaiah's life in the village was already one of injustice. As a Dalit, he had always been oppressed. Nonetheless, he could make a living and support his family by cultivating his two acres of land – an unusual holding for a Dalit. Also, unfair as it was, he could see and accept his place in his society. But as Venkaiah's farming nightmare unfolded, he saw this social system break down, well beyond the unfairness he already knew. He witnessed the end of life as he had known it.

He had trusted the multinational company that gave him the seeds, daring to hope they would bring some freedom. But his relationship with the company soon became just another manifestation of the corruption that he had been accustomed to all his life. Even worse, his sense of self-respect, arising out of owning his own farm, was shattered when he lost it. That feeling of self-respect had upheld him in the past, in dealing with the other farmers and people in the village who were higher caste. But he no longer had that either and his experience of the caste system became even worse.

Furthermore, in the village, Venkaiah was chided, marginalized, and rejected – but at least he was known to everyone there. He had an identity and was recognized as a person. He had a sense of belonging and solidarity with his Dalit community. Even more, his experience of exclusion and segregation brought him an element of freedom within that Dalit group. But in leaving the village Venkaiah lost his sense of belonging. In the city, there is greater anonymity and a diminishing of the Dalit spirit; this very anonymity could lead to alienation.

Notwithstanding Venkaiah's nightmare, his experience with the hybrid seeds and his initial experience of freedom in the city opened his eyes. It helped him, if only temporarily, break out of the bounds of the caste system into the anonymity of the city and a few more material things. He experienced being a fuller human being, able to act, able to move from being a victim to being an actor. But after the chili prices collapsed, most of this glimpse of freedom was taken away from him, yet the experience had offered him a new way of seeing how things could be and how he could be.

That experience also made him more attentive. He was exposed to market forces – to something bigger than his village – and to variations in the structure of his society. He could now compare the city and the village and how the caste system operated in each place. From this, he gained an understanding of the market forces and social structures that he didn't have before. However, he did not have the freedom to choose among many alternatives or to effect any positive changes in the caste system or his financial situation. He therefore could not address the root problems. So he learned and grew, but at the same time could not do anything with this new knowledge. His knowledge of Dalit oppression may offer him hope (to fight for justice) or it may reinforce despair (and a feeling of inevitability) in the future. This is unclear.

One could see Venkaiah's choice to move to the city either as an act of desperation, made under duress, or as a sign of strength, a strength that stemmed from the Dalit spirit of survival and risk-taking. We can further see it as an act of freedom, a resolve to make the one decision left to him in the face of the larger world of caste and bankruptcy over which he has no control. He was able to experience the most basic of human freedoms: to choose life and hope in the city, over death (suicide) and desperation in bankruptcy. However, there are few other human freedoms left to him.

But one thing we can expect that Venkaiah took with him from the village to the city was his sense of responsibility and belonging in his family. Family is a driving force in his life. It is the source of energy and love that leads him to overcome the shame caused by the bankruptcy. It motivated him to leave the village, where he would have remained only a coolie, a wage worker, and a Dalit, and go to the city to try to build a new life. Family allows him to continue to struggle and to live, rather than kill himself. He finds hope and love in his family – and thus is able to be for others. Traditional patriarchy helps him do this. His son is his hope for the future. He hopes his son will not suffer from Dalit oppression as strongly as he has, and that, as a result, he will be able to make a good life for himself and have more economic security. It is a thread of hope.

But in the wider world – outside his family and the Dalit community – Venkaiah does not have much hope. He sees the injustice in his predicament, and is angry toward some of the people and groups involved, whom he sees as either corrupt or unreachable. But at the same time he also feels that his situation is simply a reflection of his unfortunate life, the way things are. It is too big a problem for him, or anyone, to solve. He has a sense of shame about losing his farm and way of life, and feels powerless to change anything.

He used to find meaning in his religion, in his karma or fate, but now, after all the disastrous events of his life, Venkaiah feels alienated from God. He feels that God is partial and unresponsive and that his karma is negative. Still, he is also able to hold the seemingly contradictory idea that God continues to care for the Dalit migrants and at least the minor gods offer them some protection. He has a deep religious orientation that seems to come partly from his culture and partly from within him. It has motivated him to work hard his whole life. It gave him resilience to survive in the face of the caste system and is now pushing him to continue to live. He has chosen the ultimate good: survival and life.

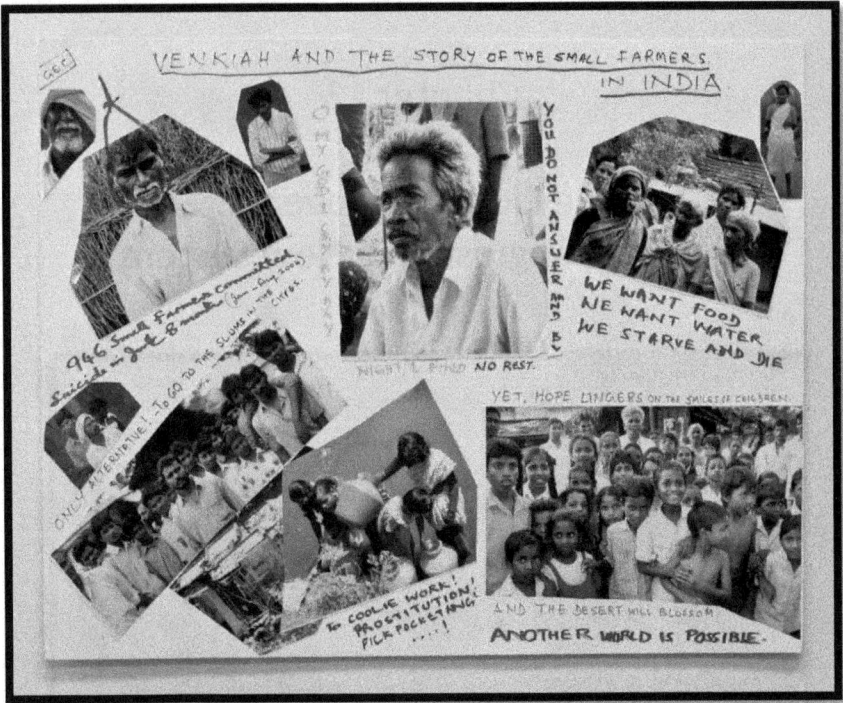

Venkaiah's mosaic tile from GEC's Fourth International Consultation

Chapter 13

Tine Ljubić in Slovenia:
Joy and Anguish in a New System

Symbols of the past and the present juxtaposed on a street in Ljubljana

NARRATOR: ROBIN SCHWEIGER, SJ

Country Director, Jesuit Refugee Service
Ljubljana, Slovenia

Narrative Summary and Economic Background

Tine's life changed with the fall of the Berlin wall in 1989 and even more dramatically in 1991, the year Slovenia became independent of the former Yugoslavia. Soon thereafter, the new nation adopted democratic rules and opted for a capitalistic economic system open to global markets. The change of political regime brought many new freedoms and economic opportunities to the country. Tine was then in his thirties and working in a small government office of the Yugoslav federal system in Ljubljana, where he grew up. Soon he saw his old job transformed, as his office became part of the ministry in charge of privatizations in the newly formed Slovene state. Tine readily accepted the capitalist principles. Eventually, facing a rising cost of living and enticed by a higher salary, he quit his government job to work for a private investment company selling international mutual funds. Tine, now in his forties, lives with his wife and two daughters in one of Ljubljana's suburbs. He enjoys his new freedoms and higher standard of living, but he wrestles with the changes that the new socioeconomic system has brought to his family and to the rest of the society.

Before independence, Slovenia's economy was interdependent with the rest of Yugoslavia, with a very high level of trade with the other six republics. With independence and the change in economic system, the level of trade with these republics, many of which were now independent countries, declined because of the war that followed. But now trade is truly international and is still a significant part of the economy: Slovenia's annual volume of trade – measured as the sum of exports and imports – remains larger than the value of its annual production. As a small country, it needs to import many goods, both for domestic consumption and manufacturing, and it exports a significant share of its production.

NARRATIVE

It was November 9, 1989, and Tine watched the television with relief and excitement. Masses of men, women, and children from East Germany were streaming through the opening in the tall, thick Berlin Wall and were greeted and cheered by thousands of West Berliners. Many jubilant people climbed to the top of the despised Wall that was covered with barbed wire and graffiti and they were shouting in triumph and celebration. The Berlin Wall had stood as a symbol of division, of the Cold War mentality between the United States of America and the Soviet Union's communist regime for decades. Now, on this day, several weeks after the resignation of East Germany's long-time communist leader Erich Honecker, Tine could see the actual physical destruction of the Wall as the East German government opened its borders to the West.

Before the Opening

Tine Ljubić grew up in the former Yugoslavia, a communist country. He was born in the region that is now Croatia but moved with his family when he was very young to Slovenia, in the north. Tine's father was an officer in the Yugoslav army and a member of the Communist Party, and was thus steeped in the country's Marxist philosophy. Tine grew up with this communist world view. Communist ideology taught his parents, and Tine, that there is no God. From the teaching of the schools and from society in general, especially the media, Tine heard the Catholic Church called "internal enemy number one." Christians suffered a great deal of discrimination in all arenas, particularly in getting leading positions in the workplace. They were treated and felt as second class citizens.

Tine respected his parents' beliefs and the Yugoslav state's promotion of socialism with atheism – but he always felt a subtle desire to search beyond these ideas. Yet he was still a man of his culture and time. He studied economics in school and then took a job in a marginal government office that was part of the federal system. On the surface, nothing was changing in Slovenia, and Tine's life seemed to be like that of most Slovenians during that time. But under the surface, communism was nearing the end of its hold over Yugoslavia, and Tine was intensifying his search for a spiritual life.

The Country Changes

The fall of the Berlin Wall brought a world of change to Central and Eastern Europe. It was the start of something new and it was exciting for people who had been living under communism. Tine visited Berlin just a few months after the Wall fell, and for him this was a time of precious opportunities that had been denied to him before. It was also the time to search for a deeper meaning in his life.

Tine visited many churches, met diverse people, and explored many different religions. When he came back from his trip, he kept traveling and also read a wide variety of religious books. Finally, he found he was most attracted to the Catholic Church and to the Jesuits in particular. In the spring of 1991, he made a guided retreat. This retreat, and the conversations he had with one of the priests, was a great help in his spiritual growth. About a month later, when he was in Medugorje in Bosnia and Herzegovina, Tine decided to join the Catholic Church. In August, he was baptized and went on a retreat with his fiancée to prepare for their wedding in October of that year.

Around the same time that Tine was on his spiritual journey, Yugoslavia was undergoing a major upheaval. After a referendum in December 1990, in which 88.5 percent of the people voted for a sovereign and independent Slovenia, it broke with Yugoslavia. This was just a few days after Tine's conversion experience. He was traveling home from Medugorje at the time and could feel the tension in the air. His train was stopped and checked by soldiers many times. Tine was frightened of this war that was happening in a country built on the once-sacred socialist spirit. He worried about what would happen to the relationships with the people of the different ethnic groups then living in Slovenia. He also worried about the members of his family who lived in the southern part of Yugoslavia.

But Slovenia's war with Yugoslavia, which followed its declaration of independence, proved to be short-lived and it claimed victory after a few days. By 1992 it was internationally recognized as a sovereign state. It immediately began an extensive transformation. The fall of the Berlin Wall had already initiated a process of liberation in Slovenia; after independence, the government moved quickly to establish a capitalist democracy. The country experienced a renewed creativity, and a sense of responsibility and solidarity, as people learned how to express their freedom while at the same time respecting the freedom of others.

Tine's Life Changes

Tine experienced changes in his life that paralleled the national shifts. For one thing, his government job was transformed. His government office, which was formerly at the periphery of the former Yugoslav federal system, was now a central decision-making ministry managing the process of privatizing government-owned enterprises in Slovenia. Tine was forced to adjust virtually overnight from being an unimportant government official in a communist state to a significant government employee in a newly-born capitalist nation.

Tine enjoyed his new work. Then, after work, he read books on capitalism, books that opened his eyes to worlds that his old economics professors had never allowed him to see. His work also gave him the chance to travel abroad to learn how to build the new economic system and how to manage the difficulties of the transition from the old system to the new. Eventually, Tine embraced wholeheartedly capitalism's principles and private ownership. He appreciated how capitalism was bringing many new freedoms and opportunities to Slovenians, who had been suffering the debilitating effects of communism. Accustomed to the Marxist rhetoric of solidarity and community, he was intrigued by the competitive and individualistic nature of capitalism, which claimed to give people freedom and to reward creative and active thinkers.

Along with the economic changes, Slovenia also revamped its education system. One of Tine's bosses recognized his talents and offered him the chance to enter a new master's program in business administration. Tine gratefully accepted the offer. The Slovenian MBA program was designed to provide to a nation of citizens familiar only with communism an education in how capitalism worked in practice. Most of the courses Tine took were taught by foreign professors with business experience in the Western world. He learned a great deal, and came to a greater understanding of capitalism and market economics.

However, Tine wanted more intellectual challenge than his government job provided. So when he was offered a position with a higher salary at one of the new private investment companies, he took it. The job involved selling international mutual funds.

In searching for a job in the private sector, Tine appreciated the significant increase in job options he had; however, he also realized that these options involved increasing competition among workers. He could see it in what was happening in local industry, which previously had produced under the state's protection and now had to compete with more efficient foreign companies. This new reality affected Tine's family directly: his wife lost her job in a textile company that could not compete with new imports from the West. She was forty-three years old and although she had professional credentials, it was not possible for her to get a job. Tine was aware of the high level of unemployment in the country and was happy that he had good work. He prayed that his wife would also find a job.

As part of the government's privatization process, it granted to its citizens vouchers that could be used to buy shares in government enterprises. Overnight, everyone became a shareholder in Slovenian companies. But many people did not know how to deal with this new wealth or the possibilities it provided. Some people became very rich by investing wisely; others simply sold the vouchers and enjoyed some of the luxuries now available.

Tine chose to sell his vouchers and used the proceeds, along with his new higher income, to buy a car and a house in the suburbs. There were dozens of attractive cars available in foreign car dealerships that had opened in Ljubljana since Slovenia's independence. Tine marveled at the impressive and luxurious technology he could now afford. Before, there had been only three or four types of cars, made in the Eastern bloc countries, from which to choose.

But Tine refused to splurge. He had misgivings about the sudden change in consumer culture. Even though some people, like him, were becoming successful and were living better, many others had not been so fortunate. He empathized with those who had suffered from the change. On the other hand, his house and his car were a great source of pride for him. Being able to say that these things were his own gave him and his family a sense of social belonging. Of course, along with the benefits of owning property came the worries of how to take care of it and make these riches grow.

Tine's Conflicts

As Tine made more money and reaped the benefits of the nation's new freedom and room for individuality, he also started to experience an increase in the cost of living. He wished he had been able to afford to buy a home in Ljubljana instead of the suburbs, but the cost of housing in the city had skyrocketed. He also now had to pay for health care and for many other services previously provided by the state, including his retirement. He had had free sports and music lessons when he was a child; now he had to pay for them for his six- and eight-year-old daughters. The children also had new extracurricular opportunities, things that hadn't been available when he was young, but they too cost money. The girls were becoming part of the e-generation, as new technology opened their world to computers and the Internet. Tine wanted his children to have these opportunities.

To meet these increased demands for money, and with his wife not able to find a full-time job, Tine started working longer hours and had much less time to spend with his family and friends. He was happy with his job but torn between the intensities of work and his desire to spend more time with his family. One thing that did make it easier for him to endure the tension was the support of his family: his parents, who never objected to his decision to become Catholic, and his wife and children, who understood the economic need for him to work long hours.

Tine couldn't help but think that this tension he felt between family and work was simply the price he had to pay for the new system. Although he was happy with the new freedoms and luxuries, he reminisced about the benefits of the old system. Communism had provided security and more time with family and friends. There were fewer job options but more job and retirement security. The health care may not have been superb but it was provided by the state. Even the option of free sports was hard to leave behind.

Tine also worried about how globalization had begun to influence local customs. A shopping center designed to satisfy new consumer demands had popped up a few miles away from Tine's new house in the suburbs. The stores were now even open on Sundays. Finding work on Sunday unfair, Tine was surprised that workers did not complain. But he knew that anyone feeling exploited was afraid of resisting and losing his or her job – especially women. The new shopping centers also provided a cultural and social setting. Tine's friends had begun going to the centers not to buy anything but just to window-shop and socialize. They could now meet people there and spend time with friends and family. Many shopping centers were even turning into cultural centers that hosted concerts and showed movies. Tine did not like the atmosphere that these shopping centers created and wished his family would not go to them.

The foreign goods, media, and new business concepts introduced to Slovenia brought completely new forms of entertainment, food, fashions, and other products into Tine's life. The new movie centers were unlike any place Tine had seen. When he took his children to see a movie after the new cinema opened, he had a choice of ten different movies to watch in the same building. Before, he had watched whatever few movies were available at the small-screen theater they had in town. Tine was apprehensive about the ongoing Americanization of his society and culture. Along with Western-style entertainment and buildings, Tine was concerned about the flood of American consumerism and media he was seeing, even at home. His daughters wanted to always eat at the new McDonald's down the road, they kept asking their mother to buy them the newest foreign style of shoes and clothes, and they loved to watch the funny American shows on television.

Tine struggled with these tensions. On the one hand, he was content with the comfortable lifestyle afforded by the freedom and economic benefits of capitalism. On the other hand, he experienced the demands and fatigue of market competition and never-ending suggestions for more material consumption. He was happy with the money he could earn now, but felt sorry for those who had failed and were disadvantaged under the new economic system. And, though his job gave him a good amount of money, he really couldn't enjoy it because he hardly ever saw his family. His work led to increasing strains on his marriage. He began asking, "Is this all there is?" and "How can I live in a burned-out marriage?" As he tried to address the anxieties that led to these questions, he began to play sports to relieve his tension. He also started to make sure he had family time on weekends.

The Present

Tine's mind finds relief as his legs begin to ache after a five-mile run. Every stride releases the accumulated stress of a full day of selling mutual funds. It is late when he finally returns home. Walking through the door, it doesn't seem that he has missed much. His daughters sit in front of the computer surfing the Internet while his wife quietly prepares dinner. They are lucky to fit in the time to eat dinner together tonight, but Tine is even more relieved that it is finally the weekend and he did not have to bring any work home with him.

Saturday morning he wakes his wife to go on a walk. They usually find time to spend alone together on the weekends to make up for the busyness and distance of the week. After the walk, he puts his daughters' bikes in the back of the car and drives his family to the park. There, he and his wife sit together quietly as the girls ride by. His younger daughter asks if they can go to McDonald's for lunch and maybe even see a movie afterwards. The girls look happy and satisfied. He is exhausted but thankful to be with his family. Tine thinks ahead to the prayers he will offer in church tomorrow. He knows that his only hope and trust are in God's love and help.

CULTURAL ANALYSIS

Tine's Traditional Culture

The Slovenian culture goes back a thousand years, even though the Slovenian people developed a national consciousness only in the nineteenth century. Bordered by Austria and Italy on one side with Hungary and Croatia on the other side, the culture is more akin to that of Western Europe than to the other groups in the former Yugoslavia.

1. *Industriousness and frugality.* Hard work is perhaps the most commonly mentioned trait of the Slovenian people.

2. *Appreciation of political freedom.* An appreciation of political freedom – to associate, to speak, to write, to travel, and so on – grew out of centuries under foreign rule and decades under communism.

3. *Appreciation of economic opportunity.* Slovenians value the chance to achieve economic success.

4. *Strong nuclear family.* The core family unit, in contrast to the extended family, is highly valued.

5. *Deep Christian religious roots.* Deep Christian values have persisted, despite the many years of atheistic communist rule.

Tine's Critical Decisions

1. He decided to pursue an MBA when his government job gave him the chance to do so.

What were his options? He did not have to go into the degree program; he had the option of declining the offer.

What cultural values lay behind his decision? He was interested in capitalism and wanted to learn more about it. But what really motivated him was his desire for improvement, for economic success. The degree was an investment in his future, a way for him to advance. His wife, and many other people, losing their jobs also made him aware of the better training now necessary to have a good job.

What cultural values were reflected in the reactions of the other people in his life to this decision? We have no information on the reactions of other employees in his government office or his family.

2. Tine decided to leave his government job and take one in the private sector.

What were his options? He could have stayed in his current job; there was no pressure to leave. In fact, his work had grown in importance and prestige since the country's independence.

What cultural values lay behind his decision? He wanted to succeed economically. He realized that the private sector offered better opportunities for success than the public sector. He knew that he would have to work harder, and that the competition would be greater, but he was willing to accept these drawbacks in light of the potential benefits.

What cultural values were reflected in the reactions of the other people in his life to this decision? We have no information about this, but because of the privatization effort in the country, many other people were probably taking similar actions.

3. He decided to put the money he received from the government vouchers toward buying a house and a car.

What were his options? Tine could have used the money to invest in the emerging stock market, which would have been a wise long-range investment strategy – and a move in keeping with his desire for economic success. He also could have used it for personal consumption, such as clothing, entertainment, and so on.

What cultural values lay behind his decision? Buying a house and a car benefited his family in a direct and immediate way and was also a personal investment.

What cultural values were reflected in the reactions of the other people in his life to this decision? We have no information about this; but many people in the country did similar things with the vouchers.

Note: In Tine's decisions to get an MBA and to work in the private sector, he is motivated by his great appreciation of *economic opportunity*. He also shows the trait of *industriousness*: those choices required not only change but hard work. His decision to invest the voucher money in a house expresses *frugality*. *Family bonds* are also important to him. Under all of his decisions, one can see a man exercising his newly acquired *freedoms*. Other Slovenians who made similar decisions – working in the private sector and investing their voucher money – were also motivated by *economic opportunity, industriousness, and frugality*.

Changes in Tine's Life

Major and sudden sociopolitical changes have taken place in Tine's world and they are all rooted in the political changes of 1989. Two years after that, Slovenia became an independent nation for the first time in its history and the communist system fell after a forty-five year reign. Democracy was officially established, new political institutions emerged, and a capitalistic economic system was adopted. In 2004 Slovenia joined the European Union. In 2007 it became the thirteenth member of the Euro zone and a member of the Schengen area of citizens' free circulation within the E.U. Any one of these changes would have been significant; taken together, they caused a complete restructuring of Slovenian society and Tine's life.

Consumption

Kakršna je setev, takšna je žetev: What you sow, you harvest.

Slovenia's increased opening to international trade and investment resulted in a much greater availability of goods and services in every category in the economy. Today, Tine has a much higher income, as well as many more consumption and investment options than were possible under communism, when the choices were very limited. He can choose from a greater variety of things, and often higher-quality things, than before.

When he bought his car, he could choose from among many cars made in the West, instead of only the three Yugoslav-made cars previously available.

Western businesses such as McDonald's are widespread, shopping malls are springing up, and American television shows are becoming very popular. His family has a computer and Internet access. But all these new possibilities bring more choices and more decisions to make and this creates a great deal of stress for him. Also, the changes are affecting the traditional culture around him. Tine worries about the impact of all this foreign influence on the Slovenian sense of identity.

However, Tine's new freedom to choose is limited by several factors. For one thing, these new foreign goods tend to be more expensive than the domestic ones previously available. New opportunities, such as some of the children's extracurricular activities, are expensive. Others that used to be free because of government subsidies now charge a fee. In addition, the government no longer provides many of the basic social services that it did formerly, such as health care, so they must be bought in the private market. Because of this, he worries about what will happen when he retires.

The cost of living has gone up and the pressure to earn an ever-higher income has increased. But, overall, Tine is able to afford more material things and enjoys a great freedom to choose among them.

Production

> *Zrno na zrno pogača, kamen na kamen palača:* Grain to grain: bread. Stone to stone: castle. Or: step by step you can build big things.

The old communist system was a command system; it provided relatively predictable and undemanding working conditions, and job security, but there was little opportunity for personal economic success. Many more opportunities exist now in the market-driven system: new jobs and new ways for people to make money. The choices available to Tine have grown dramatically.

He used to work in a small government office in the former Yugoslavia; it was a stable position that made few demands on him. After Slovenia opened its economy, his job became central to the government's policy of privatizing government assets. Later, Tine left that job and joined the private financial services industry. Tine was glad he could take advantage of this kind of job flexibility, which did not exist under the old communist system.

But along with more flexibility and more opportunities for success has come greater competition. Slovenia is filled with a wide range of good-quality imports from countries with cheaper labor or more advanced technology. Local inefficiencies have been exposed and domestic sales have suffered. This led to about one-third of the domestic work force being made redundant, causing significant unemployment. Tine's wife, who used to work in a textile company, lost her job when the company could not compete with imports from the West. She was able to find part-time work but not permanent employment. Tine finds that his job is more competitive as well. He sells financial investment advice and mutual funds to people with savings to invest, work that demands quality and production efficiency. His income, at least in part, depends on how many mutual fund shares he sells, and he has to work more hours than he did in his government job. In addition, before, Tine and his wife shared more or less equally in supporting the household; now he is the primary breadwinner.

In general, Tine has more interesting work and a higher income than he did before. But he feels he is paying a price for this greater opportunity: he must work harder and has less time for family and friends, and always worries about job security. At times he feels tormented and wishes he could "get off the treadmill."

Migration

> *Vera gore premika:* The faith moves the mountains. With God you can do everything.

The city of Ljubljana has become a very expensive place to live, especially for young couples and families. Many people are moving from the city to the outlying areas. This is a reversal of the migration pattern of some decades ago, when people from the rural areas came to live in the cities.

Tine and his family are part of this migration; they moved to the suburbs of Ljubljana in order to live more economically. Other than this, migration impacts Tine's life only marginally. He could in theory take a job in Brussels; his education and Slovenia's membership in the European Union make this a possibility, though it is a remote one.

Social Relations

Lepa beseda, lepo mesto najde: A kind word finds a nice place. A kind word finds a good response in the other person... opens horizons...creates new things.

The demands of Tine's new job allow him much less time with his family, and when he is with them he is not always fully there. His job leaves him exhausted. This places great stress on his marriage. As a couple, they are tired and have little to give each other. In many such situations marriages break down, but the two of them are persisting. Tine also has come to value his role as a parent more and more, but his lack of time to focus on it adds to the conflict he feels. This is a quiet war within him, the battle between the value of work and the value of family, but it is taking a devastating toll on him and on his family.

The nature of Tine's interactions with his coworkers and customers has changed from what it was under the communist system. Formerly, his coworkers were in a similar situation to Tine's; there was no need to compete with each other for economic opportunities. But now they have to operate within a broader world that includes international competition, a world that produces winners and losers. Some of the losers are Tine's wife and friends. This situation has created some stress for Tine and his wife. He finds, too, that he is concerned about the social inequalities he sees.

Tine has new options for socializing. Now he can go to a shopping mall for entertainment and to meet people, and the mall is even open on Sundays. There is a new movie theater and a McDonald's. This is all new, but Tine is not sure it offers an improvement in his social relationships.

New foreign social influences also entered into Tine's life with capitalism and freedom of choice. The media in particular plays a major role in exposing people to new ideas and ways of life. For the most part, these influences have greatly expanded Tine's horizons. He has gone from relating only with Slovenians to potentially being able to relate with the whole world. But he is critical of some of the things he sees on the TV and the Internet, and he worries that they will have a negative impact on his children. He is concerned about what he sees as non-judgmental assimilation of the values portrayed by the media. He also is troubled by the replacement of many Slovenian customs and small businesses with Western consumer-oriented traditions and large businesses.

Tine's social relations have expanded since his country's opening to the new global market. He has links to many more people, and different kinds of people in new roles and situations, than he did before. But there are some significant losses as well. Tine is not at peace with all the changes.

Political Power Relations

Ne vrži puške v koruzo: Do not throw the rifle in the cornfield. Do not give up without a fight.

The political changes affected Tine in many different areas. He has a new freedom to think as he chooses and, even more important, he has the freedom to express those thoughts. He can choose whether or not to practice his faith or to emigrate. If he wants to join with other people in advocating for something, he can do that. He can choose whom to support in elections. These choices were not available to him under the communist regime.

Various political parties have emerged and there are also many nongovernmental organizations working to influence society. The press, too, is free to report on political activities. Additionally, there has been a growth in unfettered communication and information dissemination, with the advent of independent television and radio and the Internet. Even Tine's children use the Internet. Tine has noticed that one effect of this has been an Americanization of the culture (as with TV programs), but at the same time it has led to an affirmation of Slovenian culture and identity. He also sees that Slovenians feel a deeper connection with their European identity, perhaps related to their accession to the European Union.

Tine has seen a change in that people have more respect for the rule of law and the state now. It used to be more common to "cheat" the state. He sees too that some people don't trust the new system, because many of the officials from the old system are working in the new one. But now there is freedom to talk about corruption; under communist rule it was unthinkable. There is also a greater concern in the country for the environment, something that is important to Tine.

The new freedoms have brought Tine much greater political choice than he ever had before. They also affected him and his family directly, because in his job he helped develop policies and procedures for privatization as part of the government's implementation of the new capitalism. He sees the political opening in very positive terms and he feels hopeful about it.

Tine has a much higher income, as well as many more consumption and investment options than were possible under communism, when the choices were very narrow. He can choose from a greater variety of things, and often higher-quality things, than before. When he bought his car, he could choose from among many cars made in the West, instead of only the three Yugoslav-made cars previously available.

Religious Experience and Expression

Holy faith be your light and mother tongue be the key to the redeeming of national civilization: This is a famous saying of the first Blessed Slovene, Anton Martin Slomšek (1800-1862).

The collapse of communism in Slovenia brought religious freedom to the country. The Catholic Church and Christian practice are no longer suppressed and people are free to choose and practice a faith. Masses are broadcast on TV and radio, and so is religious information. None of this was possible before. Under the old regime, the Catholic Church was seen as enemy number one. Military personnel and directors of corporations, for example, had to be atheists. Now chaplains are part of the army and soldiers can get spiritual guidance if they wish. It is a big shift. The Catholic faith has moved from being the "faith of the persecuted" to being the "faith of free people." It went from a faith linked to revolt against political oppression to a faith that by itself does not make a political statement but does try to influence the public sphere.

Tine's personal religious journey began with being brought up in the atheism required by the communist system. He had no formal religious education. His parents are still atheists. But his systematic search into different religions and spiritualities, which he began before Slovenia's independence, led to him converting to Catholicism when he was thirty-three. Today, Catholic values permeate how he looks at the world. Initially he was able to practice his faith to a limited extent, at the price of restricting his options under the communist government. But shortly thereafter, religious freedom became part of the new nation. Now he is free to belong openly to the Catholic Church and he feels added responsibilities because of it. He is now a member of a free church and he feels his new duties include looking at it with a critical eye. He sees a shift in the country from the values of brotherhood and cooperation, which were dominant at least in the rhetoric of communism, to the values of individualism and competition, which prevail under capitalism. At the same time, his Catholic religion calls for solidarity and a preferential option for the poor. Tine often feels caught among these conflicting beliefs.

But Tine continues to practice his faith and he takes his family to church every Sunday. He has not changed these rituals, and they give him strength.

INTERPRETATION

Slovenia's Economic Globalization and Tine

Like all the Eastern European countries that became independent and abandoned communism in the late 1980s and early 1990s, the political and economic changes Slovenia launched in 1991 were monumental. Every single existing institution in the society was affected; many of them were eliminated and some new ones emerged. However, for Slovenia this was somewhat less traumatic than for other Eastern European countries. Even when it was part of Yugoslavia, Slovenia was recognized internationally as one of Yugoslavia's economic powerhouses. Thanks to its physical proximity and historical cultural ties to the West, Slovenia was able to be more efficient than most of the other republics in the former Yugoslavia.

Unlike many of the other countries undergoing this great transition, Slovenia already had a tradition of industriousness and appreciation for economic opportunity.

When the political transition took place in Slovenia, Tine was already an adult with a high degree of education, even though it was framed by communist ideology. He was able to take advantage of the new opportunities quickly and educated himself to cope with the new system. Still, despite a full appreciation of the new freedoms and opportunities that he enjoys, he feels great tensions in the transition. One can only surmise the effects of the changes on people less fortunate than Tine because of a lack of education or just being associated with one of the disappearing businesses and institutions. Tine's wife is one of many who lost their jobs with the advent of the new economic system and competition. Also like many others, she has not been able to find a full-time job. The rapid transition in the economic system made little allowance for the adjustment necessary for the many people like Tine's wife – the economic losers in the new system.

Tine as a Person

In the midst of all the new political and economic changes, Tine, along with other Slovenians, is forging a new national identity. With other people, Tine feels that the changes that followed independence – particularly political freedom and the new opportunities of an open economy – were a liberation from the communist system and reflected who they truly were as a people. In addition, the Slovenian identity always ran closer to the Western than the Eastern world. When independence came, this Western-oriented identity grew even stronger. However, the bridge to the new Slovenian identity has been full of foreign influences. Tine is mingling the old with the new influences with an element of judgment. However, he worries about his children's future identity.

Tine already had a good education when the changes took place in Slovenia and used this base to learn about the new forces that affected him and his country. He studied capitalism, as both political and economic systems. His MBA program gave him an intellectual understanding of what was happening in Slovenia. So he is not an uncomprehending observer who has no concept of the whirlwind that has hit him. His knowledge is a strength that helps him make sense of things. He is not a passive victim of the forces of change. He has been able to draw upon the traits of his culture – industriousness, a drive to succeed, an appreciation for freedom – to not only cope but actively take advantage of the new opportunities to get ahead in many ways. Tine acts and helps shape his world.

In the economic area, there is little clash between Tine's old values, which communism suppressed, and the values of the new system. He uses many of the traditional Slovenian traits to navigate and blossom in the new economic environment: the new opportunities offer him a chance for economic and social success and he takes that chance. It is not so much a blending of old and new disparate values as a natural fit of the new with the old. Tine feels that life is better now, with all the new choices available to him. He appreciates the new political freedom he has as well, and his social relations have broadened enormously. He has many more people, and a greater variety of people, with whom he can relate. He likes the fact that he is defining his own life in this more open world.

Yet at the same time, these choices produce tensions in him. He still can feel overwhelmed by their sheer number, after so many years under the old system when choice was severely limited. And he is working very hard to afford these choices – so hard that it creates problems in his family and with other relationships. He also finds he is asking himself questions such as: Even though he can purchase many items, should he? What should he give up? What should he keep? Is the meaning of the new consumption choices for which he works so hard merely to have more? These are challenges and they create a lot of stress in him.

Yet despite the tensions between the new economic success and its cost in terms of meaning and personal relationships, he is able to go beyond himself, to be for others as well as for himself. He reaches out to his family; he fights to carve out time for his wife and children. His family is a positive force in his life that helps him deal with the negative effects of the economic changes. It gives him comfort and strength and a purpose to his economic success. He is concerned about other people as well. He works to reach outside of himself; he transcends himself. His challenge in this new freedom remains how to rebuild good relationships with the people closest to him.

Tine's faith remains important to him, and it is connected with the new freedom he is experiencing in interesting ways. His faith is making it hard for him to reconcile the good things he has gained from this freedom – a good job, the chance to succeed – with its negative consequences. His faith has given him a more critical perspective on some of the less desirable changes in Slovenian society. He sees the individualism and inequalities that have been created by capitalism, things that cause much suffering. He is aware of all the people around him who have not been able to flourish in the new environment. He personally is not much affected by these negative things, but Tine sees himself as part of a greater whole and the dichotomy bothers him and lessens his enjoyment of his new life. What makes it worse is that the Catholic Church in the country, which is now free for the first time, is unwilling to address these problems. He feels a spiritual anguish.

But at the same time his religion also helps him deal with the new tensions. It supports him as he faces the difficulties of his working conditions. It also leads him to make some decisions in response to the dichotomies he sees around him. For example, he does not buy the most expensive car available to him, even though he has the money to do so. And he and his family do not take luxurious vacations; they travel locally and often stay in tents, rather than in hotels. Still, he seems unable to figure out how to blend the new political and economic system he trusts with the negative impact of the system on some segments of the Slovene society.

Tine experiences God's love in the commitment he feels to his family and in their love and support for him. He also experiences it in the new choices now available to him. He sees these choices as God's gifts and he is grateful for them. For him, it is less the success and the things he can acquire that are important so much as the freedom he now has to work for them. The eyes of faith also lead him to really see the people who cannot benefit from the changes. He is starting to look outside of himself and to others. His new freedom is the springboard that allows him to transcend himself and be for others.

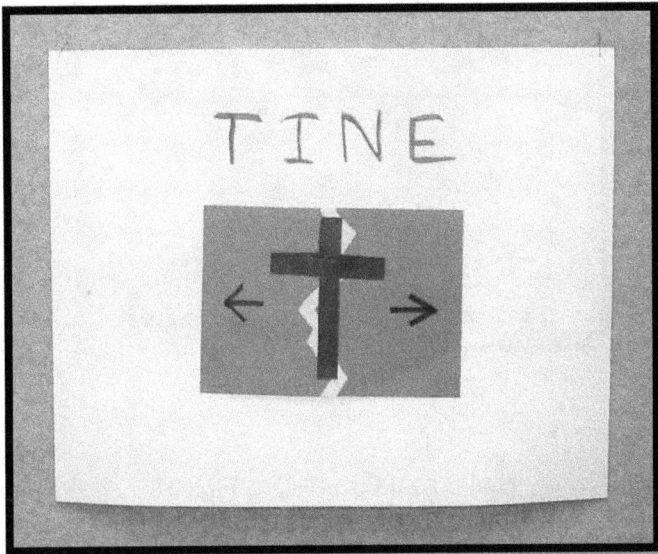

Tine's mosaic tile from GEC's Fourth International Consultation

Chapter 14

Mee-rah in South Korea:
A Labor Organizer in a Changing Nation

Mee-rah leading a demonstration

NARRATOR: CHONG-DAE KIM, SJ

"A Window on Life" Café
Jesuit Research Center for Advocacy and Solidarity
Inchon, South Korea

Narrative Summary and Economic Background

Mee-rah, a single woman now in her thirties, was born and grew up in Seoul. In 1991, after finishing high school, she started working in one of the small factories in Suwon, the capital city of Kyeonggi-Do, a neighboring province of Seoul. Appalled by the treatment the workers received at that factory, she tried to appeal to the established labor union, but the union was ineffective. She then tried to change the union's functioning and was fired by management. But because the political environment was changing, she succeeded in getting herself reinstated. Ever since, she has been involved in labor organizing. Since the financial crisis in 1997, she has been working in a printed circuit board (PCB) factory in Inchon. It produces some of the newest technology, but working conditions are very difficult and there is no union, not even a bad one, in place. In 2001 Mee-rah is contemplating how to create a labor union that would represent workers from the different factories and industries in the Inchon area.

When Mee-rah entered the South Korean labor force in 1991, the country was embarking on new policies of economic and political liberalization. In 1995, it lowered import barriers with the implementation of the Uruguay Round of trade negotiations. In 1996 South Korea committed to an even higher standard of liberalization when it joined the Organization for Economic Cooperation and Development (OECD). At the core of the Korean economic growth there has been a policy of relying on manufacturing for the export market. Now, South Korea was moving into high technology manufacturing that required higher-skilled labor, such as the PCB factory where Mee-rah works. In the new political space of the 1990s, a more open discussion of workers' rights became possible, enabling Mee-rah's activism in the labor movement. Except for the financial crisis years, South Korea's economy experienced very high rates of economic growth while it moved from agriculture to manufacturing and services. It also went from being a large recipient of foreign aid (since 1953, when the Korean War ended) to being a net international lender in the 1990s.

NARRATIVE

As they left the company lodging house, the workers could hear the steady chanting. They came to the factory and walked slowly past the group of protesters standing at the entrance. Most of the workers were half-asleep from working overtime the previous night and they paid no attention to the protesters. It was a familiar sight. A few of the workers who used to work with the protesters glanced furtively at them as they passed but tried not to meet their eyes. Four months had gone by since the protestors were fired, and each morning since then had brought the same spectacle. Mee-rah stood in the middle of the circle and led the protesters in their next chant, her voice rising up to the factory windows.

Many people Mee-rah's age were still at the university, following the path that Mee-rah had expected to take. They were competing for better grades, while she was fighting for fairer working hours. She too had hoped to get an advanced education and she had the mind and the determination to succeed. But that did not happen.

Mee-rah's Early Life

Mee-rah was born in Seoul, South Korea in 1971. Her parents had moved to Seoul from a small rural village in Chungchong-Do, a province southwest of Seoul. They did not have any land to farm and went to the city looking for opportunities. Many small factories had sprung up in the cities as part of South Korea's push for development, and they relied on cheap labor from the countryside. These factories offered good job possibilities. The lifestyle and values Mee-rah's parents found in Seoul were very different from those in their village, but they found some consolation in getting to know other rural families who were also resettling in the city.

Growing up, Mee-rah lived with her parents, three sisters, and a brother crowded into a small house in one of the poor sections of Seoul. Her parents finally saved enough money to buy a house that was larger. But they needed more money, so they rented that house out to other families and continued renting in a smaller place. Mee-rah lived on a diet of noodles, which were less expensive than the traditional rice, and put her hopes for the future in education. Her parents encouraged her, because they dreamed of giving her a better life than their own.

As she neared the end of her three years of middle school, Mee-rah hoped to continue her education at a university. A university degree would be her ticket to financial and social security. So she entered a high school where she prepared for the university entrance exam. But by the time she graduated, Mee-rah knew that her family would not be able to offer much support for her to go to a university. The money had to go for her older brother's schooling, though he was not very interested in studying. Like other Korean families, hers favored the oldest son and put his education and expenses first. Mee-rah's older sisters had not been able to go to university either, even though they wanted to. So she did not even ask her parents to allow her to study further. Mee-rah decided instead to find a job in the city and be independent. Her family, friends, and teachers were all surprised at this and tried to persuade her to continue her studies so she could raise her social status. Education is highly valued in Korea. Some students who do not get into the university and then go to work feel they have failed. Factory workers especially have a sense of inferiority. But Mee-rah stuck with her decision. She left home in 1991, shortly after turning twenty, and moved to Suwon, the capital city of Kyongi Province, close to Seoul.

The Electric Fan Company

Mee-rah had neither a university education nor highly-skilled labor experience but was able to find an entry-level job at a small electric fan company. It was very hard work. Mee-rah was used to going to class for eight hours a day, so she found working sixty hours a week very draining. The days were even longer for Mee-rah than for most employees because she lived in a lodging house owned by the company, which was attached to the factory. The supervisor of the lodge made hard rules for the residents and imposed penalties on them for not complying. She also demanded large amounts of overtime work, including work on Sundays. Mee-rah came to see the lodging house as the company's tool for controlling the workers. She felt disrespected and abused. To escape this treatment and gain some independence, the following year she moved to a small room in a house close to the company.

The foreman of Mee-rah's production line intimidated the workers. When he demanded that Mee-rah work almost seventy hours of overtime in one month, she reluctantly obeyed. She sometimes wanted to refuse, but feared being transferred to another production line where the working conditions were even harsher. She grew angrier and angrier about how unfairly the workers were treated.

In one sense, this oppressive treatment was consistent with traditional Korean beliefs. Mee-rah too had been taught these beliefs as a child. She had learned that people could be categorized and that some were better than others. The world was organized in hierarchies: businessmen and laborers, older people and younger people, men and women, and so on. In the factory, she saw this Korean attitude in action: factory work was seen as inferior and factory workers were indeed treated as inferior. But Mee-rah felt that this view could not justify the way workers were being treated. She believed that people should be accepted for who they are and treated equally, independent of position, age, or gender. She began to look for ways to help workers resist exploitation.

She turned to the company's labor union – but found out that it couldn't do anything. She learned that it belonged to the Federation of Korean Trade Unions and that the government financially supported it through that Federation. As long as the company's union depended on the government, it could not be expected to fight effectively on behalf of the workers. Moreover, union members did not elect either the union delegates or its chairperson. There was no accountability. This explained why the foremen could control the workers with impunity. The workers had no voice and no labor protection.

South Korea's former military government had never tolerated significant labor protests or allowed democratic unions to be formed. But popular protests in 1987 had begun to open the political space a bit and the people had begun to be more exposed to ideas of independence and rights. These ideas materialized in 1993, when Kim Youngsam was elected to the presidency.

By the closing months of 1994, Mee-rah could no longer endure the workers' situation and decided to take action. About twenty of her close coworkers supported her and agreed to join her resistance. Together they would take on the company and its union. Things had changed since the time of the military dictatorship and they were able to get some advice from several NGOs as well.

Mee-rah and her coworkers focused their efforts on gaining the right of workers to directly elect delegates to the union. She and some other people in the group decided to run for election themselves and put up campaign posters. The company was quick to fight back; it tore down the posters. When Mee-rah put up more, they were removed even faster. Eventually, the company disciplined Mee-rah and her associates. But Mee-rah would not stop fighting and took her message of resistance to oppression to the rest of the factory's workers. She called the working conditions unjust. The management called her a communist. Then, in what they thought would be the final blow, the management fired Mee-rah and her friends – before they had had the chance to run for the delegates election. However, the action did not have the desired effect. Mee-rah began protesting in front of the factory. For almost four months she stood by the entrance of the factory, leading the other former employees in protest rallies as the workers came in every morning.

During the protest, Mee-rah's parents called her many times. The company had sent them letters accusing Mee-rah of holding communist ideas and demanding that she reject them. Her parents were afraid of her involvement in protests. They pleaded with her to stop resisting, to get married instead. Her mother told her that as a woman she was not meant to work away from the home, but was meant to be a mother and a housewife. Or, they said, she should at least find another, better job.

But Mee-rah felt that living a good, fair life was more important than having a prestigious job or a lot of money. She was proud of the work she did and identified strongly with her job. When she introduced herself, she would say, "My name is Mee-rah, I am single, and I work at the electric fan company." She explained to her parents that she did not start the labor protest because she thought it would be easy. She simply wanted to live in a better world. Contrary to their wishes, Mee-rah persevered in her fight against injustice.

She and her fellow protesters made an appeal to the local Labor Relations Commission of the Ministry of Labor. But the commission rejected their case. Then they met with a member of the national Congress. Finally, they went to the local media; they informed a newspaper of their plight. This was effective. The company felt great pressure from the newspaper and finally agreed to negotiate with Mee-rah and her associates. They reemployed some of them at the end of 1995. This was Mee-rah's first taste of labor organization and protest. It would not be her last.

But after she returned to the factory, the atmosphere became even worse. The company tried to alienate the other workers from Mee-rah and her friends. About this time, Mee-rah's company had to reduce production because the demand for electrical fans was decreasing. The big car and electric appliance companies that bought the fans were seeing their own sales drop. So Mee-rah's factory began to fire people to cut costs. Working conditions got worse and relationships hardened. Mee-rah dreamed of having a good labor union and an environment with a human touch. But she felt powerless to change her situation. Finally, in the middle of 1996, she left the fan company.

Mee-rah leading a protest at the factory

The Farm

She worked at a newspaper for a year, covering agriculture and learning about the plight of farmers. She asked herself, "What is my role for making a better world?" She thought that working closer to nature might be the answer to her questions and desires. She left the newspaper and, with some of her friends, moved to a rural area to try to live out her new dreams. But farming was harder than she thought.

This was around the end of 1997 and something else was happening: a financial crisis was enveloping the country and spreading to the rest of Asia. The South Korean government had found itself unable to repay the huge amounts of short-term foreign debt it had accumulated and sought aid from the International Monetary Fund (IMF). However, to receive this support, it had to agree to implement austere economic policies and engage in a Structural Adjustment Program. The new policies were a severe blow to the South Korean people. Millions of men lost their jobs. There was great suffering.

Out in the country, Mee-rah felt the effects of the crisis in the steep rise in prices for farming supplies, frustrating her as she tried to succeed in this new endeavor. She read about what was happening all over the country and was disheartened as she saw the society crumble. She also felt isolated from the world. She enjoyed the harmony she experienced working in the fields, but she could not forget the strong friendships she had formed with workers in the city and longed for the interaction of the factory. Finally, Mee-rah abandoned her attempt at farming and returned to the urban working world in the middle of 1998.

The Circuit Board Factory

Mee-rah found work at another small factory, one that was part of the new surge of high-tech production sweeping the country at the time. It was located in the Namdong industrial district in Inchon, next to Seoul and the third largest city in Korea. Along with four hundred other workers, she made printed circuit boards. The hours at this new job were strenuous: the first shift began at nine in the morning and finished at nine at night and the second shift began at nine at night and finished at nine in the morning. Every month she rotated shifts. So Mee-rah's working conditions were even harder now than at the electrical fan factory. People did not last long in her new factory. She also did not feel respected by the factory management and she knew that the other workers felt the same way.

But employment in this environment of financial crisis was insecure and it was hard to find jobs at all. This made the workers unwilling to complain. Many of them were married women who were the sole providers for their families – their husbands having lost their jobs in the crisis – and so they felt they could not make any trouble. In fact, the factory management preferred to hire married women, for that very reason. It would take advantage of the women's situation and demand that they sign a contract to work at night, which was against the law. Technically, labor law stipulated that when women and any workers younger than eighteen are asked to work at night, an agreement should exist between the workers and the company. But the workers did not have a union, so there was no place the women could go for help, even if they dared ask for it.

Mee-rah kept working at the factory and began to think of ways to establish a labor union. It was an immense challenge. Her main obstacle was the long hours the employees worked. The only times available to meet were before or after one of the two twelve-hour shifts, either early in the morning or late at night, and that would mean sacrificing the little rest and relaxation they had. Furthermore, those who experienced the harshest conditions – married women – could hardly get involved with the union because they also had duties at home.

Mee-rah herself still faced constant pressure from her parents to marry or find better work. She missed having strong relationships with friends and family outside of work. She actually would have liked to get married and start a family of her own, but she knew that she might never get married. Rather, her desire to help organize workers, to fight for their well-being, filled her heart and left little room or time for other things. Gradually, her family and friends began to accept and respect Mee-rah's countercultural lifestyle and the choices she had made: to wear blue jeans, work more, challenge and complain about many things, and stay single.

Mee-rah was part of the bigger story of small factory workers at the mercy of a country trying to become a stronger industrial power. She was committed to promoting more egalitarian practices between owners and workers and between men and women. A new government seemed more open to changes, but the economy had made conditions for the workers even worse. After thinking about the situation, Mee-rah saw the need for a different type of union. Hoping for wider influence, she decided to launch a local labor union made up of workers from different factories in the area. She began getting together regularly with labor organizers from other factories in open rooms at the Labor Apostolic Office of the Inchon Diocese.

Every day, Mee-rah lives a life exhausted by work and pressured by the traditional culture, yet she is at peace in her purpose...

Mee-rah: 2001

Her ears ring from the evening shift's bell and her legs are weak from twelve hours of standing. For a few short moments, her eyes close, her hands relax, and her lips turn up. There is not a noise to distract her. Her body refreshes itself with every second it can sit and not have to move. She will not have to be at the factory again for another eleven hours. Sleep creeps slowly towards Mee-rah as her mind empties from the day's monotony. Then, without warning, a knock sounds on the door and Mee-rah jumps up to answer it. She peeks through the window and sees a handful of her friends, also sluggish. The Labor Office fills with more tired bodies and the conversation takes on a heavy tone. Mee-rah has known these workers only for a few months, but their thoughts come closer together every night. Tonight they discuss plans to register officially as a union. Mee-rah's eyes, though heavy, look out in delight at the faces of the people in the small room. They are taking another small step in their mission and they are not alone.

Even though their mission is local – one union in one city – Mee-rah feels connected with other people in other places who are also struggling for justice. She stays in touch with people through her cell phone and stays informed about events from all over through the Internet. She calls herself a *netizen*, a person who is linked to many others through the Internet.

Walking home under the hazy streetlights, Mee-rah feels revived. She has eight hours before starting again on the production line. Only a few hours are left before she begins another day of living her vocation. She finally reaches her bed and enjoys a moment of stillness and quiet in her one-room apartment. She needs only an instant to fall asleep. Tomorrow morning she will be exhausted and hungry, but her heart will be at peace.

CULTURAL ANALYSIS

Mee-rah's Traditional Culture

Korea's culture, thousands of years old, mixes an ancient shamanistic faith with religions that came in later from elsewhere in Asia: Confucianism, Buddhism, and Taoism. Each of these religions has influenced the culture. Today, Christianity is also very much a part of the culture. The cultural elements most relevant to Mee-rah's story are:

1. *Confucian ideals of harmony and ethical behavior.* Harmony – among individuals, in society, and between people and nature– is highly valued. This is coupled with a belief in doing what is right, rather than what is advantageous, and treating other people as you yourself want to be treated.

2. *Buddhist principle of valuing all living things.* Tolerance and inclusiveness of everything and everyone mark Buddhist thought.

3. *Community.* There is a strong sense of the group and of everyone having a place in it. There is also a feeling of solidarity with others. Helping one another was part of life among poor people; farmers would work together to transplant rice seedlings.

4. *Hierarchical structure and male-dominated society.* There is a great respect for authority and social status is very important. Jobs are seen as either good or bad, as high or low status. Women are assigned a lower place in the social structure. Marriage is considered the proper role for women; so single women are looked down upon.

5. *Strong family bonds. The family is core in soci*ety. Children must respect and be loyal to their parents; it is part of maintaining Confucian harmony. Part of children's duty includes having children and carrying on the family line.

6. *Value of formal education.* Education is seen as the way of getting a good job and improving one's social status. It is also one way children show respect to their parents.

7. *Reverence for ancestors and shamanistic rituals.* One's ancestors are seen as remaining part of the family circle, in a spiritual form. Korean families hold rituals several times a year to

honor them. Shamanism is an ancient belief in a world filled with spirits. Korean Shamans – who are mainly women – perform rituals for people who want help from the spirit world.

8. *Hard work and perseverance.* This is also a core value in the culture, for which they are known around the world.

Mee-rah's Critical Decisions

1. She decided to get a factory job after high school.

What were her options? She could have tried harder to raise money to go to the university. She could have followed the traditional path for women in Korean society and gotten married.

What cultural values lay behind her decision? She wanted to be independent and she knew that as an unmarried woman, she had to work to survive.

What cultural values were reflected in the reactions of the other people in her life to this decision? Everyone around her was surprised at her decision and tried to talk her out of it. They all thought that factory work was low-status work, only for inferior people.

2. She decided to try farming.

What were her options? She could have gotten a different job. She could have stopped working and gotten married.

What cultural values lay behind her decision? She felt a pull to the land, where her parents came from. She also wanted to make a better world by helping a group of people with little power or status.

What cultural values were reflected in the reactions of the other people in her life to this decision? Her family didn't like her working with this marginalized group. Some of her friends felt the same way she did and went with her to do this agricultural work.

3. She decided to become involved in the labor movement, first at the fan factory and then at the electric circuit board factory.

What were her options? She could have ignored the workers' plight and not protested. She could have quit either job and gotten married, as her parents wanted her to do.

What cultural values lay behind her decision? She felt that it was more important to try to make a better world than to follow society's expectations for women.

What cultural values were reflected in the reactions of the other people in her life to this decision? Her parents were frightened by her labor work and they worried about her. They wanted a secure life for her, but in the end, out of love for her, they respected her decision. Management at both factories opposed her involvement; they were influenced by the values of hierarchy and status, as well as male domination.

Note: Mee-rah is influenced by some of the core Korean values – *ethical behavior, harmony,* and *community* – yet she expresses them in her own way, applying them to marginalized groups. She rejects other values, such as the *hierarchical structure, education,* and *male dominance.* Her decisions also reflect the ideal of *hard work.* As an individual, she values *equality* and *independence* and they too affect her decisions. In fact, most of her choices went against the conventional wisdom of her society in one way or another. Her parents' reactions reflect the values of *family, the hierarchical structure,* and *education.* The management at the factories where she worked reflected the value of *hierarchy.*

Changes in Mee-rah's Life

When Mee-rah began working in 1991, South Korea was in the middle of an economic and political opening. But the opening was rooted in the country's pattern of development over the last several decades: industrialization and high economic growth led by exports. Some of the policies affecting Mee-rah's life had been put in place not long after the Korean War (1950-53). But the rate of change accelerated significantly with the political and economic opening of the 1990s.

Consumption

When Mee-rah's parents were young, the South Korean government stressed the need for people to work hard and save money for the good of the country. Modernization was the national slogan that everyone accepted and the dream they worked for – but it meant they had to strongly curtail their consumption.

Now a different attitude prevails. The economy is stronger and growing and people have more disposable income. The pressure to save and curtail consumption is not as pervasive. And, as South Korea opened its economy, there has been greater exposure to Western goods, media, and advertising. Mee-rah, like many South Korean young people, dresses in blue jeans and other Western clothes. She uses tools in her daily life that were unimaginable not that long ago: the cell phone, the computer, and the Internet. She gets her news and information from a variety of media sources. She consumes differently from the way her parents did, and some of this difference results simply from her having a higher income than they did when they first came to Seoul.

However, Mee-rah's consumption is basically quite moderate. She wears simple clothes and does not use make-up. She lives on her small income, spending her money on rent, meals, transportation, clothing, and her computer. Sometimes she goes out with her friends to restaurants and coffee shops. She is able to save some money, though she isn't sure she will ever be able to buy a house, which her parents did, because this is now a luxury. This does not bother her, though, because her consumption is influenced by the working class, with which she identifies. Sometimes she is fearful because the path she has chosen will not guarantee any material improvement in her life. But she is at peace because she is following her dream.

Production

Mee-rah's income since 1991 has come from working in factories and a brief attempt at farming. As an unmarried woman, a job is a matter of survival. But the work that has given meaning to her life since the mid-1990s has been that of labor organizer.

Her first job, in an electric fan company, was almost a textbook example of the growth of South Korean industry and the pressures facing it. South Korea had been gaining ground for some time in international markets, increasing its exports to the rest of the world. And behind this export success of big South Korean companies was the flexibility that small business subcontractors afforded them. Any unexpected change in export demand could be accommodated by intentionally changing or dropping subcontractors. The subcontractors in turn, in order to survive, had to squeeze all they could out of their labor force. The low prices they received for their products allowed for little investment in things like better working facilities. This situation probably existed in the early days of South Korea's industrialization in the 1960s and 1970s, but seemed to get worse over time.

In her first factory job Mee-rah saw harsh labor conditions, especially for lower-level workers. Employees often worked sixty hours a week, and then foremen regularly demanded additional – and illegal – overtime. This stemmed partly from the economic situation of small, marginal subcontractors, but much of it came from traditional Korean culture, which sees factory jobs as negative and factory workers as inferior. The management had higher status and all the power and felt free to exploit the workers.

Mee-rah, however, had a different – and countercultural – view of work. She believed that one's job is less important than who one is, and that everyone should be respected equally and treated fairly. So she was outraged at the unjust way she and the other workers were treated by the company and indignant when she discovered that the company labor union would do nothing to help.

She saw that management was hostile toward independent labor unions, an attitude that seemed to be common in industry and was shared by the government. In fact, the labor movement was commonly regarded as affiliated with communism and a threat to the country, a perception arising out of South Korea's conflict with North Korea. So when Mee-rah decided to run for delegate to the union, her company prevented her.

Despite Mee-rah's difficulties, the political environment still was more open than it had been in the past, under military rule, when the government was much more repressive. Things had changed enough that Mee-rah could, and did, stage a protest and pressured the company to rehire her. This would not have been possible less than a decade earlier.

Mee-rah's second factory job is in a printed-circuit boards (PCB) company. This kind of job arose because South Korea was concentrating on producing high-end technology items, rather than the heavy industry of earlier years. Working conditions in this company were even worse than in her first factory. There was not even a workers' union.

Furthermore, with the high unemployment rate in the country after the 1997 financial crisis, there was little hope of organizing one. But, with the political opening making some change possible, Mee-rah decided on a new way of organizing labor: instead of having the union formed around the workers in a given factory in an industry, she started trying to organize workers from different factories working in the same area. This work provides meaning for her and she is at peace.

Migration

Be careful in Seoul not to lose your nose: A comment on the commercial mindset of city people.

Internal migration has been a reality in South Korea for some time, starting at the time the country began to industrialize. Many people left the rural areas to take jobs in the new factories located in and near the cities. Mee-rah's parents, who came to Seoul in the 1960s to make a better life for themselves, were among them. They found themselves part of the new urban poor, a reserve group of workers who provided cheap labor for South Korea's burgeoning industries.

Some years later, though, Mee-rah discovered that migration wears a different face now. At the circuit board factory, she found that the migrants come from other, low-wage countries. These foreign workers have replaced the earlier wave of rural South Koreans who moved to the city. She saw, too, that these foreign workers are even more victimized by the company management because they are afraid to stand up for themselves. They are a cheaper, and usually compliant, labor source that management wants to keep. They are generally treated much worse than even the lowest-level South Korean worker.

Mee-rah actually attempted a reverse migration when she went to work on the farm. Despite living and working in the city, Mee-rah feels a bond with the country and farming. But she felt isolated there and missed her family and friends, and was frustrated by the problems she encountered. She still feels she failed there.

Social Relations

Instead of living with her parents, which most young unmarried women do, Mee-rah lives alone. She is single, even though marriage is the expected path. She works at a low-status factory job, instead of trying to get more education or higher-status work. She devotes her time and energy to organizing a union for workers. Everything she is and does flies in the face of what is expected of her socially. Children are expected to respect and obey their parents. A woman is expected to be a wife and mother. Workers are expected to obey their superiors. Mee-rah does not conform to these expectations. Her actions challenge core social traits of her culture: obedience to parents, the role of women, the emphasis on education, the need for hierarchy. And it is not just that Mee-rah has gone against her culture in the abstract. She has stood up to authority, in the very concrete form of her parents and the company management.

Young women would not have behaved this way a generation ago. They probably did not even dare to think this way. Mee-rah's life would have been much more circumscribed then. But she has been exposed to new ideas and possibilities that came in with the country's opening, and that has made things very different.

Mee-rah relates to other people out of autonomy, rather than out of the strict hierarchical strictures of her culture. She can act on her belief in mutual respect and equal value among people. She has also added a new community to her life, the community of the Internet, which has opened a social world to her bigger than that of her immediate surroundings. She identifies herself as a *netizen*. She can escape the confines of the local culture and find companions with similar interests.

As a worker, Mee-rah is alienated from the hierarchical society around her and is indifferent to how traditional society characterizes her. She has found a sense of solidarity and community with her companions in the labor movement. She is enthusiastic about her mission and is at peace with herself because her work has given her a way of living out her values.

Political Relations

As South Korea started to industrialize, relying on its growth in exports, it also began to interact more with the Western world's economy. The access of its exports to foreign markets was accompanied by an increasing influence of Western standards in such areas as political freedoms and human rights. However, the political opening did not happen all at once; it was a gradual process that accelerated in the 1990s with the first democratically elected president. By the end of the 1990s, things had opened quite a lot.

Mee-rah's parents lived most of their lives under a military rule that, while it pushed for economic growth, did not allow for much freedom of expression or human rights. The country's history of fighting communism, and the eventual partition, tended to reinforce this trait. By the time Mee-rah started working, the country was being exposed to Western ideas and attitudes, along with Western consumer goods and services. There was more room for resistance against the government and greater freedom to criticize authority. The movement to establish nongovernmental organizations (NGOs), which are now present in South Korea, began with the protest movements under the dictatorship. More recently, these groups have been collaborating in planning policy.

By the time Mee-rah started working, agitation for human rights and labor unrest had become more common, although the legacy of the Korean War meant it was associated with communism in many people's minds. Labor unions had existed before, but they functioned in a top-down fashion and for limited goals: the national leadership would negotiate for better wages for the next year, but little else. Now, in an environment of greater openness, unions became more grass-roots. Mee-rah and a small group of people could recognize and name the injustice that they saw in the workplace and try to change it. They could organize the protest at the fan company and talk to the press and, later, work to organize a union.

Communication also has opened up dramatically, with TV, radio, telephones, cell phones, and the Internet everywhere. Mee-rah is exposed to the world in a way unimaginable to previous generations. This means that it is no longer possible for the government to have a monopoly on information. Not only that; these new items have become tools for Mee-rah to use as she tries to forge a better world for workers. Through this new technology, Mee-rah has a broader cosmopolitan identity with an even greater political awareness and a new political forum. She enjoys these changes.

Religious Experience and Expression

Mee-rah's approach to life, in some ways, seems quite secular. We do not see much of Korean ancestral culture or shamanistic rituals in Mee-rah's story. She has chosen to live in a way that challenges many aspects of her culture, so she may well have challenged or rejected the religious aspects as well. However, she was raised in a Buddhist and Confucian environment, and we can discern in her the influence of some ideas from those traditions. But we do not know if there have been any changes in how she experiences and practices religion.

INTERPRETATION

South Korea's Economic Globalization and Mee-rah

South Korea went from being a rural, foreign-aid dependent country in the 1950s and 1960s to being an industrial economy with no need of foreign assistance in the 1990s. This transformation required a massive migration from the rural areas to the cities to work in the factories. It also required single-mindedness to reach the desired economic development after the country was divided at the end of the Korean War in 1953. That single-mindedness was expressed in government policies that gave preferences to certain industries favored for growth in the export market. At the top of these industries were highly concentrated private industrial structures called *chaebols*, which could produce goods for domestic consumption as well as the export market, and which were protected from imports by high tariffs. Some of this protection diminished with the Uruguay Round lowering of import tariffs in 1995, but a lot remained. Supporting the *chaebols'* growth were millions of small businesses and their workers, which supplied and depended on them. These small businesses also gave flexibility to the *chaebols*, acting as a buffer for them against changes in market forces. So the small businesses often were pressured to work with very small margins. Working conditions in these businesses have been bad for a long time and became even worse with the financial crisis of 1997. It is in these small businesses that Mee-rah works and tries to organize labor.

The conditions that Mee-rah found in the factory where she first started working in 1991 had existed for decades. What is new for her is that she found some political space to try to change, albeit unsuccessfully, those working conditions. The real test for liberalizing the Korean industrial structure, beyond the import tariff reductions of 1995, came with the 1997 financial crisis. At the time, international lenders put pressure on Korea to make its industrial structure more competitive: to allow market forces to affect every business in every industry. In the midst of the crisis changes began to take place, but the jury is still out as to whether they will eventually affect the basically concentrated and self-protected industrial structure of the country. Mee-rah, in her current job, still is witnessing the traditional adjustment of the small company to the new economy. And we can tell that, in spite of the high economic growth of the country, workers like Mee-rah continue to have basic workers' rights denied to them. She has much more financial independence than her parents had and she can consume things her parents didn't even dream of having – but she still has a very hard working life. She is allowed to struggle to form a labor union and receives support from the NGOs now allowed to operate, but her dream of a good labor union does remain only a dream.

Mee-rah as a Person

In South Korea, the economic opening had two almost opposite effects on the society. On the one hand, the increased need to compete reinforced some existing traits of the society, particularly its hierarchical structure and communitarian nature. On the other hand, globalization also created spaces, cracks, in the traditional society, and these cracks allowed some traits to be challenged and undermined. Mee-rah entered the South Korean labor force just as these changes began to permeate the society and a greater political tolerance appeared on the horizon.

A quick look at Mee-rah's story might lead to the conclusion that Mee-rah has simply rejected most of her traditional culture. She chose to be single in a society where marriage and motherhood are women's highest role. She chose to be a laborer in a world that gives high status to education and professional work. She went against her parents' wishes in a culture where children are expected to obey them. She stood up for workers' rights in a country that does not value them highly. And South Korea's opening, particularly in the political arena, allowed her to act in ways that would have been more difficult before.

The reality is more complex, however. It is true that Mee-rah challenged certain aspects of her culture that she thought negative: the hierarchical structure, the limited role of women, unquestioned obedience to parents, and education as a major indicator of status. But at the same time, she kept other aspects as part of her value system, albeit in a modified form. She has not jettisoned her traditional culture in favor of new ways; rather, she has combined the old and the new. In doing so, she acted in ways consistent with the Buddhist and Confucian ideals that have surrounded her since her childhood.

Mee-rah has not rejected the Korean notion of family, even though she does not comply with her parents' wishes in all things. But she has chosen a new family, the family of workers, to which she gives her loyalty and dedication and, in a sense, her obedience. These are values associated with the traditional family but she has applied them to a new group. Similarly, she has not rejected the old notion of community, the idea that everyone should work together for the good of all. But she has redefined it. Her community is now a community of peers; it is a society in which all members are equal, rather than the hierarchical Korean one. Family and community are as important to her as to any Korean; she simply lives these values out in her own unique way of being in her culture in a South Korea increasingly more open to global forces.

Mee-rah draws strength from her strong sense of individuality, her feeling that she has worth and should be respected simply because of who she is. For her, this trumps social role, job title, education, and status – all important criteria of her society. This sense of herself, and her courage in living it out, is not characteristic of her culture; it is truly countercultural and is, in fact, unusual in any culture. Yet hers is not a Western style of individualism. She believes that every person deserves to be respected. She has made a decision to be for others – the workers – and she wants to contribute to improving that community. Out of this come her sense of self and her sense of meaning. This focus on others guides her choices; what she accepts and rejects from her culture is all about that.

One traditional cultural trait that Mee-rah does embody is hard work and perseverance. She works hard at her jobs and she is proud of what she does, proud that she is a worker and produces things. The hard conditions did not cause her to give up. She also devotes much time and energy to her organizing efforts and here too she persevered, in the face of much opposition.

Mee-rah's core values are tolerance and inclusiveness, her acceptance of all people as having worth – values that probably come from her Buddhist tradition. This has shaped her view of things and motivates her. It leads her to believe that everyone is equal. In this she is like many other people her age in South Korea, who are more egalitarian than authoritarian. This is why she reacts so strongly to the way factory workers are treated. Coupled with this is an inner sense of right and wrong, which gives her strength in her work. This probably comes from the Confucian ideal of ethical behavior. She also has a strong desire to make things better for workers. It has become a dream for her, something that gives her life meaning. It is consistent with the traditional Confucian notion of harmony, the idea that everything in nature and in society must be in balance. She has seen the imbalance caused by the situation of workers and knows it is not the way things should be. She is trying to restore harmony to her world and this is more important to her than marrying and conforming to the traditional pattern of behavior. This ideal gives her energy and hope, even though she does not always articulate it as such. But it appears to be an integral part of her identity.

She also is able to hold opposites in her mind. She wants harmony, yet she is a troublemaker in the eyes of her culture. She values community, yet much of what she does goes against the beliefs of her society. She is able to hold these seemingly opposing values and act on them and not be disturbed by what might appear to be a contradiction. This ability helps her to shape a coherent world view, one that corresponds to her values.

Mee-rah's conduct presents a real challenge to traditional Korean society, and this creates friction. She confronts tradition and faces ignorance and discrimination. Yet she does not let the tradition crush her; she takes the very values that are the source of tension and turns them into bridges into the new Korean world. She feels anger at the workers' situation and turns it into a force to work for justice. She refused to see herself as a victim and instead became a person willing to take on politics: a labor organizer. She is a strong person who is turning her culture on its head to do what is right, making the dignity of human beings and workers her top priority and making the rest of her culture fit into it. If something doesn't fit, she throws it away and fights. If it fits, she builds on it. It is a very activist stance and the more open South Korea makes room for this activism.

She truly has taken advantage of all the changes brought about by globalization. She has actively embraced many of these changes, while not rejecting all of the tradition. She sees possibilities and evaluates them. She makes decisions, taking responsibility for her own life. She has responded to globalization by taking action: by using the new political opening to address the plight of the workers. It would even be fair to say that her independent income and the political opening associated with globalization make it possible for her to address her highest social and spiritual needs, her very meaning in life – working to improve her society.

Mee-rah's experience of God's love is manifested in the way she finds meaning in her life. She experiences God's love in her need to be related to other people and to create harmony among them. She finds this love in her awareness of social structures that are wrong and must be changed. She finds it in her desire to contribute to her chosen community, the community of workers. Finally, God is mediated to her in the affirmation she receives from others for who she is and what she does.

Mee-rah's mosaic tile from GEC's Fourth International Consultation

Chapter 15

Maurice in the United States: African-American Faith, Family, and Redemption

Maurice at his home in Washington, D.C.

NARRATOR: REV. RAYMOND B. KEMP

Senior Research Fellow, Woodstock Theological Center
Community Fellow, Georgetown University Center for Social Justice
Faculty Member, Georgetown University Theology Department
Washington, D.C., United States of America

Narrative Summary and Economic Background

Globalization entered Maurice's life through the expansion of the illegal international drug trade in the 1970s and 1980s. An African American living in Washington, D.C., in the United States, he began using and selling drugs in high school. His basketball skills helped him get into a good college but then an injury kept him from playing. He dropped out of school and started selling drugs, and developed a severe heroin habit. Eventually he was arrested for selling drugs; since his release he has gone through several cycles of overcoming his addiction and then relapsing again. He is currently in his mid-forties and is employed as a counselor at a drug rehabilitation center run by Catholic Charities.

The illegal drug trade in the United States has always been global. But the scope of this trade started expanding greatly in the late 1960s, concurrently with an increased demand for illegal drugs in the country. The growth of the drug trade was already in motion when the United States began to move towards a more open economy in the 1980s. The U.S. already had the lowest import tariffs in the world and a thriving private sector, so the new economic liberalization took the form of government deregulation of private industries, such as airlines and telecommunications – which incidentally also contributed to making drugs cheaper – and the reduction of already low government subsidies. Deregulation became a battle cry under President Reagan in the 1980s. This economic liberalization, however, was taking place at the same time that the country was proclaiming a "War on Drugs," a tougher stance against drugs that began in the 1970s. The effect of drugs in the U.S. was becoming enormous: a much greater volume of drugs was entering the country, violence and homicides increased, and many inner-city neighborhoods severely eroded. Drug use permeated not only poor urban communities like Maurice's but also wealthier ones. The introduction of low-priced crack cocaine in the mid-1980s made the situation even more explosive.

NARRATIVE

The Early Years

Maurice S. Young, born August 2, 1959, was the seventh of eleven children. He was born and raised in Southeast Washington, D.C., in a predominantly African-American neighborhood. Maurice's father had grown up in the same neighborhood and his mother had grown up in the Georgetown area of Washington. She worked as a nurse's aide at St. Elizabeth's Hospital. She was Catholic and had all the children baptized Catholic; they went to church regularly with her. They attended Bible study and Sunday school until they were twelve or thirteen, when they were allowed to decide for themselves whether to keep going. Their local parish, St. Peter's, was culturally more white than black. The music did not reflect the African-American spiritual tradition of black churches. Maurice occasionally went with his father to the Baptist church, which was more reflective of black culture.

Maurice's Neighborhood

The formation of poor black neighborhoods in Northern cities – often called ghettos – goes back to the migration of blacks from the rural South to the industrialized North. This migration began in 1865, after the Civil War, during which slavery was abolished in the U.S. Subsequent migration happened in waves: the first Great Migration happened after World War I and the second Great Migration after World War II. Through this entire period, blacks faced discrimination in housing and employment. In addition, slavery had been abolished, but in its place official segregation laws were enacted in some states, even in the North.

By 1950, most African Americans lived in neighborhoods in which the large majority was black. But despite the relative poverty of these neighborhoods, they were vibrant communities with people of all classes living there and many businesses, churches, schools, and both formal and informal social structures. The radical changes and impoverishment of black neighborhoods came in the 1960s, with two federal programs' unintended consequences. The Urban Renewal program razed a great many existing neighborhoods and often constructed new "projects" or government-subsidized housing, like Potomac Gardens near Maurice's home, exclusively for the poor. The Interstate Highway program often dislocated or physically isolated black neighborhoods. Also, between 1950 and 1970 seven million whites left center cities to move to the newly forming suburbs. Later, wealthy and middle-class blacks were able to join in this exodus. By the 1970s vibrant black communities had become poor black ghettos.

This economic marginalization and a new black power separatist movement erupted into violence beginning in 1965. Although President Johnson undertook a "War on Poverty," most programs were severely underfunded. One program that did expand was the Aid to Families with Dependent Children (AFDC), commonly referred to as welfare. This program has been criticized for eroding marriage in the black community, since it allowed single women with children to become (slightly) self-sufficient. It provided a disincentive to get married if the man was employed because it would usually mean the loss of welfare benefits.

According to 2004 census figures, African Americans make up 12.8 percent of the U.S. population and 57.7 percent of the population of Washington, D.C. In 2004, the U.S. poverty rate overall was 12.7 percent. For African Americans, it was 24.7 percent, compared to 8.6 percent for non-Hispanic whites.

Maurice's father did a variety of jobs; he was a painter, a handyman, and a landscaper. He drank heavily and became abusive towards his wife and children when he was under the influence. Maurice and his brothers tried to protect their mother at these times. His father was not around for much of their childhood and had relationships with many other women, fathering five other children outside the family. He eventually left their family.

The Young family lived less than a mile and a half from the U.S. Capitol and they were exposed to all the ills of the city and its public housing projects. Built in the 1960s, these housing projects were intended to provide low-income families and senior citizens with safe and affordable housing. But many of them, such as Potomac Gardens (which was a few blocks away from Maurice's home), became run down and crime-ridden.

Maurice's parents were not around for much of his childhood but they did manage to teach him the value of family. From his mother, he learned to treat others as he would like to be treated. From his father, he learned that it is a "dog-eat-dog world" and self-preservation is the most important thing. He also learned a great deal from his older siblings. The children were divided up roughly into three age groups. Maurice was in the youngest group and they were handed over to the group above them, who taught them "the streets." At first, when he was on the streets he tried not to step on other people's toes, but eventually he did whatever it took to make it. He was also taught a strong sense of machismo: "Real men do not cry, show emotion, eat quiche, wear pink, or carry umbrellas." To this day, he will not wear pink or carry an umbrella.

School

Maurice attended D.C. public schools for elementary and middle school. He played CYO (Catholic Youth Organization) basketball for his parish in eighth grade. In 1974, he was recruited for his basketball skills by Mackin High School, a Catholic school that served low- and middle-income African-American students. Most of the teachers there were white. Maurice was an intimidating basketball player and he saw basketball as his ticket out of the ghetto and into a rich and glamorous life. In 1975, in the tenth grade, he went on his first weekend retreat. The retreat was known as IMPAC, Improving My Personal Act with Christ, and was run mostly by black teachers. On the retreat, Maurice testified to an experience of throwing a coin into a stream as far as he could, "in the hope of throwing all the negativity in my life away and not succumbing to its power." This was the basis for many of his subsequent religious experiences and moments of conversion. On this retreat, he also began a lifelong friendship with Fr. Raymond Kemp, a priest in the Archdiocese of Washington.

In 1975, on his sixteenth birthday, Maurice was locked up in jail for drinking in public on an elementary school playground across the street from his house. Three months later he smoked marijuana for the first time; shortly afterwards, he began selling it in his neighborhood. He had been observing some of his brothers who were involved in the drug business. They tried to keep him out of it at first, telling him to stay in school and stay on the right path. They tried to buy him off by giving him whatever he wanted – new sneakers, girls, hotel rooms, etc. But Maurice wanted to be involved. Eventually he got his own "crew," a group of people with whom he sold drugs. When his brothers found out they were angry but could not stop him. Throughout high school, Maurice continued to smoke marijuana on the weekends. With four of his brothers, he also supplemented the family income by selling drugs – heroin and cocaine – in the neighborhood. Like most of the black males he knew, Maurice had run-ins with the police, many of whom were white, over issues such as driving too fast and carrying guns.

In 1978, Maurice graduated from Mackin High School and won a basketball scholarship to Howard University. Located in D.C., Howard is one of the most prestigious historically black universities in the country. He moved into one of the dormitories on campus. He did pretty well as a student and as an athlete, but he never felt that he fit in. Most of his classmates came from wealthier families and he felt that they looked down on him because of his poor background and darker skin. At one point, Maurice found out that one of the other players on the basketball team could not read or write. He was furious – furious that the coaches knew this and allowed the boy to play and that his friend had allowed himself to be moved along in school and used all these years.

In his second year at Howard, Maurice started selling cocaine on campus and around the city. In his third year, he began snorting cocaine occasionally. Later that year, he was injured and could not play basketball. He became depressed and began snorting heroin. He also arrived at the difficult realization that he was not going to make it as a professional basketball player with the National Basketball Association. This was the only dream he had for his future. He dropped out of Howard in 1982 and moved back to his neighborhood in Southeast.

Living and Dealing in the Neighborhood

Maurice lived with his mother but also stayed with the different women he was dating (generally about three at a time: "a pair and a spare"). He never lacked a place to lay his head. He worked at several part-time jobs, with D.C. Parks and Recreation and as a teacher's aide at Anacostia High School. His life centered on the neighborhood – the "hood," the community where his roots lay. He continued to use drugs and began to sell them again, forming another crew to do it. It was made up mostly of people who had grown up in the neighborhood with him, who had eaten at each other's mothers' tables. There was some degree of trust in these groups, though longer prison sentences for drug offenses later eroded it.

Maurice's standard of living remained low because all his money went to support his drug habit. His mother and girlfriends kept food on the table and he was expected to bring them some money when he came to stay. If he had money when friends or family asked for help, he shared with them, as he would have expected them to do for him. When he got depressed and was using drugs heavily, he became abusive toward his girlfriends or retreated to the attic.

On a good day (as on pay day, when "the eagle flies"), Maurice and his friends would visit the local Chinese-owned restaurant and get fish sandwiches, coleslaw, and fries, or they would get cold cut sandwiches from the Italian store. On bad days, when they had no money, they stole food from the grocery store. When Maurice and his friends were high on drugs, they ate mostly sugar – lollipops and chocolate.

Because he had gone to high school and college outside the neighborhood, Maurice had more contacts for selling drugs across the city than his peers who had stayed in Southeast. But he sold mostly around Potomac Gardens to people who knew him from pickup basketball games in the neighborhood. He was a minor player in this business. He grossed $1,200–$2,000 every week, and about $800 of that was profit. Individual transactions ranged from $10 to $50. He described himself as a "rustler" (just trying to make ends meet), not a "hustler" (in it for the money).

Drugs permeated Maurice's world. They were in his immediate neighborhood, not only in the drug users and sellers but even among the police, because some of them were "dirty." Many residents came to distrust the police even more than before. Drugs also played a part in local politics – including D.C.'s mayor at the time, who was caught using drugs – and in the lives of local and national sports figures.

The Bigger World Moves into the Neighborhood

By the 1980s, Maurice began noticing that things were changing in the neighborhood and in the drug business. Drugs and drug addicts had been around in his childhood, but back then there were only four big drug dealers in the city. In some ways they were local Robin Hoods, stealing from the rich to give to the poor. And boys then still made a reputation by being popular with girls or being good at basketball. If they weren't athletic, they might get into dealing drugs because it made them popular and well known, but there wasn't a high level of violence in it.

Maurice wasn't aware of it, but the drug trade was becoming more globalized. He got his supply of cocaine from small dealers, not kingpins, but he was at the end of a long chain of distributors that could be traced back, in the U.S., to the notorious Crips Gang in California. Before that, coca plants grew in Peru or Bolivia, were turned into cocaine in Colombia and then shipped to the U.S. His supply chain for heroin was similar. His supplier, Joe, would travel to Amsterdam himself and buy heroin that came in from Afghanistan or Pakistan. He would carry it back packaged in cigarette packs, baby powder bottles, or other containers. Joe was eventually shot and killed at his house by a man who came to his door claiming to be the postman. Some of Maurice's peers were working as "mules," driving drugs down from New York City or carrying heroin from Amsterdam and Ghana to D.C.

Then, in the mid-1980s, crack cocaine – a low-priced, highly addictive form of cocaine – came to DC, bringing with it fierce drug wars and violence. Gun salesmen from Virginia would come to Maurice's neighborhood and sell guns out of the trunks of their cars. More children got involved in the drug trade; there was a big incentive for them because they would get only "juvenile time" in prison, which meant they were released at age twenty-one. In the juvenile prison, they could come home every forty-five days for a weekend; often they would get a hit list and kill several people in that weekend, receiving about $500 for each person killed. The number of people they killed – their "body beef" – was a source of pride and reputation. It was very different from Maurice's childhood.

The government response to the increased drug trade and violence was to step up drug enforcement with police traffic stops, "stings," and undercover work. In 1986, four years after Maurice left Howard, the Drug Enforcement Administration (DEA) and the D.C. Metropolitan Police wiretapped the telephone at his home and at June's (the dealer who replaced Joe after he was shot). Maurice and his brother were arrested for a drug distribution ring called "Dial-a-Dope," in which customers called in their drug orders. June and his assistant Roger were arrested several months later. Hundreds of street sellers were arrested around this time. The federal agencies thought they were getting major drug kingpins when, in fact, they were only "cleaning the streets." Younger men scrambled to fill the places of the local dealers.

Maurice was tried, convicted, and sentenced to nine months of probation for a single count of possession of heroin. If he had been charged with all the crimes he had committed (unlawful use of the phone, conspiracy to possess, conspiracy to distribute), he would have faced at least fifty-nine years in prison.

In and Out of the Drug World

While Maurice was on probation, he was turned in to the police by a girlfriend for using heroin; he had probably been ignoring her. In 1987, he received a sentence of ten months in a federal penitentiary in Lexington, Kentucky. Most of the guards there were white. Maurice found that prison changed people, forcing them to learn the new rules of the prison culture. For example, on the street, profanity was accepted and often was a sign of affection; in prison it was disrespectful. In general, people did not have crews or gangs in prison. From his time behind bars, Maurice learned that he was "not a jailhouse guy." He came back determined to stay out of the drug game, especially since it had "gotten so nasty."

While he was in prison, he began a relationship with another inmate. They got married on October 28, 1988, while she was home on furlough. She was paroled later that year and joined Maurice in D.C.

Maurice had gotten relatively clean in jail, but despite his resolution to stay away from drugs, he returned to the same neighborhood and the same situation upon his release. He started selling and using hard drugs again. He grossed $2,000 every week from heroin sales and another $2,000 a week from crack cocaine. Whatever profits he made, say $500 to a $1,000 a week, went to support his habit and take care of his family and friends. Soon – in February 1989 – he and his wife parted company. Maurice was now on a roll, down to the bottom.

In 1989, a reporter from the *Washington Post* did a series featuring Maurice as the "drug user and seller" of the notorious Potomac Gardens.

When the front-page article was published, the photo showed his lips around a crack pipe. Fr. Raymond Kemp was then the pastor of Holy Comforter-St. Cyprian in Southeast D.C., which had a number of parishioners from Potomac Gardens. The reporter called Fr. Kemp and told him that Maurice had stood out among the many drug dealers she spoke to because of his intelligence and education. She had asked him about the role of religion in his life and he had told her, "Call Father Kemp. He'll explain it to you." Fr. Kemp believed it was Maurice's way of asking him for help.

Fr. Kemp called Maurice and it was clear to him that something was happening: he had "hit bottom." Maurice started crying uncontrollably and talked about feeling totally empty and being "emotionally bankrupt." He found his way to Holy Comforter and enrolled in a month-long residential drug rehabilitation program.

When Maurice returned from rehabilitation, he went to live and work for Catholic Charities in the newly opened Father Horace McKenna, SJ, Transitional Home on Park Road in Northwest D.C. Although most of the leadership of Catholic Charities was white, most of the workers on his level were African Americans. His job was to help people in situations similar to his stay sober through support group meetings such as Alcoholics Anonymous and Narcotics Anonymous. He also helped them with job searches and managing their funds. Maurice worked at this and other constructive work for ten years, in and out of support group meetings, in and out of prayer and church, and in and out of relationships. During this time, his father passed away. Maurice became the chief instigator in getting four of his brothers off drugs and clean and sober. A big motivating factor for Maurice and his brothers was the pain that their actions had been causing their mother. Overall, he was doing pretty well.

Of Maurice's siblings, three brothers made it out of the neighborhood without selling drugs. One of them, an older brother, left town and joined the Air Force; another got married, moved to the suburbs, and became a "functional addict: someone who used drugs but still managed to cope with everyday life." He would come to Potomac Gardens to buy heroin from Maurice and another brother, but he was never involved in the drug business. A younger brother attended Mackin and then Howard, and became a pharmacist. Maurice's sisters used drugs occasionally but never got caught. Of the four brothers who did use and sell drugs, three were eventually arrested and spent time in prison, although not as much as Maurice's ten months.

Maurice moved to Texas for four and a half years to be with a white woman, a fellow counselor from the Potomac Job Corps. In a sense, he was trying to distance himself from his old life and its temptations. In Texas, he worked as a case manager at a teenage shelter and halfway house. The relationship did not last and he returned to D.C. because his mother had another stroke. She passed away shortly afterwards.

When he returned to D.C., he moved in with an old girlfriend. He had been diagnosed with high blood pressure, but he never took the medication because the label said it "may interfere with sexual performance." In January 2000, his kidneys failed and he had to go on dialysis. He became depressed and started smoking cigarettes and taking heroin again. His body was physically ravaged. This time, his brothers came to his aid and helped him get clean again. He moved in with another old girlfriend who lived a block from where he grew up and close to where two of his brothers lived. He developed a heart problem and in the spring of 2004 had quintuple bypass surgery.

The Present

Maurice is recovering nicely and hopes to get strong enough to receive a kidney transplant. He has two prospective compatible donors. He has returned to work at Catholic Charities and is working on his college degree, taking classes at Howard University and the University of the District of Columbia. He has started going to church again, this time to a nondenominational one founded by a friend. He has been praying. Recently, one of his most joyous times was playing Santa Claus and handing out gifts to poor children on Christmas Day.

CULTURAL ANALYSIS

Maurice's Traditional Culture

Maurice lives in the United States, but the culture that has primarily shaped him is the African-American urban culture. Some aspects of that culture are the same as those of the mainstream American culture, but others are quite different.

1. *Family.* Family bonds are strong; loyalty and support for family members is stressed. This includes a respect for elders, especially older women. It also includes an easy forgiveness for the failings of family members.

2. *Community.* This is defined as a sense of solidarity with the black community. In urban settings, it is often seen as a connection with the neighborhood (or the "hood": the street life of young black men).

3. *Individualism and materialism.* These traits are prevalent in the mainstream American culture and also in the urban black culture. They act in opposition to the traditional sense of community that is part of black culture and tend to diminish it.

4. *Religion.* In the black community, the Christian churches have played a major role, serving as a refuge and a source of support and strength for people.

5. *Inner strength and strong self-preservation instincts.* These traits can lead to both resilience and to numbness. For men, they often manifest as attitudes of "machismo."

6. *Resentment of the mainstream white culture.* There is a reluctance of many African Americans to accept the values of the white majority, an unwillingness to let white society define what is important. This includes the notion of success held by most white people.

Maurice's Critical Decisions

1. He decided to use and sell marijuana, and later heroin and cocaine, while he was in high school.

What were his options? He could have decided to be different from many people in his neighborhood and not use or sell drugs. As a source of income, he could have gotten a part-time job.

What cultural values lay behind his decision? He knew it wouldn't please his mother but many other people in the "hood" were doing it. Drugs were a way of being accepted by his friends.

What cultural values were reflected in the reactions of the other people in his life to this decision? His friends saw his decision as bringing him into the group. But his brothers and his mother did not want him getting involved in the drug business.

2. He decided to drop out of college and move back to his old neighborhood after he injured himself and could no longer play basketball.

What were his options? He could have stayed in college and made other life plans for himself, since the basketball option had closed. He could have moved to another part of Washington or even to another city and looked for work there.

What cultural values lay behind his decision? He resented the mainstream white culture and the elite and wealthy black community at Howard. He wanted to keep his own cultural definition of success, rather than accepting the standard American one of school and career. He also was strongly connected to his family and his neighborhood.

What cultural values were reflected in the reactions of the other people in his life to this decision? We have no solid information about this, but can assume that his family and friends welcomed him back home, even though his mother and his brothers, especially those who had college degrees, were disappointed that he'd left school.

3. He decided on several occasions to try to break his drug addiction but often relapsed.

What were his options? He didn't have to try to break free of drugs; he could have simply given up. Doing that would have been easier for him, because the bonds of addiction are so powerful.

What cultural values lay behind his decision? He knew how destructive drugs were and all the problems they caused. He also knew his drug use was hurting his family, particularly his mother, and that bothered him. Finally, his faith pushed him to stop using.

What cultural values were reflected in the reactions of the other people in his life to this decision? His family and Fr. Kemp, out of their care for him, supported him in his efforts.

Note: Maurice's sense of *community* – his neighborhood – and a desire to be accepted by his peers influenced these decisions. The pull of the "hood" certainly contributed to his getting involved in drugs and then relapsing after getting off them. Another strong motivating factor, especially in the decision to drop out of college, was his *resentment of the mainstream white culture. Family* influenced him when he decided to use and sell drugs, because his brothers were doing it. But it also was a positive factor during the times he tried to get off drugs. *Individualism and materialism,* though prevalent in U.S. culture, do not seem to drive Maurice's decisions. *Inner strength and self-preservation,* and *religion,* were at work in his efforts to get off drugs. When the people in Maurice's family reacted negatively to his decisions to start using and selling drugs and to drop out of college, they were motivated by their strong *family* bonds. This trait also lay behind their support when he fought his addiction. Many people in Maurice's neighborhood supported the decisions to use and sell drugs, influenced by their particular sense of connection with the "hood."

Changes in Maurice's Life

Crack cocaine and the more globalized drug trade began to dramatically change the landscape in Maurice's neighborhood in the 1980s: higher sales volume, more violence, less room for the local dealers who had run things before. It made Maurice's work dealing drugs more precarious and he ended up going to prison. Later, he had to deal with all the changes in the neighborhood caused by the more intense drug trade.

Consumption

Most of the changes in Maurice's consumption over the years revolved around his use of drugs. He started in high school with marijuana and then progressed to cocaine and heroin. After he dropped out of Howard University, most of his disposable income went to support his habit. Because of this, for large portions of his adulthood he was not much better off than he was as a child, in terms of what he consumed. He depended on his mother and various girlfriends to feed and shelter him, although he also gave them money from time to time when he had extra.

Interestingly, despite the fact that he is surrounded by a culture in which acquiring things – fashion items and electronics, for example – is stressed, Maurice has never seemed very materialistic. Even his chosen work of selling drugs has never had a greater purpose than satisfying his addiction and paying the bills. It was not to amass things.

Production

When he was young, Maurice's dream was to be a professional basketball player. When an injury destroyed this dream, he reacted by leaving college and becoming a street seller of heroin and cocaine. He supplemented his drug income by working at various jobs – with the Parks Department and as a teacher's aide – but his major occupation was selling drugs. It was a small-scale operation, relatively speaking, but it was part of a global network of drug production and distribution that passed through many other countries before coming to the United States and his Washington, D.C. neighborhood.

After he came out of jail, Maurice spent the next decade or so alternating between periods of using and selling drugs, on the one hand, and going to treatment programs and working at mainstream jobs on the other. He became seriously ill in 2000 and after that, with help from some of his brothers, he was able to stop using drugs.

Then Maurice started working for a Catholic Charities transitional program, helping other people through their own recovery. He has no special training to do this; his experience with addiction is what allows him to do this work.

Migration

Maurice has spent most of his life in the neighborhood where he was born and grew up. The only significant times away from it were when he went to college and to prison and, later, a brief move to Texas with a woman he knew from work. He left his neighborhood to go to school, but still stayed close to his family and friends.

His prison experience made him realize he wanted to change his life. But when he got out and returned to his old neighborhood he went back to using and selling drugs. His time away did not seem to change things. When he went to Texas to be with the new woman in his life, he was also trying to physically distance himself from that neighborhood. But he came back as soon as the relationship ended.

Although Maurice himself has not had to migrate because of global forces, over the years he saw many people move in and out of his neighborhood. The drug business also brought in new people, and with them came weapons and more violence. Many middle-class black families, including some of his brothers, left the neighborhood to escape the problems and moved to the suburbs. At the same time, a few poor immigrants from Latin America moved in.

Social Relations

Maurice's involvement with drugs over the years strongly affected his social relations. He seems to have repeated some of his father's patterns of addiction in his own life, though it was alcohol in his father's case. As a child, he and his brothers tried to defend their mother against their father's abuse. But when Maurice started using drugs, he became abusive with his girlfriends. And, like his father, he had several girlfriends at a time; he never stayed with one woman for very long.

Drugs damaged the relationships within his family as well, particularly with his mother. Maurice's drug use also distanced him from the siblings who had chosen a different path, one that did not include drugs. But drugs did provide a connection for Maurice to the "brothers in the "hood" The drug-related community, particularly when he was first involved in it, did provide Maurice with a social network. At that time in his life, his experience of neighbors was through his drug business. And because the people in the business were all raised in the same neighborhood, there was an attempt to preserve some semblance of social order. The drug dealers and users would ensure that the young people showed respect to children and elders, especially older women: "somebody's mother."

Drugs brought widespread violence to his community, particularly after the outside drug lords moved in. He saw that people simply accepted this violence as a way of life. It became normal to just move out of the way when police came to clean up murders, then move back again. At most, people would pour some beer or wine on the ground to honor the person who had been killed.

Maurice's social groups changed with the changing circumstances of his life. Going to college marked the first time he related to people outside his neighborhood and outside his social class. It was there that he experienced the politics of color within the African-American community. He went to a prestigious, historically black college, but felt looked down on by his wealthier classmates because of his low class and darker skin. They should have been his peers but instead he felt discriminated against.

He used drugs in college and met new people that way. When he began selling them, he met still more people: his customers. Still another group in college was made up of people involved in basketball. Later, after he left school, his social circle consisted of the other people in the drug business. Still later, Maurice's social circle changed again, and became the people he got to know in his work with Catholic Charities and the ones in his support groups.

His relationships with women did not change as much. They had often been marked by abuse when he was under the influence and by his habit of maintaining several romantic involvements at the same time. This pattern continued while he battled his addiction.

Political Power Relations

Maurice's relationship with political structures is intertwined with two things, drugs and race, and the police are involved in both of them. Although Maurice's experience of the drug business was always centered on his neighborhood, that local business was becoming part of a much broader international phenomenon. As the drug trade became more globalized, Maurice was exposed, at least to a limited extent, to the larger world.

From the perspective of Maurice and his community, their relationship with the police is tainted by discrimination. Even in his childhood, police were never seen as the "good guys," but as outsiders, because most of them were white. As Maurice grew older, he had many run-ins with them; he was regularly stopped for driving too fast and suspicion of guns and drugs. As the drug business grew, all this intensified. On the national level, the War on Drugs emerged as a response to the increase in drug use, which meant even more police and more crackdowns in Maurice's neighborhood. His ultimate confrontation with the white power structure came when he went to prison, where he found most of the inmates were also black and the guards and wardens were all white.

Religious Experience and Expression

Religion has always been part of Maurice's life. It was around him as a child, when he went to a Catholic church with his mother and, occasionally, to a Baptist church with his father. In high school, he experienced God as a way of getting rid of the negativity in his life and began a lifelong friendship with Fr. Kemp. As an adult, he experienced God in his recoveries over the years and he eventually found meaning in prayer and in church. He currently goes, every other week, to a nondenominational Christian church founded by an old friend and self-proclaimed minister, that reflects black culture. His faith was – and still is – a lifeline for him but he is not overtly very religious.

Maurice has a basic moral sensibility, though it has been shaped by how he grew up. For example, he had a guilty conscience not when he sold and used drugs but when he treated his women badly or disappointed his mother. Some of this can perhaps be traced to the traditional religion brought to America by the African slaves. One can see this link in certain neighborhood customs: the respect for elders, especially mothers, and the pouring of beer or wine to honor someone who has been killed.

INTERPRETATION

U.S. Economic Globalization and Maurice

Globalization entered Maurice's life most directly through the expansion of a global industry – the production and trade of illegal drugs – that does not have a home country. Its home is the globe. It moves to wherever there is demand; it works at stimulating that demand everywhere; and it is truly multinational. It originates wherever nature provides the basic ingredients to make the products and then distributes them through worldwide channels. All of this is largely outside the control, except for corruption, of national states.

As the U.S. liberalized its economy in the 1980s, it was already fighting the War on Drugs. This addressed primarily the supply of drugs: attempts at eradication in supplying countries (such as coca plants in Bolivia) and greater law enforcement within the U.S. It made only a feeble attempt to restrict the demand for drugs in the U.S. Arguably, the reduction of subsidies to the poor that accompanied the deregulation actually might have stimulated the demand for drugs. In any case, the U.S. policy on illegal drugs has had only a very limited impact on drug use in the country.

None of this justifies Maurice's involvement with drugs, but it is a testimony to the power of international forces, even illegal ones, in a global economy. It also shows the very limited effect that U.S. drug policy had on reducing the use of drugs by people like Maurice. His time in prison for using drugs taught him that he didn't want to get caught and go back to prison. But it is the privately-sponsored Catholic Charities that has helped him in his attempts to rehabilitation, not the government.

Maurice as a Person

Drugs have dominated Maurice's life and he formed his values around drugs. For much of his life, he has navigated between two different worlds in which drugs are seen very differently. The neighborhood where he grew up and where he still lives – the "hood"– revolved around drugs. Even the self-image he adopted as he grew out of childhood came from the "power" linked to drugs. The "hood" pulled him toward addiction, violence, and prison. But Maurice also lived in the world represented by his mother, a world of being drug-free and responsible. His ties with his mother pulled him toward health and good relationships, and when he was very young those ties helped form him, even though as he grew older they could not compete with the drugs all around him. The rest of his family also is also part of that positive world. They never abandoned him; they loved and accepted him through all his problems. And his love for them was part of his motivation when he tried to break his drug addiction. More concretely, when he did finally stop, some of his brothers helped him do it. His family was a bridge for him in his journey toward recovery and healing.

Outside his family Maurice has always been part of two communities, which overlap with each other: his African-American neighborhood and the people in the drug business. The neighborhood forms a core part of his identity and is where he feels at home, where he belongs. He still maintains strong ties with people there, even after spending time away in prison and in Texas. When he joined drug treatment support groups, he was able to use the community to reach out to others. Maurice also has great respect for the wider black community's struggles in the past, and this gives him strength. In many ways, the rituals of family, friends, and neighborhood are the most resilient things in Maurice's life.

On the other hand, the neighborhood was also an enabling environment for developing his addiction and his drug business. It was also a narrow, limited community, especially after many middle-class people moved out because of the drugs and violence. The people who were left were more economically depressed and less diverse, and were thus even more marginalized than before from the rest of society.

Maurice's other community, made up of the people in the drug business, was connected to the neighborhood, at least in the earlier years of his addiction. There was a semblance of trust and honesty in this early drug community, which was based on shared history: growing up in the same neighborhood and eating at each other's mothers' tables. Yet this community based on drugs was intrinsically destructive and had primarily a negative effect on Maurice – his health, his relationships, his education, his work life, and so on.

Maurice only feels comfortable in these two overlapping communities. He never envisioned for himself the standard – white – American dream of success through higher education and business. Characteristic of the African-American culture, he resents the mainstream white culture and has rejected its dream. He chose instead, at least in his earlier life, the dream of the street. As a seller of drugs, success is redefined to mean survival: staying alive, out of jail, and making enough money to support his habit. In the world of the "hood," life probably looked like a dead-end street for Maurice as he was growing up. He did not expect to make it to age thirty, thinking he would be killed by then. He found it hard to conceive of himself as a productive person.

Over time Maurice saw things change and he had to grow and change along with them, with his family, teammates, girlfriends, Howard classmates, even his jail mates. What was once local – "I know you, I'm Maurice, son of ___" – became, once he entered the drug culture that was expanding with the global economy, a bartered, economic, socially structured relationship. Relationships now became more objective, with others and self becoming objects to be manipulated and used for power or pleasure. Maurice saw this objectification in college, when he saw what he thought was the abuse of some of his teammates by the coaches and the school. He also saw how relationships in the drug business were too often controlled by violent behavior. So he has experienced some profound changes – but despite them, Maurice seems to be able to keep a lifeline of loving family and some friends and church.

Maurice has made many bad decisions in his life. He was very young when he began using drugs; even so, no one forced him to do it. In fact, his brothers tried to dissuade him from taking that path. On the other hand, over the years, he did try several times to break his addiction and escape the world of drugs. Each time, he would succeed for a while and then relapse. He struggled to overcome something very tenacious, not only socially and emotionally but physically. Once addicted, he did not just take the easiest path and give in to the world of drugs; he kept trying to leave it. He has an inner strength that helps him carry on and survive in tough times. He draws on the resilience of his culture. Maurice is a subject, trying at different periods in his life to take action and take charge of his life.

As time passed, he has redefined his communities. His globalized drug community is no longer made up of his drug business friends, and acquaintances, but instead revolves around his new job, around helping people get off drugs rather than selling them. They are positive relationships rather than negative ones. In his own support groups (self-help groups that helped him stay off drugs), and in his work helping others, he is reaching out to people, a sign of growth.

For an African American, America's history of racial discrimination, including slavery, is always in the background. It is not surprising that Maurice holds strangers, especially people of different races and classes, at a distance. In general, he has problems dealing with the world when it becomes too big. It is easier for him to move in the small circles where he is comfortable (family, neighborhood) and not venture far away. This sharply limits his horizons in a globalizing world.

Understandably, Maurice also has difficulty trusting. He cannot trust "the man"– those in authority – especially the police and prison guards. He could not even trust the people at the historically black university, who proved themselves untrustworthy when he realized they were, to his mind, exploiting some of his teammates and looking down on him for his social class. This problem with trusting, like his holding people unlike him at a distance, limits his ability to grow.

But along with his new work and new community, Maurice has a new definition of success, a more constructive one. It is no longer the drug-based definition of mere survival but one of staying sober and making it through each day. More than that, his religious world view has expanded as well. But Maurice's hopes and dreams of the future are not on a grand scale. They are limited by his fear of success. After his cycles of addiction and recovery, he knows that the higher he is able to climb, the worse the fall will be when he relapses. So he confines his dreams to small things, within the world that he knows.

Religion is the one area of his life where Maurice seems to be able to integrate the "opposites" that make up his life. Despite all the negatives and guilt about drugs, academic failure, and authority struggles, for Maurice, religion and the church seem to be the lifeline that makes him feel good (or at least a little good) about himself. God is a source of strength for him, and he discerns God's presence through other alcoholics and in his prayer life. He has a strong impulse toward growth and healing, which impelled him to try to beat his addiction and then continue his education. He also has a moral sense, evidenced in his moving from healing himself to wanting to heal others in his work. He sees children as a sign of hope and an embodiment of what is good in life.

The Exodus narrative in particular resonates with him. The cycle of slavery, exodus, and then re-enslavement seems to represent Maurice's life – and the African-American experience in general. His experience of full human freedom seems limited, whether by the disease of addiction or by social structures. But despite failed relationships, drugs, and violence, he seems to be able to relate back to his mother's love and a meaningful religious experience. His life cycle through basketball hopes, college failure, prison time, and on to Catholic Charities, seems almost to be a postmodern-global-urban retelling of the Paschal Mystery. That might be too neat or too optimistic but, indeed, it seems to be Maurice's only bridge to confronting reality and becoming a free-acting subject rather than a victim.

Chapter 16

Marie in Cameroon:
A New Way of Being
a Cameroonian Woman *

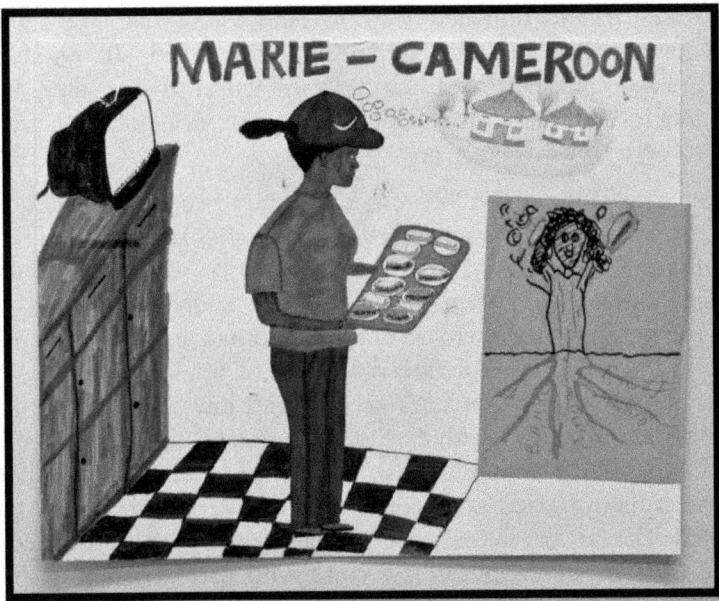

Marie's mosaic tile from GEC's Fourth International Consultation

NARRATOR: JEAN JACQUES TENE

Provided early version of narrative and cultural analysis
Yaoundé, Cameroon

* For an experimental application of Phase II methodology to the story of
Marie, see the Appendix, "A New Way of Seeing Marie – A Controlled
Experiment in Applying Phase II Methodology" that follows Chapter 17.

Narrative Summary and Economic Background

Marie's life changed drastically in 1996, when she lost her job as a secretary in a government-owned company in Yaoundé, Cameroon's capital. The company had been privatized as part of Cameroon's Structural Adjustment Program (SAP) and the new owners began dismissing employees to increase productivity. The job had provided status, security, a small but steady income, and a way for her to help her family and clan in the village. Suddenly, in her thirties, Marie had to find new ways to fend for herself. She started selling sandwiches in a bar. When this effort failed, she opened a small restaurant. She found herself in the world of struggling, hustling micro-entrepreneurs. Her challenge was not only to survive but to forge new meanings and values.

Starting in the mid-1980s Cameroon faced economic deterioration, which reached crisis proportions in the 1990s. It resulted most directly from a worldwide decline in the prices of its commodity exports: oil, coffee, cocoa, and cotton. To address the crisis, the government devalued the currency and adopted austerity measures; later, in 1994 and more seriously in 1996, it implemented an SAP under the IMF. These policies kept salaries low and reduced government subsidies in health care, education, and social services. As part of the SAP, the country also began a program of privatization of government-owned companies, such as the one in which Marie worked. The cost of living went up sharply and people struggled to make ends meet. People in the cities who used to support their families in the rural areas found this much harder to do. Unlike many other countries undergoing economic restructuring, agriculture became an even more significant portion of the economy. Already important in the mid-1990s, with a share of 28 percent, agriculture has accounted for an average of 42 percent of the nation's output since the new measures were introduced. Surprisingly, the service sector – where Marie now works – lost relative importance in the economy. Cameroon's economic fate has been tied to the fluctuations in world prices of the commodities it exports. Its annual rate of growth per capita has been as high as nearly 20 percent, when oil production began, and as low as negative 10 percent, when world commodity prices collapsed.

NARRATIVE

The office was crowded with boxes and sluggish workers. Along with a few other secretaries, Marie packed up the few personal items on her desk and said her goodbyes. The workers' salaries had been decreasing gradually over the last ten years but now the company was being privatized and she had lost her job altogether. It was a real shock to her.

Coming to the front door of the office building, Marie sighed pensively before stepping outside. She headed home to be with her two children, wondering where she could find work and how they would survive. For the first time in a long time, Marie looked to her Christian God for help and protection.

Marie had worked as a secretary in a government-owned company in Yaoundé, Cameroon's capital, for a number of years. She had lived in the city her entire life, ever since her parents had come from their village to look for jobs. But she had kept close ties with the village, as most Cameroonians in the city did, particularly after her parents moved back there. She regularly sent money from her salary to her extended family and supported them in other ways as well. For a long time, Marie was able to live comfortably herself and still help out. In return, her parents and family in the village regularly sent her vegetables, fruit, and tubers, which meant she didn't have to spend as much money on food. These gifts were not only a way of helping one another; they also expressed their desire to maintain good relations and remain at peace with the ancestors.

Marie was very much part of the village tradition, where everybody cared for others in the community (especially the elderly and disabled) and accepted help in turn. They were interdependent, living in a network of mutual aid and reciprocal obligations. However, Marie was the family member working in the city and making the most money, so she was the one most responsible for financially supporting her relatives.

Marie's ability to provide this support began to erode in 1986 with the collapse of world commodity prices, on which Cameroon depended heavily for its exports. To cope with the impact of the crisis, Marie's company began to reduce its employees' salaries. At first the reduction was somewhat bearable. She could still manage, even with the pay cuts, because of the food her village sent her. That support helped her get by. But the systematic reduction continued at increasingly higher rates, finally reaching nearly 70 percent. Then in 1996 the company was privatized and Marie lost her job.

The Country Struggles

The economic crisis put a great deal of pressure on the existing political system, which was basically a one-party system. A few years after the crisis erupted, political opening and a multi-party system began to emerge. Marie, along with many others, was fed up with the current regime, which now could not even deliver economic stability. She wanted greater accountability and transparency in the government. The single-party system had discriminated against and even banned other parties and newspapers that criticized the government. As a result, there had been virtually no opposition to political leaders, even in the midst of corruption and persecution.

Marie held the government responsible for her situation, accusing it of poor organization and empty legislation. The law, in her eyes, was simply decoration and completely ineffectual. She thought the new political opening would allow for more transparency and the possibility of people defending their rights against abuse. So, seeing democratic action as a way of improving her situation, Marie became actively committed to politics. In particular, she got involved in fighting for the appropriate use of public revenue, a viable economic situation, and rights for women.

In 1990, Marie decided to become a member of the main opposition party, the Social Democratic Front (SDF). Life as a member of the SDF was not easy. She knew that associating with this party would lead to discrimination, but she supported its vision strongly enough to face the consequences of opposing the majority. Because of fear, many members hid their affiliation with the SDF. Marie refused such anonymity and would not keep her views or attitude a secret. She would rather be a martyr for democracy than a timid and muted victim. So in 1996, when she was dismissed from the newly-privatized company by the new owners, who were active members of the incumbent government, she concluded that this was her political martyrdom.

Conflict

When Marie lost her job, she and her family wondered how they would all survive. The economic crisis, and the economic measures meant to deal with it, had had a very negative impact on her whole family. Those living in the village, including her parents, needed more and more help – but Marie was becoming less and less able to provide money for them. Not only had she lost her job, the cost of living kept going up and government subsidies for things like health and education had gone down. It was impossible for her to fulfill her family duties. Before, Marie had been able to contribute financially to relatives in the village, helping with things like funerals, educating the children, and caring for her parents. Now, she could only afford to give money to her parents and care for her own children.

Even before she was fired, Marie had been encountering growing disappointment and resentment from her family in the village. Her aunts and uncles and some of her cousins did not believe that she was too poor to give them more money. They had seen the life of city dwellers and did not think it was possible to be poor in the city. They began to mistrust Marie, believing that her economic problems were only a cover-up for her selfishness. Her parents and children understood her difficulties, and her friends and neighbors in the city sympathized with her. They could see her generosity in the midst of her struggles. Her extended family, however, could not and they only complained more. Nonetheless, they continued sending food to her – expressing their desire to maintain a good relationship.

Marie felt she had no options. She had lost her only source of income and was still unemployed. Because of her well-known political affiliation, it was very hard for her to find a job.

Taking Action

To begin with, Marie wanted another job like the one she had. She looked very hard for it, going to many companies and talking to many people. She knew she had the skills. But these places had nothing for her.

Then Marie felt that God gave her some practical and tangible support: she discovered a group of women who offered to help her find work. These women belonged to the same tribe as Marie and had formed a *tontine*, a voluntary association organized to give its members financial

and other kinds of support. Long a tradition in Cameroon, *tontines* originally focused on social activities. Recently they had turned to financial and
other projects in response to the economic crisis created when the government reduced many social services. Many *tontines*, like Marie's, became
official non-governmental organizations (NGOs). The women gave Marie
the support and community that she badly needed. Her traditional solidarity with family and village had been weakened by living and working in the
city, but the group provided a new type of solidarity.

The women gave Marie affirmation and reassurance. Since they realized Marie would probably not be able to find a good job like the one she
had had before, they suggested that she start her own business. She had
never thought it possible to take such an initiative in entrepreneurship,
but felt she had no other real alternative. So, empowered by the group,
she decided to start her own business selling sandwiches at a bar.

The women's group, though not physically working with her, gave
Marie much support. They advised her on how to operate in her new job
and provided a network of people and resources for her. So Marie began
making and selling sandwiches to the many city dwellers looking for
quick, cheap food. She made them during the day and sold them every
evening from 6:00 p.m. to 11:00 p.m. On weekends she could sell sandwiches as late as 4:00 a.m. to the night owls relaxing at the bars. On an
average, Marie would make about 5000 CFA every night. She was amazed,
when she thought about it from time to time: she had gone from being a
secretary in a government-owned company to an entrepreneur with a new
small business. But not everybody back in the village saw it that way.

Marie had become the breadwinner and caretaker for her family, but
not a figure of authority. A woman was not supposed to hold authority
over other adult family members, especially over men. She discovered that
the same notion applied to business. Because she did not have a regular
job with an employer, many people thought she did not have a job at all,
and considered her business activity illegitimate. Moreover, as a woman in
business she received no respect from many of these people. Some even
considered her a prostitute since, they thought, no female could truly succeed in making a profit without sleeping with men. But for Marie, her new
job, though it didn't bring in a great deal of money, gave her a sense of
self-respect and appreciation along with freedom and independence. She
was exercising talents and gifts she never knew she had.

Adjusting to a New Life

But other things made it hard for Marie to adapt. She now had a very long work day and had little time for the children; the older child had to take care of the younger one. Still, time had never been of much concern to her in her old job or to her family, and so efficiency in her business suffered. The notion of competition was also foreign to her. Adjusting to her new job created mixed feelings in her. It was different from what she was used to and so there was some discomfort. She feared losing her identity in her national tradition. But she desired a better life and enjoyed the feeling of being current and individual.

Around the time Marie began her sandwich business, the country's economic liberalization was opening the door more widely to Western culture. Foreign media came in, providing more choices and better quality programs. Although this media invasion was largely due to the prevailing poor Cameroonian programming, it nonetheless came at the expense of national media, so it was even more difficult for local programs to succeed. The media and the products now available in the stores introduced Marie to consumer goods that improved the quality of her life. Her children even began taking advantage of the Internet. Media provided entertainment and education, the Internet gave her children information through e-learning, and cell phones made communication even easier.

However, access to foreign media gradually also created a drive to Westernize that pulled Marie away from her traditional culture and influenced the attitudes of her children. Learning from watching television, Marie started to keep her house differently and changed her hairstyle and wardrobe. She was not alone: the captivating plot, scandals, and intrigues of American and Latin American soap operas such as *The Bold and the Beautiful, Dallas,* and *Isaura* engrossed the whole city of Yaoundé. Every Friday night, virtually everyone with access to a television set would drop everything to watch these shows. But Marie was frustrated with the ways the shows influenced her children's attitudes toward their elders and sexual behavior. Since their education now relied primarily on schools and teachers rather than on family, she thought they were at risk of being affected by this alternative lifestyle portrayed on TV more than by their own personal heritage. But even Marie was addicted to the stories and thought that it was good for her children to at least be exposed to other cultures and be challenged to know more about the world.

As well as changing Marie's lifestyle and loosening her ties to tradition, this infatuation with media affected her business as well. Every Friday evening, from 9:30 pm to 10:15 p.m., the streets of Yaoundé emptied. Hoping to catch every minute of the riveting new episode, Marie's clients rushed to the nearest small screen, usually forgetting to pick up a sandwich. Marie finally decided to stop selling once the shows started, so that she too could keep up with the latest soap stories. As a result, she cut her hours on Fridays to 6:00 p.m. to 9:00 p.m. and made less than half as much money, only 2000 CFA.

Finally, the owner of the bar where Marie sold her sandwiches allowed a female friend of his to start selling sandwiches there also. Eventually Marie was forced to shut down her sandwich business. Having lost the sandwich business, Marie decided to try again for another office job. But nothing was available to her. Some people she contacted even suggested that they might have a job for her, if she would be willing to provide certain personal services in return – sexual services. Marie rejected this option and instead looked for help from her women's group again. Armed with their encouragement, and with the experience and business sense she had gained from her sandwich business, Marie decided to open a small restaurant. The women's group advised her on how to open and run an official, registered restaurant and she took out a loan to get underway.

Soon the new restaurant started to generate some profits, but still not enough to provide more support for the extended family in the village. But Marie was more at peace now that she considered her family to consist first of her parents and children and only secondarily her other relatives. She did not let the extended family interfere with her business. She was also changing her concept of neighbor and community. She now identified herself not only by village, town, bloodline, and ethnicity, but also by her worth as a restaurant owner, her interests, and her political party. However, this greater freedom and individualism often was accompanied by loneliness. Marie had children and friends, but living in the city, it was possible for her and people around her to be sick or poor and have no help or support from anyone. Had it not been for the women in the NGO, she could have cried about her problems for hours, walking through the city, bumping into thousands of people but never embracing any of them.

Contributing to Marie's sense of isolation was the situation in her personal life. Years earlier, she had married a man and neither one had told their parents, which according to the traditional culture was highly disrespectful. Having already started to think of herself less in local and ethnic terms, she had no problem marrying a man from a different tribe and religious denomination. But since she had not told her parents about her marriage, she could not look to them for support, advice, or consolation when it was struggling. The marriage ended in divorce. Her parents did not even find out about her husband until they had had two children and had gotten divorced. His parents to this day do not accept either Marie or the children.

Marie's parents did not resent her marriage and offered their support when she came back home to the village. But they did press her to offer a sacrifice to the ancestors to placate them for their anger about her marriage and divorce. Like most Cameroonians, her parents held a strong belief in the ancestors and attributed any problems to somehow angering them. They thought that Marie's losing her job and her inability to find another one were a punishment for her transgressions. But Marie refused to offer any such sacrifices, and this was not typical. She considered them a violation of her Christian faith.

Even though she continued to feel a strong bond with her ethnic group in the village, by now she was developing a modern understanding of society and of personal freedom, especially of women's rights, that she could not reconcile with village life. Even if she could have been better off financially and emotionally in the village, Marie refused to move back. She could not accept her role as a woman there, nor the power that the village elders exerted on everybody in the village.

Marie's Day

In spite of economic problems, Marie's restaurant continues to operate and she is content living in the city where she was born and raised.

She tallies up the week's totals as the helper gets the dining room ready for the next day and closes up the kitchen. The screeching sounds of tables being shoved across the tile floor echo against the low ceilings. The smell of the night's menu wafts past Marie's nose as she calmly stacks the money. Counting the meager profits, she compares her own earnings to the monthly bills. She should still have enough to send some to her parents. She adds up the day's final numbers once again before placing her chair upside down on a small round table.

Locking the front door of the restaurant, Marie looks at her watch to catch the time. It's just after 11:00 p.m. and she thinks about her children. They will have finished watching *The Bold and the Beautiful* and should be in bed. She thinks of her cousins and her surviving aunts and uncles in the village. Having not talked to any of them for a while, Marie hopes that their harvest is good. She also remembers that tomorrow will be Sunday, but once again she will not have time to go to Mass. She has to be back in the restaurant by 6:00 a.m.

CULTURAL ANALYSIS

Marie's Traditional Culture

Even though Marie grew up in the city and still lives there, she was brought up within the traditional culture by parents who had just migrated to the city. She also maintains close contacts with her village, where her parents have gone to live. The traditional culture is still very much a part of her life.

1. *Solidarity.* The community is emphasized over the individual. Each person is seen as "being with," living in a web of relationships rather than in isolation. Human relations take precedence over material things. This value finds expression in sharing, mutual aid, and a sense of reciprocal obligation. It is very important for people to have a sense of belonging; conversely, rejection is feared.

2. *Vertical culture.* There is an ordered sense of hierarchy and authority. Parents, chiefs, and elders exert a great deal of control over people's lives. They are highly respected and people are reluctant to challenge their authority. This system includes strict gender roles, with women generally not allowed to have any authority.

3. *Strong family bonds.* The family plays a major role in the culture and it is the extended family, rather than the nuclear family.

4. *A strong sense of the "spirits" world.* Spirits are both evil and good. They are the mystical powers that help good people and punish others for wrongdoing.

5. *A spirit of enterprise.* In Marie's ethnic group, this spirit is a common trait.

Marie's Critical Decisions

1. She decided to sell sandwiches at a bar after she lost her office job and then, when that business failed, to open a small restaurant.

What were her options? When she lost her job, she looked for a job in another company in the city. But she couldn't get one because of her involvement with the opposition party. She could have taken a job offered her in one company – in exchange for sexual favors – but she refused. She also could have moved to her parents' home village but didn't want to do this. Later, when she was forced out of her sandwich business, her other options were the same: prostitution and returning to her village. Again, she rejected these choices and chose to stay in business.

What cultural values lay behind these decisions? When she lost her office job, she worried at first that the spirits were punishing her because she had not been taking care of her obligations to her relatives back in the village. But she put aside this concern. She relied on the women's group that was helping her for advice and funds as she worked to succeed in business. Business is one of the favorite activities of people from her tribe; they are known to be very skillful entrepreneurs.

What cultural values were reflected in the reactions of the other people in her life to this decision? To the people in her village, a woman running a business was unacceptable. They thought that a woman in business must be a prostitute because she encounters so many men that she may be tempted to go beyond a professional relationship. But her neighbors in the city understood Marie's situation. They were supportive and hospitable, offering her encouragement and helping care for her children.

2. She decided to reduce the financial support she would offer to her extended family in the village.

What were her options? Her first option was to continue providing this support, but Marie felt she could not do this. Her economic circumstances were so dire that she did not think she could afford to keep it up.

What cultural values lay behind her decision? Marie thought the demands made upon her by her extended family were not fair. She valued the independence that came with living in the city and working for herself, and she was not willing to let village norms dictate her behavior. But she worried about the consequences in her relationship with the village and possibly the ancestors' spirits punishing her for withdrawing support.

What cultural values were reflected in the reactions of the other people in her life to this decision? People in the village assumed that Marie's financial situation was better than theirs and that she was being selfish in not providing support for them. They resented her because they believed she was learning foreign ways in the city and rejecting the traditional village obligation of supporting the family.

Note: Marie's decision to go into business was consistent with her tribe's characteristic trait of a *spirit of enterprise*. The reaction of the people in her village to this decision shows the traits of a *vertical culture* and the *subordinate role of women*. In contrast, Marie was rebelling against those traits. The reactions of her neighbors to her decision reflected the trait of *solidarity*, but a new solidarity as it has been redefined in the city. Marie's decision to reduce her financial support showed her ambivalence about the traditional trait of *solidarity* with the extended *family and clan*. She could not accept it, and she adapted it to meet her changed circumstances, although she worried about punishment from the *spirits*. She redefined *family* as her children and her parents, instead of including the extended family dictated by tradition. The people in the village, however, continued to hold the traditional view of *solidarity* with the extended family and they condemned her decision.

Changes in Marie's Life

Marie lost her job and her income when her company was privatized, and she had to find a new way to make a living. But she had to make many other changes as she navigated her way through life in a globalized world. She was forced to reevaluate many of the basic values that had been part of her life.

Consumption

> *Ku oza burya esaazi neiwe ozirya:* When you go to where they eat flies, you also eat them. In a new place, you can learn from existing practices.

> *Enkinko eshonda eki eramire:* A hen bites what it can swallow. Be modest and keep to your means and capacity.

> *Man skui ngaya aje kledlao man skui ngaya a mbay vao ndev gnaya:* If you have much, give your goods; if you possess little, give your heart. Everyone always has something to share with others.

With Cameroon's greater exposure to the global economy, Marie has more imported consumer goods available to her now, especially Western ones. Often they have lower prices than local goods. In general she feels these new goods have improved her quality of life in many ways. She and her children like these new things and often choose Western clothing, food, and hairstyles. It is a new lifestyle for her – but one that marks her as different from some members of her tribe, especially those back in the village.

She now has access to foreign media. The new TV programs are better quality than the local ones: Marie especially enjoys watching Western soap operas. Television is a major influence on her consumption choices. Also, the new media and the Internet give her access to more information than she had in the past and therefore more choices in the political arena. The media has broadened her horizons and opened her to a wider world. It helps her deal with the tensions she experiences in the new environment. For example, when she sees single mothers on TV, it helps her feel more comfortable with her own situation. And her children use the Internet for information and learning.

But Marie believes that much of the new TV and radio has a negative effect on how she raises her children, and that there aren't enough controls over things like pornography. These popular Western TV shows also have tended to give her both unrealistic expectations about family life and aspirations to a Western lifestyle.

Despite her increased consumption choices, Marie is finding that some critical domestic services, such as education and health care, now cost more because government subsidies for them have been reduced. So the total amount of things she can buy with her income, even though it is higher than before, has actually decreased.

These economic changes have altered how Marie spends her income in an even more profound way. She has fewer resources with which to help her extended family in the village. She cannot provide the same support to them as before, although she continues to receive help from them in the form of food. This situation creates great conflicts for her. She can no longer give the gifts that show her desire to have good relations with the people in the village. She feels alienated from her traditional culture and is afraid that her choices are making her a foreigner to her own people.

Production

> *Wadar a kele me gnaya a mbay ka de a hecheket a ka de pere'e:* The jujube never falls into the mouth; it is necessary to go and pick it. Even the free wild fruit asks for an effort to obtain it. Nothing is obtained effortlessly.

> *Koa ndi houdgui ngaya cumba ka heche ndaf ngaya aringnaya:* The clan is merely a multitude. You cannot always depend on the group; you must be responsible for yourself.

> *Nyenge nyenka akeenga mabi:* He who said let me brew alone brewed bad beer. If you work alone, you are likely to make mistakes.

Marie went from being a secretary in a government-owned company to being an entrepreneur in a new small business: the restaurant business. Her old job was relatively stable and she was a wage earner working for a supervisor. Now her work is less stable and the profits in her enterprise depend on hard-to-predict business forces. Instead of working under someone who is above her, she works for herself and her business fate depends on her customers and on business people such as her restaurant suppliers.

She suffered a loss of prestige among her friends and family when she lost her company job. Among workers, those who work for the government get more respect in her society than those who don't, even if they don't make much money. Also, in traditional thinking, the notion of "job" is associated with working for someone else. So a person working alone will feel jobless, even when earning a lot of money. Marie has yet to accept that her business is her job.

Marie felt angry and afraid when she lost her secretarial job. She was angry because she suspected that her affiliation with the opposition political party led to her firing and she was afraid because she didn't know how she would support herself and her children. When she went into business for herself she felt tension because in the traditional Cameroonian culture women are not supposed to be producers outside the household.

Migration

> *Akanyonyi Katagyenda tikaanya eyibwezire*: A little bird that does not travel does not know where there is a rich harvest of millet. Don't be too comfortable with where you are.

> *Omwana otagyenda agyira ngu nyina niwe ateka kurungyi*: A child who does not travel thinks his mother is the best cook.

> *Man ka sun sem diman ka ndepe mbi war shived man ka check tepa*: When you do not know where you go, look where you come from. The origin helps us to find the road to follow.

Strictly speaking, Marie is not a migrant because she was born in the city. She still lives in the city and prefers living there; it gives her joy and hope. But her immediate family lives in the village. Her parents originally migrated from the village to the city and then moved back there after retirement. She often goes there to visit them and the village elders. In spite of her new independence and her enjoyment of city life, the village and its traditions still have a powerful hold on Marie, even when she deliberately chooses not to follow those traditions. However, she wouldn't go to live there, even if financially and emotionally she could be better off in the village.

Social Relations

> *Ri mandi a pen ri gloa, ri gloa pen ri mandi:* One hand washes the other.

> *Goali ngaya ndar hecheket waff man ka paodi aseem dra'a aman ka ndickanda sema ndokwa ndar woufhi man ndawa ndawa a guidna:* The clan is like a cluster of trees which, seen from afar, appear huddled together, but which stand individually when approached more closely. The individual is real, and his or her individuality cannot be diminished by membership in a human community.

Marie's relationships today are very different from what they were when she worked as a secretary. They differ even more sharply from what they would have been in her parents' village. In the village, she would have related only to members of her family and her ethnic group. In the city, she relates to her neighbors and to other people, who may be from a different ethnic group than her own. They form her primary social circle. Since she started her sandwich business and the restaurant, her relations have actually expanded. The women's group to which she belongs is a focus for her new social relationships, which now include her customers and the suppliers to her business. But she also has less time for other relationships because of the long hours she has to spend working. She feels very bad that she has less time to spend with her children and cannot afford to visit the village as often.

Living in the city, Marie has to a large extent broken away from the social dictates of traditional village culture. She owns her own business, so she is a producer and, to a certain extent, an authority figure. She married a man from another tribe and now lives apart from her family as a single mother. She decided that she could no longer support all of her extended family in the village. All these things challenge the traditional Cameroonian view of women, which does not allow women to be independent or to have authority.

Marie decides for herself what work she will try to do, what consumer goods she will buy, and how much support she can provide to the village. She likes this freedom. She knows that in the vertical culture of the village, many of these decisions would be made for her, by family members, village chiefs, and other authority figures. The fact that she is forging her own way and has made decisions that go against traditional customs has led some people in the village to criticize her.

In adopting a more Western lifestyle and assuming the responsibility and authority required to run her own business, Marie is considered to have gone "beyond the norms of decency" in the traditional social interactions between men and women, the young and the aged, and with one's extended family. Back in the village, a woman refusing to comply with these social traditions would likely be considered bewitched and even get killed. In the city, Marie can escape these traditions, but not the censure from those who remain tied to the village culture.

Her choices have created tension in Marie. She has no doubts about the path she has chosen – she is confident she is doing the right thing – but she knows that her independence has weakened her ties to the village. She reacts to this situation with desire and fear: desire because she really enjoys her new independence and would like to grow in it, and fear because she would also like the extended family and the village to understand and accept her situation.

Political Power Relations

Wafukaana nomuhango orahendeka: If you wrestle with a big person, you break down. Before you take on a fight, weigh your strength against your opponent.

Man ndohi tele te zub giguile asem tsad ndo man ndeb ada dzana azembay: If all the people were to carry the heavens, no one individual would become humpbacked.

Babukiika tibwo bwengye: Holding a meeting will not necessarily bring wisdom. Don't rely just on group advice.

Cameroon's political opening was accompanied by the emergence of a multiparty system that gave people more political choices. Marie, who was fed up with the oppression of the former one-party regime, was able to get involved in politics and she became active in the main opposition party, the Social Democratic Front. The opening also meant there was more tolerance for her new role as a businesswoman, at least in the city, even though she did not come from the ruling party's tribe. So she had more political options and took advantage of them.

But the ruling party still has near absolute power and most "formal" jobs are controlled by members of this party. Marie found herself the subject of retaliation in the privatized company because of her affiliation with the opposition party and could not find a "formal" job afterwards. She believes that corruption in the political system, as well as fear of the authorities, are leading to a stifling of any serious civil society political engagement.

However, despite this state of affairs, Marie still experiences a greater degree of freedom than before. There is certainly more access to information, with the greater presence and availability of media in the country. She sees that this has improved governance and transparency and that people are generally more interested in knowing how the country is governed. There is also a new civil society in Cameroon, with a greater presence of nongovernmental organizations. Marie has more options for political involvement than she did before. Her *tontine*, now an NGO, is a good example of this development. The *tontine* also reflects the increasing participation and leadership of women in Cameroon, especially in business. They have been in the forefront of responding to the country's economic crisis.

Marie is at peace with her challenge to the traditional authority and her participation in the new political structures. She is disappointed that some of them, such as the opposition party, have not measured up to her expectations. But she is happy with her involvement with the *tontine*.

In the village, Marie also sees the authority of the tribal ruler eroding, partly as a result of the political opening. But Marie believes that the political reality in the country still is one of two coexistent worlds: the narrow political world of the traditional culture, as lived in the village and in the tribal associations in the cities; and the broader and more national in scope world of the modern culture of the city dwellers, especially those who were born and raised in the cities. She sees a backlash from the defenders of the traditional political relationships and is fearful that the forces of oppression both in the city and the village may not be overcome, since they are so much a part of the country's mentality. She fears the oppression from the traditional power structure in the village the most because it has a mystical character to it. The chief's authority in the traditional setting is not just political; it is also religious. It is seen as sacred, and there is a great reluctance to criticize it. Overall, however, she feels a sense of relief from what she calls political oppression from both the traditional power and the modern power of a single-party government.

Religious Experience and Expression

> *Bachwezi njuna nagawe oteireho*: The gods will help you but with your own effort, too. If you ask God for help, put in your effort, too.

> *Ndo man achike te giguile a ndikkanda ahoudgui ndohay:* When a person descends from heaven, he or she descends into a human society.

> *Giguile ango ndo yao a gidhakda agui ndzekendia:* God only sketched the human being; it is on earth that each builds itself up. We have to build our fate; God does not predestine us.

Marie is Catholic but she also has roots in traditional African religion. This religion – belief in spirits and the power of ancestors, and practices like polygamy and female mutilation – remains strong among people in the village. This includes her parents. Because she lives in the city, Marie's ties to traditional religion are not as strong as her parents' are. When she lost her job, she refused to return to the village to offer sacrifices to appease the ancestors, as her parents wanted her to do. This is highly unusual for anyone in her culture. In the world of the village, the spirits are angered when someone does not adhere to traditional customs, which Marie does not in many ways. This continues to be a source of tension with her parents and others in the village, who cannot accept Marie's refusal to acknowledge her transgressions or offer sacrifices in compensation.

But Marie says she feels very close to God, whom she finds in her Catholic faith and her daily life. This is a loving God who helps her overcome the many tensions in her life and who watches over her and her children. For her, since losing her job, this is a personal experience of God and it seems to be more satisfying and gives greater purpose to her life than just belonging to the institutional Church or taking part in rituals. At the same time, however, she feels a tension with the traditional Catholic sacramental life and emphasis on the hierarchy.

INTERPRETATION

Cameroon's Economic Globalization and Marie

The economic situation that triggered Cameroon's SAP was unsustainable; it needed to be addressed. Long before Marie lost her job, her wages already had been declining for some years. In addition, foreign lenders demanded that market liberalization policies be adopted in order to forgive Cameroon's huge unsustainable foreign debt. Assuming that the government-owned enterprise where Marie worked was run inefficiently, the privatization could have increased the company's productivity. However, the new owners were members of the incumbent political party and this raises some questions about the way the company was privatized. We do not know what happened to this company after Marie was dismissed. The reduction in the number of employees, by itself, would have increased productivity if these employees were really redundant. But if the new management just exchanged the old employees for new ones more loyal to them, then nothing was accomplished from the point of view of the country's economy.

But, even if one assumes that the privatization of Marie's company was done properly, and that the new management improved productivity, questions remain about the human cost paid by the employees who were dismissed: the many Maries who lost their jobs. In her case, though, Marie's character and entrepreneurship seem to give credibility to the premises of classical economic theory: she finds another way to make herself productive to the country, running a restaurant eventually. She might even be making more money than what she did before, certainly more than what she made towards the end of her job in the government-owned company. Unfortunately, because of the elimination of consumer subsidies, she faces higher prices and she might not be better off in purely economic terms.

Marie as a Person

When Marie lost her job, she was a victim of circumstances beyond her control – and those circumstances were much bigger than her life; they were national and even international. Her life was – and continues to be – touched by Cameroon's opening to the global economy. She was confronted with all the changes that were associated with that opening, and in the process of responding to those changes she herself was transformed. Yet through this process, she has been, and remains, an active subject who makes choices about what she does. She was born a Cameroonian, and is very much connected with the traditional life of the village. That too is part of her world. As she confronts the new world, she draws on that tradition. She starts with the traditional village culture and then blends the modern culture, so influenced by the global economy, into it, forming something new. It helps that she lives in the city, which allows much more individual freedom than the village does. But that too reflects her decision, because staying there, rather than going to live in her parents' village, is a choice she has made. For example, her ethnic group has a reputation for being enterprising. She took this traditional trait and adapted it to her life in the city.

She keeps some of the traditional cultural elements and rejects others. Still others she keeps, but adapts them to what she believes is right for her in the new situation. Family is very important in the tradition, as well as to Marie. But she does not accept it wholesale. She manifests the bonds of family in a way more appropriate to her new situation, and it is different from the village way. She loves and supports her family, but she has redefined what family means to her. She has reduced the number of family members that she feels obliged to support, from the traditional large African extended family to just her children and parents. In smaller matters, she has also changed the ways in which she relates to her family. For example, she plans things, and likes to be informed ahead of time when someone from the village is coming to visit her. For some funerals, she may not return for the rites but she will send a condolence card. So she expresses her family ties in a modified way and does not allow the village to determine how she will express them.

Likewise, the traditional expression of solidarity is also central in Marie's life – but again, she has adapted it. In the village, the focus is on the community, on the network of relations. The support she was expected to provide her extended family was part of this. But now Marie is not able to meet the financial demands of solidarity as it is understood in the village. Nonetheless, solidarity is still very much a part of her new, expanded world. She has formed bonds with her neighbors, her business associates, and above all with her women's group, the *tontine*. She has kept the traditional value of solidarity, of being connected, of reaching out to others, but she has redefined it so the concept of "neighbor" in the city now includes many affiliations outside of tribe and family. Marie finds joy and hope in these new relationships.

Marie has redefined solidarity in another way as well. Traditional solidarity is associated with vertical structures and authoritarianism. Yet Marie has discovered in her new situation that she highly values individualism and freedom and has accepted this element – individualism – from the new global culture. She has shaped a style of solidarity that incorporates a Western and urban style of individualism. Her relationships are more horizontal, more egalitarian than those in the traditional culture. In the village, the chief is an authority figure who exerts control over people's relationships. But in the city there are no such authority figures. Marie's new environment allows her to be liberated from the old restrictive structures, although not without doubts sometimes. And since she started to run her own business, Marie does not even have a supervisor. She chooses the people with whom she relates and she relates with some, like her customers, only for business reasons. Marie believes that the global economy gives people more freedom to be who they would like to be.

Marie has rejected categorically the traditional cultural element of a subordinate role for women. In the village, it is not acceptable for a woman to be a single mother, to live independently of a man, or to be in business alone. Marie does all three. She refuses to let traditional norms tell her who she is. Her expanded social group and connectedness to the rest of the world are a source of support and identification in how she lives, as she appreciates being able to escape what she sees as "the tyranny of the traditional village social structure." At the same time, though, she has kept some related cultural norms, such as the one that prohibits sex outside of marriage. And she still keeps her village ties. In a sense, she is asserting that she can be different from what is expected but still be attached.

The country's new focus on freedom manifests itself in a greater political openness, something Marie appreciates and accepts. The new system has led Marie to political self-centeredness, a concept foreign to the village culture. Her expressions of respect now are with regard to merits of the individual, not the person's position in the political structure. Yet the political opening has brought mixed results for Marie. It made it possible for her to dream of a better and more democratic country, tribe, and village – but it has not yet delivered the dream. It gave her more opportunities for her to exercise political power, but she has little time to do so because of her long working hours. She now does not have any faith in what government can do and derives no meaning from her work with the opposition party, although she refuses to join the incumbent party. Her greatest exercise of political power is in the new civil society, with the women's group. This has been the most positive side of the political opening for her: something local, rather than national.

Marie does reject one element of Western-style individualism: unquestioning consumerism. She does not accept uncritically all aspects of the market economy. It is true that her consumption horizon has expanded. She can buy many imported things that were not available before, while the traditional items are still available. But in her choices, Marie negotiates her place amid competing claims from the traditional and modern lifestyles. She increasingly opts for the Western ways, but again chooses carefully among them. For example, she carefully monitors what her children watch on television so they do not see things her culture finds offensive. The media sometimes presents consumption patterns of which she disapproves, but it also enables her to reflect on her experience and see its ties to what is going on in Cameroon and the world.

Marie has had to confront the consequences of the greater freedom and individualism of her life in the city: loneliness and alienation. She also realizes that her increased freedom of choice carries with it an enormous responsibility to judge whether what is chosen is not just a selfish desire. To do this, she draws on both her own sense of individuality and her traditional culture. When she was faced to choose what kind of work she would do, she contemplated her choices and did not do what was most expedient: prostituting herself. So she has some clarity on how she will deal with her changed environment. She has found a place in the new reality and has some control on what that place is. Together, people like Marie and her neighbors are shaping a new culture that blends the old and the new. In the process the traditional social relationships within a vertical, male-dominated culture are being challenged.

With religion, Marie's world contains both the old and the new. She is Catholic, but the traditional African religion still influences her. She does not follow the traditional religious practices, but finds that some of the concepts, like that of the spirits, can still affect her. She won't offer sacrifices to the ancestors but worries about it sometimes. The old ideas are still a part of her. But she continues to have basic goodness of reaching out and helping others.

Her Catholic faith is a positive element for her and it has deepened over time. Before, when she was working as a secretary, it did not play a major role in her life. But her experience of hardship – being unemployed and then running a business and working long hours – strengthened it. She changed from being a superficial Catholic to someone with a deeper faith, who relies on God for comfort and hope for the future. She doesn't have time to go to Mass or be very involved in a faith community. Rather, hers is a personal religion, arising out of her felt experience of God. It offers her solace and hope. But she has freely chosen her faith and she does not allow the standard way of being Catholic dictate how she will practice it.

Marie finds meaning in the life she has fashioned for herself since she lost her job with the privatization of the company where she worked as a secretary. She is proud of her accomplishments as an independent business woman and she cherishes her new social relations, especially the women's group that has supported her in business. She continues reaching out to others and offering her support, but she adjusts the traditional ways of doing it in the Cameroonian village and before the new opening of the country. She fits her care for others to her changed situation in a Cameroon more integrated into the global economy. She draws on the strength of her culture and finds new ways to express her cultural roots in her changed world. She is helping to create a better Cameroon within the limits of her situation.

Marie experiences God's love in her sense of his presence in her life as she perseveres in the face of difficulties and despair. She experiences it in the joy she feels because she can be herself. She finds it in her relief from the oppression of some of the traditional structures and in her experience of freedom and respect for human dignity. Finally, she finds it in her sense of peace as she works to shape a new life for herself.

PART IV

THE BROADER VIEWPOINT

Chapter 17

Stepping Back and Looking Forward

From its inception, we wanted this book to reflect an understanding of the meaning of globalization from the perspective of the poor person, as he or she saw and felt and reacted to globalization. This is in contrast to understanding it from the perspective of the researcher analyzing general descriptions and socioeconomic statistics, which is not to deny the importance of those figures for planning and monitoring socioeconomic progress.

From the beginning, we thought our goal required seeing the world through the eyes of individual people who live within a specific cultural context: the culture and religion that give meaning to their way of life. So the underpinnings of the project have been narrative stories of the lives of specific individuals, the protagonists of our narratives, which were enriched with as much cultural contextual data as possible. Those who told and helped research the stories of our protagonists, the narrators, were Jesuits (with the exception of two diocesan priests) and their partners in ministry at Jesuit social centers around the world. They already knew the protagonists and often were born and raised in their same cultural tradition, or had lived in the country for many years.

We also thought that to capture the poor person's perspective on the meaning of globalization, we had to acknowledge her as a decision-maker – not just a victim of the economic changes taking place. So from early on in the project, we tried to focus on the decisions that these individuals made as they confronted the specific ways in which globalization entered their world. It is from these decisions that we expected to get an understanding of what they valued within the context of their own culture and, therefore, what globalization truly meant to them. However, as pointed out in the "Research Methodology Highlights" section in Chapter 1, and elaborated in more detail in Chapters 3 and 4, we found that developing the research tools to arrive at the perspective of the poor is not so easily done.

In the remainder of this chapter we first look back at the eleven narratives that we analyzed in Parts II and III. In the next section, "A Retrospective View of the Narratives," we summarize how globalization entered into the protagonists' lives and how the protagonists dealt with the imbalances created in them by globalization. Having done this short summary of the narrative chapters in the book, we take a broader perspective and report our findings when, towards the end of the project, we took a look at the narratives as a whole. The chapter then concludes with comments on some of the implications of our findings for development policy. The Appendix to this chapter, "A New Way of Seeing Marie – A Controlled Experiment in Applying Phase II Methodology," illustrates some of these implications.

A RETROSPECTIVE VIEW OF THE NARRATIVES

How Globalization Entered the Protagonists' Lives: A Review

Globalization entered the lives of our protagonists indirectly in many and diverse ways, as their communities began to be exposed to a larger world; and directly, as when they lost their job because the company where they worked was privatized. We systematically surveyed and compared the conditions that prevailed in the protagonists' lives and in their communities before and after the major globalizing economic decision we had identified in the given country. We did this by using the changes that had taken place in the six selected analytic themes mentioned earlier: consumption, production, migration, social relations, political power, and religious experience and expression. All these changes required many decisions on the part of the protagonists about how to respond to them at different levels. But some of the changes brought about by globalization affected them much more directly. These changes were a major focus of the narrative stories and required decisions on the part of the protagonists that often changed their way of life profoundly. Not surprisingly, given the economic nature of the current wave of globalization through liberalization of markets, most of the protagonists' major decisions involved changing their way of making a living in order to contend with the effects of their countries now being more exposed to that market liberalization. From a personal ethical perspective, the crux of their problem was how to change their way of making a living in a new and different world while remaining true to the balance of values that had guided their lives before globalization entered them.

The box below summarizes the most direct way in which we saw globalization entering into the lives of the respective protagonists and the protagonists' major decisions in response to that event. The chapter numbers in parenthesis identify the chapters in this book where the full narrative and our analysis appears.

Globalization Major Event and Protagonists' Major Decision/Action

Shanti, in Agaria Tola, Jharkhand, India (Chapters 5 and 6)

Globalization major event: Expanding coal mine stops her from picking coal at the mine pit and destroys the village spring.

Protagonist's major decision/action: Shanti picks coal off the road and organizes a protest against the mine destroying the spring.

Chanda, in Lusaka, Zambia (Chapter 7)

Globalization major event: Elimination of agricultural subsidies dooms agricultural production in Chanda's village.

Protagonist's major decision/action: Chanda accepts being sent to the city and once there sells cigarettes one at a time on the streets of Lusaka.

Núria, in Barcelona, Spain (Chapter 8)

Globalization major event: New opportunities for entertainment and involvement in global causes and care for the environment become more available in Barcelona.

Protagonist's major decision/action: Núria spends more time in Barcelona, away from her family in Lleida, to take advantage of these new opportunities.

Jorge Enrique, in El Salto, Jalisco, Mexico (Chapter 9)

Globalization major event: Allegedly because of international competition, management closes the tire factory where Jorge Enrique works after failing to gain concessions from the labor union.

Protagonist's major decision/action: Jorge Enrique refuses to accept the liquidation payment offered by management; he also becomes more active in the company's labor union and helps with domestic chores at home.

Joseph, in Qingdao, China (Chapter 10)

Globalization major event: Increased efficiency in agriculture reduces the number of laborers needed in Joseph's home village, while jobs become increasingly abundant in the city.

Protagonist's major decision/action: Joseph leaves the village and moves to the city of Qingdao to work in a factory.

Telma and Pedro in the Pastoral Obrera (PO), in Brasilia, Brazil (Chapter 11)

Globalization major event: The labor situation changes with rural migration to the cities, increases in factory productivity, and growing unemployment.

Protagonist's major decision/action: Telma and Pedro expand the structure of the PO to include workers in the informal economy and the unemployed, in addition to the traditional members – factory workers.

Venkaiah, in Andhra Pradesh, India (Chapter 12)

Globalization major event: Foreign investment brings new seed technology to farming.

Protagonist's major decision/action: Adoption of the new technology leads to Venkaiah losing his farm and he migrates to the city.

Tine Ljubić, in Ljubljana, Slovenia (Chapter 13)

Globalization major event: A capitalistic economic system is adopted, including privatization of government-owned companies.

Protagonist's major decision/action: Tine leaves his government employment and becomes a mutual funds salesperson.

Mee-rah, in Inchon, South Korea (Chapter 14)

Globalization major event: Industrialization and competition both grow, and working conditions worsen.

Protagonist's major decision/action: Mee-rah becomes a labor organizer.

Maurice, in Washington, D.C., United States (Chapter 15)

Globalization major event: The global illegal drugs trade intensifies in Washington, D.C.

Protagonist's major decision/action: Maurice, after being involved in consuming and selling illegal drugs, recovers and helps others in the process of drug rehabilitation.

Marie, in Yaoundé, Cameroon (Chapter 16)

Globalization major event: Privatization of the company where Marie works leads to her dismissal.

Protagonist's major decision/action: Marie begins selling sandwiches in a bar and then establishes a small restaurant.

The above provides the basic development facts on which we build our value-ethics approach.

IMBALANCES CREATED BY GLOBALIZATION AND HOW THE PROTAGONISTS BALANCED DYNAMIC TENSIONS

In each narrative chapter, the final section offers the authors' reflections on the understanding we gained on the meaning of globalization to the protagonists of that narrative. In Chapters 6-10, we applied both Phases I and II of the methodology. In those chapters, the relevant section is under "Researchers' Reflection" and is entitled "Getting to Know the Protagonist: Our Journey." In Chapters 11-16, we applied only Phase I of the methodology, and the relevant section is under "Interpretation," entitled "The Protagonist as a Person."

By way of providing a summary of the kaleidoscopic mosaic that emerged from looking at the tiles contributed by our narratives, in this section we present a synopsis that highlights the newly-created imbalances in the tensions at different levels in the scale of values and how the protagonists addressed them. We do this only for the stories to which we applied the Phase II methodology. We detected similar tensions in the narratives to which we applied only the Phase I methodology, but we couldn't articulate them as well with the tools we had available at that stage.

A partial view of the "kaleidoscopic mosaic" of the global economy that emerged when the artwork from the "narrative mosaic tiles" were juxtaposed at the end of the GEC project's Fourth International Consultation (2004) appears in the pictures that follow.

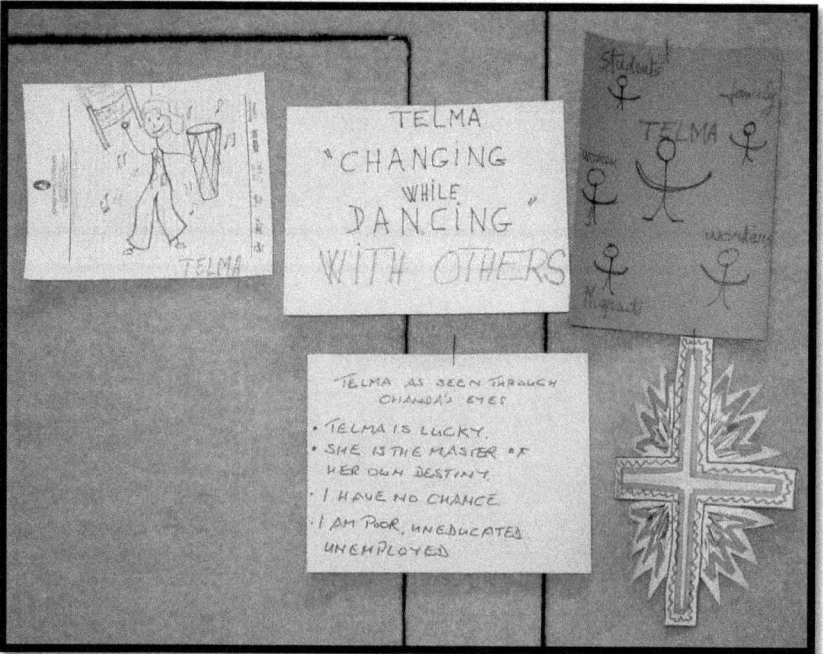

Shanti (Chapters 5 and 6)

When Shanti in India organizes a protest against the mine destroying the village spring, she is protesting the changes in tribal life brought about by the expanding mines. She has accepted and even valued other changes, as when she came to appreciate the use of money instead of bartering. But taking away the village spring goes too far. Interestingly, her protest also challenges certain village traditions: the role of women and the village's apparent acquiescence to the power of the mines. With the protest, she is challenging critical economic and political structures that provide cohesiveness to the village community. She is taking responsibility for her personal actions to the point of putting her in conflict with the power structures of the village. One can sense the tension within Shanti between what she values in the old tradition of her culture and the values of the more independent new ways she is adopting. This tension risks alienating her from others in the village, if she decides in favor of the new; and personal stagnation, if she decides in favor of tradition. It can be seen as an impasse in what Shanti values at the cultural level. Curiously, balance between these tensions is restored rather than exacerbated with Shanti's decision to organize the protest. In doing this, she is guided by her sense that her dignity (a personal/moral value) has been violated, as well as her sense of justice and the presence of the Divine in the spring (a religious value). It is her religious and moral values that bring coherence and balance to the tensions that she experiences between her new assertiveness and what she values in the power structures of the village tradition as she goes on to organize the protest and adopt other changes in her way of life. Shanti remains at peace, saddened by the loss of the forest and the spring to the mines, but creatively adjusting to the new world and dealing with new tensions while maintaining her personal integrity.

Chanda (Chapter 7)

Chanda's world in Zambia is turned upside down as he leaves his home village to make a living selling cigarettes in the capital, Lusaka. The ways of making a living in the village are irrelevant in the city. The socioeconomic and political structures that he valued in the village are of little use in the city. There are enormous tensions between what he valued socially and culturally in his old world in the village and what he must find of value in the new world in the city, where he needs to survive. He still values the traditional moral responsibility to support his family when they need him, which his traditional culture also values, but to do so he has to accept a job in which he sees little dignity (selling cigarettes on the streets) and he does not get any assistance from the tradition to do this. He has to find new meanings and new values in what he must do in the city, without the support of the village traditions – other than the value they place on his helping his family. Again, we can sense the new imbalance in the tensions that he must deal with between the old values and the values of the forces of change. He brings balance to the tensions by turning to his personal/moral and religious values. Beyond the value that the tradition places on supporting his family, it is love for his family and his reliance on God that help him make sense of the *muchanga boy* job he must accept in the city, and take responsibility for and give meaning to it. It is what he values at the religious and personal level, and how he finds ways to express those values, that helps him break the impasse created by the confrontation of city values with his traditional rural values at the social and cultural levels. The adaptation required is enormous. He might have responded by pursuing a criminal life or disintegrating into utter depression. But he doesn't. He maintains his moral integrity and creatively adapts to his new situation as well as he can. Without rejecting the communal uniformity of the village, he enters into social relationships and new tensions that are different from those in village life and embodies a new pluralism in the restored balance of his everyday life.

Núria (Chapter 8)

For Núria in Barcelona, Spain, globalization already enters her life as she grows up in Lleida, but she first reacts to it as a young adult when she goes to study at the university in Barcelona. There she finds the traditional differences between life in the city and life in the town. But in her case, it also involves a city very much exposed to global influences and opportunities to participate in global causes. Her social structures change a good deal when she goes to Barcelona, and she comes to value the new things that Barcelona has to offer. But these new values create an imbalance in the tension with the tradition that she learned to value socially and culturally, and even morally, growing up in Lleida. Núria's cultural tradition values spending time with the family and helping with siblings, and this applies even to university students. However, the youth culture of university life in cosmopolitan Barcelona values socializing with peers and getting involved in global causes – such as care for the environment and world peace – above family responsibilities. The two sets of values come into open conflict as Núria decides what to do in her spare time: to go back home to be with the family, as her tradition values, or to stay with friends in Barcelona taking advantage of the new opportunities globalization offers to develop new interests. The tensions Núria experiences between her traditional cultural values and the new values of her culture in Barcelona, in turn, create tensions at the personal/moral level of values. A greater tension then emerges at this level between the traditional responsibility of caring for her family and the responsibility of developing as an adult. This calls for a true moral discernment in which selfish motives compete for attention. Given Núria's religious training, this might call for finding what is right in the eyes of God. But we are not sure Núria does this in the traditional religious way. However, she solves the dilemma of imbalance, at least to some extent, in favor of allocating more of her free time doing things in the city and less time with the family back home. She brings balance between what she values at the moral level, we believe, in a manner consistent with her implicit religious values. But, regardless of the moral comfort she achieves, she is forging an identity as a young adult in the cosmopolitan city, an identity that is different from what it would have been back in Lleida.

Jorge Enrique (Chapter 9)

In the case of Jorge Enrique in Mexico, his social structure changes greatly from one day to the next when the tire plant where he works closes in response to labor problems. His decision to refuse the liquidation settlement offered by the tire company (and consider going to work in the U.S.) further changes the social structure of his life. It changes even more when he becomes a more active union member. He had achieved what he thought would be a good job, and now the forces engendered by the global market are taking that away from him. He hopes that his new "job" of participating in the union actions against the company, and helping with domestic chores at home, is temporary and that the economic gamble will result in either getting his old job back or a better financial settlement. Nonetheless, his decision leads to great changes in his social structures and those changes now expose him to the world of union activism and the international labor movement. His decision creates new tensions between what he values in his cultural tradition and a new set of values associated with change as he joins the culture of the union. In the tradition, union activism is not so highly regarded and *machismo* influences the role of men at home. Imbalance in favor of the values associated with his new union activism risks alienation from others in *el rancho* and those who accepted the liquidation. Imbalance in favor of adopting the old values risks doing just what is economically expedient, but without much meaning to him. But his personal/moral values reinforce his decision as the right thing to do: to stay with his family and hope for a resolution to the closing of the plant that provides better financial support for the family. His sense of dignity as a person and his sense of fidelity to the demands of relationship with his family are the underpinning of what he considers the right thing to do. His faith in God, whom he trusts, reinforces the moral decision and helps him maintain his moral integrity, while creatively adapting to the changes and dealing with new tensions in employment associated with globalization.

Joseph (Chapter 10)

For Joseph in Qingdao, China, his decision to leave the village to seek economic opportunities in the city represent a giant change in his social structures. He does achieve the economic improvement that he seeks in the city. But this requires exchanging the communal social work structures of the village for the anonymous structures of work in a city factory. These tensions at the level of social structures, in turn, create other tensions: between the communal, trust-based, cultural values that gave meaning to his life in the village and the individualism embedded in the market economy of the city, which he needs to adopt to improve his and his family's economic situation. The tensions between these two sets of values are not easily balanced. He is brave and is willing to accept cultural change. However, in excessively embracing the new world in the city at the expense of his traditional values, he risks losing himself in the loneliness there. Excessively embracing the tradition, however, dooms his efforts to improve his and his family's living standards. Joseph succeeds in bringing balance between the tensions that exist between these two poles as he relies on his personal/moral values. Fidelity to relationships with his family is the key. Being able to provide more financial support for his parents back in the village and for his new family in the city is better done while working in the city. He also has great trust that God will take care of him and his family in this endeavor. This religious value guides and maintains his integrity and helps him balance the tensions between the values of the two worlds in which he lives as he adjusts creatively and lives with new tensions.

OUR FINDINGS: A BROADER PERSPECTIVE

It should be obvious that it was not our intention to structure the GEC project to assess the net impact of globalization on the poor, particularly in socioeconomic terms. We were after much more. We were after gaining a deeper understanding of what was happening within the hearts and minds of poor people, as full human beings, in their particular encounters with globalization. We wanted to see beyond what is needed for proper economic survival, basic as that is. And in all this, we were seeking a new ethics for development professionals so that they would include the poor in creatively new and vital ways, as agents of change in the process of development and globalization.

In each narrative, we invested a good deal of effort into understanding the facts of the changes in the protagonists' and their communities' lives introduced by globalization. We also tried to understand what they did in response to these changes: the decisions they made, which often involved a change in the way in which they made a living. Already during Phase I of the project, their decisions revealed that each one had had to navigate a number of specific and often major tensions that globalization had introduced into their traditional culture. Globalization required the protagonists to evaluate many such tensions. Moreover, for each decision they made in response to those tensions, they also had to make adjustments in the rest of their lives.

During Phase I of the project, the traits of the culture of each of the protagonists provided a helpful context to understand the balancing act that the protagonists had to negotiate as they blended their old world with the one in which they found themselves in a more globalized environment. In Phase I, we could see and describe how the protagonists' love for family and community, and in some cases explicitly for God, provided the energy for making the necessary tradeoffs among traditional cultural traits and conflicting values – tradeoffs reflected in what they had decided to do in the new environment. But this took us only so far.

In Phase II of the project, in the narratives presented in Part II, we went further. In those narratives we looked at the protagonists' critical decisions in terms of what might have been going on within them at different stages of consciousness, and we explicitly considered the role the scale of human values played in their decision process. In doing this, we could properly begin to deconstruct and appreciate what was happening from the protagonists' point of view. Exploring step-by-step what must have been going on within the protagonists at different stages of consciousness made us fully enter into their world. We could now focus on in much greater detail, and much better feel with the protagonists, what they were experiencing in the new environment that global forces had brought into their lives. We could much better appreciate what was involved in their coming to understand their new world in such a way that they finally decided to follow the course of action that we observed. Only then did we really start to see the protagonists' world through their eyes. In the process, we also gained a much better appreciation of them as intelligent decision-makers, who encountered and successfully dealt with great tensions in what they valued at the vital, social, cultural, personal/moral, and religious levels of values. When in each narrative we looked in detail at the complex package of decisions, tradeoffs, and adjustments that our protagonists had to confront, the picture that emerged was one of courageous human beings who successfully renegotiated the meanings and values of their old world in light of the new world brought about by globalization. And, in the process, they succeeded in maintaining their personal integrity, one of the highest values of sustainable development. It is at this level that our findings emerged, particularly when we stepped back and looked at the narratives as a whole.

When we applied the Phase II methodology to the narratives in Chapters 6-10, we went a long way into understanding what was going on within the protagonists in each of the selected instances. As the protagonists went from experiencing the new situation to reaching a decision to cope with it, we saw the specific tensions that had been created by the encounter of the new world and the old one at each level in the scale of values. As the protagonists moved to implement the decision, we saw how they proceeded to change the weights they gave to values within each level and among levels of values in order to resolve the tensions embedded in the decision. But, as we came to the end of the project and looked at the narrative analysis as a whole, we realized there was even more going on within the protagonists that we had failed to grasp. Chapters 6-10, in particular, did a good job of describing the tensions that must have been going on within the protagonists and the changes in weights of values they must have undergone to adapt to the new situation. But at this point, we realized that in focusing on the changes in weights, somehow we had lost track of the dynamics in the tensions they were attempting to rebalance at each value level, if they were to keep their integrity. We had done a good job in describing what must have been happening within the protagonists, but we were not yet explaining it. There was a grander picture that we had failed to understand. To reveal this picture, we had to focus on the dialectics created by the tensions between certain forces. On the one hand were the forces embedded in the tradition encouraging stability and harmony in the community, and on the other were the forces associated with globalization encouraging change and development.

Let's take the most pervasive change that took place in the lives of our protagonists: finding a different way of making a living in order to support themselves and their families in a world now more exposed to global forces. Obviously, their economic situation changed. After the change in jobs, some protagonists appeared to do better in meeting their economic needs. For others the new policies had devastating effects, and for still others we couldn't tell for sure with the data we had. But, generally and not surprisingly, those protagonists who started with more education tended to do better and at least avoided economic devastation. This is not a particularly revealing finding about the economic impact of globalization. But much more was taking place. An important change had been introduced into the protagonists' social structures overall that often challenged the traditional structures valued by the protagonist and her community, and this change required a rearrangement of what they valued at the social level. The economic, social, and political structures on which they depended to support themselves and their families had shifted.

Here is where our value-ethics methodology began to yield new insights. At a higher level, at the level of cultural values, many of the meanings and values of their lives before this encounter with global forces – the traditions that they valued – often did not fit their new situation well. The old values now often were in tension with those embedded in the newly introduced social structures. It is at that point that we really began grasping the extent of the negotiations that had to be taking place between the forces for change that the protagonists valued in the new situation, and the forces for stability embedded in social institutions and cultural values from the tradition. We got in touch with the many elements and tradeoffs that the protagonists had to consider, and which were integrated into their actions. Then, we realized the depth and breadth of the internal negotiations necessary for them to successfully implement their decisions.

The tensions that the protagonists had to negotiate internally as they confronted the new global economy brought disarray into their sense of being and belonging in their society. Failure to re-establish balance between the old and the new cultural poles could have left our protagonists at risk of either falling prey to alienation from their society or inability to function in the new environment. To succeed with integrity in bringing balance between the poles of tradition and change that they were negotiating at the social and cultural levels, they had to engage their moral/personal values and religious values to decide where the greater goodness lay. Thankfully, our protagonists found the moral compass necessary to re-establish balance among the tensions created at these levels of value. We believe that the protagonists' successful balancing between the new and the old worlds at each value level was possible because the protagonists the narrators chose were "good people." In addition, the narrators had a relationship of friendship with the protagonists that allowed the narrators to better accompany the protagonists as development professionals. In this balancing act the protagonists forged new meanings and values that allowed them to remain true to themselves in the midst of the new structures. Every protagonist in the project learned to adapt to the new world in creative ways and, in their responses, succeeded in blending what they cherished in the old world with what they found of value in the changing environment. In resolving these tensions, our protagonists emerged as *agents for change, for ethically sound (i.e., sustainable)* development within their context, even when their own economic situation might not have improved.

Our work was simplified by the fact that all the narrators believed that their respective protagonists, despite what they often considered to be deteriorating economic and social conditions, were "at peace" with the actions that they had taken to contend with the great changes taking place in their lives. They had maintained their integrity as a person. If so, these individuals had achieved an immense rebalancing operation. This rebalancing of tensions embedded in value decisions is crucial to the protagonists acting as agents of their own destiny, as well as to their understanding of globalization. In the midst of major upheavals in their personal lives, they had succeeded as human beings in responding creatively, while maintaining their personal integrity – even when not satisfied with their new economic reality. We could now really see the protagonists as true actors in their own history, even though that history often presented them with limited options and the outcome was not necessarily an improvement in living conditions.

After applying Phase II individually to each of the five narratives where we did so, we were awed by the power of each of our protagonists to successfully blend their old values into the new situation while remaining at peace. When, having gained this understanding, we looked again at the kaleidoscopic mosaic that emerged from putting the tiles represented by each of the narratives side by side, we were astounded at the magnitude of what they had accomplished. Then we could better see the pattern of pitfalls they had avoided and challenges they had conquered in their success in blending the two worlds. This is not to say that they were happy with their new world (although often they had not been fully satisfied either with the old world before they encountered the new global forces). But they had maintained their personal integrity, sometimes against great odds, and had recovered some balance so they could continue to deal with new tensions creatively.

We set out to find the meaning of globalization as seen through the eyes of the poor, and in our protagonists we encountered the power of humanity at the margins of society.

IMPLICATIONS FOR DEVELOPMENT POLICY

What We Have Learned that Could Be of Value to Development Policy

In transferring what we have learned from our narratives to its implications for development policy, we must first make explicit the major differences between our research approach, with the narrative of specific individuals, and the usual scope of development policy. For the professional seeking to develop and implement policies that support socioeconomic development in a community or a country, the approach is much broader than ours. For the development professional, development refers at least to a whole community and often to a whole country, not just individuals. But communities and countries are made up of individuals who interact with one another and make decisions based on their values. Thus, what we learned from working with the individuals in our narratives can be extrapolated to working with communities and countries – as long as one is willing to approach development from the point of view of the people who are expected to be the beneficiaries of the development process, and as long as one acknowledges them as integral human beings with needs and desires beyond the limits of economic rationality. If so, one would be willing to find new ways of designing the involvement of these people in the development and implementation of policy, ways that we have found necessary if we are to tap into their creativity and full human potential.

In addition, the protagonists of our narratives were *exemplars*. Some of their exemplary traits resulted from the way in which the narrators selected the protagonists of their stories. They were all very good people worthy of admiration. The narrators also found them to be "at peace" with their decisions. However, they were not necessarily "at peace" with the situation in which they found themselves. They had done the best that they could – sometimes heroically and often creatively – with the options that were available to them, but this did not mean that they were happy with their state of affairs as an improvement over the previous situation. For the professional engaged in development policy, obtaining an improvement in the socioeconomic environment of the community or country is of paramount importance. This is not the goal that we analyzed. But if the development professional can both achieve an improvement in socioeconomic measures AND have the community "at peace" with the decisions they must make, that development will be sustainable.

So, what have we learned that could be of value to development policy? Foremost, we have learned that our value-based approach to development ethics can reasonably provide a framework to understand how individuals, (and, if such, communities) adjust to change successfully, in a sustainable manner. Specifically, this approach requires:

1. Entering into the world of the poor from their own perspective. This requires an understanding of how they themselves experience and understand their world and, therefore, go about reaching decisions in that world. In this respect, we found that analyzing their decisions in terms of the various stages of consciousness to be extremely useful.

2. Articulating explicitly ALL the levels of value relevant to the subjects involved in development – not only measurable socioeconomic values, but also cultural, moral, and religious values.

3. Recognizing that values at each level exist in dynamic tension. There is an ongoing tension within each level of value that the individual tries to balance: between the values associated with traditional social structures and new ones that might be more effective; between cultural values upheld by the community and values that provide individual meaning. In a stable situation, the forces behind these poles of tension are in balance.

4. Identifying how development breaks any existing balance in the tensions between the two poles at each value level. It creates a skewed situation where one pole flourishes at the expense of the other. To restore this balance requires involving higher levels of value. An imbalance at the socioeconomic level (the target of economic development), for example, created by the introduction of new technologies to traditional farming, also creates imbalances at the cultural and moral levels. The restoration of balance at any level of value must begin at the next higher level and ultimately requires balancing at the highest levels – moral and religious levels – to be sustainable. Religious and moral values shape the meaning given to cultural values.

In our narratives we came to understand the intelligence and creativity that the protagonists brought to their adaptation to globalization. We saw the great power that they brought to bear in this process. The challenge for the development professional is how to learn to marshal these forces in the service of economic development. More specifically, the challenge is how to develop venues and tools that allow both the development professional and the community or country to get in touch explicitly with their values in the interrelated and dynamic fashion we have seen.

For some assessment of the possible impact of applying our value-based approach to development ethics, see the Appendix to this chapter, "A New Way of Seeing Marie – A Controlled Experiment in Applying Phase II Methodology." In this Appendix one can see how one student of economic development changed his perspective and approach to development after applying Phase II methodology to the story of Marie.

What Might Our Approach Look Like in Practice?

For starters, it means that the development and implementation of any development policy requires envisioning in some detail the changes in behavior that it would require at the individual level. This change in behavior, in turn, will require identification of the specific decisions these individuals would have to make for the policy to be successful. At this point, traditional economics would argue in favor of providing economic incentives to induce the necessary decisions and behavioral changes. But, we argue that this is not enough and it might even be counterproductive if these economic incentives run too much counter to the traditional cultural, moral, and religious values of the community and exacerbate the imbalances caused by economic changes. We argue for explicitly exploring the imbalances between the values of the community's tradition and the values of change that the given development policy would create. This must be done not only at the social level of value (e.g., when introducing competitive modes of production into a traditional communal way of working). We also must examine the ramifications of the imbalances created between the values of the tradition and the values associated with change at the cultural and moral levels of value. A more competitive production method will surely introduce imbalances at the cultural level in a tradition that places the community above the individual. And this imbalance, in turn, will disrupt any existing balance between the moral responsibility to the community and the responsibility to self. We propose that, ultimately, balance can be restored only by going beyond "what is the right thing to do" and appealing to "what is the loving thing to do" – what we have called ultimate or religious values.

But how do we get in touch with the people's values at different levels and the balance or lack of balance in the tensions between the tradition and the forces for change? We see no way other than involving the people directly and interactively. And by this involvement we do not mean taking a survey asking directly about their values. We mean creating venues that facilitate the relevant community discussing their values within a decision-making context. For example, discussing cases in another culture can facilitate identifying their own cultural values. Also, providing simplified situations that the given development policy would produce and asking the people how they would go about reaching decisions in this context. There are many possible approaches, but the constants are: (1) it is the people who are asked to discuss their decisions; (2) the facilitator's role is only to make sure to elicit a discussion of all value levels – not just the immediate socioeconomic ones. Hence development professionals give pride of place to field personnel, that is, to development practitioners at the grass roots level.

Such initial involvement of the people in the identification of their values and tensions at each level in the scale of value can be quite useful in suggesting alternative approaches to implement a given development policy. It also generates ownership of the policy among those who will be most affected by it. But, from our perspective, this is not the end. This consultation process should be seen as an ongoing one with a clear communication loop. It is one thing to anticipate how the policy will operate and another one to experience the actual policy. New issues involving new values and new tensions between the forces of change and tradition will emerge as the policy moves from development to implementation. As the policy implementation proceeds, this consultation process also is likely to become a social support effort that facilitates the adjustments that the people must make as they work to reestablish balance between the values of the tradition and the values for change. One of the roles of development professionals at every level is to accompany the community in this process.

Of course, this approach does run the "danger" that when the people become engaged, the policy favored by the development professional might be rejected as not being consistent with the cultural and moral values of the community. This presents a confrontation between the tradition that the community values and the values of the development professional. In some extreme cases, like emergencies when lives are at stake, the humanitarian values should win the day. But, in most cases, the sustainable answer would rely on education and a dialogue between the development professional and the community – a dialogue in which all social levels in the community should participate.

Future Research

Our protagonists were all "good people" whose moral and religious values guided their decisions. We suspect that as we expand the size of the group involved, we will have to deal with the human fact that not everybody is "at peace" with their decisions. And even when they are at peace, there are biases. Some are as straightforward as personal selfishness, but there are also biases in the community. Not all parts of the cultural tradition support what is good (e.g., discriminatory behavior). Any future research and assessment will have to sort out these biases, as well as address the implications of the changes introduced by globalization – not an easy task. In addition, any assessment must include all the institutional actors in the community, although the poor should always have a preferential role. The picture that emerges from the analysis of the narratives in this project lacks the contribution that might have come from the other actors themselves reflecting on the narrative data. Future research should include participants from the worlds of business, government, NGOs and religions.

Finally, moreover, the key to sustainable development policies lies in balancing the highest human values of openness to transcendence and love, values that are in tension with self-preservation and a closed world. According to our theological anthropology framework (the overarching assumption behind this study), there is a constant need to rebalance the tensions that emerge from the development process. This recovery of balance is the highest "redeeming" value that we can observe in our protagonists. And this recovery always requires some form of heroic courage in overcoming dehumanizing forces. We pay tribute to the heroes of this book who teach us new things.

APPENDIX:

A NEW WAY OF SEEING MARIE –
A CONTROLLED EXPERIMENT IN APPLYING
PHASE II METHODOLOGY

A close-up of Marie's mosaic tile from the Fourth International Consultation

TEST RESEARCHER: FRANCOIS PAZISNEWENDE KABORE, SJ

Doctoral Student at American University, Washington, D.C.
West Africa Jesuit Province, Burkina Faso

This Appendix reports on an experiment to test the net contribution of applying Phase II methodology. To this end, we asked a third party, a person knowledgeable about development economics, to be a test researcher. We asked him to apply Phase II methodology to a narrative previously unknown to him. The original narrator and the WTC researchers already had applied Phase I methodology to this narrative. We selected the story of Marie in Cameroon – the narrative presented in Chapter 16, "Marie in Cameroon: A New Way of Being a Cameroonian Woman."

The experiment involved three distinct steps that the WTC researchers asked the test researcher to perform:

Step 1: Reflect on Marie after reading Chapter 16, which is based on applying only Phase I methodology.

The test researcher was asked to address the following questions:

a. How does the test researcher understand Marie at this point?

b. What are the implications for development policy?

Step 2: Apply Phase II methodology to the Marie narrative.

This had the test researcher generate materials comparable to those found in the section "Meanings and Values as Reflected in Her Choices" in Chapters 6-10. This section in those chapters was created by the respective narrators and the WTC researchers as they applied Phase II methodology to those narratives.

Step 3: Reflect on Marie after applying Phase II methodology.

The test researcher was asked to address the following questions:

a. How does the test researcher understand Marie now? Has there been a change?

b. What are the implications for development policy of any new understanding?

This involved the test researcher in a reflection comparable to the ones presented by the narrator and the WTC researchers in the section

"Researchers' Reflection" in Chapters 6-10, as part of applying Phase II methodology.

Any differences between the reflections in Step 1 and Step 3 could then be attributed to the knowledge gained from applying Phase II methodology to the Marie story.

For this experiment the third-party researcher was Francois Pazisnewende Kabore, a doctoral student at American University specializing in Development Economics and Political Economy. Kabore lived for some time in Cameroon, but he is a native of Burkina Faso. He has never met Marie in person. His initial knowledge of her for the experiment came only from reading Chapter 16, which contains the Marie narrative and the analysis resulting from the narrator and WTC researchers applying Phase I methodology. In doing his work Kabore, unlike the narrators, had limited interaction with the WTC researchers.

The remainder of this chapter constitutes Kabore's work in following the three steps listed above, with the WTC researchers contributing only copyediting. Elements of what Kabore has written differ from the scope of what the WTC researchers and the narrators wrote in the corresponding section in Chapters 6-10. First, Kabore's knowledge of the protagonist Marie and her culture was considerably more limited than that of the original narrator. Secondly, he applies the Phase II Methodology with the limitations of someone who is in the process of learning how to apply it. For these reasons, what is written in this chapter does not have as comprehensive an approach as what is written in Chapters 6-10. However, a comprehensive application of Phase II methodology was not the objective of this experiment.

Our goal was to compare Kabore's understanding of the protagonist before and after applying the Phase II methodology and the policy implications of these different understandings. In this regard, we can say that this experiment was successful. Applying Phase II methodology did change Kabore's understanding of Marie – from the "objective" point of view of the economist/researcher to an "empathetic" point of view, that of Marie herself, the subject of the development process.

Kabore's reflections illustrate in his own words the change that he experiences as he moves from viewing the protagonist as a victim to viewing her as an agent of development. The WTC researchers believe that what Kabore has written does reflect an enhanced understanding of Marie as he struggles to integrate the insight he has gained from applying the Phase II Methodology and the traditional approach of development economists.

STEP 1: REFLECTIONS ON MARIE AFTER READING CHAPTER 16

My Understanding of Marie:
What Did I Learn about Her in This Chapter?

Marie's story epitomizes the experience of the "global majority" in Africa: people who had very high expectations after the political independence of their home countries, but who eventually came to feel trapped in a political process that does not deliver. Marie is one of those many Africans who feel that the distribution of economic resources is biased. They are disenchanted with the political process that is supposed to regulate social life and ensure a fair distribution of economic resources. In another respect, Marie's story also reflects the experience of the "few" in the new generation of Africans who are born in the richness of their ancestral culture, raised in a more multicultural environment, and "condemned to survive" in a globalizing world. To that extent, Marie is part of the Africans who are migrating away from their villages, not only physically but also, and above all, culturally. But, as it turns out, Marie has not moved from one "cultural place" to another; she has not abandoned one cultural identity for another. She is in the process of forging a new cultural identity that borrows from both her original culture and modernity.

Economically, Marie can be considered as one of the numerous people in urban areas who were part of the formal sector but who end up in the informal sector as a result of an economic downturn. She, however, prefers living in the city; not only because of her reluctance to live in a village, but also because the expectation of finding a good job is higher in the city than in the village. Being fired, Marie is now required indeed to sell her labor to other people in a country where unemployment is already high. Searching for a job in the formal sector is so unsuccessful that the best option appears to be to find an alternative in the form of entrepreneurship in the informal sector. From a development perspective, it is interesting to notice that this suggestion didn't come from some formal micro-finance institution, but from within Marie's traditional culture. Marie is struggling for survival. She is fighting for a better future for herself and her children. To follow up on the suggestion, she needs some money and she relies on a loan from a solidarity group to start the business.

Culturally, since the time she chose to marry a man without the approval of her parents, Marie has made it clear that she wants to be the main actor in her own life and this is a departure from the tenets of her own culture, with regard to women. Self-determination will, however, allow Marie to dare to invent the future as an entrepreneur and, eventually, to find the peace of mind and heart she lost. She is now able again to earn a living and provide for the needs of her family, which she would no longer define as the entire tribe or village. She was also spiritually challenged. How can she not consider her misfortune a result of her disobedience of the ancestors' will? The new Marie is a self- conscious person, eager to make things happen, to enjoy modernity, while staying rooted in her tradition in many respects: spiritually, socially, culturally.

Implications for Development Policy:
A Memo to the Development Minister

Given that the goal of your office is to fight against poverty, break the cycle of poverty intergenerational transmission, and improve Cameroonians' well-being, the following ideas could help meet that goal.

Promote corporate good governance. I do not know if Marie was fired because of her political views or if firing her was a necessary condition for her firm to improve efficiency. In any case, despite the global economic downturn that affects Cameroon, it looks obvious that better corporate governance would have helped prevent such a case or, at least, either anticipate it or mitigate its negative impacts. Moreover, Marie does not seem to have received any compensation for her dismissal. Such compensation would have facilitated her, and others', adjustment process.

Establish an employment resource database. After she lost her job, Marie had only herself to rely on to find a new job in the formal economy, which eventually she could not find. It would be useful to the development process to facilitate the job search of those in frictional or structural unemployment. Establishing a database of jobs available, so that job seekers know where there are jobs, would be of great help.

Support micro-finance institutions. The decision of Marie to go into business was made possible by the financial support of her cultural solidarity group, which granted her a loan through a *tontine.* It is very likely that a substantial number of people unemployed like Marie would like to go into business; but because they are credit constrained, they are not able to do so. The government can encourage entrepreneurship in many ways: (i) building micro-credit institutions where people can come individually or collectively to ask for credit; (ii) helping to finance existing solidarity organizations such as the *tontines*; (iii) encouraging the creation of new culturally-based solidarity groups; (iv) helping to establish new types of solidarity organizations such as profession-based groups, so that those who are not part of an organized culturally-based group can benefit from their services. It is important, for the sake of efficiency, that these solidarity groups be independent from the government to avoid too much political interference in their management.

Encourage a spirit of entrepreneurship. Although Marie's experience as an entrepreneur is pretty successful, she went into business only because she did not have another option. It is important for the government to help strengthen the private sector and promote a culture of entrepreneurship. One can earn a better living as an entrepreneur than as a civil servant. As a matter of fact, recent statistics show that the average income of a successful businessperson or of a worker in a private firm is higher than the income of the average "honest" civil servant. Even in the informal sector, people engaged in the "dynamic informal sector" (vs. the traditional stagnant informal sector) end up having higher living standards than "honest" civil servants, who content themselves with their salaries and do not resort to corruption.

Conclusion. Ultimately, by promoting good governance, the government will increase job security for its citizens and that will result in better corporate management. By gathering the data to manage frictional and structural unemployment, the government helps to reduce the costs of job searching for the unemployed. Last but not the least, by promoting micro-finance and a spirit of entrepreneurship, the Development Ministry can open new job opportunities for people who are credit constrained or who lack the human skills necessary to go into business. People do not often expect too much from their government: what they need is the freedom to create wealth and economic opportunities for themselves, their families, and their nation. An important input of the government, namely of your ministry, could therefore be to help reduce the constraints and create an environment conducive to private entrepreneurship.

STEP 2: APPLYING PHASE II METHODOLOGY
TO THE MARIE NARRATIVE

Action: Marie, not being able to find a job in the formal sector, starts her own business first selling sandwiches and then establishing a small restaurant.

A. *What can we infer goes on within Marie as she experiences the new economy and moves on to decide to take this action? What questions may Marie have been raising and what answers seem consistent with reaching that decision? (Note: This refers to the stages of consciousness, experiencing to deciding; see Chapter 4, p. 88ff.)*

There is a multiparty system and Marie chose to belong to an opposition party in order to show her discontent with the incumbent party: she *experiences* political freedom, at least *de jure*.

In the aftermath of privatization, Marie loses her job and concludes that she lost her job because of her political affiliation. She does not believe that she was fired just because the company wanted to cut expenses to improve efficiency. She *experiences* despair, revolt, and frustration. Thinking about the consequences of her being unemployed fills her with horror. She will no longer be able to earn a living or take care of her children – not to mention help her family back home as she used to. She will no longer be able to meet other people's financial expectations. At first she is hopeful that she will still be able to find another job in the formal sector. After the hardships of an unsuccessful job search, she asks herself about possible alternatives to a job like the one she had. In her questioning, she comes across the idea of getting in touch with a *tontine*.

She eventually comes to *understand* that whatever the reasons for her being fired, she will not necessarily be able to get another job in the formal sector. She has to take responsibility for her situation. She reasons that, after all, her situation is not necessarily that desperate: the *tontine* suggests that there are other alternatives.

She *judges the facts* and concludes that she can take advantage of the trading skills tradition in her tribe and that she can indeed benefit from the support offered by her cultural women's solidarity group.

She *judges it worthwhile* going into business, namely selling sandwiches and later opening a restaurant, given her new situation. She *decides* to stop looking for a job in the formal sector and instead to go into business in the informal sector.

B. What values appear to drive Marie's decision? What are the good things that she seeks? (Note: This refers to the scale of values; see Chapter 4, p. 95ff.)

Marie is driven by her *religious, cultural, social, and moral/personal values.* When she loses her job she first looked to her Christian God for help. When it became clear to her that she should find an alternative to continuing in a costly job search, she realizes that God is offering her some practical and tangible support through the women's solidarity group. Her *cultural values* support her decision, as this solidarity group is from her ethnic group. When she was earning a good living she kept good ties with her family and helped her extended family, but now she turns to her closest family and her *tontine* group to look for help to settle in business. In this new situation her *personal/moral values* are in play. From the start, she wanted to take responsibility. That is why she married the man of her heart, although he was not from her tribe. Unfortunately, they eventually divorced. She should take responsibility once more. She cannot go back to the village; her strong personality and moral values suggest that she find a way to survive by herself. She never thought about going into business but now she has to. In the entire process, Marie's self-esteem, optimism, and inner strength are the driving forces that help her hold firmly to her moral, social, religious, and cultural values.

C. How does Marie's new knowledge and decision change the horizon of meaning in her world?

Marie respects her extended family. But her family has become a financial burden for her. Now she is getting to know another aspect of her extended family through her ethnic-based *tontine.* Her extended family, which now includes the *tontine*, is also her "insurance" during "rainy days" when she faces the negative economic shock of a job loss. In Marie's world, the importance of a solidarity group as an informal insurance device or coping strategy becomes reality. She turns for help to her new extended family, first to begin selling sandwiches and then to start a restaurant.

Marie never before thought about going into business. Women who are in business, especially those who are very successful, are even considered to be morally suspicious women. Her tribe values entrepreneurship, but the acceptable role of women as entrepreneurs is limited to things like selling home-grown vegetables. But Marie goes much further. She uses her creativity to establish a business away from home and in the city, and she is proud of this. Her business now is a source of self-respect for her.

D. *Given Marie's new horizon of meanings, what can we infer goes on within her as she moves to implement her decision? What questions may she have been trying to answer as she puts her decision into action? What values of Marie are engaged in this implementation? (Note: This refers to the stages of consciousness, from deciding to acting; see Chapter 4, p. 90ff.)*

Marie was not sure in the first place if she should really give up looking for a job in the formal sector: should she really dare going into business? Is this the right thing to do? If she dares, can she really succeed? How will her parents and family welcome such a change? Going into business, selling sandwiches in bars, and opening a restaurant hurts how she has perceived herself and how she is perceived by others. Can she therefore really afford to let people change their mind about her? Can she really accept the fact that she will no longer be perceived as the civil servant who can afford to send money to her extended family? Why and how can God allow this to happen to her, in the first place? Such a situation makes her question her social, religious, moral, and personal values. But she adapts those values.

She first tried to cut off or stay relatively distant from her culture, but she actually ended up relying on her cultural solidarity group. For practical reasons, she redefines what a family is. She will care first and foremost for her nuclear family. Last, but not least, her perception of business has changed. And the decision she took was to meet her *basic and vital values.* She has been struggling to reconcile the ideals and values of "what should be," as defined by her society, her religion, and family, with the reality of "what is" in her current situation. To do so, she had to first question and then adapt the *social, religious, moral, and cultural values* that she inherited from her culture to fit her current situation.

E. *Do we detect changes in the relative weights Marie now places on different values within a given level of values and among different levels of values? Does Marie seem comfortable with her decision and action? (Note: This refers to tensions within and among the levels of values; see Chapter 4, p. 102ff.)*

She seems to place a greater weight on her Christian *religious values* since she lost her traditional job and had to venture into the informal economy. A higher sense of dependence on God guides her life now.

Marie looked at her traditional culture with much suspicion at the beginning. She thought that freedom and happiness might consist in keeping herself away from her own culture. But she eventually realizes that not everything from her culture is bad. The women's solidarity group and their spirit of entrepreneurship helped her find a solution to her new situation. She re-evaluates her *cultural values.*

Also, her social perception of business becomes more positive. Business is nothing but a livelihood-coping strategy. That helps her meet her basic needs. She redefines her family to focus more on her nuclear family, so the needs of her extended family carry a lesser weight than before. Her *social values* are redefined.

Overall Marie is now more pragmatic and mature in some sense. She could, for example, have stuck by the initial weighting of her social, religious, and cultural values. But that would have meant to accept that: "I, Marie, am destined to work in the formal sector, in an office. Such a respectable person like me should not engage in business…" Only her ability to reweight her different values allowed her to "move on," take responsibility, and feel respectable and comfortable in her new decision.

STEP 3: REFLECTIONS ON MARIE AFTER APPLYING PHASE II METHODOLOGY

My New Understanding of Marie

First, with regard to the application of the methodology itself, I make some observations. In contrast to the linear approach of the methodology, Marie's actions are not in a clear sequence. They are not clearly separate from each other but rather are intertwined, concomitant. She has to sort out many decisions at the same time. I also notice the complexity of the many values (religious, social, cultural) that simultaneously drive Marie's decisions.

The Phase II methodology allowed me to see that:

1. Marie appears to adjust her own aforementioned values. She discerns what is eventually good for her. She is fighting to survive and she re-evaluates the importance and weights of the different values that drive her.

2. As a result of her decisions, Marie is a new person in many respects. She went through a tough life experience, in which things seemed to be falling apart around her. But she was able to survive and looks peaceful and comfortable with the decisions she has taken.

3. Marie is an iron-lady: she trusts herself, is realistically optimistic, values her dignity and personal opinion, and she does not give up when facing a difficult situation.

When I compare my understanding of Marie before and after applying the Part II methodology I find that:

1. Before applying the methodology, Marie was just someone, an "anonymous" person who, somewhere in Africa, suffered from the consequences of globalization like many other people in Sub-Saharan Africa. I felt sorry for her. But, well, I did not have any reason to feel sorrier for her than for the others. Marie was definitely a mere statistic in the sense that there is one more unemployed person, one more person in the informal sector, and just one more economic victim of globalization.

2. After applying the methodology there seems to be some familiarity with Marie. She is no longer just some person who suffered the consequences of globalization somewhere in Sub-Saharan Africa. Now she is that particular lady named Marie, who went through a difficult decision-making process and who was able, thanks to her internal strength, religious, social, and cultural values, to overcome the difficulties. Marie has a name from now on and even if there are many people who experienced the same situation as hers, her story remains unique.

3. Moreover, Marie epitomizes an economic victim of globalization who is able to face globalization by relying on her cultural, social, and religious values.

4. I even feel some kind of intimacy with Marie. Although I was the one who tried to understand what was going on within Marie, it surprisingly looks like Marie shared her story with me in a way she would not necessarily have done with anyone else and probably not in public. This more intimate knowledge I have of her calls also for respect: that is, I have more respect and consideration for her, because I know what she went through and what she was able to overcome.

Implications for Development Policy:
Revisions to Memo to the Development Minister

My new understanding of Marie leads me to add the following to my earlier memo to the Development Minister.

Promote tontines or micro-finance institutions. The point here is to help those who are liquidity-constrained and suffer financial exclusion because they cannot have access to formal credit for many reasons, including lack of collateral.

Marie and the women in the *tontine* value solidarity with their group highly. They also seem to be able to assess local market needs, take initiatives, and help one another. Such solidarity-based local organizations can be an instrument of development in Marie's society beyond credit providers, particularly if supported with necessary information and training to execute their plans. More specifically, in supporting micro-financing, the importance that solidarity plays in the decisions of Marie and her community suggests that a lending system based on this value could rely on trust, in contrast to physical collateral, to ensure efficient use of credit and hence repayment.

Learn by examples; share positive stories. It is important to acknowledge that there are people such as Marie who go through very difficult situations and who are strong enough to make the necessary decisions to overcome their difficulties. Success stories such as Marie's should be made public to allow other people who are struggling to know that they can get through their own situation. Community groups should be brought together to share their stories and inspire one another.

Train the unemployed. It should first be made clear that this training is not the first step of a job offer. However, it should (i) allow people who are currently unemployed to manage successfully their transition from their previous job to another one; and (ii) offer if possible skills-building training.

Indeed, Marie was able to transition from the formal to the informal sector (i) because of her capacity to rely on her cultural, social, and religious values and (ii) because of her entrepreneurial spirit that is pretty common to her ethnic group. The first aspect of the training is to help people turn from economic victims of globalization to survivors who rely on their values. For people who do not necessarily have particular skills in entrepreneurship, the second aspect of the training is aimed at helping them build some useful skills. Training should also be aimed at rebuilding community ties, so as a person benefits from the new training the whole community can participate in development.

Marie's story is a success story, but Marie "the civil servant" is not exactly the same as Marie "the business woman." She is willing to go out of her own comfort zone, accepting and re-evaluating certain things she deems important, and she adjusts and re-weights her own values. This requires going through internal struggles and subsequent discernment and it is not necessarily easy. To survive globalization and development, Marie becomes a new person, not another person: she is transformed in the process. This new person can be happy and peaceful only if she accepts the re-weighting that globalization imposes without completely uprooting or losing herself. The development process should allow room and provide support for the community explicitly undergoing this adjustment process. The first aspect of the training should therefore be to help people turn from being economic victims of globalization to survivors who rely on their own values.

The development process should rely more on Marie's and her community's capabilities of reaching and implementing their decisions based on their own values. The development project should try to, first, trust people and second, get them involved in the development project. People should not be treated as "patients" – i.e., people who have to "undergo" development – but be treated as actors of their own development, as Marie is.

INDEX

www.ingramcontent.com/pod-product-compliance
Lightning Source LLC
Chambersburg PA
CBHW060322100426
42812CB00003B/855